THE
OHIO SPORTS ALMANAC
★

ORANGE
FRAZER
PRESS

THE
OHIO SPORTS ALMANAC

★

By The Editors of
Orange Frazer Press

──────── ★ ────────

research editors
Patric Jones
Dave Stephenson

drawings
Jim Borgman

design, formatting, and composition
Annette Bickel and the Designer Set
Studios of Wilmington, Ohio

production supervisor
Michael Houck

cover design
Brooke Wenstrup

assistance
Beth Carpenter
Susie Doan

ISSN: 1061-8368
ISBN: 0-9619637-8-6

Ordering information: Additional copies of the Ohio Sports Almanac
may be ordered directly from:

       Customer Service Department
       Orange Frazer Press, Inc.
       Box 214
       37 1/2 West Main Street
       Wilmington, Ohio 45177

Telephone 1-800-852-9332 for price and shipping information

The Ohio Sports Almanac is a registered trademark of Orange Frazer
Press, Inc.

The information in this edition was compiled from the most current data
available. Any errors, inaccuracies, or omissions are strictly uninten-
tional.

Cover: © J.V. Marcu, 1992

Photography, page v: Jay Paris

"We tried to get in shape for Sandusky on November 9 but they cancelled since they were out of condition and Father Conn scheduled us for a game at Fremont on that date. We were terribly over-confident and out of condition ourselves but all alibis aside, the score stood 0 to 0 after the game. The referee was a robber and the umpire a thug; in short they penalized us a total of 195 yards—a small part of which we rightly deserved. But let bygones be bygones, in the words of the poet, and cast all memories of the game into oblivion..."
—An account of the Findlay-Fremont game, 1918, The Blue and Gold, the yearbook of Findlay High School

Table of Contents

Special considerations

Particular thanks to:

—The Sports Information Directors of Ohio's colleges and universities, and the Public Information Officers of Ohio's professional teams, all of whom patiently fielded dozens of arcane questions and righteously mailed out sheets of statistics, media guides, and photographs

—The Ohio High School Athletic Association, who shared their files and records

The drawings were furnished by special permission of King Features Syndicate, and *Jim Borgman*. The editors note that it is their strong impression that Mr. Borgman would enjoy being droll with the Cleveland Indians but, unfortunately, he lives in Cincinnati and doesn't get out much. Therefore, the weight of his drollery is brought to bear largely upon the Cincinnati Reds.

Continuing thanks to *Jim Schwartz* of Wright State University's lake campus, whose intelligence about computers is surpassed only by his robust good nature and inspired quest for the perfect taco.

Sources of photography: Page 15, Cincinnati Post, Pro Football Hall of Fame; 38, Ohio Historical Society; 40, Blegen Library, Archives and Rare Books Department, University of Cincinnati; 93, 97, Cleveland State University Library; 98, Cincinnati Post; 100-101, Blegen Library; 103, Youngstown State University; 117, Ohio State University; 119, Xavier University; 122, 127, 133, Cleveland State University Library; 153, Kenyon College; 155, Denison University; 181, National Baseball Library

THE PERENNIAL ROOKIE

THE
OHIO SPORTS ALMANAC

ORANGE
FRAZER
PRESS

a field guide to Ohio, featuring its most sporting fellows, the champions, changers, innovators, pace-setters, and record-breakers who mastered the nation's collegiate and professional games

Paul Brown

When Cleveland's new football franchise held a contest to name the team in 1946, the most popular entry was Browns, a telling tribute to the just-hired coach, whose spectacular records at Ohio State and his hometown high school in Massillon were already rendering him a football icon. Brown's Massillon Tigers took six consecutive state titles and were twice named the nation's scholastic champions, and in 1942, he led OSU to the national collegiate title in only his second year as coach. The magic continued from the 1940's through 1950's, when Cleveland and "the Paul Brown System" dominated pro football with seven national championships. In 1968, Brown started the Cincinnati Bengals, whom he coached until retiring to their front office in 1975. Brown's contributions to the game include the messenger playcall system, face guards on helmets, and putting players in classrooms, where he even graded their playbooks. He crossed pro football's invisible color line by signing blacks and his "alumni" comprise an all-star cast of the nation's coaches and players. One of football's all-time winningest coaches, Brown was the only man who (1) took both college and NFL teams to national championships, (2) founded two teams, and (3) had a pro team for a namesake.

Wayne Woodrow "Woody" Hayes

A writer once said that Hayes wore a scarlet "O" cap for so many years that it seemed to be part of his head. A most astute observation, considering that before Hayes came to Columbus, Ohio State University was called the graveyard of college football coaches, thanks to the ardent, but acutely fickle, Buckeye fans. Hayes changed all that, lasting through twenty-eight Ohio autumns because he did precisely what the impassioned inhabitants of Ohio Stadium wanted him to do: win football games. Between 1951 and 1978, Hayes had 205 wins, ten ties, and only 61 losses. He took 13 Big Ten conference titles and five national championships, coached 58 All-Americans, and won four Rose Bowls. Often, when a game wasn't going his way, he peeled off his trademark cap and stomped on it. Some said

his well-publicized tirades were mere theater. Others saw it as the pure raging of a football perfectionist frustrated by an imperfect world. Though Hayes alternately cuffed his players and mother-henned them, he brought Ohio State football into modern times with his curiously old-fashioned brand of "three yards and a cloud of dust" football. Like his hero, Billy Sherman (known to the rest of the world as General William Tecumseh), Hayes preferred a methodical ground-based attack to the razzle-dazzle of taking to the air. His strategy worked beautifully in the golden years 1968-76, when he lost only thirteen games, and was the big fish in the Big Ten's pond. Hayes became one of the five winningest college coaches in football, which to him was a metaphor for life. "With out winners, there can be no civilization," he wrote. But in his zeal to win, Hayes's behavior became uncivilized, and finally, he slugged–on television for all the world to see–a Clemson player during the 1978 Gator Bowl. Hayes was never bitter about his firing, although his wish to die on the 50-yardline would never come true. In Columbus, he came to be regarded with the gentle affection reserved for patriarchs, and when he died in 1987, flags flew at half-staff across the city. "If Woody isn't a legend," said one cohort, "he'll do until one comes along."

John Heisman

Born in Cleveland in 1869, Heisman was a pioneer of modern football. He lobbied for game quarters and the forward pass, taught teams to start plays with voice signals, invented the snap from center, and developed the "Heisman shift," the granddaddy of the I and T formations. Heisman was a natural who earned one of the first football letters at Penn, but he cut his coaching teeth at Oberlin College, where his undefeated 1892 season was the springboard for a career that took him to schools from Texas to Pennsylvania. A trained actor, Heisman often sowed flowery phrases on the field of play, but his pretty words never belied his aggressive winning style. In his hand book, The Principles of Football, he wrote, "A coach has no time to say 'please' or 'mister,' and he must be occasionally severe, arbitrary, and something of a czar." The Heisman Trophy, awarded annually to the best college football player, is named in his honor.

Jack Nicklaus

When he won the U.S. Open in 1962, Nicklaus was only 22, the youngest golf champion in nearly four decades. They put his picture on the cover of Time. Not bad for a kid from Columbus, the blond, burly "Golden Bear," who with the dew from the links at Ohio State still fresh on his clubs, toppled America's golf king, the venerable Palmer, and sent "Arnie's Army" into retreat. With his concentration and powerful swing, Nicklaus dominated golf for a quarter of a century. A multi-time PGA Player of the Year, he is the only man to win the five major tournaments—U.S. Open, Masters, PGA, U.S. Amateur, British Open—twice, and his career earnings exceed $5 million. But his most impressive record, and a telling measure of his greatness, is his endurance. When he won the U.S. Masters in 1986, he was 46, the oldest champion of any decade, and his win put the incomparable Nicklaus signature on the mantle of Time.

Jesse Owens

He was the toast of the 1936 Berlin Olympics, but Owens' dash to fame began at a Cleveland junior high school, where even then his untrained legs took him 100 yards in a record ten seconds. Owens' given name was James Cleveland, but Records should have been his middle one, because setting new marks in track and field was his specialty. In high school, he owned three--the 100-yard dash, the 220-yard dash, and the broad jump—and in 1935, wearing the Scarlet and Gray of Ohio State at a track meet in Ann Arbor, he became the only person to ever establish six records in one day, a feat made all the more remarkable because Owens achieved them in only 45 minutes. But if Michigan was a piece of cake for him, then Berlin provided the frosting. Owens took four gold medals—the 100-meter dash, the 200-meter dash, the 400-meter relay, and broad jump—and his shining victory was moral as well as athletic. He, a black American, had with enormous dignity and grace stolen the Olympics out from under the racist nose of Adolph Hitler.

Branch Rickey

They called him "Mr. Baseball" and "The Mahatma." The accolades stemmed from Rickey's talent for finding and developing good ball players, and this was the particular genius with which he founded three baseball dynasties. Rickey was born in 1881, in the hardscrabble southern Ohio hill country to a farm couple who eventually moved to Lucasville so that their bright boy could enjoy the advantages of a town school. From his athletic father, Rickey inherited the genes that put him on the Ohio Wesleyan baseball team, and from his Scripture - reading mother, he got the philosophy that kept him off the diamond on Sundays. When tuberculosis interrupted his playing career, and hard times undermined his law pratice, Rickey turned to major league baseball, becoming a scout, manager, and finally executive. Players knew him as shrewd and something of a skinflint, but if Rickey ran his teams with an iron hand in a leather glove, he was also considered humane and impeccably fair-minded. His leadership of the St. Louis Cardinals (1917-1942), Brooklyn Dodgers (1942-1950), and Pittsburgh Pirates (1950 - 1960) made powerhouses and pennant winners of them all. Along the way, Rickey signed more than a few baseball greats - Campanella, Clemente, Newcombe; and he made two contributions that changed the game forever - the farm team in 1919, and racial integration in 1947. Rickey broke major league baseball's long ban on black players by signing Jackie Robinson to the Dodgers. His famous decision not only strengthened baseball, but also, ultimately, the country by calling attention to the national hypocrisy about civil rights. It is said that Rickey waited forty years to find the right man with the intelligence and moral courage to successfully integrate baseball. The virtue of Rickey's patience was no less than could be expected from someone who called the notebook where he tracked potential players, the "Bible."

Pete Rose

His pinnacle came in Cincinnati on September 11, 1985, when Rose, on the fifty-seventh annversary of Ty Cobb's last game, surpassed said Mr. Cobb's 4,191 base hits, the record that conventional sports wisdom said could never be broken. Rose—in his hometown, at the overripe age of 44, playing for the Reds with whom his major league career began twenty-three years before—had defied the odds, thus elevating himself to the small pantheon of baseball dieties. Years before, no less than the mythic Mickey Mantle had pegged Rose as "Charlie Hustle," an acutely apt sobriquet for a man who over- compensated for his lack of a "natural ability" with a sheer, unabashed love of the game. Whatever the thorns in his personal life, Rose wore both his heart and soul on his uniform sleeve, and his phenomenal desire to play carried him to giddy status in the litany of baseball mosts-hits, at- bats, games, winning games, singles, seasons with 200 or more hits. And he is the only man in baseball to have played 500 games at five positions-first, second, and third base, left and right field.

Rose the Player yielded to Rose the Manager in 1986, but not before he had tacked another 64

base hits onto his record, thus ensuring a long haul for any would-be equal. The life-long goal of this perpetual Boy of Summer was, of course, the Baseball Hall of Fame, and his remarkable record certainly should have made him a shoo-in. But Rose was shut out on August 23, 1989, when the commissioner of baseball banned him from the game for life after a scandal over his betting on sports.

Denton "Cy" Young

As a young man, he could throw a baseball so hard that it reminded folks of a cyclone, and thus "Cy" Young found his nickname and began carving out his incomparable place on the mound in the Ohio towns near his Tuscarawas County farm. He began his major league career with the Cleveland Spiders in 1890, pitching (and winning) in his first season a doubleheader that signaled the greatness yet to come. He played in the first forerunner of the World Series (1903; his Boston Red Sox won); pitched three no-hit, no-run games and the first perfect game (1904); and until 1968, held the record for the most games pitched (906). Though Young quit in 1911, three of his lifetime records still stand: most wins (511), completed games (751), and innings pitched (7,377), and he remains the only pitcher to win 200 games in both leagues. He was, of course, a shoo-in for the Baseball Hall of Fame and the annual Cy Young Award, given to baseball's best pitcher, fittingly bears the name of the Ohioan who set the pace for generations of pitchers. Young spent most of his major league career in Cleveland, and upon retiring his splendid arm, he returned home to his Tuscarawas County farm.

Stalwart Ohio Firsts

Johnny Vander Meer, Cincinnati Reds
First and only major league pitcher with back-to-back-no-hitters, against Braves and Dodgers, June 11 and 15, 1938.

Joe Nuxhall, Cincinnati Reds
Twentieth Century's youngest major league baseball player, age 15, 1944

Bill Wambsganss, Cleveland Indians
Made first unassisted triple play in World Series, October 10, 1920

Neal Ball, Cleveland Indians
Made first unassisted triple play in major leagues, July 19, 1909

Les Horwath, Ohio State
First and only Big Ten Quarterback to win the Heisman Trophy, 1944

James Madison Toy, Cleveland, American Association, 1887
First American Indian to play major league baseball

Charles Follis, Wooster
First black professional football player, Shelby (Ohio) Blues, 1904-06

Moses and Welday Walker, Mt. Pleasant
First black players in major league baseball, Toledo, 1884

Frank Robinson, Cleveland Indians
First black major league manager, 1975

Bob Feller, Cleveland Indians
First opening day no-hit game in baseball history, 1-0 over the White Sox, April 16, 1940.

Ray Chapman, Cleveland Indians
First and only major league player killed by a pitched ball (thrown by the Yankee's Carl Mays), August 16, 1920

William DeHart Hubbard, Cleveland
First black American to win an Olympic Gold Medal (broad jump, 24 feet, 5 1/8 inches), 1924

Lawrence Eugene Doby, Cleveland Indians
First black baseball player in the American League, 1947

Elwood Parsons, Dayton
First fulltime black scout in major league baseball.

Marge Schott, Cincinnati
First woman to purchase a major league sports team, the Cincinnati Reds, 1984

Archie Griffin, Ohio State University
First and only college football player to win Heisman Trophy in consecutive years, 1974-75

Ohio State football team
First Big Ten school to play in all major Bowl games-Rose, Orange, Cotton, Sugar, Fiesta, 1921-1987

First NFL player to rush for 10,000 yards
Jim Brown, Cleveland, 1964

First NFL playoff game
Chicago Bears 9, Portsmouth Spartans 0, December 18, 1932

William Howard Taft, President,
United States of America
Having warmed up during his Cincinnati youth as a sandlot catcher, he started the baseball tradition of the President tossing out the season's first ball, doing the honors for the Washington Senators, April 14, 1910.

Monday Night Football
To the delight of die-hard fans and the chargin of their spouses, Cleveland Browns' president Art Modell teamed up with network TV to host the first Monday matchup, the Browns tuning out the Jets 31-21, on September 21, 1970.

Professional baseball
The Cincinnati Baseball Club, a.k.a. the Red Stockings, became in 1869, the first all-paid touring team. Though their record–64 wins, no losses, one tie–was spectacular, their net profit–$1.39–was not.

Night baseball

Cincinnati manager Larry McPhail, the "Barnum of Baseball," not only put the Reds under the lights but also got President Roosevelt to throw the switch for the first major league night game, May 24, 1935

Air travel, professional basketball

The first flight involving pro basketball occurred at the end of the 1939-40 season during the three-game playoff for the National Basketball League's Eastern Division. After losing the second game, the Akron Firestone Nonskids flew home to rest up for the final game, which they won. As usual, the Detroit Eagles drove.

NCAA Basketball Tournament

The event began in 1939, at the suggestion of Ohio State basketball coach Harold Olsen, who also chaired the the early committees of the tournament that has become the Super Bowl of college basketball.

Penalty flags

In 1941, Youngtown College football coach Dike Beede provided flags to referees as a subtitute for their confusing horns and whistles. One referee, Jack McPhee, used his flag in an Ohio State-Iowa game in Columbus, where the Big Ten commissioner liked what he saw so much that the conference immediately adapted the idea, thus triggering a silent revolution in football.

NFL Midwives

Teams present at the birth of pro football, Canton, Ohio, 1920

Canton Bulldogs
Akron Pros
Massillon Tigers
Cleveland Indians
Dayton Triangles
Decatur Stanleys
Hammond Pros
Rochester Jeffersons
Rock Island Independents
Muncie Flyers
Racine Cardinals

When Ohio flexes its muscles, athletic collarbuttons pop all over America. One never knows exactly where or when a Buckeye—or even worse, a team of Buckeyes—might drop by and carry off all the trophyware.

There's an old story about the fabled Jim Thorpe getting off the train to represent Carlisle at a track meet, and when the opposing college's representative asked where the team was, Thorpe said, "I'm it." Then, single-handedly, won the meet. In the spring of 1991, however, seven young women representing Central State University got off the plane for the NAIA track and field championships and—shades of Thorpe—did the same thing. Not only did the seven women win the national championship, they set three relay records, and all seven were named All-American.

When it comes to athletics, no sport is sacred. Buckeyes will outdribble, outshoot, outhit, outreach, outride, outrun, outjump, outbox and outfox whomever shows up.

Outrageous.

They'll do it to you in a major way (pro baseball) or in the minors (Little League). They'll do it to you in competitions you just barely heard of—bridge, water-skiing, and hot air balloon racing—and some you *never* heard of—summit-climbing, orienteering, and stair-climbing.

Faced with this exercise in exercise, there is but one bit of advice, and that from another one-time Buckeye athlete, Satchel Paige of the Cleveland Indians: *Don't look back. Somebody might be gaining on you.*

The odds are it's an Ohioan, with a trophy gleam in his or her eye.

Archery
Straight arrow

Pan-Am Games—Darrell Pace, Hamilton, individual gold, archery. Pace, a two-time Olympic gold medalist and at 34 still a contender, was also part of the Pan-Am gold medal three-man archery team.

Badminton
Shuttle service

National Junior Badminton Championships, boys and mixed doubles titles—Christopher Stanton Hales, Wooster

Ballooning
Air Dayton

World Hot Air Balloon Championship—Albert Nels, Beavercreek, for the second time.

Baseball
Stealing home

Starter, The All-Star Game—catcher Sandy Alomar Jr., Cleveland Indians (American League).

Basketball
Dribblers

Coach of year, U.S. Basketball Writers Association and Associated Press—Randy Ayers, OSU basketball coach, who in his second year coached the Buckeyes to a 25-3 record, a No. 5 national ranking, and a share of the Big Ten title.

World Basketball League Championship—Dayton Wings, over the Calgary 88's, 120-89, and a 3-0 series sweep, in its first year of existence.

AAU/USA Junior Olympic National Basketball Championship—Hocking Valley, 12-and-under category, 47-46 over Missouri Valley on Amy Tatman's shot at the buzzer. Tatman was tournament MVP.

Basketball Hall of Fame—Bobby Knight, Orrville and OSU; Nate Archibald, Cincinnati Royals.

Highest paid pro basketball player—John Williams, Cleveland Cavaliers. $4 million signing bonus, $1 million in salary.

All-American—Vonda Ward, the 6-foot-6 Trinity (Cleveland) High player was named co-player of the year by *Parade*.

Division III men's player of the year—Brad Baldridge, Wittenberg.

Division III women's player of the year—Ann Gilbert, Oberlin, who averaged 31.2 points a game.

Top prep shooting guard in America—Damon Flint, a 6-5 junior from Cincinnati Woodward, ranked by recruiting experts. Flint averaged 22.2 points a game as a sophomore.

Concensus first team All-American, 1990-1991 season—Jimmy Jackson, OSU sophomore.

Championship Moments from Cincinnati

Starter, The All-Star Game—third baseman **Chris Sabo**, Cincinnati Reds (National League).

Most Likely—**Barry Larkin**, Cincinnati Reds shortstop, was named by a poll of professional baseball's general managers as the player with whom they would most like to start a baseball team.

The 1991 Hutch Award—**Bill Wegman**, Cincinnati and the Milwaukee Brewers, who, after surgery on shoulder and elbow, came back with a 15-7 record and a 2.84 ERA.

The Cincinnati Reds—won National League home run crown (164) while leading the league in total bases (2,215) and hitting percentage (.403). **Jose Rijo**, according to the Elias Sports Bureau, was the NL's top starter, and **Rob Dibble** its best reliever.

Youngest Major League player in 35 years to drive in 100 runs—**Ken Griffey Jr.**, of Moeller High, and the Seattle Mariners.

Number One high school baseball team in America—**Fairfield High School**, named by USA Today after winning the 1991 Ohio Division I state baseball title.

United States Slo-Pitch Softball Association Hall of Fame—**Velma Lehmann**, leftfielder and lead-off hitter for Cincinnati Empress. Lehmann, a member of three world championship teams, is only the 11th player to be inducted.

The Babe Ruth World Series amateur championship—**The Storm Club** (ages 16-18) of Cincinnati, who, appropriately enough, won the title in Massachusetts after waiting out Hurricane Bob.

Connie Mack World Series championship—**The Midland Redskins** (ages 17-18), whose team also won national titles in 1984, '85, and '89.

Pony League 13-under World Series—**Morgenroth** of Cincinnati beat Brooklyn 5-0 for the title after finishing the season 66-1.

The Hamilton Little Leaguers won a berth in the Little League World Series, finishing in the consolation bracket.

The Cincinnati Bulls played for the title of the National Amateur Baseball Federation Major World Series.

Empress Chili finished second in the World Series for women's slo-pitch softball. Empress won three world championships, from 1986 through 1988, and finished second the last two years. ▶

Boomerang
Adult boomers

World Indoor Boomerang Championships—Greg Snouffer, Deleware, at Perth, Australia. Brother Chet Snouffer, also of Delaware, won the U.S. Boomerang Association's championship.

Bowling
Super bowl

American Bowling Congress Tournament, doubles title—Jimmy Johnson, Columbus. He was also a member of the group winning the team all-events title.

Boxing
The big knock

U.S. Amateur Boxing Championships—Timothy Austin, Cincinnati, fly weight class title. Austin, at 112 pounds and ranked No. 2 in the world, also won his division in the U.S.-USSR amateur boxing meet, the U.S. Olympic Festival title, and the Golden Gloves championship.

U.S. Olympic Festival—Larry Donald, Cincinnati, super heavyweight and ranked No. 3 in the world, gold medal. Donald also won the U.S. Boxing Championship in his class.

IBF Light-heavyweight Championship—Charles Williams, Mansfield.

National Golden Gloves Tournament—Dezi Ford, Alliance, 132-pound title.

World Boxing Organization—Manning Galloway, Columbus, welterweight title.

Bridge
A warm hand

Jeff Meckstroth, Reynoldsburg, called "one of the world's great bridge players," won the prestigious *Spingold Knockout Teams championship* in Las Vegas, making him one of the few bridge players to win all three major titles.

The Von Zedwitz Gold Cup—Doug Simson, Columbus, for winning the Life Masters Pairs title in bridge.

Canoeing
Up an Olympic creek

U.S. Olympic Festival—Jim Terrell, Milford, dominated canoe events, winning 4 gold medals.

U.S. Nationals—Greg Steward, Williamsburg, first in the 500 and 1,000-meter canoe events.

Climbing
Peak-a-boo

Jack Bennett became the only Ohioan certified by the Highpointers Club to have climbed the highest summit in each of the fifty states.

World Stair Climb Record—Russell Gill, Columbus, 10 hours, 32 minutes, 39 seconds, at the Rhodes Tower.

Equestrianism
Horse sense

Intercollegiate Horse Show Association National championship—OSU, western style division.

Fencing
Swordsman

U.S. Olympic Festival—Donald Anthony Jr., Cincinnati, gold, men's sabre. He was also a member of the festival's gold-medal fencing team.

Flying
Plane geometry

The 1991 Top Gun Invitational Aces Championship, team large-scale radio controlled airplanes—Geoff Combs, Pickerington, and Kim Foster, Mansfield.

Football
Turf Heads

NCAA Division I-AA national championship—Youngstown State, 25-17 over Marshall University. Defensive tackle Pat Danko of Warren John F. Kennedy High named AP first team Division I-AA All-American. Coach Jim Tressel named I-AA Coach of the Year.

California Bowl—Bowling Green, 28-21, over Fresno State.

Heisman Trophy—junior Desmond Howard, Cleveland and Michigan, second-largest vote-getter in history. Howard also won the Maxwell Award, which goes to the nation's outstanding college player, and his margin of votes was the largest in the history of the 55-year-old event.

NCAA Division III coach of the year—Mike Kelly, University of Dayton.

First-round selection, Green Bay Packers—defensive back Vinnie Clark, OSU and Cincinnati CAPE.

First Division III player ever selected for college football's biggest all-star game, the Hula Bowl: Keith Rucker, 6-4, 340-pound defensive lineman from Ohio Wesleyan.

NCAA Division III freshman records—Brad Hensley, Kent and Kenyon, total offense (2,554 yards), most passing yardage (2,520), and most passes attempted (384).

Longest completed pass—Adam Fried, Andy Goss and Tom Nigro, to the 101st Airborne in Saudi Arabia. The OSU students mailed the football 6,000 miles to U.S. Troops and four months later it was thrown back to Columbus, autographed: "Go Bucks, HQ, 2nd Air Assault BDE."

Consecutive attempts without an interception—Cleveland Browns quarterback Bernie Kosar, 308, new NFL record.

College Football Hall of Fame—Dave Maurer, Wittenberg, who in 15 years won 129 games and lost only 23, including three undefeated seasons, and two national titles.

National High School Sports Hall of Fame—Bron Bacevich, Cincinnati's Roger Bacon High. In 20 years his teams won 150 games and lost 40, including seven league championships and a national coach-of-the-year title in 1973.

National Football Foundation and Hall of Fame Scholar-Athlete Award—Greg Frey, OSU quarterback who lettered three times in football and twice in baseball for the Buckeyes, and was one of 11 players in America to win the prestigious graduate fellowship.

Pro Bowl—Cincinnati Bengal offensive tackle Anthony Munoz, 11th consecutive year, and regarded as the NFL's premiere player at his position. Also: Michael Dean Perry, Cleveland Browns nose tackle.

Associated Press All-Pro team—Massillon's Chris Spielman (Detroit Lions) and St. Henry's Jim Lachey (Washington Redskins)

United States Flag and Touch Football League National Championship—Mr. E's Raiders of Cleveland, 14-13, over Norton's Silver Bullets of Dayton.

Rose Bowl Hall of Fame—All-American quarterback Rex Kern, OSU, who was the Rose Bowl MVP in 1969 when he led the Bucks to a come-from-behind win over USC.

Parade Magazine All-American—Ty Douthard, Cincinnati LaSalle senior running back.

Golf
Tee and sympathy

U.S. Senior Open and PGA Seniors titles—Jack Nicklaus, Columbus. It was his fifth U.S. Open title, as he became the only man to win major U.S. Golf Association titles in five decades.

National Match Championship, Putt-Putt Golf—Roger Beckerman, South Euclid.

Gymnastics
King of spring

1991 World University Games—Mike Racanelli, OSU, gold, floor exercise.

Hockey
High sticks

U.S. Olympic Festival, gold, women's field hockey team—Jibs Thorson, Pataskala.

Jump rope
Rhythm methodology

World Double Dutch Invitational Tournament championship—Double Forces, the Columbus YMCA five-man jump rope team.

Boys and Girls Clubs of America 1991 Jump Rope Championships—Channon Jackson, Cincinnati, age 9 and under girls title.

Orienteering
Plotters

By out-navigating their competitors, these Ohioans won national orienteering events: John Simonsen, Columbus, 1st at the *Heartland Championships*, age 35-39 advanced course. Amy Wells, Oberlin, women's open champion on the intermediate course at the *U.S. Orienteering Federation Convention Meet*. Steve Hughes, Amelia, won the Open Short Elite Course title at the *U.S. Intercollegiate Championships*.

Championship Moments—*In two unrelated and unprecedented events, three Ohio divers survived chute failures. At Waynesville Airport,* **Mike Hussey** *and* **Amy Adams** *fell from 13,500 feet with a shredded parachute and were saved by falling into a bush. In Cleveland,* **Jill Shields** *fell 10,500 feet after her chute failed to open and landed in a swamp. None was seriously injured.*

Racing
Bigfoot

All Pro Winter Nationals, Modified Division title—Frank McCammon, Cincinnati, 8.310 and 157.85 mph.

Racquetball
Bad seed

Gerri Stoffregen and Shelley Ogden, Cincinnati, *National American Amateur Racquetball Association Doubles Championship*, 40-and-over.

Amy Kilbane, Rocky River, and Shane Vanderson, Dublin, *World Junior Racquetball titles.*

Elaine Hooghe, Columbus, *World Intercollegiate Racquetball title.*

Doug Ganim, Columbus, gold medal, racquetball doubles, *U.S. Olympic Festival.*

Roller skating
Honor roll

National Ball Hockey Roller Skating Championships—The Louisville Raiders, Louisville, Ohio, Bronze Division crown.

Pan Am Games—April Dayney, Maumee, demonstration gold medal, figures and freestyle.

United States Roller Skating Championships—Andrew Crissman and Christina Raedel, Brookpark, Elementary Dance title, and Gary Stark, Austintown, Masters Men's Figures crown.

Rowing
Gently down your stream

American Rowing Championships—The Cincinnati Rowing Center won seven gold medals, including five in women's events, and the team title.

National Collegiate Rowing Championships—OSU, lightweight men's eight crew. In lightweight eight rowing the boat can average no more than 155 pounds per man, and no rower can weigh more than 160 pounds. The Bucks covered the 2000-meter course in just over six minutes.

Sailing
Arts in crafts

Pan American Games gold medal in the Soling class went to Matt Fisher, Westerville. Columbus's George Fisher, Matt's father, was the *Lightning*

Second Bananas

Second at the U.S. All-Around Speed Skating Championships—**Tony Meibock**, Fairview Park.

Second at the 22nd Annual World Series of Poker—**Don Williams**, Bellvue, $66,500, Seven Card High competition.

Second in the nation, 100-meter dash—**Jonathan Burrell**, John Marshall High, 10.41 seconds.

Second in the National Golden Gloves Tournament—**Fred Neal**, Cleveland, 125-pound class.

Second in Intercollegiate Horse Show Association Nationals—**Miami University**, English Style division.

Second best NCAA Division III football team—**University of Dayton**, who lost to Ithaca, 34-20, in the Amos Alonzo Stagg Bowl.

Second best NAIA Division I football team—**Central State University**, who lost the championship to Central Arkansas, 19-16, on a field goal with six seconds to play. ▶

Masters North American champion, defeating 18 other boats. Greg Fisher, George's son, is the *Thistle Midwinter champion*. Craig Tovell, Hilliard, and Mike Gaber, Columbus, were crewmates on the boat winning the *Interlake Nationals*. Tovell also won the *Cape Cod Frosty National Championship*.

Senior Olympics
Golden retrievers

U.S. National Senior Olympics:

John Florance, Delaware, gold, men 60-64, 50-meter freestyle swimming.

Janet Freeman, Napoleon, gold, women 55-59, 1500, 800, 400 and 200-meter track events.

Beverly Myers, Toledo, six gold medals, women 55-59.

Cliff and Lucille Sampson, Middletown, gold, discus, he with a 138' toss in the 65-69 age group, and she with 71' 6" in the 60-64 category.

Mary Bowermaster, Cincinnati, gold, women 70-74, 100-meter dash, l7.2.

Vadine Koenig, Cincinnati, gold, women 70-74, 10K road race.

Skeet
Top guns

Champion of Champions seniors division title, Grand American Trapshoot—Claude Freeman, Lebanon, a perfect 100 of 100.

U.S. Olympic Festival—Jonathan Frazer, Wheelersburg, rapid-fire gold medal.

Pan-Am Games—Dean Clark, Garrettsville, member of the gold medal skeet team that set a world record, 445 out of 500 points.

Soccer
Kicks

U.S. Olympic Sports Festival—Wane Lobring, Cincinnati, gold, soccer team. Lobring was the leading scorer with five goals and two assists in four games. He was also on the Pan-Am Games gold medal team, and is a member of the U.S. National team.

National coach of the year—Mike Pilger, Kenyon soccer, Division III. Pilger's team was 18-0 during the regular season, the only undefeated, untied team in NCAA Division III.

U.S. Junior Olympic Taekwondo Championships—Anna Kim, Cleveland, 13-16 age group, national title, her third straight.

Pam Kalinoski, N. Olmstead, a senior midfielder, had three assists and a goal while leading North Carolina to soccer wins over Wisconsin and Virginia—its sixth NCAA title in a row. Kalinoski set NCAA career assist (51) and season (28) records.

Swimming and Diving
First water

At the Ohio High School Swimming and Diving Championships, Joe Hudepohl, a St. Xavier (Cincinnati) High junior, won four state titles, the first Ohioan to ever do so—and broke three national records, in the 200, 100 and 50-yard freestyle races. He also won the 200-meter freestyle in the Los Angeles Invitational.

NCAA Division III Swimming and Diving Championships—Kenyon, as usual, both men's and women's titles. It was the 12th consecutive championship for the men, which is the most titles by any school, in any sport, in any division. Coach Jim Steen was coach of the year and All-American senior Cami Mathews was the Division III swimmer of the year.

Dexter Woodford, 77, Akron, holds the National Masters' record in the two-mile swim. He also has national records in the 500, 1000, and 1650-yard freestyle. He has world records in the 400, 800 and 1500 meter freestyle.

North American Maccabi Youth Games—Adam Katz, Cleveland, boys 15-16 fly, gold.

United States Long Course Championships—Kathy Hoffman, Dayton Raiders, 1500-meter freestyle. She is currently ranked sixth in the world in her event.

U.S. Olympic Festival—Mark Bradshaw, Columbus, gold, 3-meter springboard diving.

The 1991 Speedo/U.S. Diving Junior Olympics—Angie Trostel, Oxford, girls 14-15, one-meter springboard title

U.S. Indoor Diving Championships—Pat Evans, Cincinnati, men's platform and 1-meter titles. Evans, considered one of best half-dozen divers in the world, also won the 1991 Alamo Challenge 1-meter title, and the Phillips 66 Indoor platform and 1-meter crowns.

U.S. Diving Championships—Patrick Jeffrey, OSU, 3-meter springboard title.

NCAA Championships—Dean Panaro, Cincinnati, 1-meter springboard title.

NCAA Championships— David Pichler, OSU, 10-meter platformtitle.

Pan-Am Games—Jill Schlabach, Fairfield and University of Cincinnati, gold, women's 1-meter springboard.

Synchronized swimming
Twin peaks

The 1991 U.S. Olympic Festival, the 1991 Pan Pacific Championship, and the World Championship—Sarah and Karen Josephson, OSU, duet synchronized titles. For the World title in Perth, the twins earned the highest overall total for a duet in the history of international synchronized swimming.

Pan Am Games—Diana Ulrich, OSU, gold medal, duet synchronized swimming crown; Kim Ochsner, Cincinnati, and Tia Harding, Columbus, gold medals in team synchronized swimming at the 1991 Pan Am Games.

Team Play
Pan-Am teams—Mark Coleman, Columbus, wrestling; Scott Klingenbeck, OSU and Cincinnati, baseball; Jim Jackson, OSU and Toledo, basketball; Rick Oleksyk, Parma, and Bryant Johnson, Columbus, handball team.

U.S. Junior World Team—Jody Radkewich, 15, triathlon, three-time national champion.

U.S. National Rowing Championships—Kelly Marie Sherman, Sylvania, winning team, Women's Lightweight Eight.

U.S. Squash Racquets Association National Junior Women's Team—Libby Eynon, Cincinnati.

U.S. Freestyle B Team, Snow-skiing—Rick Emerson, Cleveland, who beat World Cup point leader Edgard Grospiron.

Tennis
Another racquet

North American Macccabi Youth Games, gold, tennis—Scott Marshall and Brad Goldberg, Cincinnati, boys 15-16 doubles,

Junior National Indoor Tennis Championship—Josh Osswald and Brad Goldberg, Cincinnati, Boys 16 title.

Tiddlywinks
Wink, wink, nod, nod

World Singles Tiddlywinks Singles Championship—Larry Kahn, Cleveland.

Track and Field
Making tracks

Jumbo Elliot Award—Mark Croghan, OSU and Greensburg, top male collegian in American track and field. Croghan won the 1991 NCAA outdoor 3,000-meter steeplechase, and the Mobil National Track and Field Championship, which he finished in 8 minutes, 21.46 seconds, the fastest time in the world during 1991.

NCAA Division III Track and Field Championships—Keith Rucker, Ohio Wesleyan, discus and shot put titles; Kevin Luthy, Case Western Reserve, decathlon title for the second straight year.

U.S. Olympic Festival—Jane Brooker, West Chester, women's 800-meter run title.

NAIA National Track and Field Championships—Central State University, women's title. CSU won first place in seven events with only seven women on the team. CSU sophomore Carolin Sterling was named as the meet's outstanding female athlete. The CSU women swept the relay events and set three new NAIA meet records.

NAIA Track and Field Championships, mens' mile relay title—Central State, 3:19.02.

Volleyball
Net Worth

U.S. Olympic Festival, gold, volleyball—Laurie Maxwell, Granville, and Tammy Schiller, New Carlise, members of the South team.

Water Skiing
Turning tricks

The *slalom and tricks National Water Ski Champion*—Lucille Borgen, Akron, Womens Division, 75-and-over.

American Barefoot Club National Championship—David Reinhart, Defiance, overall title, He also won the trick and jump titles.

Weightlifting
Iron guys

National Junior Weightlifting Championships—David Novak, Bedford, 110kg class.

United States Power Lifting Federation Tournament—John Black's Health World powerlifting team, Cleveland, first place.

Ohio members of *Team USA* in the triathalon—Winston Allen, Dublin, 60-64 age group; Jody Radkewich, Hudson, junior division; Anne Guist, Cincinnati, 25-29 age group.

American Weightlifting Association National Championships—Howard Prechtel and Noi Phamchaona, Cleveland. Prechtel successfully defended his title in the 242-pound class, and his wife, Phamchaona, set three U.S. records defending her title in the 114-pound class.

Wrestling
Armed and at it

The *1991 University National Championships*—Brian Wallis-Keck, Brecksville, Greco-Roman wrestling title.

The 1991 *Espoir World Championship* of freestyle wrestling, in Czechoslovakia—Alan Fried, Lakewood. Fried, a three-time Ohio champion from St. Edward High, became the first American to win the gold medal since 1987.

National AAU-USA Wrestling Championships—Aaron Zistler, Cincinnati, gold, sombo wrestling. Zistler, 10, also won a silver medal in Greco-Roman competition.

Research assistance by Dave Stephenson, reprinted from Ohio Magazine.

Football
State Champions

Associated Press			United Press International		
1947	*Barberton*				
1948	Massillon				
1949	Massillon				
1950	Massillon				
1951	Massillon				
1952	Massillon				
1953	Massillon		1953	Massillon	
1954	Massillon		1954	Massillon	
1955	Canton McKinley		1955	Canton McKinley	
1956	Canton McKinley		1956	Canton McKinley	
1957	Cleveland Benedictine		1957	Cleveland Benedictine	
1958	Alliance		1958	Marion Harding	
1959	Massillon		1959	Massillon	
1960	Massillon		1960	Massillon	
1961	Niles McKinley		1961	Massillon	
1962	No final poll announced		1962	Toledo Central Catholic	
1963	Niles McKinley		1963	Niles McKinley	
1964	Massillon		1964	Massillon	
1965	AA	Massillon	1965	AA	Sandusky
	A	Dovert St. Joseph		A	Marion Catholic
1966	AA	Columbus Watterson	1966	AA	Columbus Watterson
	A	Marion Catholic		A	Marion Catholic
1967	AA	Upper Arlington	1967	AA	Upper Arlington
	A	Portsmouth Notre Dame		A	Versailles
1968	AA	Upper Arlington	1968	AA	Upper Arlington
	A	Newark Catholic		A	Cory Rawson
1969	AA	Upper Arlington	1969	AA	Upper Arlington
	A	Norwalk St. Paul		A	McDonald
1970	AAA	Massillon	1970	AAA	Massillon
	AA	New Lexington		AA	New Lexington
	A	Portsmouth Notre Dame		A	Portsmouth Notre Dame
1971	AAA	Warren Harding	1971	AAA	Warren Harding
	AA	Steubenville Central Catholic		AA	Steubenville Central Catholic
	A	Marion Pleasant		A	Marion Pleasant
1972	AAA	Massillon	1972	AAA	Massillon
	AA	Columbus Watterson		AA	Columbus Watterson
	A	Marion Pleasant		A	Marion Pleasant

Note: State football championship playoffs began with the 1972 season

CLASS A

	Champion	Coach		Runner-up	Coach	
1972	Marion Pleasant	Don Kay	vs.	Lorain Clearview	Wayne Ross	20-14
1973	Middletown Fenwick	Jerry Harkrader	vs.	Montpelier	Hobert Krouse	27-7
1974	Middletown Fenwick	Jerry Harkrader	vs.	Fremont St. Joseph	Ricky Wonderly	21-0
1975	*Carey	Thomas Geschwind	vs.	Newark Catholic	J. D. Graham	15-7
1976	West Jefferson	Gene Keel	vs.	Ashtabula St. John	Paul Kopko	21-0
1977	Crooksville	Craig Spring	vs.	Ashtabula St. John	Paul Kopko	8-7
1978	Newark Catholic	J. D. Graham	vs.	Lorain Clearview	Tom Hoch	21-0
1979	**Mogadore	Norman Lingle	vs.	Covington	Larrie Tisdale	23-17

CLASS AA

	Champion	Coach		Runner-up	Coach	
1972	Akron St. Vincent	John Cistone	vs.	Columbus Watterson	Ron Shay	28-7
1973	Cleveland Benedictine	August Bossu	vs.	Ironton	Bob Lutz	38-13
1974	Norwalk	Robert Hart	vs.	Louisville St. Thomas Aquinas	Frank Sakal	27-17
1975	Cleveland Holy Name	Richard Donovan	vs.	Cincinnati Wyoming	Bob Lewis	19-14
1976	Elyria Catholic	Jim Rattay	vs.	Brookville	John Barsala	34-10
1977	Cincinnati Wyoming	Bob Lewis	vs.	Elyria Catholic	Jim Rattay	26-14
1978	Brookfield	John Delserone	vs.	Hamilton Badin	Terry Malone	28-0
1979	Ironton	Bob Lutz	vs.	Akron St. Vincent-St. Mary	John Cistone	7-6

Paul Brown at Massillon: Other coaches knew how to develop a game plan, but none had ever stepped back and devised a program.

Massillon, Ohio: The Cradle of Football

In the early 1980s, when Detroit Lion **Chris Spielman** was just making a name for himself as all-state linebacker and Wheaties poster lad, his team, the Massillon Tigers, was about to end a record to which no other Ohio high school had even come close—state football titles in each decade of the past half-century. Massillon was runner-up in 1980 and 1982, but it brought home no championship. If, however, Massillon has been overshadowed in the last decade by Johnny-come-latelies like Cincinnati Moeller and Cleveland St. Ignatius, consider that in those four decades before, Massillon won 83 per cent of its games, including 17 state championships, produced more than 114 all-Ohio players, was named the finest high school in America seven times, and drew 5.8 million fans. What is an off decade in the face of such staying power?

Massillon football was invented by favorite son, **Paul Brown**, the skinny but scrappy Tiger quarterback who put the town on the gridiron map then went on to invent the professional game in Cleveland. Brown became the head coach in 1932, taking over a team that had just been 2-6-2. The dirt field had to be sprinkled before games to keep the spectators from choking, and the band wore old military uniforms. Brown lost four games his first year, two the next, and then only two in the entire next decade. In 1940, Massillon beat the competition by an average score of 48-.6, and the entire starting team was named All-State by the United Press.

Before Brown left for Cleveland-through-OSU, his teams won six straight state titles. His last team annihilated a good Kent State team in a scrimmage and Brown later would muse about whether that last Massillon team could have beaten his first OSU team. Brown left town with, said writer Alan Natali, a status akin to "a combination of Amerigo Vespucci, the Inca of Peru, Benjamin Franklin, and a splinter from the True Cross."

Lesser luminaries went on later to coach at the Chicago Bears (**Chuck Mather**), Ohio State (**Earle Bruce**), Cornell (**Tom Harp**), Iowa (**Bob Commings**); Kent State (**Leo Strang**), and Baldwin-Wallace (**Lee Tressel**). Other program alumni include **Harry Stuhldreher**, one of Notre Dame's Four Horsemen; **Jim Houston**, late of the Browns; **Robert Vogel**, Baltimore Colts All-Pro; and Spielman, the OSU All-American linebacker now with the Detroit Lions. **Don James**, who last season coached Washington to a national title, was one of four James boys to play for Massillon, but **Tommy James** is the local legend. He played on three straight state title teams, scored the first TD at Tiger Stadium, then went with Brown to OSU. He followed Brown to Cleveland, too, where he played with his old high school teammates, **Horace Gillom** and **Lin Houston**. James, an All-Pro defensive back, played in eight straight league championship games. In Coach Earle Bruce's initial year with Massillon, there were some 50 Tigers playing college ball.

In Massillon, the 1980s was an aberration. Each male child born in the town is still presented a football by the Tiger Booster Club. Wrote Natali: "This is a town where arthritic seventy-year-olds and middle-aged steelworkers alike can, for a fourth of a year, return to a fine youth unsullied by acne traumas and rejection complexes." ❱

CLASS AAA

	Champion	Coach		Runner-up	Coach	
1972	Warren Western Reserve	Jospeh Novak	vs.	Cincinnati Princeton	Pat Mancuso	37-6
1973	Youngstown Mooney	Don Bucci	vs.	Warren Western Reserve	Joseph Novak	14-3
1974	Warren Harding	Ed Glass	vs.	Upper Arlington	Pete Corey	41-8
1975	Cincinnati Moeller	Gerry Faust	vs.	Lakewood St. Edward	Michael Currence	14-12
1976	Cincinnati Moeller	Gerry Faust	vs.	Gahanna Lincoln	Neal Billman	43-5
1977	Cincinnati Moeller	Gerry Faust	vs.	Canton McKinley Senior	John Brideweser	14-2
1978	Cincinnati Princeton	Pat Mancuso	vs.	Berea	Tom Madzy	12-10
1979	Cincinnati Moeller	Gerry Faust	vs.	Parma Padua Franciscan	Tim Kohuth	41-7

* Overtime
**Two Overtimes

DIVISION I

	Champion	Coach		Runner-up	Coach	
1980	Cincinnati Moeller	Gerry Faust	vs.	Massillon Washington	Mike Currence	30-7
1981	Canton McKinley Senior	Terry Forbes	vs.	Cincinnati Moeller	Ted Bacigalupo	13-0
1982	Cincinnati Moeller	Steve Klonne	vs.	Massillon Washington	Mike Currence	35-14
1983	Cincinnati Princeton	Patrick Mancuso	vs.	Akron Garfield	William McGee	24-6
1984	Toledo St. Francis DeSales	Richard Cromwell	vs.	North Canton Hoover	Ed Glass	17-14
1985	Cincinnati Moeller	Steve Klonne	vs.	Canton McKinley Senior	Thom McDaniels	35-11
1986	Fairfield	Ben Hubbard	vs.	Lakewood St. Edward	Al O'Neil	21-20
1987	Cincinnati Princeton	Patrick Mancuso	vs.	Youngstown Boardman	Bill Bohren	14-7
1988	Cleveland St. Ignatius	Chuck Kyle	vs.	Cincinnati Princeton	Patrick Mancuso	10-7
1989	Cleveland St. Ignatius	Chuck Kyle	vs.	Cincinnati Moeller	Steve Klonne	34-28
1990	Warren Harding	Phil Annarella	vs.	Cincinnati Princeton	Pat Mancuso	28-21
1991	Cleveland St. Ignatius	Chuck Kyle	vs.	Centerville	Robert Gregg	24-21

DIVISION II

	Champion	Coach		Runner-up	Coach	
1980	Youngstown Mooney	Don Bucci	vs.	Lebanon	Jim VandeGrift	50-0
1981	Cleveland Benedictine	Augie Bossu	vs.	Trotwood Madison	John Butler	28-7
1982	Youngstown Mooney	Don Bucci	vs.	Toledo St. Francis DeSales	Richard Cromwell	12-0
1983	Brecksville	Joe Vadini	vs.	Celina	Jerry Harris	12-6
1984	Steubenville	Reno Saccoccia	vs.	Col. Whitehall-Yearling	Jeff Jones	12-9
1985	Galion	Lee Owens	vs.	Youngstown Mooney	Don Bucci	6-0
1986	Cincinnati Purcell Marian	Herb Woeste	vs.	Willoughby South	Don Hoffman	26-7
1987	Akron Buchtel	Timothy Flossie	vs.	Steubenville	Reno Saccoccia	26-14
1988	Akron Buchtel	Timothy Flossie	vs.	Steubenville	Reno Saccoccia	28-21
1989	Cleveland St. Joseph	William Gutbrod	vs.	Fostoria	Richard Kidwell	21-14
1990	St. Marys Memorial	Skip Baughman	vs.	Columbus DeSales	Bob Jacoby	14-3
1991	Fostoria	Dick Kidwell	vs.	Uniontown Lake	Jeff Durbin	21-6

DIVISION III

	Champion	Coach		Runner-up	Coach	
1980	Cleveland Benedictine	Augie Bossu	vs.	Hamilton Badin	Terry Malone	9-3
1981	Akron St. Vincent-St. Mary	John Cistone	vs.	Washington Court House	Paul Ondrus	48-7
1982	Akron St. Vincent-St. Mary	John Cistone	vs.	Ironton	Bob Lutz	21-14
1983	Elyria Catholic	Jim Rattay	vs.	Urbana	Ray DeCola	14-9
1984	Elyria Catholic	Fred Schmitz	vs.	Cincinnati McNicholas	George Marklay	45-20
1985	Columbus DeSales	Tony Pusateri	vs.	Orrville	Moe Tipton	21-13
1986	Cincinnati Acad. of Phys. Ed.	Steve Sheehan	vs.	Chagrin Falls Kenston	Paul Koballa	7-6
1987	Youngstown Mooney	Don Bucci	vs.	Thornville Sheridan	Paul Culver	30-7
1988	Akron St. Vincent-St. Mary	John Cistone	vs.	Ironton	Mike Lutz	14-12
1989	Ironton	Bob Lutz	vs.	Campbell Memorial	Edward Rozum	12-7
1990	Hamilton Badin	Terry Malone	vs.	Richfield Revere	Joe Pappano	16-6
1991	Mentor Lake Catholic	John Gibbons	vs.	Cincinnati Acad. of Phys. Ed.	Steve Sheehan	45-20

DIVISION IV

	Champion	Coach		Runner-up	Coach	
1980	Garfield Heights Trinity	Mike Hall	vs.	Cincinnati Mariemont	Tom Crosby	19-14
1981	Nelsonville-York	John Boston	vs.	Tontogany Otsego	Dan Cocke	34-16
1982	West Jefferson	John Sines	vs.	Archbold	John Downey	6-0
1983	Columbus Ready	Paul Nestor	vs.	Orrville	Morris Tipson	43-15
1984	Louisville St. Thomas Aquinas	Jack Rose	vs.	Columbus Hartley	Dick Geyer	23-0
1985	Cincinnati Acad. of Phys. Ed.	Steve Sheehan	vs.	Louisville St. Thomas Aquinas	Jack Rose	27-0
1986	Columbus Hartley	Richard Geyer	vs.	Castalia Margaretta	John Zang	47-0
1987	Columbus Academy	Paul Bernstorf	vs.	Gates Mills Hawken	Cliff Walton	21-0
1988	Canton Central Catholic	Lowell Klinefelter	vs.	Versailles	Al Hetrick	21-6
1989	Wheelersburg	Ed Miller	vs.	Warren John F. Kennedy	Dennis Zolciak	14-7
1990	Versailles	Al Hetrick	vs.	Loudonville	Mike Warbel	29-26
1991	Warren Kennedy	Tony Napolet	vs.	Springfield Catholic	Steve DeWitt	20-7

	Champion	Coach		Runner-up	Coach	
1980	Tiffin Calvert	Roger M. Kirkhart	vs.	Newark Catholic	J. D. Graham	22-0
1981	Tiffin Calvert	Roger M. Kirkhart	vs.	Newark Catholic	J. D. Graham	3-0
1982	Newark Catholic	J. D. Graham	vs.	Fostoria St. Wendelin	Eugene Peluso	14-7
1983	McComb	Bill Banning	vs.	Newark Catholic	J. D. Graham	6-0
1984	Newark Catholic	J. D. Graham	vs.	Middletown Fenwick	Richard Martin	14-6
1985	Newark Catholic	J. D. Graham	vs.	Delphos Jefferson	Kevin Fell	19-0
1986	Newark Catholic	J. D. Graham	vs.	Defiance Ayersville	Craig McCord	28-27
1987	Newark Catholic	J. D. Graham	vs.	Mogadore	Norm Lingle	16-13
1988	Archbold	John Downey	vs.	Mogadore	Norm Lingle	42-14
1989	Minster	Ken Newland	vs.	McDonald	Andrew Golubic	16-7
1990	St. Henry	Tim Boeckman	vs.	Sandusky St. Mary's	Toby Hammond	20-17
1991	Newark Catholic	J.D. Graham	vs.	Bluffton	Dennis Lee	34-13

Graham's legacy

Newark's J.D. Graham Exits At Top Of Game

When **J.D. Graham** resigned as the head football coach at **Newark Catholic High School** in March, 1992 to pursue a new career in the insurance industry, he left a legacy as one of the most successful prep football coaches in the state. A native of Wellston, he graduated in 1965 from St. Vincent DePaul High School, where he made the All-Ohio football team at quarterback. He went to Saint Joseph's College in Indiana on a football scholarship, and his entire 23-year teaching career was spent at Newark Catholic, where he became athletic director and head football coach of the Green Wave in 1971.

During his 21-season stint, Graham composed a stellar 220-30-1 record coaching teams that took fourteen league championships and were state Division V football champions seven times (1978, 1982, 1984, 1985, 1986, 1987, and 1991), an Ohio record equalled only by the Division I powerhouse Cincinnati Moeller. Graham's teams were state runners-up in 1975, 1980, 1981, and 1983; played in state championship games for eight consecutive years; and set state records for the most appearances in state championship games (11); the most playoff appearances (16); and the most playoff game victories (45). They were also selected the AP Division V state champions seven times and the UPI state champions seven times. Moreover, since Graham became athletic director, Newark Catholic's girls and boys teams have won a total of 32 state championships in football, basketball, volleyball, baseball, and track.

As keys to his success, Graham credits the strong academics, disciplined environment, and tremendous parental support at Newark Catholic, where every year between 70 and 80 of about 120 boys in the student body try out for football.

Among the more successful players that Graham coached are **Shane Montgomery**, the Division V back of the year in 1984, who went to North Carolina State, where he broke every passing record in the history of the university; and another 1984 grad, **Jeff Uhlenhake**, who became an All-American at Ohio State and is starting center for the Miami Dolphins. But probably Graham's final coaching season was the most satisfying of all for him, because in 1991, Green Wave football was truly a Graham Family affair. Not only was his daughter Michael a varsity cheerleader, but Graham also coached a state championship team that included his son Brian, who was selected an All-Ohio quarterback and kicker.

Ohio's Ten Most Popular Nicknames

1. Tigers
2. Panthers
3. Wildcats
4. Eagles/ Golden Eagles
5. Bulldogs
6. Indians
7. Warriors/ Golden Warriors
8. Vikings
9. Falcons
10. Cardinals, Trojans (tie)

Football
Championship Records

DIVISION I

MOST POINTS
Individual—24—Mark Brooks, Cincinnati Moeller vs. Massillon Washington at Cincinnati, 1980
One Team—43—Cincinnati Moeller vs. Gahanna Lincoln at Akron, 1976
Both Teams—49—Cincinnati Moeller (35) and Massillon Washington (14) at Ohio Stadium, 1982
49—Warren Harding (41) and Upper Arlington (8) at Akron Rubber Bowl, 1974

MOST TOUCHDOWNS
Individual—4—Mark Brooks, Cincinnati Moeller vs. Massillon Washington at Cincinnati, 1980
One Team—6—Warren Harding vs. Upper Arlington at Akron Rubber Bowl, 1974
6—Cincinnati Moeller vs. Gahanna Lincoln at Akron Rubber Bowl, 1976
6—Cincinnati Moeller vs. Parma Padua Franciscan at Akron Rubber Bowl, 1979
Both Teams—9—Cincinnati Moeller (4) and Cleveland St. Ignatius (5) at Ohio Stadium, 1989

MOST FIELD GOALS
Individual—2—Bill Williams, Warren Western Reserve vs. Cincinnati Princeton at Akron Rubber Bowl, 1972
One Team—2—Warren Western Reserve vs. Cincinnati Princeton at Akron Rubber Bowl, 1972
Both Teams—2—Warren Western Reserve (2) and Cincinnati Princeton (0) at Akron Rubber Bowl, 1972

MOST YARDS GAINED (RUSHING)
Individual—196—Mike Nicholson, Toledo St. Francis DeSales vs. North Canton Hoover at Ohio Stadium, 1984
One Team—379—Cincinnati Princeton vs. Akron Garfield at Ohio Stadium, 1983
Both Teams—490—Cincinnati Princeton (379) and Akron Garfield (111) at Ohio Stadium, 1983

MOST YARDS GAINED (PASSING)
Individual—347—Adam Hyzdu, Cincinnati Moeller vs. Cleveland St. Ignatius at Ohio Stadium, 1989
One Team—347—Massillon Washington vs. Cincinnati Moeller at Ohio Stadium, 1982
Both Teams—658—Cincinnati Moeller (347) and Cleveland St. Ignatius (311) at Ohio Stadium, 1982

MOST PASSES ATTEMPTED
Individual—40—Adam Hyzdu, Cincinnati Moeller vs. Cleveland St. Ignatius at Ohio Stadium, 1989
One Team—40—Cincinnati Moeller vs. Cleveland St. Ignatius at Ohio Stadium, 1989
Both Teams—67—Cincinnati Moeller (40) and Cleveland St. Ignatius (27) at Ohio Stadium, 1989

MOST PASSES COMPLETED
Individual—21—Adam Hyzdu, Cincinnati Moeller vs. Cleveland St. Ignatius at Ohio Stadium, 1989
One Team—21—Cincinnati Moeller vs. Cleveland St. Ignatius at Ohio Stadium, 1989
Both Teams—33—Cincinnati Moeller (21) and Cleveland St. Ignatius (12) at Ohio Stadium, 1989

LONGEST FIELD GOAL
49 yards—Tony Milink, Cincinnati Moeller vs. Massillon Washington at Cincinnati, Nippert Stadium, 1980

LONGEST TOUCHDOWN RUN FROM SCRIMMAGE
79 yards—James Valentine, Warren Harding vs. Upper Arlington at Akron Rubber Bowl, 1974

LONGEST SCORING PASS PLAY
80 yards—Mark Ruddy from Joe Pickens, Cleveland St. Ignatius vs. Cincinnati Moeller at Ohio Stadium, 1989

LONGEST PASS INTERCEPTION SCORE
32 yards—Mike Larkin, Cincinnati Moeller vs. Parma Padua Franciscan at Akron Rubber Bowl, 1979

LONGEST FUMBLE RECOVERY FOR A SCORE
47 yards—Stephen Weis, Cincinnati Moeller vs. Canton McKinley Senior at Ohio Stadium, 1985

LONGEST PUNT RETURN FOR A SCORE
None

LONGEST KICKOFF RETURN FOR A SCORE
None

DIVISION II

MOST POINTS
Individual—12—Michael Hardie, Youngstown Cardinal Mooney vs. Lebanon at Upper Arlington, 1980
12—John Klein, Youngstown Cardinal Mooney vs. Toledo St. Francis DeSales at Akron Rubber Bowl, 1982
12—Joe Johnson, Steubenville vs. Whitehall-Yearling at Ohio Stadium, 1984
12—Ricky Powers, Akron Buchtel vs. Steubenville at Ohio Stadium, 1988
12—Casey McBeth, Fostoria vs. Cleveland St. Joseph at Ohio Stadium, 1989
One Team—50—Youngstown Cardinal Mooney vs. Lebanon at Upper Arlington, 1980
Both Teams—50—Youngstown Cardinal Mooney (50) and Lebanon (0) at Upper Arlington, 1980

MOST TOUCHDOWNS
Individual—2—Michael Hardie, Youngstown Cardinal Mooney vs. Lebanon at Upper Arlington, 1980
2—Joe Johnson, Steubenville vs. Whitehall-Yearling at Ohio Stadium, 1984
2—John Klein, Youngstown Cardinal Mooney vs. Toledo St. Francis DeSales at Akron Rubber Bowl, 1982
2—Ricky Powers, Akron Buchtel vs. Steubenville at Ohio Stadium, 1988
2—Casey McBeth, Fostoria vs. Cleveland St. Joseph at Ohio Stadium, 1989
One Team—7—Youngstown Cardinal Mooney vs. Lebanon at Upper Arlington, 1980
Both Teams—7—Youngstown Cardinal Mooney (7) and Lebanon (0) at Upper Arlington, 1980

7—Akron Buchtel (4) and Steubenville (3) at Ohio Stadium, 1988

MOST FIELD GOALS
Individual—2—John Paul Case, Cincinnati Purcell vs. Willoughby South at Ohio Stadium, 1986
One Team—2—Cincinnati Purcell vs. Willoughby South at Ohio Stadium, 1986
Both Teams—2—Cincinnati Purcell (2) and Willoughby South (0) at Ohio Stadium, 1986

MOST YEARDS GAINED (RUSHING)
Individual—206—Ricky Powers, Akron Buchtel vs. Steubenville at Ohio Stadium, 1988
One Team—268—Akron Buchtel vs. Steubenville at Ohio Stadium, 1987
Both Teams—395—Akron Buchtel (254) and Steubenville (141) at Ohio Stadium, 1988

MOST YARDS GAINED (PASSING)
Individual—195—John Paul Case, Cincinnati Purcell vs. Willoughby South at Ohio Stadium, 1986
One Team—195—Cincinnati Purcell vs. Willoughby South at Ohio Stadium, 1986
Both Teams—303—Cincinnati Purcell (195) vs. Willoughby South (108) at Ohio Stadium, 1986

MOST PASSES ATTEMPTED
Individual—24—Jeff Wiley, Celina vs. Brecksville at Ohio Stadium, 1983
One Team—24—Celina vs. Brecksville at Ohio Stadium, 1983
Both Teams—41—Trotwood-Madison (21) and Cleveland Benedictine (20) at Akron Rubber Bowl, 1981

MOST PASSES COMPLETED
Individual—13—John Paul Case, Cincinnati Purcell vs. Willoughby South at Ohio Stadium, 1986
One Team—13—Cincinnati Purcell vs. Willoughby South at Ohio Stadium, 1986
Both Teams—22—Cincinnati Purcell (13) and Willoughby South (9) at Ohio Stadium, 1986

LONGEST FIELD GOAL
42 yards—Tom Tupa, Brecksville vs. Celina at Ohio Stadium, 1983
42 yards—John Paul Case, Cincinnati Purcell vs. Willoughby South at Ohio Stadium, 1986

LONGEST TOUCHDOWN RUN FROM SCRIMMAGE
74 yards—Ricky Powers, Akron Buchtel vs. Steubenville at Ohio Stadium, 1988

LONGEST SCORING PASS PLAY
59 yards—Pass play from Tom Tupa caught by Brian Cook for 19 yards followed by a backward pass to Kevin Good, Brecksville vs. Celina at Ohio Stadium, 1983

LONGEST PASS INTERCEPTION SCORE
55 yards—James Bonitace, Youngstown Cardinal Mooney vs. Lebanon at Upper Arlington, 1980

LONGEST FUMBLE RECOVERY FOR A SCORE
27 yards—Brian Roddy, Cleveland Benedictine vs. Trotwood-Madison at Akron Rubber Bowl, 1981

LONGEST PUNT RETURN FOR A SCORE
65 yards—Brian Brown, Cleveland St. Joseph vs. Fostoria at Ohio Stadium, 1989

LONGEST KICKOFF RETURN FOR A SCORE
None

At play in Ohio

The top five football games in attendance over the 18 years of the playoffs

1982 Division I and II Championship Games at OSU Stadium   31,412
***Cincinnati Moeller** (35), **Massillon Washington** (14);*
***Akron St. Vincent-St. Mary** (21), **Ironton** (14)*

1973 AAA Championship at Akron—   29,720
***Youngstown Mooney** (14), **Warren Western Reserve** (3)*

1980 Region 4, Division I Championship at Cincinnati—   27,000
***Cincinnati Moeller** (28), **Cincinnati Princeton** (3)*

1980 Division I Championship at Cincinnati—   22,692
***Cincinnati Moeller** (30), **Massillon Washington** (7)*

1982 Division I Championship at Akron—   20,325
***Canton McKinley Senior** (13), **Cincinnati Moeller** (0)*

DIVISION III

MOST POINTS

Individual—18—Bryan Thomas, Elyria Catholic vs. Brookville at Akron Rubber Bowl, 1976

18—Chris Dolle, Cincinnati Wyoming vs. Elyria Catholic at Akron Rubber Bowl, 1977

18—Frank Stams, Akron St. Vincent-St. Mary vs. Ironton at Ohio Stadium, 1982

18—Al McKinney, Elyria Catholic vs. Cincinnati McNicholas at Ohio Stadium, 1984

One Team—48—Akron St. Vincent-St. Mary vs. Washington Court House at Upper Arlington, 1981

Both Teams—65—Elyria Catholic (45) and Cincinnati McNicholas (20) at Ohio Stadium, 1984

MOST TOUCHDOWNS

Individual—3—Bryan Thomas, Elyria Catholic vs. Brookville at Akron Rubber Bowl, 1976

3—Chris Dolle, Cincinnati Wyoming vs. Elyria Catholic at Akron Rubber Bowl, 1977

3—Frank Stams, Akron St. Vincent-St. Mary vs. Ironton at Ohio Stadium, 1982

3—Al McKinney, Elyria Catholic vs. Cincinnati McNicholas at Ohio Stadium, 1984

One Team—7—Akron St. Vincent-St. Mary vs. Washington Court House at Upper Arlington, 1981

Both Teams—9—Elyria Catholic (6) and Cincinnati McNicholas (3) at Ohio Stadium, 1984

MOST FIELD GOALS

Individual—1—Tony Donelly, Louisville St. Thomas Aquinas vs. Norwalk at Dayton Welcome Stadium, 1974

1—Rich Cassano, Hamilton Badin vs. Cleveland Benedictine at Parma, 1980

1—Robert Pinkerton, Urbana vs. Elyria Catholic at Ohio Stadium, 1983

1—Jim Molnar, Elyria Catholic vs. Cincinnati McNicholas at Ohio Stadium, 1984

One Team—1—Cleveland Benedictine vs. Ironton at Massillon, 1973

1—Louisville St. Thomas Aquinas at Norwalk at Dayton Welcome Stadium, 1974

1—Brookville vs. Elyria Catholic at Akron Rubber Bowl, 1976

1—Hamilton Badin vs. Cleveland Benedictine at Springfield, Evans Stadium, 1980

1—Urbana vs. Elyria Catholic at Ohio Stadium, 1983

1—Elyria Catholic vs. Cincinnati McNicholas at Ohio Stadium, 1984

Both Teams—1—Cleveland Benedictine (1) and Ironton (0) at Massillon, 1973

1—Louisville St. Thomas Aquinas (1) and Norwalk (0) at Dayton Welcome Stadium, 1974

1—Brookville (1) and Elyria Catholic (0) at Akron Rubber Bowl, 1976

1—Hamilton Badin (1) and Cleveland Benedictine (0) at Springfield, Evans Stadium, 1980

1—Urbana (1) and Elyria Catholic (0) at Ohio Stadium, 1983

1—Elyria Catholic (1) and Cincinnati McNicholas (0) at Ohio Stadium, 1984

MOST YARDS GAINED (RUSHING)

Individual—166—Al McKinney, Elyria Catholic vs. Cincinnati McNicholas at Ohio Stadium, 1984

One Team—293—Youngstown Mooney vs. Thornville Sheridan at Ohio Stadium, 1987

Both Teams—368—Youngstown Mooney (293) and Thornville Sheridan (75) at Ohio Stadium, 1987

MOST YARDS GAINED (PASSING)

Individual—143—Mark Snyder, Ironton vs. Akron St. Vincent-St. Mary at Ohio Stadium, 1982

One Team—194—Cincinnati McNicholas vs. Elyria Catholic at Ohio Stadium, 1984

Both Teams—277—Cincinnati McNicholas (194) and Elyria Catholic (83) at Ohio Stadium, 1984

MOST PASSES ATTEMPTED

Individual—19—Mark Snyder, Ironton vs. Akron St. Vincent-St. Mary at Ohio Stadium, 1982

One Team—28—Cincinnati McNicholas vs. Elyria Catholic at Ohio Stadium, 1984

Both Teams—32—Cincinnati McNicholas (28) and Elyria Catholic (4) at Ohio Stadium, 1984

MOST PASSES COMPLETED

Individual—12—Brent Wilcoxon, Ironton vs. Akron St. Vincent-St. Mary at Akron Rubber Bowl, 1979

12—Mark Snyder, Ironton vs. St. Vincent-St. Mary at Ohio Stadium, 1982

One Team—13—Ironton vs. Akron St. Vincent-St. Mary at Ohio Stadium, 1982

12—Mark Snyder, Ironton vs. Akron St. Vincent-St. Mary at Ohio Stadium, 1982

13—Cincinnati McNicholas vs. Elyria Catholic at Ohio Stadium, 1984

Both Teams—16—Cincinnati McNicholas (13) and Elyria Catholic (3) at Ohio Stadium, 1984

LONGEST FIELD GOAL

35 yards—Tony Donelly, Louisville St. Thomas Aquinas vs. Norwalk at Dayton Welcome Stadium, 1974

LONGEST TOUCHDOWN RUN FROM SCRIMMAGE

78 yards—Bryan Thomas, Elyria Catholic vs. Brookville at Akron Rubber Bowl, 1976

LONGEST SCORING PASS PLAY

53 yards—Al McKinney from Keith Rybarczyk, Elyria Catholic vs. Cincinnati McNicholas at Ohio Stadium, 1984

LONGEST PASS INTERCEPTION FOR A SCORE

46 yards—Ron Traut, Elyria Catholic vs. Cincinnati McNicholas at Ohio Stadium, 1984

LONGEST FUMBLE RECOVERY FOR A SCORE

65 yards—Bryan Thomas, Elyria Catholic vs. Cincinnati Wyoming at Akron Rubber Bowl, 1977

LONGEST PUNT RETURN FOR A SCORE

75 yards—Al McKinney, Elyria Catholic vs. Cincinnati McNicholas at Ohio Stadium, 1984

LONGEST KICKOFF RETURN FOR A SCORE

95 yards—Bryan Thomas, Elyria Catholic vs. Brookville at Akron Rubber Bowl, 1976

DIVISION IV

MOST POINTS
Individual—24—Terrence Davis, Columbus Hartley vs. Castalia Margaretta at Ohio Stadium, 1986
One Team—47—Columbus Hartley vs. Castalia Margaretta at Ohio Stadium, 1986
Both Teams—58—Columbus Bishop Ready (43) and Orrville (15) at Ohio Stadium, 1983

MOST TOUCHDOWNS
Individual—4—Terrence Davis, Columbus Hartley vs. Castalia Margaretta at Ohio Stadium, 1986
One Team—7—Columbus Hartley vs. Castalia Margaretta at Ohio Stadium, 1986
Both Teams—8—Columbus Bishop Ready (6) and Orrville (2) at Ohio Stadium, 1983

MOST FIELD GOALS
Individual—2—Mark Athon, Cincinnati Academy of Physical Education vs. Louisville St. Thomas Aquinas at Ohio Stadium, 1985
One Team—2—Cincinnati Academy of Physical Education vs. Louisville St. Thomas Aquinas at Ohio Stadium, 1985
Both Teams—2—Cincinnati Academy of Physical Education (2) and Louisville St. Thomas Aquinas (0) at Ohio Stadium, 1985

MOST YARDS GAINED (RUSHING)
Individual—230—Jewell Jackson, Columbus Bishop Ready vs. Orrville at Ohio Stadium, 1983
One Team—468—Columbus Bishop Ready vs. Orrville at Ohio Stadium, 1983
Both Teams—552—Columbus Bishop Ready (468) and Orrville (84) at Ohio Stadium, 1983

MOST YARDS GAINED (PASSING)
Individual—230—Chris Lorentz, Louisville St. Thomas Aquinas vs. Columbus Hartley at Ohio Stadium, 1984
One Team—230—Louisville St. Thomas Aquinas vs. Columbus Hartley at Ohio Stadium, 1984
Both Teams—230—Louisville St. Thomas Aquinas (230) and Columbus Hartley (0) at Ohio Stadium, 1984

MOST PASSES ATTEMPTED
Individual—25—Mike Coukart, Castalia Margaretta vs. Columbus Hartley at Ohio Stadium, 1986
One Team—25—Castalia Margaretta vs. Columbus Hartley at Ohio Stadium, 1986
Both Teams—30—Louisville St. Thomas Aquinas (24) and Columbus Hartley (6) at Ohio Stadium, 1984

MOST PASSES COMPLETED
Individual—15—Chris Lorentz, Louisville St. Thomas Aquinas vs. Columbus Hartley at Ohio Stadium, 1984
One Team—15—Louisville St. Thomas Aquinas vs. Columbus Hartley at Ohio Stadium, 1984

Lonesome polecat

Pro football's hottest offense—the run-and-shoot—was invented three decades ago in Middletown, Ohio

The newest professional offensive wrinkle, the run-and-shoot, as plied by the Houston Oilers and the Detroit Lions, is actually an old offensive wrinkle as plied by an Ohio high school team in 1958. That was when Middletown Middies coach Glenn "Tiger" Ellison arranged his offense to match his personnel.

Ellison had small linemen and smaller backs so he devised what he called "the lonesome polecat," a quarterback under center and everybody else spread out. Essentially, the offense tries to stretch a defense from side-to-side, utilizing speed and elusiveness. It worked so well (the Middies went 38-7 in four-plus seasons), Ellison wrote a book on it, which came out in 1963, the year he went to OSU as an assistant coach.

Mouse Davis introduced it into pro football when he coached with Jack Pardee and the USFL Gamblers in the early 1980s, but he first learned about it by reading Ellison's book, and adapting it to his Oregon high school team, which then won the state championship. Thus football, like literature, revolves its characters around the same basic plots; they only seem different. ▶

Source: Cincinnati Enquirer; Jerry Nardiello, Middletown Journal

Both Teams—15—Louisville St. Thomas Aquinas (15) and Columbus Hartley (0) at Ohio Stadium, 1984
LONGEST FIELD GOAL
42 yards—Dave Seagraves, Brookville vs. Elyria Catholic at Akron Rubber Bowl, 1976
LONGEST TOUCHDOWN RUN FROM SCRIMMAGE
64 yards—Trent Galentin, Nelsonville-York vs. Tontogany-Otsego at Groveport-Madison, 1981
64 yards—Ed Miller, Columbus Ready vs. Orrville at Ohio Stadium, 1983
LONGEST SCORING PASS PLAY
67 yards—Ken Baltes from Jaime Mescher, Versailles vs. Canton Central Catholic at Ohio Stadium, 1988
LONGEST PASS INTERCEPTION FOR A SCORE
63 yards—Randy Miller, Tontogany-Otsego vs. Nelsonville-York at Groveport-Madison, 1981
LONGEST FUMBLE RECOVERY FOR A SCORE
65 yards—Randy Miller, Tontogany-Otsego vs. Nelsonville-York at Groveport-Madison, 1981
LONGEST PUNT RETURN FOR A SCORE
None
LONGEST KICKOFF RETURN FOR A SCORE
None

DIVISION V

MOST POINTS
Individual—24—Pat Sauder, Archbold vs. Mogadore at Ohio Stadium, 1988
One Team—42—Archbold vs. Mogadore at Ohio Stadium, 1988
Both Teams—56—Archbold (43) and Mogadore (14) at Ohio Stadium, 1988
MOST TOUCHDOWNS
Individual—4—Pat Sauder, Archbold vs. Mogadore at Ohio Stadium, 1988
One Team—6—Archbold vs. Mogadore at Ohio Stadium, 1988
Both Teams—8—Newark Catholic (4) and Defiance Ayersville (4) at Ohio Stadium, 1986
8—Archbold (6) and Mogadore (2) at Ohio Stadium, 1988
MOST FIELD GOALS
Individual—2—Pat Ariss, Middletown Fenwick vs. Newark Catholic at Ohio Stadium, 1984
One Team—2—Middletown Fenwick vs. Newark Catholic at Ohio Stadium, 1984
Both Teams—2—Mogadore (1) and Covington (1) at Akron Rubber Bowl, 1979
2—Middletown Fenwick (2) and Newark Catholic (0) at Ohio Stadium, 1984
MOST YARDS GAINED (RUSHING)
Individual—135—Tim Musselman, Newark Catholic vs. Middletown Fenwick at Ohio Stadium, 1984
One Team—300—Defiance Ayersville vs. Newark Catholic at Ohio Stadium, 1986
Both Teams—359—Mogadore (179) vs. Covington (180) at Akron Rubber Bowl, 1979
MOST YARDS GAINED (PASSING)
Individual—324—Jeremy Montgomery, Newark Catholic vs. Defiance Ayersville at Ohio Stadium, 1986
One Team—324—Newark Catholic vs. Defiance Ayersville at Ohio Stadium, 1986
Both Teams—412—Newark Catholic (324) and Defiance Ayersville (88) at Ohio Stadium, 1986
MOST PASSES ATTEMPTED
Individual—29—Jeremy Montgomery, Newark Catholic vs. Defiance Ayersville at Ohio Stadium, 1986
One Team—29—Newark Catholic vs. Defiance Ayersville at Ohio Stadium, 1986
Both Teams—44—Newark Catholic (29) and Defiance Ayersville (15) at Ohio Stadium, 1986
44—Newark Catholic (27) and Mogadore (17) at Ohio Stadium, 1987
MOST PASSES COMPLETED
Individual—21—Jeremy Montgomery, Newark Catholic vs. Defiance Ayersville at Ohio Stadium, 1986
One Team—21—Newark Catholic vs. Defiance Ayersville at Ohio Stadium, 1986
Both Teams—27—Newark Catholic (21) and Defiance Ayersville (6) at Ohio Stadium, 1986
LONGEST FIELD GOAL
38 yards—Pat Ariss, Middletown Fenwick vs. Newark Catholic at Ohio Stadium, 1984
LONGEST TOUCHDOWN RUN FROM SCRIMMAGE
91 yards—Joe Schmidt, Covington vs. Mogadore at Akron Rubber Bowl, 1979
LONGEST SCORING PASS PLAY
43 yards—Chuck Ritzler from Tim Sieslove, Tiffin Calvert vs. Newark Catholic Mansfield, Arlin Field, 1980
LONGEST PASS INTERCEPTION FOR A SCORE
None
LONGEST FUMBLE RECOVERY FOR A SCORE
95 yards—Jamie Bright, Marion Pleasant vs. Lorain Clearview at Ohio Wesleyan, 1972
LONGEST PUNT RETURN FOR A SCORE
70 yards—Tom McCoy, Ashtabula St. John vs. Crooksville at Akron Rubber Bowl, 1977
LONGEST KICKOFF RETURN FOR A SCORE
None

High School Football All-Star Games

Year	Where Played	North Score	South Score	Winning coach
1946	Toledo	6	21	F. Leahy (Notre Dame)
1947	Canton	6	6	Tie—Ray Eliot (Illinois)—Wes Fesler (Ohio State)
1948	Canton	20	0	Harry Strobel (Barberton)
1949	Massillon	13	20	Glenn Ellison (Middletown)
1950	Toledo	33	7	Bup Rearick (Canton McKinley)—A. Morningstar (Mansfield)
1951	Middletown	7	20	C. Thackera (Hamilton)
1952	Akron	19	21	George Vlerebome (Zanesville)
1953	Canton	18	7	Chuck Mather (Massillon)
1954	Springfield	28	6	Jim Robinson (Canton Lehman)
1955	Mansfield	26	13	Mel Knowlton (Alliance)
1956	Canton	19	19	Tie—Wade Watts (Canton McKinley)—R. Webster (Columbus East)
1957	Canton	0	26	Hugh Hindman (Columbus North)
1958	Canton	26	0	Hilton Murphy (Toledo DeVilbiss)
1959	Canton	19	0	Fred George (Cleveland Latin)
1960	Canton	18	8	Leo Strang (Massillon)
1961	Canton	6	14	Jim Eby (Dayton Wright)
1962	Canton	12	18	Bob Wion (Martins Ferry)
1963	Canton	6	12	Bron Bracevich (Cincinnati Bacon)
1964	Canton	8	20	Mel Adams (Logan)
1965	Canton	16	6	Earle Bruce (Massillon)
1966	Canton	8	18	Dick Walker (Columbus Watterson)
1967	Canton	12	40	Lou Florio (Hamilton Garfield)
1968	Canton	12	12	Tie—Bill Wilkins (Shelby)—Dick Haines (Dover)
1969	Canton	16	8	Ron Chismar (Canton McKinley)
1970	Canton	6	7	Abe Bryan (Steubenville)
1971	Canton	14	7	Bob Commings (Massillon)
1972	Canton	13	6	Tom Batta (Warren Harding)
1973	Canton	25	0	Babe Flossie (Akron Garfield)
1974	Canton	21	0	Don Bucci (Youngstown Cardinal Mooney)
1975	Columbus	27	19	Ed Glass (Warren Harding)
1976	Columbus	13	12	Bill Jones (Findlay)
1977	Canton	14	0	Bill Ricco (Walsh Jesuit)
1978	Canton	0	23	Fred Zechman (Miami Trace)
1979	Canton	15	7	Paul Starkey (Louisville)
1980	Massillon	17	14	Pat Gucciardo (Toledo Whitmer)
1981	Akron	3	7	Dale Robertson (Hamilton)
1982	Massillon	32	0	John Cistone (Akron St. Vincent)
1983	Massillon	11	10	Tom Madzy (Berea)
1984	Massillon	3	7	Tom Kocica (Colerain)
1985	Massillon	31	10	Dick Kerschbaum (Lakewood)
1986	Massillon	12	6	Thom McDaniels (Canton McKinley)
1987	Massillon	24	14	Glenn Sutherin (East Liverpool)
1988	Massillon	15	17	Lou Cynkar (Forest Park)
1989	North	0	23	Leonard Rush (Lima Senior)
1990	Massillon	26	0	Dick Kidwell (Fostoria)
1991	Massillon	12	21	Bill Goodwin(Allen East)
Totals		*688*	*532*	

Victories

South Victories 18
North Victories 25
Tie Games 3

Shut Outs

South 3
North 8

The Harbin Football Team Rating System

As modified and used by the Ohio High School Athletic Association

Purpose

The purpose of this system is to provide a fair and objective method of determining the high school football teams in each division that will qualify for the post season playoffs.

Based solely on a team's record, this system does not reflect each team's accomplishments during the current season.

Basis

This system is based on how successful each team is against its opponents and how successful these opponents are during the season. Rating points are awarded in various ways, the total of these points determines a team's ultimate standing.

This system DOES NOT rank teams on the basis of potential team strength.

The score by which a team may win DOES NOT affect that team's ultimate point total or ranking.

These ratings DO NOT predict the outcome of any games remaining to be played.

These ratings DO NOT compare the relative strength of teams in different parts of the state.

These ratings DO NOT reflect the personal opinion of anyone.

Authorization—This system and many modifications may have been approved and authorized by the Board of Control of the Ohio High School Athletic Association.

Point system

On the first level:

    Points are earned for each game a team wins. *(Full value)*

    Points are earned for each game a team ties. *(One-half value)*

On the second level:

    Points are earned for each game a defeated opponent wins. *(Full value)*

    Points are earned for each game a defeated opponent ties. *(One-half value)*

    Points are earned for each game a tied opponent wins. *(One-half value)*

    Points are earned for each game a tied opponent ties. *(One-fourth value)*

Points are earned on the following basis:

	Win	**Tie**
Division V	1.0 points	0.50 points
Division IV	1.5 points	0.75 points
Division III	2.0 points	1.00 points
Division II	2.5 points	1.25 points
Division I	3.0 points	1.50 points

Awarding of First Level Points

1) For all teams playing a 10 game schedule:

    a. Points are earned for each game a team wins *(full value)*

    b. Points are earned for each game a team ties *(half of full value)*

    c. No points are awarded for game lost.

2) For all teams playing fewer than 10 games:

    a. Add total first level points earned as explained under #1, section a, b, c.

    b. This total is then divided by the number of games actually played. To determine total first level points, the quotient is then added to the total points earned, once for each open date.

Awarding of Second Level Points

Second level points are awarded as a result of a team defeating or tying an opponent or, sometimes, an open date according to the following formula:

    1) Defeating an opponent awards the winner the loser's first level points.

    2) Tying an opponent awards the winner the loser's first level points.

    3) No second level points are awarded for losing to any opponent.

4) Defeating a nonmember OHSAA school. The school is assigned a point value based upon male enrollment in grades 9-11. Second level points are awarded based upon the point value of the OHSAA nonmember school multiplied times the number of victories by the nonmember school. (one-half value for a tie)

5) A schedule open date. Second level points are totaled, divided by the number of games played and the quotient divided by 2 ten added to the second level point total.

6) An unscheduled open date (opponent on strike, closed for economic reasons, fails to honor contract, etc.). Second level points points are totaled, divided by the number of games played and the quotient added to the second level point total.

Calculation of Total Points:

The sum from the Awarding of Second Level Points above will be added to the first level points credited from Awarding of First Level Points to determine the total points.

Example: Team A plays a nine game schedule consisting of seven (7) OHSAA member schools, two (2) nonmember schools with one open date. Team A won eight (8) games losing one (1) to a nonmember school (out-of-state). The eight opponents defeated consisted of four Division I teams at 3 points each, three Division III teams at 2 points each and one nonmember team at 2 points which won 6 games during the season.

First level points are calculated as follows:

Division I	4 schools at 3 points	=12 points
Division III	3 schools at 2 points	=6 points
Division III	1 nonmember school at 2 points	=2 points
	20 TOTAL FIRST LEVEL POINTS	

Total First Level Points earned	20	
Divided by number of games played	9	
Equals	2.2222	quotient
Add	20	Total first level points earned
Plus	2.2222	First level value for one open date
Equals	22.2222	Total first level points credited

Second level points are earned and credited based upon the victories attained by OHSAA member schools over their opponents. Team A earned 92.5000 second level points.

Since Team A had one open date on their schedule, defeated one nonmember school and lost to one nonmember school, adjustments are made to credit Team A at the second level for the one open date and the one victory over a nonmember school. No second level points are credited in the game lost to a nonmember school.

Calculation:	92.5000	Second level points credited from OHSAA member schools
Divided by	7	Number of games played against OHSAA member schools
Equals	13.2143	Average value of each win at second level
	92.5000	Second level points credited from OHSAA member schools
Plus	6.6072	Second level value for one open date (1/2 of 13.2143)
Plus	12.0000	Second level value for win over nonmember school (2 points x 6 wins)
	111.1072	Total second level points credited
Summary:	22.2222	First level points
	111.1072	Second level poinnts
	133.3294	Total points

Compilation

Due to a complexity of the system, computer services are used to record and tally the points earned by each team. The computer operates only on the data fed into it—that is, did a team win, tie or lose. The margin of victory is not a factor. A win by one point or 20 points counts only as a win—nothing more.

Coaches Hall of Fame

1970
John Brickles—New Philadelphia
Paul Brown—Massillon
C. O. Cartledge—Steubenville
Glen Ellison—Middletown
Ernie Godfrey—Wooster
Charles Mather—Massillon
Jack Mollenkopf—Toledo Waite
Jim Robinson—Canton Lehman

1971
H. O. Beck—Warren Harding
Dick Gallagher—Ironton
Woody Hayes—New Philadelphia
Merle Hutson—Crestline
Mel Knowlton—Alliance
Mack Pemberton—Columbus West
H. B. Rearick—Canton McKinley
George Vlerebome—Zanesville

1972
Bill Kidd—New Philadelphia
John Knapick—Compbell
Carl Schroeder—Massillon
Gil Smith—Van Wert
Ralph Webster—Columbus East

1973
Mike Hagely—Columbus North
Lou Meszaros—Toledo Woodward
Mary Moorehead—Upper Arlington
Elmo Lingrel—Middletown
Eddie Wentz—Akron St. Vincent

1974
John McAfee—Youngstown South
Chester McPhee—Youngstown Chaney
Dr. Lee Tressel—Mentor-Massillon
George Wertz—Piqua
John Wirtz—Cleveland St. Ignatius

1975
Dick Barrett—Youngstown East
Bron C. Bacevich—Cincinnati Roger Bacon
Hilton H. Murphy—Toledo
Ralph Robinette—Youngstown Rayen
Schuyler "Sky" Wharton—Coshocton

1976
Abe Bryan—Steubenville
Edwin "Bud" Bucher—Lisbon
Junie Ferrall—Barberton
Joseph A. Rich—Mineral Ridge
Henry "Hank" Schroth—Carlisle

1977
Fred Brideweser—Navarre
Michael Krino—Akron
Gertrude H. Schroeder—Massillon
Carlton H. Smith—Columbus
Charles C. Thackara—Hamilton
Ben Wilson—Warren

1978
James Bowlus—London
Jack Llewellyn—Bay Village
Earl McCaskey—Lorain
Bob McFarren—Wintersville
Dr. George M. Wilcoxon—Alliance

1979
Bill Edwards—Fostoria
Fred Garretson—Hamilton
Gordon Larson—Akron
Leo Strang—Massillon
Lou Venditti—Canton
Fritz Howell—Columbus

1980
James W. Aiken—Canton
Harold Castor—Arlington
Dan Flossie—Akron
Sid Gillman—Philadelphia Eagles
Robert S. Kettlewell—Wintersville
Joseph Rufus—Cleveland

1981
James Eby—Dayton
Hugh Hindman—Columbus
Russ Pastuck—Munroe Falls
Tom Phillips—Laramie, Wyoming
Robert H. Whittaker—Put-In-Bay

1982
Mel Adams—Logan
Tom Campana—Kent Roosevelt
James Dutey—Coal Grove
Ted Federici—Oregon Clay
Bob Lewis—Wyoming
Richard Armstrong—O.H.S.A.A.

1983
Tom Armstrong—Dover
Gerald Faust—Dayton
Ralph Quesinberry—Chagrin Falls
Herald Roettger—Lockland
Bob Wion—Worthington

1984
Augie Bossu—Benedictine
Thomas Carey—Youngstown
Pierre F. Hill—Martins Ferry
Gene Keel—West Jefferson
Robert D. Smith—Fremont

1985
John "Jack" Britt—Painesville
Wilbur "Weeb" Ewbank—Oxford
Doyt L. Perry—Florida
Lawrence ArtTeynor—New Philadelphia
Wade Watts—California

1986
William J. Gutbrod—Cleveland
Jerry Harkrader—Middletown
Dick Kerin—Cincinnati
Robert McNea—Columbus
Harold Meyer—Florida
Bill Ricco—Stow

1987
Joe Vadini—Brecksville
William Shunkwiler—Warren Harding
Don Hertzer—North Canton
Frank Howe—Northland
Blair C. Irvin—Covington

1988
Bill Hoffeld—Cincinnati
Jack Ryan—Columbus
Fred Dafler—Columbus
Ned Booher—Northmont
Bill Jacobs—Cleveland
Frank Alberta—Canton

1989
Al Carrino—Bristolville
George Daniel—Lorain
Cliff Foust—Garfield
Wilbur Rutenschroer—Cincinnati
Paul Starky—Louisville
Bob Stuart—Columbus

1990
Tom Ballaban—St. Xavier
L. C. Boles—Fostoria
Charles Buckenmeyer—Napoleon
Joe Carlo—Berea
Billie J. McFarren—Dalton
Paul Keltner—Albany

1991
Larry L. Fruth—Wauseon
David Hurst—Sycamore
Howard Sales—Oakwood/Kettering
Doug Thompson—Fostoria/Lorain
Tom Walters—Southeast/Jefferson
Ralph Haffner—Jewitt-Scio

All-Ohio Team

Columbus—The 1991 Associated Press Division I All-Ohio high school football team, selected on the recommendations of a state-wide panel of sports writers and broadcasters

Division I

First Team Offense

Pos.	Player	School	Hgt.	Wgt.	Class
End	Aaron Gralak	Findlay	6-3	185	Senior
End	Ronnie Burr	Canton McKinley	6-2	174	Senior
End	Omar Provitt	Warren Harding	6-1	165	Senior
End	Thad Persinger	Talawanda	5-10	156	Senior
End	Jeff Cummings	Reynoldsburg	5-9	160	Senior
Line	Korey Stringer	Warren Harding	6-5	298	Senior
Line	Juan Porter	Cleveland St. Ignatius	6-4	315	Senior
Line	Eric Wendt	Moeller	6-5	275	Senior
Line	Jim Rosko	Youngstown Boardman	6-2	225	Senior
Line	Larry Nosse	Euclid	6-8	235	Senior
QB	Jeff Stewart	Reynoldsburg	6-3	170	Senior
QB	Tim Austing	Elder	6-1	190	Senior
Back	Chris Jaquillard	Toledo Woodward	6-0	205	Senior
Back	Travis McGuire	Massillon Washington	6-0	185	Senior
Back	Tracy McDaniel	Fairborn	6-1	190	Senior
Back	Brian Thomas	Grove City	5-8	165	Senior
Back	John Mandato	Eastlake North	5-10	185	Senior
Back	James Olverson	Princeton	6-0	180	Senior
Kicker	Josh Jackson	Logan	5-11	160	Senior

First Team Defense

Pos.	Player	School	Hgt.	Wgt.	Class
Line	Terry Cole	Springfield South	6-1	210	Senior
Line	Paul Conn	Mansfield Senior	6-4	235	Senior
Line	Darius Card	Lakewood St. Edward	6-1	220	Senior
Line	Tim Robbins	North Canton Hoover	6-5	236	Senior
Line	Corey Glass	Princeton	6-1	195	Senior
LB	Jayson Gwinn	Columbus Brookhaven	6-3	230	Senior
LB	Marty Kilbane	Cleveland St. Ignatius	6-3	225	Senior
LB	Josh Johnson	Princeton	6-1	195	Senior
LB	Benny King	Dublin	6-1	215	Senior
LB	Eric Wright	Massillon Washington	5-11	200	Senior
Back	Corey Sewell	Fremont Ross	6-1	185	Senior
Back	Gary Kuhn	Toledo Start	6-3	210	Senior
Back	Lee Struck	Grove City	6-1	195	Senior
Back	Dan Colson	Middletown	6-0	185	Senior
Back	Tony Everhart	Middletown	6-1	185	Senior
Back	Steve Poston	Lancaster	5-11	170	Junior
Punter	Matt Hirsch	Colerain	6-0	165	Senior

Backs of the Year: Chris Jaquillard, Toledo Woodward; Travis McGuire, Massillon Washington.
Lineman of the Year: Korey Stringer, Warren Harding.
Coach of the Year: Bryan Deal, Dublin.

Division II

First Team Offense

Pos.	Player	School	Hgt.	Wgt.	Class
End	Bob Cotter	Marysville	6-4	220	Senior
End	Wesley McDaniel	Dayton Dunbar	6-0	185	Senior
End	Kevin Marn	Cleveland V.A.-S.J.	6-4	215	Senior
Line	Jack Anders	Miami Trace	6-2	250	Senior
Line	Scott Tripp	Uniontown Lake	6-4	275	Senior
Line	Chris Gee	Fostoria	6-11/2	213	Senior
Line	Rex Rosmus	Urbana	6-0	250	Junior
Line	Dan Wasniak	Solon	6-1	225	Senior
Line	Paul Collins	Norwood	6-2	265	Senior
Line	Dan Casar	Louisville	6-4	228	Senior
QB	Derek Kidwell	Fostoria	6-4	225	Senior
Back	Marc Edwards	Norwood	6-2	210	Junior
Back	Michael Parker	Portsmouth	5-9	185	Junior
Back	Kim Herring	Solon	5-11	190	Junior

Back	Bill West	Tiltonsville Buckeye	5-9	190	Junior
Back	Chuck Penzenik	Richfield Revere	6-0	185	Senior
Kicker	Jim Watts	Lemon-Monroe	6-1	170	Junior

First Team Defense

Pos.	Player	School	Hgt.	Wgt.	Class
Line	Tom Breitigam	Fostoria	6-0	229	Senior
Line	Darrell DeWitt	Bay Village Bay	6-0	230	Senior
Line	Nate Burress	Steubenville	6-2	230	Senior
Line	Mical Brown	Akron Buchtel	6-3	215	Senior
Line	Davon Battles	Dayton Dunbar	6-2	220	Junior
Line	Kevin Zerowski	Chstrind W. Geauga	6-6	220	Senior
LB	Matt Christopher	Uniontown Lake	6-3	227	Senior
LB	D. J. Jones	Lebanon	6-5	262	Senior
LB	John Williams	Parma Holy Name	6-0	210	Senior
LB	Jon McCray	Akron Buchtel	6-2	220	Senior
LB	Ray Long	Clyde	6-2	200	Senior
Back	Kai Walkr	Col. Linden-McKinley	5-11	170	Senior
Back	Mike Elston	St. Marys Memorial	6-4	220	Junior
Back Dan Iwan		Solon	5-10	155	Senior
Back Richard Brown		Dayton Dunbar	6-3	170	Senior
Back	Jevon Brunston	Columbus Eastmoor	6-1	170	Senior
Punter	Andy Tracy	Bowling Green	6-2	192	Senior

Back of the Year: Derek Kidwell, Fostoria.
Lineman of the Year: Matt Christopher, Uniontown Lake.
Coach of the Year: Jeff Bayuk, Hubbard.

Division III

First Team Offense

Pos.	Player	School	Hgt.	Wgt.	Class
End	Joe Jurevicius	Mentor Lake Catholic	6-5	205	Junior
End	Chris Campbell	Akron St. V.-St. M.	6-1	175	Senior
End	James Farley	Medina Buckeye	6-2	185	Senior
End	Jeremy McClure	Wintersville	6-0	160	Junior
Line	Joe Watts	Minerva	6-2	240	Senior
Line	Matt Jones	Bucyrus	6-7	320	Senior
Line	Frank Hall	Ashtabula Harbor	6-1	270	Senior
Line	Chad McGarry	Youngstown Mooney	6-1	207	Senior
Line	Norman Ayers	Bellaire	6-3	290	Senior
Line	Brian Jones	Springfield Northeastern	6-5	270	Senior
QB	Matt Knee	Springboro	6-3	170	Senior
QB	Shawn Buescher	Williamsport Westfall	6-1	175	Senior
Back	Cliff Foght	Bucyrus	5-9	175	Senior
Back	Lou Mongenel	Ashtabula Harbor	5-7	165	Jr.
Back	Jerome Christian	Girard	6-2	195	Senior
Back	Terry Killens	Purcell Marian	6-3	205	Senior
Back	George Brandon	Twinsburg Chamberlin	6-0	175	Senior
Kicker	Steve Brinkman	Kettering Alter	5-9	150	Senior

First Team Defense

Pos.	Player	School	Hgt.	Wgt.	Class
Line	Luke Fickell	Columbus DeSales	6-5	240	Senior
Line	Eric Bronson	Mentor Lake Catholic	6-3	250	Senior
Line	Chris Holbrook	St. Paris Graham	6-3	265	Senior
Line	Jason May	Byesville Meadowbrook	6-3	305	Senior
Line	R. C. Jones	Youngstown Mooney	6-3	241	Senior
Line	Steve Jarrett	Castalia Margaretta	6-0	182	Senior
LB	Mike Barwick	Cape	5-8	200	Senior
LB	Matt Crutcher	Washington Court House	5-9	205	Senior
LB	Bill Hubans	Oak Harbor	6-3	205	Senior
LB	Marty Loncar	Mentor Lake Catholic	6-0	195	Senior
LB	Chris Elias	Bexley	5-10	175	Senior
LB	Joe Heinzer	Canton Central Catholic	6-2	200	Senior
LB	Nick Bosh	Magnolia Sandy Valley	6-3	205	Senior
Back	Mike Burcham	Ironton	6-2	215	Senior
Back	Mike Sechrest	Bellaire	6-3	205	Senior
Back	Nick Magistrale	Columbus DeSales	6-2	180	Senior
Back	Rashawn Byrd	Cape	5-9	170	Senior
Back	Andy Hulse	Circleville Logan Elm	6-4	183	Senior

| Punter | Curt McGuire | Uhrichsville Claymont | 6-2 | 185 | Senior |

Backs of the Year: Cliff Foght, Bucyrus; Terry Killens, Purcell Marian.
Lineman of the Year: Luke Fickell, Columbus DeSales.
Coaches of the Year: Joe Jeswald, Girard; Randy Felumlee, Utica.

Division IV

First Team Offense

Pos.	Player	School	Hgt.	Wgt.	Class
End	Roger Plowman	Cardington-Lincoln	6-2	190	Senior
End	DaWann Gray	Beachwood	5-10	165	Junior
End	Tim McNeil	Warren Kennedy	5-11	180	Senior
End	Chris Wisvari	Hannibal River	6-1	160	Senior
End	Aaron Erter	Springfield Catholic	5-10	170	Senior
Line	Matt Meyer	Bloomdale Elmwood	5-10	180	Senior
Line	Matt Spellman	Andover Pymatuning Valley	6-2	215	Senior
Line	Brian Fortman	Sidney Lehman	6-4	226	Junior
Line	Kevin Hyme	Columbus Ready	6-4	285	Senior
Line	Tim Zinni	North Lima South Range	6-4	245	Senior
Line	Chris Kirkendall	Wheelersburg	6-2	230	Senior
QB	Tony Britt	Beachwood	6-0	170	Senior
Back	Andy Bish	Bloomdale Elmwood	6-2	175	Senior
Back	Doug Hesson	Marion Elgin	5-9	175	Senior
Back	Karlin Adams	Campbell Memorial	6-0	180	Senior
Back	Chad Lytle	Chillicothe Huntington	5-9	165	Senior
Back	Nathan Rose	Montpelier	6-0	180	Senior
Back	Aaron Bable	Columbiana Crestview	5-10	180	Senior
Back	Ed Daugherty	Orwell Grand Valley	5-9	175	Senior
Kicker	Pat Hannon	Springfield Catholic	6-0	180	Senior

First Team Defense

Pos.	Player	School	Hgt.	Wgt.	Class
Line	David Stanwick	Steubenville Catholic	6-4	225	Senior
Line	Travis Ritter	Carey	6-2	220	Senior
Line	Ryan Price	Brookville	6-5	210	Senior
Line	Randall Sampson	Columbus Hartley	6-0	205	Senior
Line	Jerod Conley	London Madison Plains	6-4	200	Senior
LB	Chris Ellis	Wheelersburg	6-4	210	Senior
LB	Jim Kitchen	West Jefferson	6-0	215	Senior
LB	Steve Stout	Mt. Blanchard Riverdale	6-0	185	Senior
LB	Corey Marshall	Bloomdale Elmwood	6-0	195	Senior
LB	Shane Patrone	Columbiana Crestview	5-10	200	Senior
LB	James Hardiman	Gates Mills Hawken	5-10	175	Junior
Back	Eric Clark	Marion Elgin	6-0	175	Senior
Back	Chris Kazmarek	Lorain Clearview	5-10	170	Senior
Back	Brian Beight	Columbiana Crestview	6-2	185	Junior
Back	Ryan O'Dear	Akron Manchester	5-10	160	Junior
Punter	Joel Gallimore	Batavia	6-3	185	Sophomore

Back of the Year: Andy Bish, Bloomdale Elmwood.
Lineman of the Year: Matt Spellman, Andover Pymatuning Valley.
Coach of the Year: Brian Hessey, Bloomdale Elmwood.

Division V

First Team Offense

Pos.	Player	School	Hgt.	Wgt.	Class
End	Chad Koontz	Bluffton	6-1	220	Senior
End	Reuben Kittle	Glouster Trimble	5-9	145	Junior
End	Josh Havens	Lockland	6-1	175	Senior
End	Trevor Foster	Williamsburg	6-5	250	Senior
Line	Brett Smith	Bainbridge Paint Valley	5-10	210	Senior
Line	Mac Davis	Bluffton	6-3	240	Senior
Line	Chad Ulm	Delphos St. John's	6-2	230	Senior
Line	Jeff Burgemeir	Fenwick	6-2	220	Senior
QB	Bo Hurley	McGuffey Up. Scioto Valley	6-3	205	Senior
Back	Rob Kelly	Newark Catholic	6-3	195	Senior
Back	Mike Rafter	Mariemont	6-3	205	Senior
Back	Bob Santangelo	McDonald	6-0	190	Senior
Back	Tim Bissell	Reedsville Eastern	6-0	164	Senior
Back	Mike Pike	Gates Mills Gilmour	5-10	180	Senior

Back	Andy Hutchison	Malvern	6-0	185	Senior
Kicker	Brian Graham	Newark Catholic	6-0	165	Senior

First Team Defense

Pos.	Player	School	Hgt.	Wgt.	Class
Line	Nick Toth	Fairport Harbor Harding	6-2	217	Senior
Line	Jeff Remish	Columbiana	5-10	180	Junior
Line	Ronnie Bowman	New Miami	6-3	233	Senior
Line	Rich Shout	Dalton	6-0	225	Senior
LB	Steve Schumacher	Woodsfield	6-1	205	Senior
LB	Nathan Puckett	Newark Catholic	5-10	185	Senior
LB	Beau Parry	Country Day	5-11	220	Senior
LB	Tony Borges	Minster	6-0	200	Senior
LBLB	Bubba Webb	Portsmouth Notre Dame	5-10	215	Senior
Back	Brandon Felger	Fairport Harbor Harding	5-11	187	Senior
Back	Chuck Barker	Fenwick	5-10	160	Senior
Back	Randy Pierce	Mogadore	6-2	210	Senior
Back	Eric Cusick	Columbiana	5-9	145	Senior
Back	Mark Turner	New Bremen	5-10	160	Senior
Back	Scott Elwer	Delphos St. John's	6-0	185	Senior
Punter	Chris Gallagher	Fenwick	6-0	175	Junior

Back of the Year: Rob Kelly, Newark Catholic.
Lineman of the Year: Beau Perry, Country Day.
Coaches of the Year: Lowell Bacon, Columbiana; Dan Cox, Union City Mississinawa Valley.

Ohio State Recruits, 1992 freshman class

Player	High school, city	Position	Size	Comment
Jimmy Bell	Youngstown Ursuline	lb	6-6, 225	Will play linebacker, defensive or tight end
Matt Christopher	Lake	lb	6-3, 235	A Chris Spielman clone
Dan Colson	Middletown	db	6-0, 170	Top defensive back in Ohio; 84 tackles
LeShun Daniels	Warren Harding	line	6-3, 265	Teamed with top pick Stringer at Warren
Luke Fickell	Columbus DeSales	de	6-5, 240	Top wrestler; Division III lineman of year
Eddie George	Philadelphia	rb	6-3, 225	2,572 yards, 37 TDs in 2 years at Fork Union
Jayson Gwinn	Columbus Brookhaven	lb	6-3, 230	Rated one of top five players in Ohio
Neil Hawkins	Bucyrus	line	6-5, 240	Diamond in the rough
Ty Howard	Columbus Briggs	db	5-11, 180	4.4 speed in the 40
Darrell Jones	Lebanon	te	6-5, 250	22 catches, 306 yards
Robert Jones	Youngstown Mooney	line	6-4, 245	Projected as outstanding pass rusher
Rob Kelly	Newark Catholic	db	6-3, 195	Has height, weight to sparkle
Max Langenkamp	Cincinnati Moeller	te	6-4, 240	4.8 speed, projected at tight end
Travis McQuire	Massillon	rb	6-0, 195	1,414 yards, top running back in Ohio
Mike Mezgec	Eastlake North	line	6-4, 250	Very agile for the size
Ryan Miller	Allen Park, Mich.	lb	6-3, 210	Steal from Michigan; 122 senior tackles
Eric Moss	Belle, W.Va., DuPont	te	6-5, 260	Considered blue-chipper in West Virginia
Juan Porter	Cleveland St. Ignatius	line	6-5, 310	Heavily recruited by Michigan
Steve Sheets	Columbus West	line	6-5, 265	Blue Chip All-American
Brian Smith	Nitro, W. Va.	line	6-6, 270	Outstanding quarterback sack prospect
Tommy Stokes	Texas	lb	6-2, 225	Sought by all Southwest Conference schools
Korey Stringer	Warren Harding	line	6-6, 290	Top offensive line prospect in midwest
Lorenzo Styles	Farrell, Pa.	lb	6-3, 230	250 tackles, 12 sacks in two years
Michael Tillman	Steubenville	wr	6-2, 180	Reminds scouts of Joey Galloway
Louis Willard	Grove City	rb	6-2, 210	Blue-chipper before knee injury

Source: Jack Patterson, Akron Beacon Journal

Top Ohio Football Prospects, 1992

#	Name	Pos	Ht	Wt	Time	School	City
1.	Korey Stringer	OL	6-5	290	5.0	Warren Harding High	Warren
2.	Eric Boykin	QB	6-3	200	4.6	Meadowdale High	Dayton
3.	Jayson Gwinn	LB	6-3	225	4.7	Brookhaven High	Columbus
4.	D.J. Jones	TE/DL	6-5	253	4.9	Lebanon High	Lebanon
5.	Dan Colson	DB	6-0	180	4.5	Middletown High	Middletown
6.	Luke Fickell	DL/TE	6-5	240	4.8	St. Francis DeSales High	Columbus
7.	Matt Christopher	LB	6-2	225	4.7	Lake High	Uniontown
8.	Travis McGuire	RB	6-0	185	4.4	Massillon High	Massillon
9.	Ty Howard	RB/DB	5-11	180	4.3	Briggs High	Columbus
10.	Derek Kidwell	QB	6-4	227	4.8	Fostoria High	Fostoria
11.	Ray Edmonds	DL	6-4	255	5.0	Akron Hoban High	Akron
12.	Ty Douthard	RB	6-2	200	4.4	Cincinnati LaSalle	Cincinnati
13.	Louis Willard	RB	6-0	205	4.5	Grove City High	Grove City
14.	Juan Porter	OL	6-5	310	5.3	St. Ignatius High	Cleveland
15.	Eric Wendt	OL	6-5	275	5.1	Moeller High	Cincinnati
16.	Chris Campbell	WR/DB	6-2	183	4.5	St. Vincent High	Akron
17.	R.C. Jones	DL	6-4	243	5.0	Cardinal Mooney High	Youngstown
18.	LeShun Daniels	DL	6-3	260	5.1	Warren Harding	Marion
19.	Rob Kelly	DB/RB	6-4	210	4.5	Newark Catholic	Newark
20.	Terry Killens	RB/DB	6-1	205	4.5	Cincinnati Purcell	Cincinnati

Source: *The Ohio Football Recruiting News*,
reprinted by permission of editor Bill Kurelic, Westerville, Ohio

State Champions, Boys

Year		Champion	Coach	Runner-Up	Coach
1923	A	Lorain—15	A. W. Collins	Bellevue—14	Willis Fulton
	B	Plattsburg—16	Paul Glenn	Bellpoint—15	Guy Zimmer
1924	A	Dayton Stivers—30	Harry Wilhelm	Columbus East—16	Robert Kasch
	B	Bellpoint—24	Guy Zimmer	Archbold—20	Chester Henry
1925	A	Springfield—32 (2 OT)	Oliver Matheny	Lakewood—30	Jerry Ross
	B	Bellpoint—42	Guy Zimmer	Oberlin—24	John Atkinson
1926	A	Zanesville—40	Gail Vanorsdall	Akron East—27	Warren Vanorsdall
	B	Oberlin—32	John Atkinson	Miamisburg—13	Ralph Ness
1927	A	Dover—23	Joe Herman	Toledo Waite—21	Bill Zorn
	B	Kent State—20	Glen Francis	Oberlin—16	Lars Wagner
1928	A	Dayton Stivers—25	Floyd Stahl	Canton McKinley—20	Dwight Peabody
	B	Hillsboro Marshall—20	Noah Emery	Manchester—17	Gilbert Buriff
1929	A	Dayton Stivers—36	Floyd Stahl	Dover—22	Peterka
	B	Akron St. Marys—26	Leo Engler	Bluffton—26	Dwain Murray
1930	A	Dayton Stivers—18	Floyd Stahl	Akron East—16	Warren Vanorsdall
	B	Lancaster St. Marys—34	Clarence Joos	Rome—3	Phoney Smith
1931	A	Portsmouth—20 (1 OT)	Dick Hopkins	Canton McKinley—19	Dwight Peabody
	B	Austintown-Fitch—26 (2 OT)	Harold Riekert	Lancaster St. Marys—24	Clarence Joos
1932	A	Akron West—26	Rus Beichly	Columbus North—17	A. C. Jones
	B	Castalia Margaretta—26 (1 OT)	Clayton R. Cook	Ostrander—24	C. N. Stevenson
1933	A	Dover—34	Herman Rearick	Marietta—23	Frank Sutton
	B	Lawrenceville—36	Bill Armstrong	Henrietta—24	John Salisbury
1934	A	Dayton Roosevelt—46	Paul Nelson	Portsmouth—30	Richard Hopkins
	B	Waterloo—40	M. E. Hairston	Mark Center—26	Wendell Devore
1935	A	Akron North—47	Luther Hosfield	Coshocton—15	Schuyler Wharton
	B	Waterloo—25	M. E. Hairston	Oxford Stewart—22	D. P. Walton
1936	A	Newark—32	Clifford Orr	Findlay—23	Carl Bachman
	B	Sandusky St. Marys—25	L. L. Zieroff	Leesburg—22	Louis Pausch
1937	A	Hamilton—37	Lewis Hirt	Massillon Washington—32	Paul Brown
	B	Upper Arlington—43	Walt Heischman	Lockland—25	Harold Roettger
1938	A	Newark—28	Clifford Orr	New Philadelphia—27	Paul Hoememan
	B	Canal Fulton—42	Philip Heim	Enon—21	Frank Long
1939	A	Akron North—47	Luther Hosfield	Cincinnati Roger Bacon—38	John Wiethe
	B	North Canton—24	Raymond Swope	Sandusky St. Marys—23	L. L. Zierolf
1940	A	New Philadelphia—30	Paul Hoememan	Canton McKinley—22	Herman Rearick
	B	New Carlisle—43	Hubert Cole	Canfield—26	Merle Rosselle
1941	A	Martins Ferry—37	Floyd Baker	Lakewood—30	Jerry Ross
	B	Glenford—48	Nolan Swackhammer	Canfield—28	Jack Guy
1042	A	Xenia Central—51	Tom Blackburn	Toledo Central—33	Adolph T. Scheme
	B	Somerset—49	Frank Sowecke	Bremen—42	Harold Grimes
1943	A	Newark—47	Max Douglas	Canton McKinley—42	Herman Rearick
	B	Yorkville—54	Ted Sims	Tipp City—30	Joe Brammer
1944	A	Middletown—50 (1 OT)	Royner Green	Toledo Woodward—46	Homer Hanham
	B	Akron Ellet—49	John Scott	Lima St. Johns—39	Richard Bechtel
1945	A	Bellevue—36	Harry Strobel	Middletown—34	George Houck
	B	Dayton Northridge—51	Ben Ankney	Columbiana—42	John Cabas
1946	A	Middletown—42	George Houck	Akron North—37	Robert White
	B	Farmer—36	Ollie Zedaker	Worthington—32	Ray Heischman
1947	A	Middletown—47	Paul Walker	East Liverpool—29	Merrill Hall
	B	Columbiana—43	John Cabas	New Knoxville—34	Roger Stauffer
1948	A	Findlay—51	Carl Bachman	Hamilton Catholic—36	Harold Mouch
	B	Eaton—45	Gene Ellington	Lima St. Rose—36	Fred George
1949	A	Hamilton—70	Warren Scholler	Toledo Central—52	Larry Bondy
	B	Delphos St. John's—47	Dick Bechtel	Lockland Wayne—43	Joe Martin
1950	A	Springfield—53	Elwood Pitzer	Akron South—48	Bill Satterlee
	B	Miller City—44	Norris Simpson	Eaton—36	Gene Ellington
1951	A	Columbus East—57	Bucky Walters	Hamilton—39	Warren Scholler
	B	Grand Rapids—52	Dale Reichenbaugh	Waynesburg—51	Walter Headley
1952	A	Middletown—63	Paul Walker	Steubenville—53	Ang Vaccaro
	B	Lockland Wayne—56	Joe Martin	Nelsonville—46	Alfred Cole
1953	A	Middletown—73	Paul Walker	Newark—35	Max Douglas
	B	Mariemont—87	Norman Kusel	Philo—44	Paul Jackson

Year	Div	Champion	Coach	Runner-Up	Coach
		Champion	*Coach*	*Runner-Up*	*Coach*
1954	A	Hamilton—66	Warren Scholler	Columbus South—56	George Hood
	B	New Lexington—65	Robert Fowle	Delphos—63	Bob Amzen
1955	A	Zanesville—56	Wayne Ashbaugh	Cincinnati Hughes—42	Howard Grimes
	B	Lockland Wayne—64	Joe Martin	Willshire—56	Bob Games
1956	A	Middletown—91	Paul Walker	Canton McKinley—69	Herman Rearick
	B	Arcanum—72	Glenn Harter	Columbus St. Marys—71	Ken Nevilce
1957	A	Ayersville—74 (1 OT)	Lee Himmeger	Gratis—73	John Buriff
	AA	Middletown—64	Paul Walker	Kent Roosevelt—54	Harold Andreas
1958	A	Northwestern—60	J. Daniel Baker	Holmes Liberty—56	Clarence Jewell, Jr.
	AA	Cleveland East Tech—50 (2 OT)	John Broski	Columbus North—48	Frank Truitt
1959	A	Edgerton—57	G. D. "Babe" Shoup	Lynnwood-Jacksontown—53	Jack E. Gill
	AA	Cleveland East Tech—71	John Broski	Salem—51	John A. Cabas
1960	A	Salem Local—74	William Hupp	Frazeysburg—59	Myron Cline
	AA	Dayton Roosevelt—51	John A. Woolums	Cleveland East Tech—41	Joe Howell
1961	A	Defiance Ayersville—40	Lee Himmeger	Youngstown Liberty—38	Peter Prokop
	AA	Portsmouth—50	George Heller	Urbana—44	Sam Marchio
1962	A	New Lebanon Dixie—74	Columbus Hines	Berlin Hiland—62	Robert Schrock
	AA	Hamilton Taft—59	Frank McCollum	Cleveland East Tech—52	Joseph Howell
1963	A	Dresden—48	Jack Van Reeth	Jackson Center—46	Frederick M. Gross
	AA	Columbus East—41	Bob Hart	Marion Harding—32	J. Daniel Baker
1964	A	Dresden—71	Richard Longaberger	Celina Immaculate Conception—61	Robert J. (Bob) Guinta
	AA	Dayton Belmont—89	John Ross	Cleveland East—60	Charles Lyons
1965	A	West Salem Northwestern—55	Ray S. Bates	Springboro—45	Gerald Saunders
	AA	Columbus South—54	John Colmery	Cincinnati St. Xavier—53	Dick Berning
1966	A	New Lebanon Dixie—75	Columbus Hines	Rossford—63	Cot Marquette
	AA	Dayton Chaminade—55	Jim Turvene	Toledo Liberty—52	Burt Spice
1967	A	Strasburg—54	Charles Huggins	Arcanum—47	Richard Graeff
	AA	Columbus Linden McKinley—88	Vince Chickerella	Cleveland East Tech—56	John Chavers
1968	A	Mansfield St. Peters—73	Robert Frye	Petersburg Springfield—50	Leigh Klingensmith
	AA	Columbus East—64	Robert Hart	Hamilton Garfield—60	Robert R. Sweeten
1969	A	Arcanum—84	Richard Graeff	Bridgeport—59	Frank Baxter
	AA	Columbus East—71	Robert Hart	Canton McKinley—56	Robert Rupert
1970	A	Cincinnati Lincoln Heights—62	John Hillard	Sebring McKinley—60	Rick Brook
	AA	Dayton Chaminade—69	Jim Turvene	Rossford—47	Joe Stalma
1971	A	Ft. Recovery—70	Allen Souder	Marion Pleasant—57	Stanley Kirby
	AA	Canton Lehman—68	Don Eddins	Warren Champion—63	Roger Rogos
	AAA	Columbus Walnut Ridge—76	Jack M. Moore	Dayton Dunbar—63	George Galloway
1972	A	Gnadenhutten Indian Valley So.—59	Charles Huggins	Morral Ridgedale—41	Don Wendell
	AA	Columbus Ready—59	Patrick Penn	Lexington—47	John Barr
	AAA	Cleveland East Tech—78	John Chavers	Cincinnati Princeton—67	John W. Hillard
1973	A	Marion Pleasant—42	Stan Kirby	Gnadenhutten Indian Valley So.—37	Charles Huggins
	AA	Columbus Ready—79	Patrick Penn	Delphos St. John's—66	Bob Arnzen
	AAA	Cincinnati Elder—60	Paul Frey	Akron Central-Hower—53	Joseph Siegferth
1974	A	Lorain Clearview—74	Bob Walsh	Pitsburg Franklin Monroe—69	Phil Dubbs
	AA	Akron Manchester—72	Bernard Conley	Columbus Hartley—52	Dick Geyer
	AAA	Cincinnati Elder—60	Paul Frey	Canton McKinley—54	Bob Rupert
1975	A	Maria Stein Marion Local—59 (1 OT)	Irv Besecker	Gnadenhutten Indian Valley So.—56	Charles Huggins
	AA	Warsaw River View—77 (1 OT)	Walter Harrop	Dayton Stivers—72	Earl Johnson
	AAA	Columbus Linden McKinley—77	Jene Davis	Cleveland Heights—72	Jim Cappelletti
1976	A	Gnadenhutten Indian Valley So.—63	Charles Huggins	Pettisville—53	Phil Rychener
	AA	Dayton Roth—82	Michael Haley	Lorain Catholic—81	Jim Lawhead
	AAA	Barberton—82	Jack Greynolds	Middletown—70	Paul Walker
1977	A	Fort Loramie—63	George Hamlin	Mansfield St. Peters—50	Pat Maurer
	AA	Cleveland Cathedral Latin—69	Don Gacey	Columbus Mifflin—65	John Smith
	AAA	Columbus Linden McKinley—80	Jene Davis	Barberton—74	Jack Greynolds
1978	A	Mansfield St. Peters—78	Pat Maurer	Tipp City Bethel—60	John Whitehouse
	AA	Portsmouth—63	Richard Hopkins	Cleveland Cathedral Latin—62	Don Gacey
	AAA	Kettering Alter—68	Joe Petrocelli	Akron Central-Hower—52	Joseph Siegferth
1979	A	St. Henry—64	Fran Guilbault	Mansfield St. Peters—57	Pat Maurer
	AA	Dayton Jefferson—65	John Watkins	Cleveland Cathedral Latin—63	Don Gacey
	AAA	Columbus East—74	Larry Walker	Cleveland St. Joseph—65	Robert Straub

		Champion	Coach	Runner-Up	Coach
1980	A	Sandusky St. Mary's—62 (1 OT)	Wally Ambum	Cincinnati Summit Country Day—56	Joe Cruse
	AA	Hamilton Ross—45	Ron Chasteen	Portsmouth—44	Richard Hopkins
	AAA	Akron Central-Hower—52	Joe Siegferth	Lorain Admiral King—48	Mitch Gilliam
1981	A	Kalida—58	Richard Kortokrax	Gahanna Columbus Academy—44	Jack MacMullan
	AA	Napoleon—60	Fred Church	New Lebanon Dixie—48	Gary Peffly
	AAA	Dayton Roth—73	Mike Haley	Wadsworth—66	Dave Sladky
1982	A	Middletown Fenwick—64	John Rossi	Racine Southern—44	Carl Wolfe
	AA	Dayton Roth—68	Mike Haley	Youngstown Rayen-56	Frank Cegledy
	AAA	Cincinnati Roger Bacon—71 (1 OT)	Bob Callahan	Barberton—67	Jack Greynolds
1983	A	Delphos St. John's—55	Bob Arnzen	New Washington Buckeye Central—48	Steve Mohr
	AA	Columbus Bexley—77	Gene Millard	Oak Harbor—58	David Christie
	AAA	Toledo St. Francis DeSales—58	Val Glinka	Akron Central-Hower—59	Mike Meneer
1984	A	Monroeville—66	Dave Augsperger	Columbus Wehrle—62	Chuck Kemper
	AA	Akron St. Vincent-St. Mary—75	Joe Suboticki	Wheelersburg—71	Mike Lovenguth
	AAA	Canton McKinley—79 (1 OT)	Mike Riley	Dayton Dunbar—75	Mike Haley
1985	A	Jackson Center—63	Jerry Harmon	Graysville Skyvue—61	Mark Huffman
	AA	Youngstown Raven—50	Frank Cegledy, Jr.	Columbus Linden McKinley—46	Jim Hollern
	AAA	Cincinnati Purcell Marian—65	Jim Stoll	Mansfield Senior—57	Joe Prats
1986	A	Columbus Wehrle—72	Chuck Kemper	Dayton Jefferson—58	Ben Waterman
	AA	Oberlin—74	Bob Walsh	Springfield Greenon—70	Lyle Falknor
	AAA	Akron Central-Hower—70	Mike Meneer	Columbus South—44	Dick Ricketts
1987	A	Fort Loramie—68	Dan Hegemier	Bucyrus Wynford—50	Rob Sheldon
	AA	Columbus St. Francis DeSales—71	Vince Chickerella	Dayton Jefferson—64	Ben Waterman
	AAA	Dayton Dunbar—70	Mike Haley	Canton McKinley—65	Dave Cady
1988	I	Cincinnati Woodward—107	Larry Miller	Columbus Linden McKinley—70	Steve Dickerson
	II	Portsmouth—54	Joseph Suboticki	Chesterland West Geauga—47	Cliff Hunt
	III	Hamilton Badin—68	Gerry Weisgerber	Zoarville Tuscarawas Valley—63	Bob VonKaenel
	IV	Columbus Wehrle—71	Chuck Kemper	Kalida—54	Richard Kortokrax
1989	I	Toledo Macomber-Whitney—75	Bart Schroeder	Cleveland St. Joseph—72	Mike Moran
	II	Lexington—89	Greg Collins	Cleveland West Geauga—57	Cliff Hunt
	III	Akron Hoban—52	Vince Gross	Cincinnati North College Hill—49	Steve Collier
	IV	Columbus Wehrle—83	Chuck Kemper	Lima Central Catholic—81	Bob Seggerson
1990	I	Toledo Scott—64	Ben Williams	Cincinnati Woodward—53	Jim Leon
	II	Dayton Colonel White—71	Tom Clements	Portsmouth—57	Joe Suboticki
	III	St. Henry—71	Fran Guilbault	Youngstown Liberty—60	Bob Patton, Sr.
	IV	Columbus Wehrle—67	Chuck Kemper	Springfield Catholic Central—58	Tim Sullivan
1991	I	Cleveland Villa Angela-St. Joseph—76	Mike Moran	West Chester Lakota—72	Mike Mueller
	II	Lexington—55	Greg Collins	Dayton Chaminade-Julienne—53	Joe Staley
	III	Haviland Wayne Trace—77	Al Welch	Chillicothe Unioto—55	Ron Lovely
	IV	St. Henry—71	Fran Guilbault	New Madison Tri-Village—45	Lee Falknor
1992	I	Lakota—88	Mike Mueller	Lima Senior—86(OT)	Paul Whitney
	II	Cleveland Villa Angela-St. Joseph—61	Mike Moran	St. Charles—48	Jim Lower
	III	Orrville—78	Steve Smith	Hamler Patrick Henry—65	Dave Krauss
	IV	Berlin Hiland	David Bielak	Gates Mills	Perry Reese, Jr.

Tournament Records, Boys

CHAMPIONSHIP GAME

MOST POINTS
Individual—51—Clark Kellogg, Cleveland St. Joseph's vs. Columbus East, 1979
One Team—107—Cincinnati Woodward vs. Columbus Linden McKinley, 1988
Both Teams—177—Cincinnati Woodward (107) and Columbus Linden McKinley (70), 1988
MOST FIELD GOALS (2-point)
Individual—21—Clark Kellogg, Cleveland St. Joseph vs. Columbus East, 1979
One Team—39—Middletown vs. Canton McKinley, 1956
Both Teams—66—Middletown (39) and Canton McKinley (27), 1956
MOST FIELD GOALS (3-point)
Individual—4—Chip Jones, Cincinnati, Woodward vs. Columbus Linden McKinley, 1988
One Team—6—Cincinnati Woodward vs. Toledo Scott, 1990
Both Teams—7—Cincinnati Woodward (5) and Columbus Linden McKinley (2), 1988
7—Cincinnati Woodward (6) and Toledo Scott (1), 1990
MOST FREE THROWS
Individual—12—Jerry Lucas, Middletown vs. Kent Roosevelt, 1957
One Team—31—Columbus Linden McKinley vs. Cleveland Heights, 1975
31—Dayton Belmont vs. Cleveland East, 1964
Both Teams—52—Dayton Belmont (31) and Cleveland East (21), 1964
FEWEST POINTS
One Team—14—Bellevue vs. Lorain, 1923
Both Teams—29—Lorain (15) and Bellevue (14), 1923
LOWEST WINNING SCORE
15—Lorain vs. Bellvue, 1923
WIDEST WINNING MARGIN
38—Middletown (73) and Newark (35), 1953

ANY TOURNAMENT GAME
MOST POINTS
Individual—53—Jerry Lucas, Middletown vs. Cleveland East Tech, 1956
One Team—107—Cincinnati Woodward vs. Columbus Linden McKinley, 1988
Both Teams—177—Middletown (99) and Cleveland East Tech (78), 1956
177—Cincinnati Woodward (107) and Columbus Linden McKinley (70), 1988
MOST FIELD GOALS (2-point)
Individual—21—Clark Kellogg, Cleveland St. Joseph vs. Columbus East, 1979
One Team—39—Middletown vs. Canton McKinley, 1956
Both Teams—76—Dayton Roth (38) and Newark (38), 1981
MOST FIELD GOALS (3-point)
Individual—4—Chip Jones, Cincinnati Woodward vs. Columbus Linden McKinley, 1988
One Team—6—Valley Forge vs. Cincinnati Woodward, 1988
6—Cincinnati Woodward vs. Toledo Scott, 1990
Both Teams—9—Valley Forge (6) and Cincinnati Woodward (3), 1988
MOST FREE THROWS
Individual—14—Jerry Lucas, Middletown vs. Toledo Macomber-Whitney, 1957
One Team—34—Dayton Belmont vs. Canton McKinley, 1964
Both Teams—51—Celina (28) and Cleveland East Tech (23), 1972
FEWEST POINTS
One Team—2—Bowling Green vs. East Liverpool, 1923
Both Teams—12—East Liverpool (10) and Bowling Green (2), 1923
LOWEST WINNING SCORE
10—East Liverpool vs. Bowling Green, 1923

TWO GAME TOURNAMENT RECORDS
MOST POINTS
Individual—97—Jerry Lucas, Middletown, 1956
One Team—190—Middletown, 1956
MOST FIELD GOALS (2-point)
Individual—38—Jerry Lucas, Middletown, 1956
One Team—77—Middletown, 1977
MOST FIELD GOALS (3-point)
Individual—6—Chip Jones, Cincinnati Woodward, 1988
One Team—9—Cincinnati Woodward, 1990

The Big Schools Play Classic, Come-from-behind, Overtime, Record-setting Basketball

The 1992 Ohio prep basketball Division I championships demonstrated that, in St. John Arena at least, there was no place to hide, even behind the biggest of leads. The title match between **Lima Senior** and Cincinnati's **Lakota** went into overtime—Lakota came back from a near-impossible 21-point third-quarter deficit—and the Division I semifinal was played out in two overtimes. The tourney thus was described by one observer as "hand-wringing, stomach-churning, foot-stomping, program-wadding, towel-clutching basketball." The winning coaches got trophies and a pacemaker.

The trophy for Most Luckless went to Division I **Canton McKinley** who, in the semifinal matchup, lost a first-half lead of 41-22 to Lima Senior, and a 65-50 lead in the fourth quarter. Lima's **Greg Simpson** hit what one writer called "a 38-foot prayer" that tied the game in the first overtime, and Lima went on to win 91-88 in the second. That made 23 state tournament appearances for Canton McKinley, and one title. Said McKinley coach **Dave Cady**: "It's a tough damned way to make a living."

But Cincinnati's Lakota was waiting for Lima Senior in the final, a game that by its own astonishing conclusion ranks it as one of the best title games in the history of the old arena. It was also the first time in the 70-year history of the tournament that two teams from the same league played in the final. Lima Senior coach **Paul Whitney**, whose team had lost twice to Lakota in Greater Miami Conference games, apparently knew what he was up against. "When we went up by 21, I didn't think we had it won." And, startlingly, they didn't. The T-Birds were back, 62-41, with 3:01 left in the third quarter when they began to move.

Senior guard **Brad Evans'** three-pointer with 13 seconds hit the front of the rim, bounced straight up, then dropped through the net. That tied the game at 79-79, and sent the two into overtime. Evans then opened the OT with a field goal—it was the only Lakota field goal of the OT—and had three steals. The rest was won on the foul line. Final: 88-86.

The star of Lima's show was not Ohio's two-time Mr. Basketball and OSU recruit Greg Simpson, but junior guard **Demond Lyles**, whose 43 points were the third-highest totals ever for a major-school game. Only **Clark Kellogg** of St. Joseph's (51 points in 1979) and **Jerry Lucas** of Middletown (44 in 1956) ranked higher. Lyles' eight three-pointers was a record for all divisions. Simpson, meanwhile, who had scored 47 points in each of his two previous games against Lakota, had only 23 points—his season average was 35.3—but was hobbled with a knee injury. It was his three-pointer that sent Lima into OT in the semifinal against McKinley, and he hit the winning shot with 4.7 seconds left.

Lakota's other star was **Keith Gregor**, headed to UC, who led the T-Birds with 25 points. In eight postseason games, the 6-5 forward averaged 20.8 points and 9.1 rebounds. "I'd rather have a state championship ring than average 35 points," he said.

Lakota had won only nine postseason games in its first 31 years but during the last two seasons the T-Birds went 50-6, including a 15-1 tournament record, and last year's overtime loss to Cleveland Villa Angela-St. Joseph for the title. ◗

MOST FREE THROWS
Individual—26—Jerry Lucas, Middletown, 1957
One Team—65—Dayton Belmont, 1964

THREE GAME TOURNAMENT RECORDS
MOST POINTS
Individual—59—Dick Vice, Middletown, 1952
MOST FIELD GOALS (2-point)
Individual—23—Dick Vice, Middletown, 1952
23—Bill Ross, Steubenville, 1952
MOST FREE THROWS
Individual—13—Dick Vice, Middletown, 1952
13—Charles Ellis, Steubenville, 1952

DIVISION II

CHAMPIONSHIP GAME
MOST POINTS
Individual—38—Mike Phillips, Akron Manchester vs. Columbus Hartley, 1974
One Team—89—Lexington vs. Chesterland West Geauga, 1989
Both Teams—163—Dayton Roth (82) and Lorain Catholic (81), 1976
MOST FIELD GOALS (2-point)
Individual—18—Mike Phillips, Akron Manchester vs. Columbus Hartley, 1974
One Team—36—Mariemont vs. Philo, 1953
Both Teams—64—Dayton Roth (35) and Lorain Catholic (29), 1976
MOST FIELD GOALS (3-point)
Individual—2—Will Watkins, Dayton Colonel White vs. Portsmouth, 1990
2—Darnell Hoskins, Dayton Chaminade-Julienne vs. Lexington, 1991
One Team—4—Dayton Chaminade-Julienne vs. Lexington, 1991
Both Teams—4—Dayton Chaminade-Julienne (4) and Lexington (0), 1991
MOST FREE THROWS
Individual—16—Jerry Dennis, Columbus DeSales vs. Dayton Jefferson, 1987
One Team—40—Lexington vs. Cleveland West Geauga, 1989
Both Teams—55—Lexington (40) and Cleveland West Geauga (15), 1989
FEWEST POINTS
One Team—44—Portsmouth vs. Hamilton Ross, 1980
Both Teams—89—Hamilton Ross (45) and Portsmouth (44), 1980
LOWEST WINNING SCORE
45—Hamilton Ross vs. Portsmouth, 1980
WIDEST WINNING MARGIN
43—Mariemont (87) and Philo (44), 1953

ANY TOURNAMENT GAME
MOST POINTS
Individual—38—Mike Phillips, Akron Manchester vs. Columbus Hartley, 1974
One Team—108—Lorain Catholic vs. Brookfield, 1976
Both Teams—192—Lorain Catholic (108) and Brookfield (84), 1976
MOST FIELD GOALS (2-point)
Individual—18—Mike Phillips, Akron Manchester vs. Columbus Hartley, 1974
One Team—46—Lorain Catholic vs. Brookfield, 1976
Both Teams—82—Lorain Catholic (46) and Brookfield (36), 1976
MOST FIELD GOALS (3-point)
Individual—4—Mike Singleton, Canton South vs. Dayton Colonel White, 1990
One Team—9—Dayton Chaminade-Julienne vs. Columbus Briggs, 1991
Both Teams—12—Dayton Chaminade-Julienne (9) and Columbus Briggs (3), 1991
MOST FREE THROWS
Individual—16—Jerry Dennis, Columbus DeSales vs. Dayton Jefferson, 1987
One Team—40—Lexington vs. Cleveland West Geauga, 1989
Both Teams—55—Lexington (40) and Cleveland West Geauga (15), 1989
FEWEST POINTS
One Team—36—Cincinnati McNicholas vs. Akron St. Vincent-St. Mary, 1984
Both Teams—89—Hamilton Ross (45) and Portsmouth (44), 1980
LOWEST WINNING SCORE
45—Hamilton Ross vs. Portsmouth, 1980

TWO GAME TOURNAMENT RECORDS
MOST POINTS
Individual—64—Mike Phillips, Akron Manchester, 1974
One Team—189—Lorain Catholic, 1976

Curtis McMahon, Waterloo center from Greasy Ridge: he learned to shoot on an outdoor court where missed shots rolled several hundred yards into a hollow behind the barn.

Ohio's Improbable but Favorite All-Time Cage Team

The movie, *Hoosiers*, could just as easily have been made in southeastern Ohio, in a tiny village named Waterloo, in Lawrence County. In the deeps of the Great Depression, five country kids and their 26-year-old coach won back-to-back state championships in an improbable farm-to-fame odyssey that made **Waterloo** into Ohio's all-time high school basketball legend.

The kids learned to play in a hayloft where **Orlyn Roberts**, his cousin **Wyman Roberts**, and **Stewart Wiseman** practiced with a bound handful of rags masquerading as a ball, tossed through an old iron ring off a wagon. Wiseman, a farmboy, scraped and graded his own court down by the creek. When they got to high school, there were no portents to overshadow what they would eventually accomplish. In the hayloft, the boys imagined the size of the trophy they would receive for winning the state. It would have to be, they concluded, "surely as large as a kitchen stove." They opened the 1934 season unheralded even at home but after they beat Blackfork, Pedro, Racine, a Kentucky team, and the Marshall College freshmen by a 209-122 margin, the locals began to turn out. Waterloo's playing style was unorthodox and showy; they might bounce the ball off the floor into the basket, or two players might go to the bench and eat popcorn while their teammates played three-on-five. They knew ball-handling, back-hand passing, and run-and-gun. They developed the pivot, highly uncommon then in prep play.

After their first game in the state tournament—they blasted Chandlersville 58-29—the AP wrote that the Wonders "converted the ball into a trained seal." After a relatively lacklustre semi-final win over Lowellville, they beat Mark Center, 40-26, for the title. Orlyn Roberts scored 69 points in three games, still a record.

After their first Class B championship, they began to play A schools. They didn't lose for 56 games. They barnstormed around Ohio in their 26-year-old coach's black Chevrolet sedan and, according to writer Danny Fulks, "they were, in unique combination, consummate basketball players and deliberate clowns. They mastered the range of conventional court tactics and then moved beyond them to innovations that extended the limits of the game." In mid-winter, they were to play at Painesville, east of Cleveland, but heading north they ran into a snowstorm and called Painesville to say they might not make it. When the announcement was made in the packed gym, no one left. When the Wonders arrived at 1 p.m., the gym was still full.

During the early part of February, 1935, they beat five Class A schools in six days and, the next week, beat the tallest team in Kentucky, the famous Piner Giants from Kenton County, who averaged 6'-5". Unheard-of crowds swelled primitive gyms, and the boys became celebrities, earning the program enough from 10 and 20-cent tickets to allow them to stay in hotels where they learned how to tip the bellboys and marveled at the elevators.

They lost only three games in 1935, on their way to their second state title. Author Dick Burdette pointed out that other teams have had more impressive scoring records, and may have had better defenses but none had more overall skill, showmanship, and staying power. "The odds were infinity-to-one," he wrote, "but the Waterloo Wonders became the most colorful, beloved high school combination in Ohio basketball history." ▶

MOST FIELD GOALS (2-point)
Individual—30—Mike Phillips, Akron Manchester, 1974
One Team—75—Lorain Catholic, 1976
MOST FIELD GOALS (3-point)
Individual—4—Donn Restille, Lexington, 1989
4—Will Watkins, Dayton Colonel White, 1990
4—Mark Holton, Dayton Chaminade-Julienne, 1991
One Team—13—Dayton Chaminade-Julienne, 1991
MOST FREE THROWS
Individual—21—John Williams, Warsaw River View, 1975
One Team—50—Delphos St. John's, 1973

DIVISION III

CHAMPIONSHIP GAME
MOST POINTS
Individual—25—Pat Droesch, St. Henry vs. Youngstown Liberty, 1990
One Team—77—Haviland Wayne Trace vs. Chillicothe Unioto, 1991
Both Teams—132—Haviland Wayne Trace (77) and Chillicothe Unioto (55), 1991
MOST FIELD GOALS (2-point)
Individual—11—Pat Droesch, St. Henry vs. Youngstown Liberty, 1990
One Team—28—St. Henry vs. Youngstown Liberty, 1990
Both Teams—43—Haviland Wayne Trace (26) and Chillicothe Unioto (17), 1991
MOST FIELD GOALS (3-point)
Individual—5—Bob Patton, Jr., Youngstown Liberty vs. St. Henry, 1990
One Team—10—Youngstown Liberty vs. St. Henry, 1990
Both Teams—12—Youngstown Liberty (10) and St. Henry (2), 1990
MOST FREE THROWS
Individual—11—John Brinck, Hamilton Badin vs. Zoarville Tuscarawas Valley, 1988
11—John Richter, Hamilton Badin vs. Zoarville Tuscarawas Valley, 1988
11—Dave Harmon, Cincinnati North College Hill vs. Akron Hoban, 1989
11—Russell Jewell, Haviland Wayne Trace vs. Chillicothe Unioto, 1991
One Team—37—Hamilton Badin vs. Zoarville Tuscarawas Valley, 1988
Both Teams—54—Hamilton Badin (37) and Zoarville Tuscarawas Valley (17), 1988
FEWEST POINTS
One Team—49—Cincinnati North College Hill vs. Akron Hoban, 1989
Both Teams—101—Akron Hoban (52) and Cincinnati North College Hill (49), 1989
LOWEST WINNING SCORE
52—Akron Hoban vs. Cincinnati North College Hill, 1989
WIDEST WINNING MARGIN
22—Haviland Wayne Trace (77) and Chillicothe Unioto (55), 1991

ANY TOURNAMENT GAME
MOST POINTS
Individual—35—Rob Welch, Haviland Wayne Trace vs. Cincinnati McNicholas, 1991
One Team—93—St. Henry vs. Richmond Dale Southeasterm 1990
Both Teams—138—Cincinnati North College Hill (71) and Wheelersburg (67), 1989
138—St. Henry (93) and Richmond Dale Southeastern (45), 1990
138—Chillicothe Unioto (80) and Bedford Chanel (58), 1991
MOST FIELD GOALS (2-point)
Individual—13—Matt Combs, Chillicothe Unioto vs. Bedford Chanel, 1991
13—Rob Welch, Haviland Wayne Trace vs. Cincinnati McNicholas, 1991
One Team—28—Akron Hoban vs. Bucyrus Wynford, 1989
28—St. Henry vs. Richmond Dale Southeastern, 1990
28—St. Henry vs. Youngstown Liberty, 1990
Both Teams—47—Akron Hoban (28) and Bucyrus Wynford (19), 1989
MOST FIELD GOALS (3-point)
Individual—6—Bob Plasman, Bedford Chanel vs. Chillicothe Unioto, 1991
One Team—10—Youngstown Liberty vs. St. Henry, 1990
Both Teams—12—Youngstown Liberty (10) and St. Henry (2), 1990
12—Bedford Chanel (6) and Chillicothe Unioto (6), 1991
MOST FREE THROWS
Individual—11—John Brinck, Hamilton Badin vs. Zoarville Tuscarawas Valley, 1988
11—John Richter, Hamilton Badin vs. Zoarville Tuscarawas Valley, 1988
11—Dave Harmon, Cincinnati North College Hill vs. Akron Hoban, 1989
11—Russell Jewell, Haviland Wayne Trace vs. Chillicothe Unioto, 1991
One Team—37—Hamilton Badin vs. Zoarville Tuscarawas Valley, 1988
Both Teams—54—Hamilton Badin (37) and Zoarville Tuscarawas Valley (17), 1988

FEWEST POINTS
One Team—43—Sparta Highland Morrow vs. Hamilton Badin, 1988
Both Teams—101—Akron Hoban (52) and Cincinnati North College Hill (49), 1989
LOWEST WINNING SCORE
52—Akron Hoban vs. Cincinnati North College Hill, 1989

TWO GAME TOURNAMENT RECORDS
MOST POINTS
Individual—53—Rob Welch, Haviland Wayne Trace, 1991
One Team—164—St. Henry, 1990
MOST FIELD GOALS (2-point)
Individual—20—Matt Combs, Chillicothe Unioto, 1991
One Team—56—St. Henry, 1990
MOST FIELD GOALS (3-point)
Individual—6—Bob Patton, Jr., Youngstown Liberty, 1990
One Team—14—Youngstown Liberty, 1990
MOST FREE THROWS
Individual—17—Keven McGuff, Hamilton Badin, 1988
One Team—52—Hamilton Badin, 1988

DIVISION IV
CHAMPIONSHIP GAME
MOST POINTS
Individual—35—Mike Allen, New Lexington St. Aloysius vs. Delphos St. John, 1954
35—Mike Post, St. Henry vs. Mansfield St. Peter, 1979
One Team—84—Arcanum vs. Bridgeport, 1969
Both Teams—164—Columbus Wehrle (83) and Lima Central Catholic (81), 1989
MOST FIELD GOALS (2-point)
Individual—16—Jay Byrne, Middletown Fenwick vs. Racine Southern, 1982

Jerry Lucas, All-World

Jerry Lucas was the most sought-after cage player in America. His first year at OSU, his shooting percentage from the floor was a startling 63.7.

The Legend of Middletown High

At **Middletown High** and Ohio State, **Jerry Lucas's** teams lost a total of seven games. He was considered the greatest basketball player in Ohio prep history before he was a junior. He was the first sophomore in America to be named to the Scholastic Coach Magazine All-American team. When he was a 6-8 senior, the Middies had won 76 consecutive games—a national streak—and two state titles; Lucas lost his only game by one point in the state semi-finals. He had what is likely to have been more acclaim than any high school athlete in Ohio history and yet he said, "I never had any special desire to be a basketball player," one of sports' great ironic statements.

Sought by over 150 colleges. Lucas ended up at Ohio State where he and teammate John Havlicek led the Buckeyes to the national title in 1960, and runners-up to Cincinnati in 1961 and 1962. He was a unanimous All-American as a sophomore, and twice College Player of the Year. He was a member of the U.S. team that won a gold medal at the 1960 Olympic Games, and with the Cincinnati Royals of the NBA named Rookie of the Year. He became only the third man in NBA history to average 20 points and 20 rebounds in the same season. He played on the New York Knicks' championship team of 1973, becoming one of the few athletes to ever win championships at every level of play.

Lucas was a fine student, a selfless competitor who liked to pass off to his teammates, and had a sense of humor, as well. At OSU, after dropping a direct pass, he said to Fred Taylor, "It caught me in the worst possible place, coach—the palms of my hands." ▶

One Team—36—Cincinnati Mariemont vs. Philo, 1953
Both Teams—60—Lorain Clearview (32) and Pitsburg Franklin Monroe (28), 1974
MOST FIELD GOALS (3-point)
Individual—3—Matt Mullen, Springfield Catholic Central vs. Columbus Wehrle, 1990
One Team—5—Lima Central Catholic vs. Columbus Wehrle, 1989
Both Teams—8—Lima Central Catholic (5) and Columbus Wehrle (3), 1989
MOST FREE THROWS
Individual—14—Dave Barker, Columbus St. Mary vs. Arcanum, 1956
One Team—29—Dresdin vs. Celina Immaculate Conception, 1964
29—Fort Loramie vs. Mansfield St. Peter's, 1977
Both Teams—42—Dresdin (29) and Celina Immaculate Conception (13), 1964
FEWEST POINTS
One Team—3—Rome vs. Lancaster St. Mary, 1930
Both Teams—31—Plattsburg (16) and Bellepoint (15), 1923
LOWEST WINNING SCORE
16—Plattsburg vs. Bellepoint, 1923
WIDEST WINNING MARGIN
26—St. Henry (71) and New Madison Tri-Village (45), 1991

ANY TOURNAMENT GAME
MOST POINTS
Individual—45—Dave Gray, Arcanum vs. Portsmouth Clay, 1969
One Team—84—Arcanum vs. Bridgeport, 1969
Both Teams—164—Columbus Wehrle (83) and Lima Central Catholic (81), 1989
MOST FIELD GOALS (2-point)
Individual—16—Dave Gray, Arcanum vs. Portsmouth Clay, 1969
16—Jay Byrne, Middletown Fenwick vs. Racine Southern, 1982
One Team—37—Columbus Wehrle vs. Van Buren, 1986
Both Teams—66—Columbus Wehrle (37) and Van Buren (29), 1986
MOST FIELD GOALS (3-point)
Individual—4—Terry Holliman, Columbus Wehrle vs. New Madison Tri-Village, 1991
One Team—7—Columbus Wehrle vs. New Madison Tri-Village, 1991
Both Teams—8—Lima Central Catholic (5) and Columbus Wehrle (3), 1989
8—Columbus Wehrle (7) and New Madison Tri-Village (1), 1991
MOST FREE THROWS
Individual—15—Kent Wolfe, Racine Southern vs. Windham, 1982
One Team—31—Rossford vs. Richmond Dale Southeastern, 1960
Both Teams—48—Cincinnati Mariemont (25) and Holgate (23), 1953
FEWEST POINTS
One Team—3—Proctorville vs. Lancaster St. Mary, 1930
Both Teams—20—Bellepoint (11) and Berlin Heights (9), 1923
LOWEST WINNING SCORE
11—Bellepoint vs. Berlin Heights, 1923

TWO GAME TOURNAMENT RECORDS
MOST POINTS
Individual—78—Mike Allen, New Lexington St. Aloysius, 1954
One Team—161—Lima Central Catholic, 1989
MOST FIELD GOALS (2-point)
Individual—28—Jay Byrne, Middletown Fenwick, 1982
One Team—61—Arcanum, 1969
MOST FIELD GOALS (3-point)
Individual—4—Matt Mullen, Springfield Catholic Central, 1990
One Team—6—Lima Central Catholic, 1989
6—Springfield Catholic Central, 1990
6—St. Henry, 1991
MOST FREE THROWS
Individual—24—Mike Allen, New Lexington St. Aloyius, 1954
One Team—48—Lockland Wayne, 1955

THREE GAME TOURNAMENT RECORDS
MOST POINTS
Individual—69—Orlyn Roberts, Waterloo, 1934
MOST FIELD GOALS (2-point)
Individual—29—Orlyn Roberts, Waterloo, 1934
MOST FREE THROWS
Individual—14—Ronald Peters, Lawrenceville, 1933

All-Ohio Boys Basketball Team, 1991-92

Division I

Player	School	Height	Class	Average
Greg Simpson	Lima Senior	6-1	Senior	35.3
Quinton Brooks	Akron Firestone	6-7	Senior	21.0
Bobby Sellers	Newark	6-1	Senior	19.8
Keith Gregor	Lakota	6-5	Senior	18.4
Malcolm Sims	Shaker Heights	6-4	Senior	27.9
Joe Rey	Cleveland St. Ignatius	6-1 1/2	Senior	24.8
Bryant Bowden	Canton McKinley	6-8	Senior	19.8

Player of the year: Greg Simpson, Lima Senior
Coaches of the year: Dave Cady, Canton McKinley; Phil Anderson, Xenia; Dean Washington, Columbus Marion-Franklin

Division II

Player	School	Height	Class	Average
Gary Trent	Columbus Hamilton Twp.	6-7	Senior	32.4
Richard (Tu-Tu) Brown	Dayton Dunbar	6-3	Senior	29.9
Geno Ford	Cambridge	5-8	Junior	36.5
Nate Reinking	Galion	6-1	Senior	28.2
Will Klucinec	Canfield	6-5	Senior	21.8
Adam Shea	Waverly	6-0	Senior	24.3
Andy Meyer	Kettering Alter	6-6	Senior	19.0

Player of the year: Gary Trent, Columbus Hamilton Township
Coach of the year: Joe Harold, Louisville

Division III

Player	School	Height	Class	Average
Jason Terry	Sparta Highland	7-2	Senior	22.4
Eric Caudill	Piketon	6-0	Senior	26.8
Gus Johnson	Huron	6-1	Senior	24.0
Kevin Summers	Orrville	6-2	Senior	23.4
Otis Winston	Toronto	6-4	Senior	31.9
J.R. Battista	Bellaire	6-1	Senior	26.0
Brad McNeilly	Andover Pymatuning Valley	6-3	Senior	21.8
Shelby Williams	Preble Shawnee	6-0	Senior	21.8

Player of the year: Jason Terry, Sparta Highland
Coaches of the year: Dave Hughes, Arcanum; Steve Smith, Orrville

Division IV

Player	School	Height	Class	Average
Juan Gay	Dayton Jefferson	6-1	Senior	30.6
Shawn Haughn	Canal Winchester	6-3	Junior	30.2
Anthony Hutchins	Lima Central Catholic	5-11	Senior	18.1
Randy Siefker	Miller City	6-2 1/2	Senior	23.0
Steve Montgomery	Cortland Maplewood	6-5	Senior	22.7
Junior Raber	Berlin Hiland	6-3	Senior	23.2
Mike Perrino	Mingo Junction	5-8	Senior	24.5

Player of the year: Juan Gay, Dayton Jefferson
Coach of the year: David Bielak, Gates Mills Gilmour

Source: Associated Press

Cleveland Villa Angela-St. Joseph, Orrville, and Berlin Hiland Win Titles

In the **Division II** state basketball final, **Cleveland Villa Angela-St. Joseph**, playing in front of 13,072 at St. John Arena, beat **St. Charles**, 61-48. Said Villa Angela-St. Joseph coach **Mike Moran** afterward: "I think it helped that we had two saints to pray to and they had only one."

For a time, though, VA-SJ wasn't certain it would be in the finals. It almost didn't get past **Cambridge** in the semifinals. Cambridge cut an eight-point lead to 58-57 and hung onto the ball for the final 2:06, waiting for the Armeggedon shot. One was blocked, the other was short, and as one writer noted, "Cambridge got nothing except good seats for the remainder of the tournament."

In the final, VA-SJ did what most teams found impossible: it shut off both **Bill Cain** and **Chris Kitsmiller**, and St. Charles' 48 points was its lowest total of the season.

The Vikings beat Lakota in OT in last year's Division I finals thus becoming only the third school to ever win back-to-back titles in different divisions—St. Henry and Dayton Roth were the others.

In the **Division III** championship, **Orville** went on a 12-0 third-quarter run and beat **Patrick Henry**, 78-65. The Riders had an unfair advantage: old alumnus Bobby Knight of Indiana University sent the team a "Best wishes" telegram.

Orrville's **Steve Smith**, who has won 355 games in his 19 years as coach, has had consistently good teams but not been to the state since 1980. "It's a rough racket," he said.

"I was beginning to wonder if I was ever gonna get another chance at this."

Orrville forward **Kevin Summers** paced his team with 25 points and 11 rebounds, including four-of-nine from three-point range. Patrick Henry's **Kent Seemann** was the most valu-able player on the Division III All-Tournament team, however. He set division records for points in a championship game (28), points in a tournament game (39), and for two-point game total (67). He shot 67.6 percent for the tourney. Said coach Smith about Orrville's defense, "Yeah, we did a hell of a job holding him to 28 points. Hell, he could have had 50."

In the **Division IV** matchup, **Berlin Hiland** beat **Gilmour**, 74-71, but the semifinal between Berlin and **Lima Central Catholic** was the heartstopper of the entire tournament. In that one, Lima led 62-55 with thirty seconds left, then with ten seconds left, held a 62-58 lead—and the ball. But a steal, a three-point play by Berlin's **Jr. Raber**, a missed Lima free throw, a foul on an attempted 40-footer, and three Raber free throws with a half-second left iced an incredulous Lima.

So the last of an inordinate series of tournament games that saw double-digit leads evaporate was played out in the Division IV final, with Gates Mills Gilmour losing a 14-point lead when Gilmour pulled to 72-71 in the final minutes. Berlin hung on, however, and Jr. Raber was named the outstanding player in the Division IV tournament, scoring 53 points and collecting 17 rebounds in Berlin's two wins. Raber had been with coach **Perry Reese Jr.** since Raber joined the team as a fourth-grade team manager and swept the gym floor.

Observers thought Berlin came up with the most bizarre statistic of the tournament—it won its two games and the state title, but was totally dominated on the backboards. The Hawks were outrebounded 41-20 in the semifinal win over Lima, and 41-15 by Gilmour in the final. ▶

Source: Cincinnati Post, Steve Blackledge and Ray Stein, Columbus Dispatch

Coaches Basketball Hall of Fame

Class of 1987 (Charter Members)
Carl Bachman (Deceased)—Findlay H.S.
John Cabas—Salem
Walter Harrop (Deceased)—Shawnee H.S.
Columbus Hines (Deceased)—North Lebanon H.S.
Vern Hoffman—Mansfield H.S.
Charles McAfee—Athens H.S.
Marv McCollum—Hamilton H.S.
Ken Newlon—Canton Lincoln & McKinley H.S.
Paul Walker—Middletown H.S.

Class of 1989
Roy Bates—Northwestern H.S. (Wayne Co.)
C. D. Hawhee (Deceased)—Waverly H.S.
Billy Kaylor (Deceased)—Xenia H.S.
Richard Meyer—Buckeye Valley H.S. (Radnor)
Henderson Heckie Thompson (Deceased)—Western H.S.

Class of 1991
Robert Guinta—Elyria Catholic H.S.
Don Henderson—Springfield North
Robert H. McClary—McDonald H.S.
Herb Russell—Grove City
Joe Siegferth—Akron Central-Hower
Fred Taylor—(Honorary) Coach at OSU

Class of 1988
Charles "Red" Ash—Canton South H.S.
J. Daniel Baker (Deceased)—Delaware Hayes H.S.
Fred Church—Napoleon H.S.
Jackie Moore—Columbus Walnut Ridge H.S.
Herman "Bup" Rearick (Deceased)—Canton McKinley H.S.

Class of 1990
Max Douglas—Newark H.S.
Louis Heckman (Deceased)—Ottoville H.S.
Paul V. Johnson (Deceased)—Lowelville H.S.
Gene Millard—Bexley H.S.
Wayne Wiseman—Springfield South H.S.

The elitists

Ohio's Top 10 Prep Boys' Basketball Coaches

Coach	Present school	Record	Years	Percent
Bob Arnzen	Delphos St. John's	655-268	41	.709
Richard Potts	Hannibal River	589-284	40	.675
Dick Berning	St. Xavier(Cin.)	525-256	36	.781
Richard L. Kortokrax	Kalida	516-181	31	.740
Fran Guilbault	St. Henry	501-161	30	.757
Robert Haas	Willard	479-107	26	.817
Joe Petrocelli	Alter	479-126	27	.792
Harold Daugherty	Euclid	459-216	32	.680
Rick Brook	Sebring McKinley	448-147	27	.753
Will Collins	Bellefontaine	434-194	29	.691

(Compiled of coaches active in 1990-91 season.)

Basketball
State Champions, Girls

1976-1990

Year	Div	Champion	Coach	Runner-Up	Coach
1976	AAA	Toledo Woodward—63	Susan Sweet	Columbus Watterson—59	Virginia Sawyer
	AA	Columbus Hartley—45	Beth Conway	Bellbrook—44	Ginny Greene
	A	Frankfort Adena—37	Linda Ross	Rocky River Lutheran West—35	Karen Wittrock
1977	AAA	Springfield North—47	Rollie Schultz	Columbus Walnut Ridge—44	Carol Smith
	AA	Warsaw River View—41	Jane Sikes	Pemberville Eastwood—38	Betty Bruning
	A	Delphos St. John's—61	Fran Voll	Mansfield St. Peter's—40	Georgiann Mathews
1978	AAA	Struthers—53	Dick Prest	Middletown—51	Barbara Hartman
	AA	Columbus Hartley—58	Beth Conway	Springboro—56	Donald Ross
	A	Ada—51	Sharon Pitts	Old Washington Buckeye Trail—39	David Linn
1979	AAA	Akron St. Vincent-St. Mary—35	Mary Jo Chionchio	Barberton—27	Jeff Janiga
	AA	Delphos St. John's—57	Fran Voll	Columbus Hartley—53	Beth Conway
	A	Old Washington Buckeye Trail—51	David Linn	Holgate—32	Duane Sheets
1980	AAA	Akron St. Vincent-St. Mary—55	Mary Jo Chionchio	Cincinnati Mother of Mercy—53	Mary Jo Huisman
	AA	Delphos St. John's—62	Fran Voll	West Lafayette Ridgewood—41	Mary Ann Stocker
	A	Mansfield St. Peter's—61 (1 OT)	Denny Rissler	Old Washington Buckeye Trail—57	David Linn
1981	AAA	Toledo Libbey—61	Marion Scott	East Cleveland Shaw—49	Edith Spivey
	AA	Uhrichsville Claymont—52	Rhonda Funkhouser	Canton Central Catholic—45	Doug Miller
	A	Anna—54	Jane Jones	Old Washington Buckeye Trail—52	David Linn
1982	AAA	Columbus Northland—51	Elaine Boltz	East Cleveland Shaw—46	Edith Spivey
	AA	Warsaw River View—51	Dave Mast	Reading—46	Larry Phillips
	A	Zanesville Rosecrans—71	Dave Bell	New Washington Buckeye Central—51	Vainard Spiess
1983	AAA	Shelby—71	Ellen Lawrence	Barberton—69	Jeff Janiga
	AA	Huron—52	Richard Wennes	Chagrin Falls—45	Robert Ohlich
	A	Zanesville Rosecrans—70	David Bell	Mansfield St. Peter's—37	Dennis Rissler
1984	AAA	Cincinnati Forest Park—44 (1 OT)	Mark Ehlen	Canton McKinley—41	Sue Davis
	AA	Millersburg W. Holmes—36 (1 OT)	Jack Van Reeth	Orrville—35	Al Lehman
	A	Newark Catholic—71	Bill Cooperrider	Zanesville Rosecrans—60	David Bell
1985	AAA	Pickerington—58 (1 OT)	David Butcher	Dresden Tri-Valley—55	Mary Ann Grimes
	AA	Millersburg West Holmes—54	Jack Van Reeth	New Lexington—29	Roger Hooper
	A	New Washington Buckeye Central—48	Vainard Spiess	Tipp City Bethel—44	John Whitehouse
1986	AAA	Columbus South—74	Ernie Robinson	Cincinnati Oak Hills—54	Nann Meyer
	AA	Millersburg W. Holmes—46 (1 OT)	Jack Van Reeth	Tipp City Tippecanoe—42	Thomas Rettig
	A	Tipp City Bethel—80	John Whitehouse	Richmond Dale Southeastern—71	Don Barrow
1987	AAA	Cincinnati Princeton—63	Jerry Stein	Columbus Watterson—53	Tom DiCesare
	AA	Lima Bath—58	Gretchen Prichard	Wellsville—55	Randy Young
	A	Delphos St. John's—56 (1 OT)	Jean Weber	Chillicothe Unioto—55	Cyndy Driggs
1988	I	Upper Arlington—55	Dudley Beaver	Canton GlenOak—52	Gary Isler
	II	Akron Hoban—46	Mary Ann King	Byesville Meadowbrook—42	Vic Whiting
	III	Vienna Matthews—63	Dennis Holmes	Utica—48	Tom Russell
	IV	Kalida—62	Frank R. Schroeder	South Charleston Southeastern—51	Kirk Martin
1989	I	Canton GlenOak—49	Gary Isler	Cincinnati Mother of Mercy—47	Mary Jo Huisman
	II	Byesville Meadowbrook—54	Frank Gregory	Pataskala Watkins Memorial—53	Ron Ratliff
	III	Sherwood Fairview-57	Dan English	Chillicothe Unioto—56	Cyndy Driggs
	IV	Kalida—57	Frank Schroeder	Berlin Hiland—45	Ora Shetler
1990	I	Pickerington—61	Dave Butcher	Cincinnati Mother of Mercy—42	Mary Jo Huismann
	II	Garfield Heights Trinity—70	Patrick Diulus	Elida—60	Vicki Mauk
	III	Coldwater—62	Charles Maier	Brookfield—55	Tim Filipovich
	IV	Fort Recovery—54	Diane McClung	Middletown Fenwick—41	Mike Lockhart
1991	I	Celina—53	Jack Clouse	Rocky River Magnificat—50	Ron Trzcinski
	II	Dayton Dunbar-73	Tim Montgomery	Canfield—59	Bill Wolf
	III	Heath—62	Don Hardin	Sherwood Fairview—44	Dan English
	IV	Fort Recovery—63	Diane McClure	McDonald—58	Barry Clute
1992	I	Pickerington—53	Dave Butcher	Logan—46	Ralph Taylor
	II	Urbana—65	Bill Moss	Shelby—55	Allen Lawrence
	III	Coldwater—63	Charles Maier	Loudonville—47	John Wilson
	IV	Zanesville Rosecrans—44	Larry Nash	Buckeye Central—41	Chuck Snyder

Basketball Tournament Records, Girls

DIVISION I

CHAMPIONSHIP GAME

MOST POINTS
Individual—34—Jodi Roth, Shelby vs. Barberton, 1983
One Team—74—Columbus South vs. Cincinnati Oak Hills, 1986
Both Teams—140—Shelby (71) and Barberton (69), 1983
MOST FIELD GOALS (2-point)
Individual—13—Jodi Roth, Shelby vs. Barberton, 1983
One Team—33—Columbus South vs. Cincinnati Oak Hills, 1986
Both Teams—53—Barberton (30) and Shelby (23), 1983
MOST FIELD GOALS (3-point)
Individual—2—Erin Mooney, Rocky River Magnificat vs. Celina, 1991
2—Rose Weisenseel, Rocky River Magnificat vs. Celina, 1991
One Team—4—Rocky River Magnificat vs. Celina, 1991
Both Teams—4—Rocky River Magnificat (4) and Celina (0), 1991
MOST FREE THROWS
Individual—11—Susie Cassell, Pickerington vs. Cincinnati Mother of Mercy, 1990
One Team—27—Pickerington vs. Cincinnati Mother of Mercy, 1990
Both Teams—38—Pickerington (27) and Cincinnati Mother of Mercy (11), 1990
FEWEST POINTS
One Team—27—Barberton vs. Akron St. Vincent-St. Mary, 1979
Both Teams—62—Akron St. Vincent-St. Mary (35) and Barberton (27), 1979
LOWEST WINNING SCORE
35—Akron St. Vincent-St. Mary vs. Barberton, 1979
WIDEST WINNING MARGIN
20—Columbus South (74) and Cincinnati Oak Hills (54), 1986

ANY TOURNAMENT GAME

MOST POINTS
Individual—34—Jodi Roth, Shelby vs. Barberton, 1983
One Team—74—Columbus South vs. Cincinnati Oak Hills, 1986
Both Teams—140—Shelby (71) and Barberton (69), 1983
MOST FIELD GOALS (2-point)
Individual—14—Kathryn Prest, Struthers vs. Toledo Woodward, 1976
14—Denise Duncan, East Cleveland Shaw vs. Cincinnati Mother of Mercy, 1980
14—Julie Duerring, Cincinnati Oak Hills vs. Columbus Northland, 1982
14—Marie Anderson, Barberton vs. Xenia, 1983
One Team—35—Columbus South vs. Cincinnati Oak Hills, 1986
Both Teams—55—Akron Buchtel (28) and Cincinnati Princeton (27), 1987
MOST FIELD GOALS (3-point)
Individual—3—Darlene Sheehan, Rocky River Magnificat vs. Cuyahoga Falls, 1991
One Team—4—Rocky River Magnificat vs. Cuyahoga Falls, 1991
4—Rocky River Magnificat vs. Celina, 1991
Both Teams—4—Rocky River Magnificat (3) and Cincinnati Mother of Mercy (1), 1990
4—Rocky River Magnificat (4) and Celina (0), 1991
4—Rocky River Magnificat (4) and Cuyahoga Falls (0), 1991
4—Celina (2) and Beavercreek (2), 1991
MOST FREE THROWS
Individual—14—Janet Thorpe, Cincinnati Mother of Mercy vs. East Cleveland Shaw, 1980
One Team—27—Pickerington vs. Cincinnati Mother of Mercy, 1990
Both Teams—38—Pickerington (27) and Cincinnati Mother of Mercy (11), 1990
FEWEST POINTS
One Team—27—Barberton vs. Akron St. Vincent-St. Mary, 1979
Both Teams—62—Akron St. Vincent-St. Mary (35) and Barberton (27), 1979
LOWEST WINNING SCORE
35—Springfield North vs. Mentor, 1977
35—Akron St. Vincent-St. Mary vs. Barberton, 1979

MOST POINTS
Individual—61—Jodi Roth, Shelby, 1983
One Team—141—Shelby, 1983
MOST FIELD GOALS (2-point)
Individual—22—Jodi Roth, Shelby, 1983
One Team—58—Columbus South, 1986
MOST FIELD GOALS (3-point)
Individual—3—Darlene Sheehan, Rocky River Magnificat, 1991
3—Rose Weisenseel, Rocky River Magnificat, 1991
One Team—8—Rocky River Magnificat, 1991
MOST FREE THROWS
Individual—20—Janet Thorpe, Cincinnati Mother of Mercy, 1980
One Team—49—Shelby, 1983

DIVISION II

CHAMPIONSHIP GAME

MOST POINTS
Individual—36—Amy Tucker, Springboro vs. Columbus Hartley, 1978
One Team—73—Dayton Dunbar vs. Canfield, 1991
Both Teams—132—Dayton Dunbar (73) and Canfield (59), 1991
MOST FIELD GOALS (2-point)
Individual—14—Amy Tucker, Springboro vs. Columbus Hartley, 1978
One Team—33—Dayton Dunbar vs. Canfield, 1991
Both Teams—52—Garfield Heights Trinity (27) and Elida (25), 1990
MOST FIELD GOALS (3-point)
Individual—7—Jenny Kulics, Canfield vs. Dayton Dunbar, 1991
One Team—7—Canfield Vs. Dayton Dunbar, 1991
Both Teams—8—Canfield (7) and Dayton Dunbar (1), 1991
MOST FREE THROWS
Individual—8—Julie Biermann, Bellbrook vs. Columbus Hartley, 1976
8—Amy Tucker, Springboro vs. Columbus Hartley, 1978
One Team—18—Huron vs. Chagrin Falls, 1983
18—Byesville Meadowbrook vs. Pataskala Watkins Memorial, 1989
Both Teams—29—Byesville Meadowbrook (18) and Pataskala Watkins Memorial (11), 1989
FEWEST POINTS
One Team—29—New Lexington vs. Millersburg West Holmes, 1985
Both Teams—71—Millersburg West Holmes (36) and Orrville (35), 1984
LOWEST WINNING SCORE
36—Millersburg West Holmes vs. Orrville, 1984
WIDEST WINNING SCORE
25—Millersburg West Holmes (54) and New Lexington (29), 1985

ANY TOURNAMENT GAME

MOST POINTS
Individual—39—Jane Phend, Chagrin Falls vs. Reading, 1983
One Team—90—Delphos St. John's vs. Navarre Fairless, 1980
Both Teams—146—Delphos St. John's (90) and Navarre Fairless (56), 1980
MOST FIELD GOALS (2-point)
Individual—14—Amy Tucker, Springboro vs. Columbus Hartley, 1978
14—Jane Phend, Chagrin Falls vs. Reading, 1983
14—Rhonda Winters, Orrville vs. Heath, 1984
One Team—42—Delphos St. John's vs. Navarre Fairless, 1980
Both Teams—64—Delphos St. John's (42) and Navarre Fairless (22), 1980
MOST FIELD GOALS (3-point)
Individual—7—Jenny Kulics, Canfield vs. Dayton Dunbar, 1991
One Team—7—Canfield vs. Dayton Dunbar, 1991
Both Teams—9—Celina (5) and Akron Hoban (4), 1988
MOST FREE THROWS
Individual—11—Jane Phend, Chagrin Falls vs. Reading, 1983
One Team—23—Akron Hoban vs. Tipp City Tippecanoe, 1986
23—Canfield vs. Logan, 1991
Both Teams—39—Canfield (23) and Logan (16), 1991

FEWEST POINTS
One Team—27—Cincinnati Finneytown vs. Millersburg West Holmes, 1986
Both Teams—58—Millersburg West Holmes (31) and Cincinnati Finneytown (27), 1986

LOWEST WINNING SCORE
31—Millersburg West Holmes vs. Cincinnati Finneytown, 1986

TWO GAME TOURNAMENT RECORDS

MOST POINTS
Individual—70—Amy Tucker, Springboro, 1978
One Team—152—Delphos St. John's, 1980
152—Dayton Dunbar, 1991
MOST FIELD GOALS (2-point)
Individual—26—Amy Tucker, Springboro, 1978
One Team—67—Delphos St. John's, 1980
MOST FIELD GOALS (3-point)
Individual—11—Jenny Kulics, Canfield, 1991
One Team—13—Canfield, 1991
MOST FREE THROWS
Individual—18—Amy Tucker, Springboro, 1978
One Team—33—Canfield, 1991

DIVISION III

CHAMPIONSHIP GAME

MOST POINTS
Individual—26—Annette Bergman, Sherwood Fairview vs. Chillicothe Unioto, 1989
One Team—63—Vienna Mathes vs. Utica, 1988
Both Teams—117—Coldwater (62) and Brookfield (55), 1990
MOST FIELD GOALS (2-point)
Individual—10—Laurie Maxwell, Utica vs. Vienna Mathews, 1988
10—Kristina Dupps, Heath vs. Sherwood Fairview, 1991
One Team—26—Vienna Mathews vs. Utica, 1988
Both Teams—43—Vienna Mathews (26) and Utica (17), 1988
MOST FIELD GOALS (3-point)
Individual—5—Natalie Hill, Chillicothe Unioto vs. Sherwood Fairview, 1989
One Team—5—Chillicothe Unioto vs. Sherwood Fairview, 1989
Both Teams—9—Chillicothe Unioto (5) and Sherwood Fairview (4), 1989
MOST FREE THROWS
Individual—8—Connie Alig, Coldwater vs. Brookfield, 1990
8—Kacee English, Sherwood Fairview vs. Heath, 1991
One Team—22—Coldwater vs. Brookfield, 1990
Both Teams—37—Coldwater (22) and Brookfield (15), 1990
FEWEST POINTS
One Team—44—Sherwood Fairview vs. Heath, 1991
Both Teams—106—Heath (62) and Sherwood Fairview (44), 1991
LOWEST WINNING SCORE
57—Sherwood Fairview vs. Chillicothe Unioto, 1989
WIDEST WINNING MARGIN
18—Heath (62) and Sherwood Fairview (44), 1991

ANY TOURNAMENT GAME

MOST POINTS
Individual—30—Natalie Hill, Chillicothe Unioto vs. Swanton, 1989
One Team—67—Vienna Mathews vs. Coldwater, 1988
67—Chillicothe Unioto vs. Swanton, 1989
67—Coldwater vs. Heath, 1990
Both Teams—130—Coldwater (67) and Heath (63), 1990
MOST FIELD GOALS (2-point)
Individual—11—Lori McClellan, Chillicothe Unioto vs. Swanton, 1989
One Team—29—Vienna Mathews vs. Coldwater, 1988
Both Teams—48—Swanton (25) and Chillicothe Unioto (23), 1989
MOST FIELD GOALS (3-point)
Individual—5—Natalie Hill, Chillicothe Unioto vs. Sherwood Fairview, 1989
One Team—5—Chillicothe Unioto vs. Sherwood Fairview, 1989
Both Teams—9—Chillicothe Unioto (5) and Sherwood Fairview (4), 1989

MOST FREE THROWS
Individual—14—Natalie Hill, Chillicothe Unioto vs. Swanton, 1989
One Team—23—Heath vs. Coldwater, 1990
Both Teams—40—Heath (23) and Coldwater (17), 1990
FEWEST POINTS
One Team—32—Springfield Kenton Ridge vs. Heath, 1991
Both Teams—86—Heath (54) and Springfield Kenton Ridge (32), 1991
LOWEST WINNING SCORE
49—Utica vs. Bellville Clear Fork, 1988

TWO GAME TOURNAMENT RECORDS

MOST POINTS
Individual—47—Natalie Hill, Chillicothe Unioto, 1989
One Team—130—Vienna Mathews, 1988
MOST FIELD GOALS (2-point)
Individual—18—Lori McClellan, Chillicothe Unioto, 1989
One Team—55—Vienna Mathews, 1988
MOST FIELD GOALS (3 point)
Individual—5—Natalie Hill, Chillicothe Unioto, 1989
5—Annette Bergman, Sherwood Fairview, 1989
One Team—5—Utica, 1988
5—Chillicothe Unioto, 1989
5—Sherwood Fairview, 1989
MOST FREE THROWS
Individual—14—Natalie Hill, Chillicothe Unioto, 1989
One Team—39—Coldwater, 1990

DIVISION IV

CHAMPIONSHIP GAME

MOST POINTS
Individual—43—Lynn Bihn, Fort Recovery vs. McDonald, 1991
One Team—80—Tipp City Bethel vs. Richmond Dale Southeastern in Akron, 1986
Both Teams—151—Tipp City Bethel (90) and Richmond Dale Southeastern (71) in Akron, 1986
MOST FIELD GOALS (2-point)
Individual—17—Kelly Lyons, Tipp City Bethel vs. Richmond Dale Southeastern in Akron, 1986
17—Kelly Downs, Richmond Dale Southeastern vs. Tipp City Bethel in Akron, 1986
17—Lynn Bihn, Fort Recovery vs. McDonald, 1991
One Team—32—Tipp City Bethel vs. Richmond Dale Southeastern in Akron, 1986
32—Richmond Dale Southeastern vs. Tipp City Bethel in Akron, 1986
Both Teams—64—Tipp City Bethel (32) and Richmond Dale Southeastern (32) in Akron, 1986
MOST FIELD GOALS (3-point)
Individual—3—Pam Vilk, McDonald vs. Fort Recovery, 1991
One Team—3—McDonald vs. Fort Recovery, 1991
Both Teams—3—McDonald (3) and Fort Recovery (0), 1991
MOST FREE THROWS
Individual—10—Stephenie Winegardner, Chillicothe Unioto vs. Delphos St. John's, 1987
One Team—21—Chillicothe Unioto vs. Delphos St. John's, 1987
Both Teams—37—Chillicothe Unioto (21) and Delphos St. John's (16), 1987
FEWEST POINTS
One Team—32—Holgate vs. Old Washington Buckeye Trail, 1979
Both Teams—72—Frankfort Adena (37) and Rocky River Lutheran West (35), 1976
LOWEST WINNING SCORE
37—Frankfort Adena vs. Rocky River Lutheran West, 1976
WIDEST WINNING MARGIN
33—Zanesville Rosecrans (70) and Mansfield St. Peter's (37), 1983

ANY TOURNAMENT GAME

MOST POINTS
Individual—43—Lynn Bihn, Fort Recovery vs. McDonald, 1991
One Team—80—Tipp City Bethel vs. Richmond Dale Southeastern in Akron, 1986
Both Teams—151—Tipp City Bethel (80) and Richmond Dale Southeastern (71) in Akron, 1986
MOST FIELD GOALS (2-point)
Individual—17—Kelly Lyons, Tipp City Bethel vs. Richmond Dale Southeastern in Akron, 1986
17—Kelly Downs, Richmond Dale Southeastern vs. Tipp City Bethel in Akron, 1986
17—Kelly Downs, Richmond Dale Southeastern vs. New Washington Buckeye Cental in Akron, 1986

17—Lynn Bihn, Fort Recovery vs. McDonald, 1991
One Team—34—Zanesville Rosecrans vs. Anna, 1982
Both Teams—64—Tipp City Bethel (32) and Richmond Dale Southeastern (32) in Akron, 1986

MOST FIELD GOALS (3-point)
Individual—3—Pam Vilk, McDonald vs. Fort Recovery, 1991
One Team—3—Berlin Hiland vs. Fort Recovery, 1990
3—McDonald vs. Fort Recovery, 1991
Both Teams—3—Berlin Hiland (3) and Fort Recovery (0), 1990
3—Zanesville Rosecrans (2) and Fort Recovery (1), 1991
3—McDonald (3) and Fort Recovery (0), 1991

MOST FREE THROWS
Individual—10—Joan Heidman, Rocky River Lutheran West vs. Lancaster Fisher Catholic, 1976
10—Cheryl Mast, Smithville vs. Old Washington Buckeye Trail, 1978
10—Stephenie Winegardner, Chillicothe Unioto vs. Delphos St. John's, 1987
One Team—21—New Washington Buckeye Central vs. Archbold, 1982
21—Chillicothe Unioto vs. Delphos St. John's, 1987
Both Teams—37—Chillicothe Unioto (21) and Delphos St. John's (16), 1987

FEWEST POINTS
One Team—23—New Washington Buckeye Central vs. Middletown Fenwick, 1990
Both Teams—53—Middletown Fenwick (30) and New Washington Buckeye Central (23), 1990

LOWEST WINNING SCORE
30—Middletown Fenwick vs. New Washington Buckeye Central, 1990

TWO GAME TOURNAMENT RECORDS

MOST POINTS
Individual—75—Kelly Downs, Richmond Dale Southeastern in Akron, 1986
One Team—144—Zanesville Rosecrans, 1982

MOST FIELD GOALS (2-point)
Individual—34—Kelly Downs, Richmond Dale Southeastern in Akron, 1986
One Team—60—Rosecrans, 1982

MOST FIELD GOALS (3-point)
Individual—3—Pam Vilk, McDonald, 1991
One Team—3—McDonald, 1991

MOST FREE THROWS
Individual—16—Stephenie Winegardner, Chillicothe Unioto, 1987
One Team—38—Anna, 1981

The name's the thing

The Editors' Favorite Ohio High School Nicknames

1. Beavercreek Battlin' Beavers (Greene County)
2. Cleveland East Tech Scarabs (Cuyahoga County)
3. Crooksville Ceramics (Perry County)
4. Glenville Tarblooders (Cuyahoga County)
5. Mifflin Punchers (Franklin County)
6. Shelby Whippets (Richland County)
7. Shenandoah Zeps (Noble County)
8. South Webster Jeeps (Scioto County)
9. Union-Scioto (a.k.a. Unioto) Sherman Tanks (Ross County)
10. Urbana Hillclimbers (Champaign County)

All-Ohio Girls' Team, 1991-92

Division I

Player	Team	Height	Class	Point Average
Katie Smith	Logan	5-11	Sr.	30.2
Marcie Alberts	Wooster	5-5	Jr.	18.2
Kelly Fergus	Brunswick	6-3	Sr.	22.6
Sheri Horvath	Amherst Steele	6-1	Sr.	24.0
Lisa Howard	Reynoldsburg	5-7	Sr.	18.7
Atina Harris	Dayton Dunbar	5-8	Sr.	20.3
Carey Poor	Celina	6-0	Sr.	19.5

Player of the year: Katie Smith, Logan
Coach of the year: Maggi Williams, Sidney

Division II

Player	Team	Height	Class	Point Average
Anita Jurcenko	Jefferson	5-5	Sr.	23.0
Amanda Hayes	Columbus Beechcroft	5-8	Sr.	25.2
Jannon Roland	Urbana	6-1	Jr.	29.5
Kelley Burrier	Louisville	5-10	Sr.	17.5
Dee Reeder	Galion	5-11	Sr.	19.8
Jenn Swartzwelder	Dover	5-10	Sr.	17.0
Angie Gray	Washington Court House	5-3	Sr.	17.2

Co-players of the year: Amanda Hayes, Columbus Beechcroft; Anita Jurcenko, Jefferson
Co-coaches of the year: Ron Russo, Dayton Carroll; Dick Killen, Oberlin Firelands

Division III

Player	Team	Height	Class	Point Average
Marlene Stollings	Beaver Eastern	5-10	Jr.	41.6
Denise Pickenpaugh	Heath	5-10	Sr.	23.4
Lori Montgomery	East Palestine	5-8	Sr.	19.5
Amy Siefring	Coldwater	5-7	Sr.	18.7
Holly Porter	Wyoming	5-11	Jr.	26.6

Player of the year: Marlene Stollings, Beaver Eastern
Coach of the year: Jim Verba, Brooklyn

Division IV

Player	Team	Height	Class	Point Average
Stephanie Petho	Bellaire St. John	5-8	Sr.	37.3
Krista Seifert	New Reigel	5-7	Sr.	21.9
Renee Walls	Latham Western	5-5	Sr.	34.0
Allison Day	Western Reserve Academy	6-1	Sr.	23.6
Mary Winterhalter	Danville	5-11	Sr.	17.5
Lynette Roeth	Covington	5-5	Sr.	25.8
Carrie Ferguson	South Charlestown Southeastern	5-10	Jr.	13.3

Player of the year: Stephanie Petho, Bellaire St. John
Coach of the year: Bill Drury, Southington Chalker

Source: The 1991-1992 Associated Press All-Ohio basketball team is selected
upon the recommendations of a state panel of sports writers and broadcasters

Baseball

State Champions

Year	Class	Champion	Coach	Runner-Up	Coach
1928	A	Columbus Aquinas (4)	Mike Boland	Athens (3)	Alva Hatch
	B	Centerville (20)		Oxford McGuffey (9)	
1929	A	Columbus Central (10)	Dave Parks	Canton McKinley (3)	D. V. Peabody
	B	Newcomerstown (5)	Ralph Bower	Iberia (0)	
1930	A	Martins Ferry (13)	Fred Hart	Cincinnati Woodward (4)	Winton Moeller
	B	St. Paris (12)	Harry Orders	Petersburg (6)	Roman Miller
1931	A	Cincinnati Woodward (3)	Winton Moeller	Canton McKinley (2)	D. V. Peabody
	B	Delphos (2)	Gilbert Smith	Independence (1)	Cecil Burnett
1932	A	Columbus South (2)	Rodney Ross	Cincinnati Roger Bacon (1)	Ed Burns
	B	Tiltonsville (6)	Morgan Jones	Dayton Fairmont (5)	Bill Ramsey
1933	A	Warren Harding (4)	Dwight Lafferty	Pomeroy (2)	Ray Farham
	B	Congress West-Salem (9)		Delphos (4)	
1934	A	Cincinnati Withrow (13)	Angus King	Warren Harding (1)	Dwight Lafferty
	B	Mayfield Heights (7)	H. A. Sheetz	Navarre (6)	Fred Brideweser
1935	A	Cincinnati Roger Bacon (8)	Ed Burns	Toledo Libbey (3)	Albert Jeffery
	B	Brookville (4)	Robert Warnke	Reading (3) 9	Robert Elsbrock
1936	A	Norwood (9)	Paul Ludwig	Columbus Aquinas (0)	J. B. Taylor
	B	Etna (15)	M. Z. Pond	Hamilton Fairfield Township (4)	Charles Ross
1937	A	Canton McKinley (14)	John Reed	Bedford (3)	Samuel Holt
	B	Holgate (7)	John Rudolph	Troy Elizabeth Township (6) 9	Russell Huffman
1938	A	Cincinnati Hughes (4)	Earl Klinck	Canton McKinley (2)	John Reed
	B	Sugar Grove (6)	Jim Chilcote	Springfield Pitchin (4)	Marvin Borst
1939	A	Canton McKinley (2)	John Reed	Middletown (0)	Elmo Lingrel
	B	Pemberville (8)	J. F. Huebner	Lockbourne Hamilton Township (6)	Carlton Rayl
1940	A	Columbus North (5)	Bob Sekerak	Greenfield (3)	Gerald Armstrong
	B	Powhatan Point (3)	Mac Cora	Milford Center (1)	Edgar Post
1941	A	Cincinnati Withrow (7)	Angus King	East Cleveland Shaw (6)	Roy Wisecup
	B	Beavercreek (12)	C. E. Bradstreet	New Riegel (1)	Edward Newcome
1942	A	Tiltonsville (6)	Alfred Burazio	Greenfield (4)	Gerald Armstrong
	B	Reading (10)	Jess Ellis	Yorkville (3)	Elmer Stupak
1943	A	Cincinnati Elder (4)	Walter Bartlett	Springfield (0)	Russ Paugh
	B	Leavittsburg (3)	Claude Graber	Ney (2)	Dudley Ebersole
1944	A	East Cleveland Shaw (5)	Roy Wisecup	Cincinnati Roger Bacon (3)	John Wiethe
	B	Reading (4)	Jess Ellis	Lorain Clearview (0)	C. W. Stubblefield
1945	A	Cincinnati Woodward (4)	Ed Eshman	Dayton Fairmont (0)	Ralph Fowler
	B	Plainsville (9)	George Baker	St. Henry (8)	Charles Karcher
1946	A	Cleveland Lincoln (6)	Howard Filiere	Cincinnati Elder (0)	Walter Bartlett
	B	Reading (3)	Jess Ellis	St. Henry (0)	Charles Karcher
1947	A	Cleveland Heights (3)	Bernard Zweig	Upper Arlington (1)	Doyt Perry
	B	Lockbourne Hamilton Township (3)	Dwight Black	Terrace Park (1)	Dick Avery
1948	A	Cincinnati Western Hills (8)	Paul Nohr	Warren Harding (6)	Dwight Lafferty
	B	Montgomery Sycamore (7)	Bob Wearly	Galena Orange Township (5) 8	Chester Hurd
1949	A	Cincinnati Hughes (14)	Robert Ruess	Lakewood (0)	Don Harwood
	B	North Bend Taylor (3)	Vern Ullom	McCutchenville (2)	Mirl Rosendale
1950	A	Cincinnati Withrow (6)	John Huhey	Galion (4) 9	E. Renno
	B	Amelia (1)	Stanley Anstaett	Middleport (0) 9	Don McKenzie
1951	A	Cincinnati Western Hills (2)	Paul Nohr	Columbus Linden McKinley (1)	Hal Martin
	B	Lima St. Rose (7)	Harry Schlott	Navarre (2) 11	Fred Brideweser
1952	A	Cincinnati Elder (5)	George Lemmel	Galion (0)	Dick Kerin
	B	Beavercreek (4)	Mark Stewart	Warren Howland (0)	Gerald Hiestard
1953	A	Cincinnati Purcell (2)	Jack Hanlen	Tiltonsville (1)	Alfred Burazie
	B	Beavercreek (6)	Mark Stewart	Fort Recovery (1)	Harold Knapke
1954	A	Mansfield (3)	Don Pierson	Cincinnati Elder (0)	Don Ruberg
	B	Waverly (2)	C.D. Hawnee	Sycamore (1)	Henry Roberson
1955	A	Cincinnati Elder (3)	Don Ruberg	Massillon (0)	Carl Schroeder
	B	Lockland (8)	Charles Payne	Dublin (1)	Frank Diehl
1956	A	Cincinnati Elder (2)	Don Ruberg	Cleveland Benedictine (0)	August Bossu
	B	Cincinnati Greenhills (4)	Jim McDermott	Prospect (3)	Fred McCumber
1957	A	Middleport (4)	Nolan Swackhamer	Doylestown (3)	Jerry Boggs
	AA	Reading (9)	Don Mohr	Lorain (0)	Tony Misko
1958	A	Goshen (3)	Joe Deneby	Gnadenhutten (1)	Dick Scott
	AA	Cincinnati Elder (11)	Roy Dieringer	Fremont (10)	L. R. Doren

		Champion	Coach	Runner-Up	Coach
1959	A	West Salem Northwestern (7)	Roy Bates	Spencerville (0)	Robert Brookhart
	AA	Cincinnati Elder (11)	Roy Dieringer	Barberton (7)	Lester Scarr
1960	A	Liberty Union (8)	Clifford Rollins	Convoy Union (4)	P. A. Bricker
	AA	Cincinnati Elder (4)	Roy Dieringer	Lima Senior (3)	Joe Bowers
1961	A	Liberty Union (4)	Cliford Rollins	Windham (2)	Leo Kot
	AA	Cleveland South (7)	Frank Dillon	Lima Senior (1)	Joe Bowers
1962	A	Van Wert Lincolnview (4)	Andy White	Liberty Union (0)	Clifford Rollins
	AA	North Bend Taylor (7)	Harold Betz	Niles McKinley (2)	Paul Demont
1963	A	Powhaten Point (3)	F. Bland	Dublin (0)	Dick Close
	AA	Euclid (8)	Bob Addis	Lima Senior (4)	Joe Bowers
1964	A	Liberty Union (1)	Mark Wylie	North Central-Pioneer (0)	Paul Conrad
	AA	Lima Senior (7)	Joe Bowers	Cleveland Benedictine (6)	August Bossu
1965	A	Versailles (5)	Gene Pequignot	Lucasville Valley (1)	Ron Patridge
	AA	Shaker Heights (4)	Fred Heinlein	Steubenville Catholic Cent. (0)	John Nese
1966	A	West Salem Northwestern (4)	Dale Wachtel	Lucasville Valley (0)	Don Pfleger
	AA	Kettering Fairmont West (3)	Bob Hildreth	Tallmadge (1)	Dave Young
1967	A	Nelsonville (4)	Phil Fawcett	Edon Northwest (1)	Kent Adams
	AA	Cincinnati Western Hills (8)	Dick Hauck	Youngstown Boardman (6)	Tom Ferrara
1968	A	Old Fort (6)	Jim Rosendahl	Anna (0)	Robert Anderson
	AA	East Cleveland Shaw (1)	John Hicks	Toledo Rogers (0)	Ray Steely
1969	A	New Riegel (1)	Charles Hendricks	Bridgeport (0) 9	Michael Rose
	AA	Columbus East (2)	Paul Pennell	East Liverpool (1)	James Potts
1970	A	Cincinnati Lincoln Hgts. (5)	Luther Greene	Pettisville (3)	Dave Ripke
	AA	Dayton Chaminade (6)	Richard Wessels	Garfield Heights (1)	Bill Hartley
1971	A	Russia (13)	Roger Eckenwiler	Old Fort (5)	Jim Rosendahl
	AA	Columbus Wehrle (3)	Robert Lehman	West Milton Milton-Union (2)	Roger Wise
	AAA	Findlay (10)	Arvin Curlis	Kettering Fairmont East (8)	Bob Chapman
1972	A	Anna (3)	Tom Middleton	Pickerington (0)	Jack Johnson
	AAAA	Ironton (3)	Mike Burcham	Solon (2)	Willis Woods
	AAA	Cincinnati Moeller (10)	Mike Cameron	Findlay (5)	Arvin Curlis
1973	A	Portsmouth East (5)	Lou Carson	Adena Buckeye West (3)	Gary Grove
	AA	St. Paris Graham (5)	Donzil Hall	Beloit West Branch (1)	Mike Kovach
	AAA	Cincinnati Elder (7)	Jim Massa	Cleveland Glenville (1)	Dennis Woods
1974	A	Middletown Fenwick (6)	Fred Nori	Carroll Bloom-Carroll (3)	Don Matheny
	AA	Cincinnati Reading (8)	Tom Higgins	Wooster Triway (2)	Bob McCauley
	AAA	Wickliffe (6)	Ken Ranallo	Cincinnati Princeton (5)	Howard Converse
1975	A	Lucasville Valley (5)	Doug Booth	Russia (0)	Roger Eckenwiler
	AA	Bryan (5)	Ray Sumpter	Hamilton Badin (4)	Bill Hogan
	AAA	Columbus West (28)	Dave Koblentz	Parma Senior (20)	Neil Chesney
1976	A	Leipsic (6)	Ted Miller	Cuyahoga Heights (5)	Art Massey
	AA	Elida (4)	Dick Prince	Orrville (3)	Jim Swaney
	AAA	Shaker Heights(5)	Fred Heinlen	Youngstown Chaney (4)	Bob Garcar
1977	A	Miller City (4)	Dan Kern	Versailles (2)	Bruce Stall
	AA	Cincinnati Deer Park (6)	Hank Estes	Coldwater (0)	Lou Brunswick
	AAA	Cincinnati Western Hills (11)	Ken Selby	Parma Padua Franciscan (4)	Paul Beskid
1978	A	Hicksville (11)	C. Lee Peter	Middletown Fenwick (2)	John Rossi
	AA	Coshocton(9)	Jim Shamel	Cleveland Benedictine (6)	August Bossu
	AAA	Cincinnati Elder (5)	Jerry Federle	Euclid (3)	Paul Serra
1979	A	Cardington-Lincoln (1)	William Clauss	Edgerton (0)	Bob Peverly
	AA	Columbus DeSales (7)	William Killian	Trenton Edgewood (4)	Richard Boggs
	AAA	Oregon Clay (3)	Richard Kandik	Euclid (2)	Paul Serra
1980	A	Anna (8)	Richard Ansley	New Matamoras Frontier (4)	John Hoff
	AA	Reading (10)	Tom Higgins	Petersburg Springfield (5)	Bill Wesley
	AAA	Cincinnati Oak Hills (8)	Rob Rose	Bay Village Bay (5)	Cliff Cook
1981	A	Middletown Fenwick (4)	Pat Kreke	Gahanna Columbus Academy (2)	Jim Stahl
	AA	Parma Hgts. Holy Name (4)	David Wilks	Portsmouth (3)	John Tipton
	AAA	Worthington (3)	Frank Cozze	Cincinnati Oak Hills (1)	Pat Quinn
1982	A	Gahanna Columbus Academy (12)	Jim Stahl	Dadiz (0)	Dale Edwards
	AA	Urbana (4)	Bob Brenning	Bucyrus Wynford (0)	Tom Schreck
	AAA	Euclid (3)	Paul Serra	Lancaster (2)	Tom White
1983	A	Ashtabula St. John (10)	Bill Schmidt	Miller City (2)	Dan Kern
	AA	Coldwater (12)	Lou Brunswick	Urbana (5)	Bob Brenning
	AAA	Hamilton (14)	Dan Bowling	Youngstown Austintown-Fitch (10)	Rich Coppola
1984	A	Miller City (4)	Dan Kern	Tuscarawas Central Catholic (3)	Joe Drotovick
	AA	Coldwater (8)	Lou Brunswick	Hamilton Badin (4)	Gerry Weisgerber
	AAA	Cincinnati Elder (2)	Jerry Federle	Marion Harding (1)	Larry Merchant
1985	A	Graysville Skyvue (9)	Mark Huffman	Fort Loramie (2)	Michael Anthony
	AA	Bellevue (3)	Ed Nasonti	Wellston (2)	Pat Hendershot
	AAA	Fairfield (8)	Gary Yeatts	Lyndhurst Brush (5)	Jim Humpal

		Champion	Coach	Runner-Up	Coach
1986	A	Ottawa Hills (8)	Chris Hardman	Sidney Lehman (7)	Steve Hunsucker
	AA	Akron St. Vincent-St. Mary (6)	Dan Boarman	Lancaster Fairfield Union (0)	John Nelson
	AAA	Cincinnati Western Hills (11)	Ken Selby	Westerville North (9)	Bob Haegele
1987	A	Rockford Parkway (7)	Mike Schumm	Newark Catholic (3)	John Cannizzaro
	AA	Coldwater (22)	Lou Brunswick	Mason (5)	Ken Gray
	AAA	Upper Arlington (4)	Dave Koblentz	Toledo Start (0)	Rich Arbinger
1988	A	Newark Catholic (11)	John Canizzaro	Frankfort Adena (1)	Mike Mays
	AA	Youngstown Ursuline (9)	Matt GiamBattista	Cincinnati McNicholas (5)	Ray Ayers
	AAA	Columbus Watterson (9)	Tom Pond	Parma Hgts. Holy Name (2)	Dave Wilks
1989	A	Frankfort Adena (4)	Jim Thomas	Newark Catholic (6)	John Cannizzaro
	AA	Akron St. Vincent-St. Mary (15)	Dan Boarman	Byesville Meadowbrook (6)	Tim Roller
	AAA	Cincinnati Moeller (12)	Mike Cameron	Upper Arlington (4)	Mike Matthaes
1990	A	Coldwater (13)	Lou Brunswick	Lorain Catholic (10)	Jim Macholl
	AA	Urbana (8)	Bob Brenning	Gnadenhutten Indian Valley (1)	Dave DiDonato
	AAA	Upper Arlington (20)	Mike Matthaes	Cuyahoga Falls (6)	John Anspach
1991	I	Fairfield (4)	Gary Yeatts	Youngstown Boardman (0)	David Smercansky
	II	Columbus Watterson (15)	Jack Hatem	Steubenville (0)	Fred Heatherington
	III	Hamilton Badin (2)	Mark Maus	Coldwater (1)	Lou Brunswick
	IV	Rockford Parkway (3)	Mike Schumm	Sidney Lehman (0)	Wayne Shoffner

Baseball Championship Records

Records are from the State Championship games since the first Tournament in 1928 and Semi Finals and Final games since 1971. Class AA records are from 1971 when three classifications were established.

TEAM RECORDS

Most runs by one team in one game
Class A Centerville 20 1928
Pinkerington 20 1972
Class AA Coldwater 22 1987
Class AAA Columbus West 28 1975

Most runs by one team in one inning
Class A Mayfield Heights 7 1934
Franklin Furnace Green 7 1986
Class AA Akron St. Vincent-St. Mary 9 1989
Class AAA Parma 12 1975

Most hits by one team in one game
Class A Centerville 19 1928
Class AA Coldwater 19 1987
Class AAA Hamilton 25 1983

Most stolen bases by one team in one game
Class A 4 teams tied 8
Class AA Norwalk 6 1978
Wellston 6 1985
Class AAA Westerville North 7 1986

Most home runs by one team
Class A 6 teams tied 2
Class AA 3 teams tied 2
Class AAA 5 teams tied 3

INDIVIDUAL RECORDS

Most stolen bases in one game
Class A 3 individuals tied 3
Class AA 2 individuals tied 3
Class AAA Mann, Cleveland Heights 3 1947
Karl Rhodes, Cincinnati Western Hills 3 1986

Most runs in one game
Class A R. Schulze, Russia 5 1971
Class AA Dan Ruff, Lancaster Fairfield Union 4 1986
Class AAA D. Smith, Columbus West 6 1975

Most hits in one game
Class A R. Schulze, Russia 5 1971
Class AA Bob Esselstein, Columbus DeSales 4 1979
Russ Cron, Coldwater 4 1983
Class AAA 10 individuals tied 4

Most home runs in one game
Class A S. Crosley, Anna 2 1971
Class AA Mark Frantz, Urbana 2 1949
Class AAA Marrs, Cincinnati Hughes 2 1949
Kurpiel, Dayton Chaminade 2 1970
Bob Huffman, Hamilton 2 1983

Most RBIs in one game
Class A R. Schulz, Russia 5 1971
Todd Bokolich, Lorain Catholic 5 1990
Class AA Russ Cron, Coldwater 4 1983
Nick LoBianco, Coldwater 4 1987
Matt Clevenger, St. Vincent-St. Mary 4 1989
Robert Trainer, Urbana 4 1990
Class AAA H. Williams, Columbus West 8 1975

Most strike outs by pitcher in one game
Class A Curtis, Iberia 19 1929
Class AA Dave Cornutte, Urbana 14 1982
Anthony Tolliver, Urbana 14 1990
Class AAA Hemberger, Cincinnati Elder 17 1952
Osteen, Reading 17 1957

No hit, no run game by pitcher
Jack Curby, Newcomerstown (vs. Kunkle, 2-0) 1928
Bill Hickle, Columbus South (vs. Bridgeport, 5-0) 1932
Vince Peck, Holgate (vs. Glouster, 6-0) 1937
George Buckosh, Lorain Clearview (vs. Columbus St. Charles, 1-0) 1944
Melvin Held, Florence Edon (vs. South Zanesville, 1-0) 1946
E. Dulkowski, Adena Buckeye West (vs. North Lewisburg Triad 4-0) 1973
Rick Rumer, Elida (vs. Pomeroy Meigs 1-0) 1976
Steve Engel, Reading (vs. Norwalk 1-0) 1980
Allan Anderson, Lancaster (vs. Cincinnati Withrow 6-0) 1982

High School Baseball Coaches Hall of Fame

Marty Karow	Ohio State	1972		Robert Smith	Riverside	1982
Harold Potter	Oregon Clay	1972		George Sosebee	Hudson	1982
Les Scarr	Barberton	1972		Dave Young	Tallmadge	1982
Marion Allen	Logan	1974		Ray Bates	Northwestern(Wayne)	1983
Neal Nelson	Willoughby South	1974		Robert Chapman	Fairmont East	1983
Paul Nore	Western Hills	1974		Brick Long	Rossford	1983
Ed Rennow	Athens	1974				
Mike Stewart	Beavercreek	1974		Luke Izer	Sandy Valley	1984
Bob Addis	Euclid	1975		John Anspach	Cuyahoga Falls	1985
Jim Bittengle	Shadyside	1975		Jim Hardman	Piqua	1985
Joe Bowers	Lima Senior	1975				
Bob Davis	Tecumseh	1975		Don Black	Parkway	1986
Dick Finn	Ohio State	1975		Mike Burcham	Ironton	1986
Dick Hauck	Western Hills	1975		Jim Jordan	Marietta	1986
Hank Miller	Canton McKinley	1975				
Jim Murray	Dayton Stebbins	1975		Jim Stahl	Columbus Academy	1987
Don Neff	Unioto	1975		Ray Sumpter	Bryan	1987
Garold Parrott	Deshler	1975				
				Frank Cozze	Worthington	1988
Augie Bossu	Benedictine	1976		George Hamric	Hamilton Twp.	1988
Ron Brookey	Dayton Meadowdale	1976				
Lou Carson	Portsmouth East	1976		Bernie Hovan	Nordonia	1989
Fred Heinlen	Shaker Heights	1976		Richard England	Lancaster	1989
Dick Prince	Elida	1976				
Dick Shine	Cuyahoga Falls	1976		Don Colussi	Colerain	1990
				Jim Shamel	Coshocton	1990
Jim Humpal	Charles F. Brush	1977				
Don Kelly	Rocky River	1977		Tim Miller	Canton South	1991
				John Nelson	Fairfield Union	1991
George Caso	Fairview	1978				
Lou Brunswick	Coldwater	1979				
Fred Brideweiser	Fairless	1980				
Milo Ratkovich	Akron Kenmore	1980				
Bob Wren	Ohio University	1980				
Bob Baird	Genoa	1981				
Howard Converse	Princeton	1981				
Dave Koblentz	Columbus West	1981				
John Nese	Steubenville Cen. Catholic	1981				
Fred Nocera	Whetstone	1981				
Bill Sadler	Westerville South	1981				

West Side story

Pete Rose grew up playing at Bold Face Park on the West Side. Rose's grandfather used to tell Pete he hit a ball so hard it left Bold Face Park, went over the railroad tracks, and sank a steamboat on the Ohio River.

Ohio's Most Deep-seated Baseball Neighborhood

For a hundred years in Cincinnati, the ball parks, as well as the breweries, were largely confined to the west side of town, the two, at least in the German-influenced Queen City, being not at all mutually exclusive. Perhaps it was the atmosphere of the Cincinnati Reds' ancient and honorable ballyards—it was here, after all, that professional baseball was born—or perhaps it was the work ethic of the German families. For whatever reason, twenty players from **Western Hills High** and **Elder High** became major league baseball players.

But the most amazing fact is that four West Siders became major-league managers—**Pete Rose, Jim Frey, Don Zimmer,** and **Russ Nixon.** As writer Lonnie Wheeler observed, "It doesn't seem possible that any other community in the world could produce four major-league managers from one generation." When Rose played on the West Side, he was a good ball player, but he wasn't the best. That nod usually went to another neighborhood kid named **Ed Brinkman,** a shortstop of note for Washington and Detroit. And when Rose himself finally made it to the Reds, on his first road trip, he found himself up against another West Siders, Philly pitcher **Art Mahaffey,** who sat Rose down four times. The superstar of those days was **Don Zimmer,** a shortstop and hot Dodgers prospect, until beaned by a curveball, an incident that provoked the use of helmets.

Pitcher **Jim Brosnan** is a Western Hills grad who started his career with the Cubs but was most successful as a reliever with the Reds in the early 1960s. Brosnan might have been better known as a writer; The Long Season is considered a baseball classic, as well as the first baseball diary that was actually written by the guy whose name was on the title page. Bill Veeck once said, "Brosnan was worse than a drunk. He was a practicing literate."

The Cincinnati high schools have dominated the high school state playoffs, winning nearly a third of them, notably Elder with 10, and Western Hills five. Wrote Wheeler: "It seems that Western Hills boys are born with an instinct for baseball, sort of a congenital corollary to an accumulated century of baseball culture..."

Wheeler, an astute historian of the game, was referring, of course, to the original Red Stocking, West Sider **Charlie Gould,** their first baseman, who also had an ill-fated stint as manager in 1876, that club closing up with a sickly .138 winning percentage. Gould was, however, a formidable first-sacker, at six feet bigger than most players and his long arms allowed him range when first basemen stayed on the bag. For his play, he got $800 for that first professional season of 1869.

The latest West Sider in the majors is none other than **Pete Rose, Jr.,** a plucky, likeable kid who brought with him all the notorious baggage one inherits from having a famous—as well as infamous—father. Rose the younger, in March of 1992, was a third-baseman in the Cleveland Indians' minor-league camp. He's had three years in the minors, and suffers with hitting; last season he hit .217 in Class A Sarasota, and has been plagued by a series of physical difficulties, from a pulled hamstring to a respiratory infection. The kid once said he would like to be named "Joe Smith," at least for a day. "When I step onto the field," he said, "I feel like I'm carrying the whole family with me." He is, to some degree, and more—he's carrying the West Side. ▶

State Champions, Boys

Year		Champion		Runner-up	
1908		Columbus North	19	Dayton Steele	16
1909		Toledo Central	29	Hillsboro	23
1910		Toledo Central	39	Columbus North	17
1911		Columbus North	50	Doane Academy, Granville	23
1912		Toledo Central	63	Columbus North	42 1/2
1913		Toledo Central	37	Columbus North	21
1914		Columbus East	50	Toledo Scott	23
1915		East Cleveland Shaw	37	Ashville	17 1/2
1916		East Cleveland Shaw	39 1/2	Salem	19
1917		Toledo Scott	45 5/6	Columbus North	25 1/3
1918		Toledo Scott	27 1/2	Columbus East	19 1/2
1919		East Cleveland Shaw	29 5/6	Warren Harding	21
1920		Cleveland East Tech	21	Warren Harding	18
1921	A	Cleveland East Tech	38 1/2	Lakewood	23
	B	Galion	31	Ashley	17
1922	A	Lakewood	47 1/2	Cleveland East Tech	18
	B	Ashley	27 1/3	Rocky River	24
1923	A	Lakewood	38 1/2	Sandusky	15 1/2
	B	Rocky River	24	Shaker Heights	20
1924	A	Lakewood	26	Akron West	14 1/2
	B	Rocky River	20	Bellpoint	19 1/2
1925	A	Cincinnati Hughes	22 1/2	Lakewood	21
	B	Bellpoint	29 1/2	Montpelier	19 1/2
1926	A	Lakewood	49	Columbus East	25
	B	Shaker Heights	36	Cleveland University	22
1927	A	Columbus Central	31 1/2	Lakewood	21 1/2
	B	Rocky River	22	Berea	20 3/4
1928	A	Columbus Central	34 1/4	Lakewood	32
	B	Hartwell	31	Berea	26 1/2
1929	A	Columbus Central	46 1/4	Lakewood	31
	B	Dayton Oakwood	21 2/5	Port Clinton	15
1930	A	Columbus Central	29	Lakewood	26
	B	Dayton Oakwood	32 2/3	Oberlin	21 1/2
1931	A	Lakewood	27	Salem	26 3/5
	B	Dayton Oakwood	51	Oberlin	25
1932	A	Cleveland East Tech	42	Columbus Central	29
	B	Oberlin	31	Millersburg	18 1/2
1933	A	Cleveland East Tech	31	Lakewood	25
	B	Mentor	26	Lakeside	16
1934	A	Toledo Scott	26 2/3	Cleveland Collinwood	21
	B	Delta	24	Xenia OSSO	19
1935	A	Toledo Scott	36 1/3	Cleveland East Tech & Sandusky	24
	B	Glendale	31 1/2	Upper Arlington	20 1/2
1936	A	Cleveland East Tech	32 1/2	Sandusky	27
	B	Oberlin	24	Upper Arlington	21 1/2
1937	A	Sandusky	34	Toledo Scott	22
	B	Upper Arlington	26 1/2	Glendale	26
1938	A	Toledo Scott	25	Cleveland East	19 1/2
	B	Columbiana	30	Upper Arlington	27 1/2
1939	A	Cleveland East Tech	35 1/6	Columbus North	35
	B	Upper Arlington	29	Oberlin	19
1940	A	Cleveland East Tech	51	Columbus North	22 1/2
	B	Xenia OSSO	38 1/2	Oak Harbor	16
1941	A	Cleveland East Tech & Cleveland Heights	22	*Co-Champions*	
	B	Xenia OSSO	27 3/5	Clyde	14
1942	A	Cleveland East Tech	40	Springfield	17
	B	Xenia OSSO	29 1/2	Plainville	20 1/2
1943	A	Cleveland East Tech	33	Cleveland John Marshall	22 1/2
	B	Rome Stewart	31	Beavercreek	20
1944	A	Cleveland East Tech	41	Columbus East	26
	B	Chagrin Falls Orange	21	Columbus University	17 1/2
1945	A	Mansfield	23 1/2	Columbus East	22
	B	Lockland	19	Plainville	15

		Champion		Runner-up	
1946	A	Toledo Devilbiss	18	Cleveland East Tech	17
	B	New London	21 1/10	Plainville	15
1947	A	Cleveland Central	23 1/2	Columbus Central	20
	B	Poland	16 1/2	Lockland	16
1948	A	Dayton Dunbar	22 1/2	Canton McKinley	22
	B	Independence	18	Oak Harbor	16 1/6
1949	A	Cleveland Central	33	Columbus Central	17
	B	Plainville	21 1/2	Lockland	19
1950	A	Cincinnati Central	39	Mansfield	20 1/2
	B	Wyoming	17	Poland	13 1/2
1951	A	Cincinnati Central	27 1/5	Cleveland East Tech	27
	B	Poland	22 1/3	Clyde	19
1952	A	Cleveland East Tech	30 1/2	Springfield	19 1/2
	B	Belpre	22 3/10	Anderson Township, Hamilton County	22
1953	A	Cleveland John Adams	27	Springfield	26 1/2
	B	Clyde	26 1/2	Xenia Woodrow Wilson	18
1954	A	Barberton	20	Mansfield	14
	B	Nevada	18	Cuyahoga Heights	16
1955	A	Cleveland East Tech	28	Lakewood	22
	B	Xenia Woodrow Wilson	27	Cincinnati DePorres	26
1956	A	Akron North & Cleveland John Adams	19		
	B	Xenia Woodrow Wilson	43 1/2	Cincinnati DePorres	35
1957	A	Springfield	26 3/4	Lakewood	17
	B	Jefferson Township, Montgomery County & Braceville	24	Co-Champions	
1958	A	Xenia Woodrow Wilson	26 6/7	Newton Falls Braceville	25
	AA	Springfield	32 25/28	Lakewood	18
1959	A	West Alexandria	16	Dayton Wayne Township & Petersburg Springfield Local	12
	AA	Cleveland Glenville	29	Cleveland East Tech	25
1960	A	Paulding	16	Cincinnati DePorres	15
	AA	Cleveland Glenville	31	Springfield	26
1961	A	Cincinnati DePorres	18	Fairport Harbor	14
	AA	Dayton Roosevelt	27	Cleveland East Tech	24
1962	A	Newton Falls Braceville	24	Montpelier & Smithville	13
	AA	Cleveland Collinwood	23	Dayton Dunbar	21
1963	A	Cincinnati DePorres	30	Lakeside	16
	AA	Dayton Dunbar	29 1/2	Cleveland Glenville	28
1964	A	Fairport Harbor Harding	21	Cincinnati DePorres & Batavia	12
	AA	Dayton Dunbar	18	Cleveland Glenville	17
1965	A	Fairport Harbor Harding	19	Batavia	13
	AA	Cleveland Glenville	15	Dayton Dunbar	13
1966	A	Batavia	14	Xenia Woodrow Wilson	11
	AA	Cleveland Glenville	26	Cleveland East Tech	23
1967	A	Kirtland	20	Cuyahoga Heights	18
	AA	Cleveland Glenville	26	Warren Harding	21
1968	A	Kent State High	24	Yellow Springs	12
	AA	Cleveland Glenville	17	Dayton Roth & Sandusky	16
1969	A	Arcanum	17	Middletown Madison	16
	AA	Cleveland John F. Kennedy	16	Dayton Roosevelt & Upper Arlington	13
1970	A	Cortland Lakeview	28	Montpelier	26
	AA	Cleveland Glenville	37	Dayton Dunbar	35
1971	A	Cleveland Heights Lutheran East	48	Georgetown	30
	AA	Gates Mills Gilmour Academy	30	Ottawa Glandorf	28
	AAA	Dayton Roosevelt	42	Toledo Libbey	31
1972	A	Frankfort Adena	45	Lorain Clearview	40
	AA	Ottawa Glandorf	34	Columbus Mifflin	26
	AAA	Toledo Libbey	28	Dayton Roosevelt	24
1973	A	Lorain Clearview	45	Marion Pleasant	36
	AA	Brookville	33	Leavittsburg LaBrae	25
	AAA	Cleveland Glenville	42	Cleveland Collinwood	34
1974	A	Columbus Wehrle	46	Yellow Springs	40
	AA	Huron	30	Columbus Mohawk	28
	AAA	Cleveland Glenville	32	Upper Arlington	27

		Champion		Runner-up	
1975	A	Yellow Springs	34	Columbus Wehrle	24
	AA	Columbus Mifflin	54	Dayton Jefferson	35
	AAA	Cleveland Glenville	29	Mansfield Madison & Trotwood Madison	24
1976	A	Shadyside	30	Ashland Crestview	27
	AA	Dayton Roth	55	Dayton Jefferson	48
	AAA	Alliance & Cleveland John Adams	28	Co-Champions	
1977	A	Gahanna Columbus Academy	30	Galion Northmor & Yellow Springs	28
	AA	Dayton Jefferson	54	Cincinnati Mariemont & Lorain Clearview & Columbus Briggs	26
	AAA	Columbus Linden-McKinley	32	Akron North	25
1978	A	Lorain Clearview	30	Bluffton	26
	AA	Warrensville Heights	44	Dayton Jefferson	36
	AAA	Mansfield Senior	38	Cleveland John Hay	36
1979	A	Lorain Clearview	38	Shadyside	37
	AA	Columbus Mifflin	56	Elyria	31
	AAA	Gahanna Lincoln	42	Lancaster	30
1980	A	Columbus Wehrle	32	Columbus Academy	23
	AA	Dayton Jefferson	36	Youngstown Rayen	34
	AAA	Lancaster	41	Middletown	36
1981	A	Gahanna Columbus Academy	53	New Washington Buckeye Central	32
	AA	Columbus Wehrle	37	Dayton Chaminade-Julienne & Dayton Jefferson	34
	AAA	Dayton Roth	62	Lancaster	28
1982	A	Dayton Christian	42	Gahanna Columbus Academy	36
	AA	Dayton Roth	77	Columbus Wehrle	40
	AAA	Cleveland Heights & Cleveland John Adams	32	Co-Champions	
1983	A	Columbus Wehrle	32	Covington & Leetonia	26
	AA	Dayton Jefferson	64	Bedford Chanel	56
	AAA	Marion Harding	41	Berea	28
1984	A	Leetonia	46	Cincinnati Academy of Physical Education	36
	AA	Sandusky Perkins	50	Leavittsburg LaBrae Warren John F. Kennedy	36 36
	AAA	Alliance	38	Dayton Dunbar	36
1985	A	Yellow Springs	46	Bluffton	34
	AA	Columbus Hartley	58	Dayton Jefferson	37
	AAA	Dayton Patterson	61	Lancaster	31
1986	A	Dayton Jefferson	73.5	Caldwell	36
	AA	Columbus Hartley	56	Peninsula Woodridge	33
	AAA	Greensburg Green	38	Cleveland John Adams	32
1987	A	Summit Station Licking Heights	46	Cridersville Perry	36
	AA	Dayton Jefferson	39	Cincinnati Academy of Physical Education	30
	AAA	Toledo DeVilbiss	36	Columbus Eastmoor	31
1988	A	Dayton Jefferson	74	Yellow Springs	43
	AA	Cincinnati Forest Park	48	Painesville Harvey	30
	AAA	Dayton Dunbar	45	Medina	22
1989	A	Marion Catholic	28	Columbus Grandview Hgts.	23
	AA	Cincinnati Forest Park	45	South Point	27
	AAA	Dayton Dunbar	56	Cincinnati Princeton	32
1990	I	Dayton Dunbar	59	Cincinnati Princeton	28
	II	Youngstown Mooney	28	Copley	22
	III	Yellow Springs	25	Marion Pleasant	24
1991	I	Cleveland John Marshall	42	Cleveland Hts. Cleveland John Adams	28 tied 28 tied
	II	Columbus Hartley	32	Coshocton	28
	III	Pettisville	28	Caldwell	26

Track and Field Records, Boys

DIVISION I

Event	Mark	Athlete	Location	Year
100 M. DASH	10.51	Mario Allmon, Cincinnati Princeton	Columbus	1990
	10.51	Jonathan Burrell, Cleveland John Marshall	Columbus	1991
110 M. 39" HURDLES	13.57	Chris Nelloms, Dayton Dunbar	Columbus	1990
300 M. 36" HURDLES	36.38	Glenn C. Terry, Jr., Cincinnati Sycamore	Columbus	1988
200 M. DASH	20.47	Chris Nelloms, Dayton Dunbar	Columbus	1990
400 M. DASH	45.59	Chris Nelloms, Dayton Dunbar	Columbus	1990
800 M. RUN	1:51.46	Mike Huber, Cleveland St. Ignatius	Columbus	1984
1600 M. RUN	4:05.13	Robert O. Kennedy, Jr., Westerville North	Columbus	1988
3200 M. RUN	8:45.8	Alan Scharsu, Youngstown Austintown-Fitch	Kent	1977
4 x 100 M. RELAY	41.53	Robert Boykin, Dallas Johnson, Travis Mack, Dale Burrage—Dayton Patterson	Columbus	1985
	41.4	Craig Thompson, Carlos Britton, Paris Carter, Mario Allmon—Cincinnati Princeton	Dayton	1989
4 x 400 M. RELAY	3:13.57	Paul Thomas, Melran Leach, Donald Taylor, Harold Madox—Cleveland John Adams	Columbus	1984
4 x 800 M. RELAY	7:44.29	Thurman Tyus, Westley Edrington, Charles Weaver, Donte Johnson, Cleveland John Marshall	Columbus	1991
DISCUS	204'5"	Charles Moye Jr., Akron Ellet	Austintown	1987
HIGH JUMP	7'2 1/4"	Mark Cannon, Elyria	Columbus	1987
LONG JUMP	25'5"	Todd Bell, Middletown	Mansfield	1976
POLE VAULT	16'0"	Les West, Huber Heights Wayne	Bowling Green	1975
	16'0"	Justin Daler, Toledo St. John's	Columbus	1989
SHOT PUT (12 lbs.)	70'6 1/4"	Charles Moye Jr., Akron Ellet	Mansfield	1987

DIVISION II

Event	Mark	Athlete	Location	Year
100 M. DASH	10.69	Voren Hughes, Leavittsburg LaBrae	Columbus	1986
110 M. 39" HURDLES	13.3	Dan Oliver, Wooster Triway	Columbus	1976
300 M. 36" HURDLES	37.35	Clinton Davis, Cincinnati Forest Park	Columbus	1988
200 M. DASH	21.3	Dennis Mosley, Youngstown Rayen	Columbus	1976
400 M. DASH	47.22	Laron Brown, Dayton Roth	Dayton	1982
800 M. RUN	1:51.0	John Anich, Akron Hoban	Ft. Wayne, IN	1976
1600 M. RUN	4:08.03	Scott Fry, Sandusky Perkins	Columbus	1985
3200 M. RUN	8:46.7	Scott Fry, Sandusky Perkins	Oak Harbor	1985
4 x 100 M. RELAY	41.79	Ronnie Bonner, Brian Britton, Stefan Johnson, Lorenzo Payne—Dayton Jefferson	Columbus	1981
4 x 400 M. RELAY	3:14.57	Quinthony Brown, Michael McCray, Juan Mosby, Laron Brown—Dayton Roth	Dayton	1982
4 x 800 M. RELAY	7:48.40	Jon Scheffer, John Elmers, Chris Lau, Bill Werner, Genoa	Columbus	1991
DISCUS	194'10"	Andy Pentecost, Uhrichsville Claymont	Columbus	1985
HIGH JUMP	7'1/4"	Scott Wall, Springfield Shawnee	Troy	1979
	7'1/4"	Jaye Bailey, Columbus Wehrle	Dayton	1982
LONG JUMP	24'2 1/2"	Leigh Grey, Columbus Hartley	Columbus	1986
POLE VAULT	16'4"	John Coyne, Medina Buckeye	Columbus	1986
SHOT PUT (12 lbs.)	60'7 1/2"	David Bzovi, Wauseon	Columbus	1982

DIVISION III

Event	Mark	Athlete	Location	Year
100 M. DASH	10.67	Tony Lee, Dayton Jefferson	Columbus	1988
	10.4	Tony Lee, Dayton Jefferson	Dayton	1988
110 M. 39" HURDLES	13.8	Roland James, Jamestown Greeneview	Columbus	1976
300 M. 36" HURDLES	37.73	Chris Miller, Summit Station Licking Heights	Columbus	1987
200 M. DASH	21.63	Tony Lee, Dayton Jefferson	Columbus	1988
	21.1	Tony Lee, Dayton Jefferson	Dayton	1988
400 M. DASH	47.6	Gary Linstedt, Kent State High	Mansfield	1968
800 M. RUN	1:54.1	Byron Arbaugh, Lucasville Valley	Columbus	1978
1600 M. RUN	4:13.4	Jerry Walker, Cortland Maplewood	Columbus	1980
3200 M. RUN	9:13.8	John Jones, Marion Elgin	Worthington	1967
4 x 100 M. RELAY	42.31	Clifford Clack, Paul Williams, Tony Lee, Jamiel Trimble—Dayton Jefferson	Columbus	1986
4 x 400 M. RELAY	3:21.71	Travis Douce, Dan Staley, J. R. Fox, Troy Jolliff—Bluffton	Columbus	1986
4 x 800 M. RELAY	7:58.34	Scott Hurtt, Mike Maloy, Vic Austin, Randy Mather—Frankfort Adena	Columbus	1985
DISCUS	188'1/2"	John Casler, Ashland Crestview	Mansfield	1967
HIGH JUMP	7'0"	Richard Paul Dunwoodie Jr., West Alexandria Twin Valley South	Eaton	1987

LONG JUMP	23'11"	Martin Maize, Dayton Jefferson	Dayton	1988
POLE VAULT	16'3/4"	Matt Vermilion, Lewisburg Twin Valley North	West Alexandria	1982
SHOT PUT (12 lbs.)	64'9"	Larry Kolic, Smithville	Cuyahoga Hgts.	1981

Track and Field

State Champions, Girls

		Champion		Runner-up	
1975	A	Frankfort Adena	60	Minster	43
	AA	Doylestown Chippewa	46	Dayton Jefferson	44
	AAA	Toledo Scott	60	Toledo Whitmer	34
1976	A	Minster	52	Pittsburg Franklin Monroe	30
	AA	Dayton Jefferson	68	Youngstown North	30
	AAA	Dayton Stivers-Patterson	38	Euclid & Toledo Start	33
1977	A	Minster	55	Pitsburg Franklin Monroe	37
	AA	Dayton Jefferson	45	Doylestown Chippewa	40
	AAA	Toledo Rogers	36	Upper Arlington	34
1978	A	Minster	59	Youngstown North	27
	AA	Youngstown Liberty	34	Mansfield Malabar & Avon	32
	AAA	Cleveland John Adams	40	Euclid	33
1979	A	Minster	75.33	Columbus School for Girls	38
	AA	Dayton Jefferson	30	Avon & Columbus Centennial & Zanesville W. Muskingum	22
	AAA	Cleveland John Adams	48	Toledo Rogers	25
1980	A	Minster	54	Antwerp	30
	AA	Girard	40	Springfield Catholic Central	28
	AAA	Toledo Start	39	Centerville	32
1981	A	Zanesville Rosecrans	40	Minster	34
	AA	St. Clairsville	28	Dayton Roth	24
	AAA	Centerville	36	Columbus Mifflin	28
1982	A	Minster	45	Zanesville Rosecrans	37
	AA	Columbus East	60	Sunbury Big Walnut	41
	AAA	Columbus Mifflin	56	Upper Arlington	26.75
1983	A	Zanesville Rosecran	54	Minster	45
	AA	Columbus East	30	Cadiz	28
	AAA	Trotwood-Madison	30	Celina	26
1984	A	Zanesville Rosecrans	66	Minster	49
	AA	Columbus Hartley	43	Ravenna Southeast	28
	AAA	Trotwood-Madison	38	Upper Arlington	37
1985	A	Minster	40	Ashland Crestview	34
	AA	Ravenna Southeast	31	Cincinnati Roger Bacon & Oberlin	30
	AAA	Upper Arlington	38	Toledo Macomber-Whitney	32
1986	A	Cincinnati Academy of Physical Education	36	Rockford Parkway	30
	AA	Columbus Hartley	34	Steubenville	30
	AAA	Cleveland Heights Beaumont	33	Toledo Scott	25
1987	A	Newark Catholic	42	Dayton Jefferson	39
	AA	Kansas Lakota	40	Steubenville	38
	AAA	Cleveland Heights Beaumont	44	Cleveland John Adams	34
1988	A	Baltimore Liberty Union	30	Columbus School for Girls & Galion Northmor	28
	AA	Columbus Hartley	34	Cincinnati Academy of Physical Education & Olmsted Falls	28
	AAA	Cleveland Heights Beaumont	39	Centerville	27
1989	A	Minster	57	Liberty Center/Maria Stein Marion	34
	AA	Cleveland Heights Beaumont	75	Baltimore Liberty Union	30
	AAA	Cincinnati Princeton	30	Springfield South	28
1990	I	Cleveland Heights	45	Upper Arlington	40
	II	Cleveland Heights Beaumont	98	Richfield Revere	40
	III	North Robinson Colonel Crawford	44	Sandusky St. Mary's	40
1991	I	Cleveland Heights	71	Columbus Norhland	36
	II	Cleveland Heights Beaumont	52	Columbus Bexley	38
	III	North Robinson Colonel Crawford	49	Middletown Fenwick	38

Track and Field Records, Girls

DIVISION I

Event	Time/Mark	Athlete, School	Location	Year
100 M. 33" HURDLES	13.95	Terry Robinson, Columbus Northland	Columbus	1987
300 M. 30" HURDLES	42.24	Terry Robinson, Columbus Northland	Columbus	1987
100 M. DASH	11.6	Kellie Simpson, Columbus Mifflin	Whitehall	1982
200 M. DASH	24.1	Brenda Morehead, Toledo Scott	Columbus	1975
400 M. DASH	54.86	Vicky Davis, Youngstown Woodrow Wilson	Columbus	1981
800 M. RUN	2:11.07	Lisa Breiding, Alliance Marlington	Columbus	1984
1600 M. RUN	4:48.59	Laurie Gomez, Youngstown Boardman	Arcadia, CA	1988
3200 M. RUN	10:27.74	Kristy Orre, Clayton Northmont	Columbus	1985
4 x 100 M. RELAY	47.28	Richelle Webb, Martha Meaker, Tammy Leach, Kathy DiFranci—Cleveland Heights Beaumont	Columbus	1987
4 x 200 M. RELAY	1:39.74	Adrienne Bundy, Meka Rembert, Tara Williams, Shawn Clark—Cleveland Hts.	Columbus	1991
4 x 400 M. RELAY	3:49.14	Martha Meaker, Treva Offutt, Kim Liggins, Kathy DiFranco—Cleveland Heights Beaumont	Columbus	1987
4 x 800 M. RELAY	9:08.75	Beth Crowley, Judy Crowley, Joanna Butts, Dawn Crowley—Rocky River Magnificat	Columbus	1985
DISCUS	160'2"	Julie Victor, Youngstown Austintown-Fitch	Kent	1989
HIGH JUMP	5'10"	Peggy Odita, Upper Arlington	Columbus	1985
LONG JUMP	20'1"	Laura Kirkham, Centerville	Columbus	1984
SHOT PUT (4 kg)	45'6 3/4"	Jodi Riedel, Niles McKinley	Columbus	1982

DIVISION II

Event	Time/Mark	Athlete, School	Location	Year
100 M. 33" HURDLES	14.5	Beth Harris, Thornville Sheridan	Columbus	1991
300 M. 30" HURDLES	43.21	Ebonita Williams, Cleveland Hts. Beaumont	Columbus	1991
100 M. DASH	12.03	Theresa Diggs, Columbus Hartley	Columbus	1984
200 M. DASH	24.63	Judy Ratliff, Thornville Sheridan	Columbus	1986
400 M. DASH	55.67	Jennifer Ridgely, Columbus Bexley	Columbus	1991
800 M. RUN	2:12.17	Kristi Grooms, Springboro	Dayton	1983
1600 M. RUN	4:52.23	Connie Robinson, Reading	Dayton	1982
3200 M. RUN	10:47.99	Michelle Sica, Cincinnati Roger Bacon	Columbus	1985
4 x 100 M. RELAY	48.63	Sheila Ballado, Richelle Webb, Heather Wilson, Nancy Hackett—Cleveland Hgts. Beaumont	Kent	1989
4 x 200 M. RELAY	1:42.29	Allyson Williams, Shelley Joyce, Tiffany Smith, Ronda Nutt—Columbus Hartley	Columbus	1986
4 x 400 M. RELAY	3:54.80	Richelle Webb, Gina Jefferson, Ebonita Williams, Nancy Hackett—Cleveland Hts. Beaumont	Columbus	1991
4 x 800 M. RELAY	9:14.64	Monica McHenry, Nancy Hackett, Missy Supler, Gina Jefferson, Cleveland Hts. Beaumont Jami Verhoff—Bellevue	Columbus	1990
DISCUS	170'8"	Teresa Sherman, South Point	Ironton	1989
HIGH JUMP	5'10"	Shelly Jorgenson, New Lexington	Columbus	1983
LONG JUMP	19'2 1/2"	Theresa Diggs, Columbus Hartley	Columbus	1984
SHOT PUT (4 kg)	43'9 3/4"	Tammy R. Stahl, Kansas Lakota	Columbus	1988

DIVISION III

Event	Time/Mark	Athlete, School	Location	Year
100 M. 33" HURDLES	14.96	Vanessa Albernaz, Marion Catholic	Columbus	1987
300 M. 30" HURDLES	43.92	Chris McGee, Zanesville Rosecrans Columbus	Columbus	1985
100 M. DASH	12.2	Kathy Mobley, Dayton Miami Valley	Columbus	1980
200 M. DASH	25.0	Angie Shoulders, Cleveland Hgts. Lutheran East	Columbus	1975
400 M. DASH	56.48	Lori Albers, Maria Stein Marion	Columbus	1989
800 M. RUN	2:12.76	Susan Nash, Zanesville Rosecrans	Columbus	1983
1600 M. RUN	4:55.64	Patty Metzler, North Jackson Jackson-Milton	Columbus	1983
3200 M. RUN	11:13.89	Renee Peck, Baltimore Liberty Union	Columbus	1990
4 x 100 M. RELAY	49.14	Trina Pate, Jacqueline Jordan, Tyra Gordon, Michelle McGruder—Cincinnati Academy of Physical Education	Columbus	1986
4 x 200 M. RELAY	1:44.95	Tracie Bradley, Vanessa Tower, Francine Woods, Sandy Hitchens—Lorain Clearview	Columbus	1987
4 x 400 M. RELAY	3:56.70	Lisa Young, Chris McGee, Kelly Long, Susan Nash —Zanesville Rosecrans	Columbus	1984
4 x 800 M. RELAY	9:20.75	Karen Saah, Tia Chapman, Maggie McLeod, Jibs Thorson—Columbus School for Girls	Columbus	1987
DISCUS	150'8"	Mary Jane Reighard, Liberty Center	Columbus	1986
HIGH JUMP	5'8"	Pam Deaton, New Paris National Trail	Tipp City	1985
LONG JUMP	18'7 3/4"	Patty Harris, Frankfort Adena	Columbus	1980
SHOT PUT (4 kg)	44'10 1/2"	Beverly Obringer, Maria Stein Marion	Minster	1984

Soccer
Champions

Year	Div	Champion	Coach	Runner-up	Coach
1976		Cincinnati Finneytown	Bob Muro	Broadview Hgts. Brecksville	Tony Niccoli
1977		North Olmsted	Tom Hatfield	Cincinnati Roger Bacon	Jim Williamson
1978		Clayton Northmont	George Demetriades	Cincinnati Anderson	Glen Morton
1979		North Royalton	James Castanien	Findlay	Albert Laux
1980		Dayton Carroll	Mike Donohue	Cincinnati Oak Hills	Chuck Ausman
1981	A-AA	Cincinnati Finneytown	Alan Robertson	Columbus St. Charles	John Bluem
	AAA	Broadview Hgts. Brecksville	Tony Niccoli	Centerville	Gary Avedekian
1982	A-AA	Dayton Chaminade-Julienne	Pete Hayes	Akron St. Vincent-St. Mary	Bill Gamboa
	AAA	Stow Walsh Jesuit	John Kissner	Centerville	Gary Avedekian
1983	A-AA	Columbus St. Charles	Ron Wigg	Cincinnati Finneytown	Alan Robertson
	AAA	Cincinnati St. Xavier	Dick Murphy	North Royalton	Jim Tyma
1984	A-AA	Cincinnati McNicholas	Steve Teetor	Copley	George Jalics
	AAA	Centerville	Gary Avedekian	North Olmsted	Tom Hatfield
1985	A-AA	Columbus St. Charles	Glen Morton	Springfield Greenon	Gene Pistick
	AAA	North Olmsted	Tom Hatfield	Centerville	Gary Avedekian
	Girls	Clayton Northmont	Bill Kritzline	Cincinnati Turpin	David Lawson
1986	A-AA	Columbus DeSales	Steve Rand	Cincinnati Indian Hill	Jim Vockell
	AAA	Cincinnati Turpin	John Basalyga	Stow Walsh Jesuit	John Kissner
	Girls	Cincinnati Turpin	Dave Lawson	Centerville	Don Skeleton
1987	A-AA	Chagrin Falls Kenston	Marty Dworak	Cincinnati Indian Hill	James Vockell
	AAA	Kettering Alter	Roy Bohaboy	Stow Walsh Jesuit	John Kissner
	Girls	Clayton Northmont	Bill Krintzline	North Olmsted	David Reser
1988	A-AA	Kettering Alter	Roy Bohaboy	Columbus St. Charles	Ed Geraghy
	AAA	Clayton Northmont	George Demetriades	North Olmsted	Tom Hatfield
	Girls	Clayton Northmont	Bill Krintzline	Cincinnati Anderson	Jim Henke
1989	I	Westerville South	Steve Serr	North Olmsted	Tom Hatfield
	II	Cincinnati Roger Bacon	Bob Servis	Canfield	Lee Frey
	Girls	Clayton Northmont	Bill Krintzline	West Carrollton	Wayne Novick
1990	I	Stow Walsh Jesuit	John Kissner		
		Beavercreek	John Guiliano		
	II	Cincinnati Roger Bacon	Rick Arszman	Columbus DeSales	Rob Lehman
	Girls	Westerville South	Tim Lawrence	Centerville	Don Skelton
1991	I	Worthington Thomas Worthington	Ian Hamilton	Stow Walsh Jesuit	John Kessner
	II	Bay Village Bay	Sam Massad	Columbus St. Charles	Angelo Catenacci
	Girls	Cincinnati St. Ursula	Bob Sheehan	Westerville North	Tim Lawrence

All-Ohio Soccer Team, 1991

Boys' Division I

Player	Year	School
Nathan Fairchild	Senior	Thomas Worthington
Doug Kuhlman	Senior	Stow Walsh Jesuit
Todd McCandish	Senior	Westerville South
Kyle Swords	Senior	Huber Heights Wayne
Kevin Rudolph	Senior	Centerville
Chris Malik	Senior	Thomas Worthington
Jeff Winterberger	Senior	Turpin
Doug Smith	Senior	Mayfield
Jim DeCillo	Senior	Strongsville
Jason Chiero	Senior	Westerville South
Jeff Spitler	Senior	Wooster

Player of year: Nathan Fairchild, Worthington
Coach of year: Ian Hamilton, Worthington

Boys' Division II

Player	Year	School
Scott Downing	Senior	Tipp City
Brad Cartwright	Senior	Bay Village Bay
Billy Zufall	Senior	Copley
Mike Walker	Senior	Columbus DeSales
Mike Neibling	Senior	Roger Bacon
Kevin Loftis	Senior	Springfield Catholic
Curt Rosenthal	Senior	Hunting Valley
Jason Gatten	Senior	Cuyahoga Christian
Scott Arthur	Junior	Columbus St. Charles
Eric Hauk	Senior	Finneytown
Jessie Barrington	Junior	Worthington Christian

Player of year: Scott Downing, Tipp City
Coach of year: Richard Arszman, Roger Bacon

Girls

Player	Year	School
Holly Young	Senior	Centerville
P. Angilecchia	Junior	St. Ursula
Eileen Corrigan	Senior	Rocky River Magnificat
Lisa Suttmiller	Sophomore	Westerville North
Cary Walch	Senior	Anderson
Julie McCaffrey	Senior	Glen Este
Kate Ebner	Senior	Medina
Amy Sellers	Senior	Milford
Angie Poppaw	Senior	Clayton Northmont
Kate Pendry	Senior	Sylvania Southview
Lori Helle	Junior	Brecksville

Player of the year: Holly Young, Centerville
Coach of the year: Tim Lawrence, Westerville North

Wrestling

Team Champions

Year	Div	Champion	Coach	Runner-up	Coach
1939		Cleveland John Hay	Harold Kester	Cleveland West Tech	
				Cleveland Rhodes	
				Garfield Heights	
				Shadyside	
1940		Cleveland John Hay	Harold Kester	Shadyside	Arthur Kirkland
1941		Cleveland John Hay	Harold Kester	Shadyside	Arthur Kirkland
1942		Wadsworth	Russell Doan	Shadyside	Arthur Kirkland
1943		Cleveland John Hay	Harold Kester	Cleveland West Tech	Lloyd Griffith
1944		Cleveland West Tech	Lloyd Griffith	Cleveland John Hay	Harold Kester
1945		Cleveland West Tech	Lloyd Griffith	Western Reserve Academy	Edwin Ellis
1946		Cleveland West Tech	Lloyd Griffith	Cleveland West	Harold Kester
1947		Cleveland West	Harold Kester	Euclid Shore	Clarence Eckert
1948		Lakewood	Paul Harger	Cleveland West Tech	Lloyd Griffith
1949		Euclid Shore	Clarence Eckert	Cleveland West	Harold Kester
1950		Cleveland West	Harold Kester	Cleveland Adams	Bernard McGroart
1951		Cleveland West	Harold Kester	Euclid	Clarence Eckert
1952		Euclid	Clarence Eckert	Bedford	John Trojan
				Cleveland West	Bob Lazarro
1953		Cleveland West	Robert Lazzaro	Euclid	Clarence Eckert
1954		Shaker Heights	Ed Zeinik	Bedford	John Trojan
1955		Bedford	John Trojan	Bridgeport	George Kovalik
1956		Maple Heights	Mike Milkovich	Bedford	George Beshora
1957		Maple Heights	Mike Milkovich	Bedford	George Beshora
1958		Euclid	Clarence Eckert	Maple Heights	Mike Milkovich
1959		Bridgeport	George Kovalick	Maple Heights	Mike Milkovich
1960		Garfield Heights	William Morris	Maple Heights	Mike Milkovich
1961		Cleveland John Marshall	Eugene Gibbons	Euclid	Clarence Eckert
1962		Maple Heights	Mike Milkovich	Euclid	Clarence Eckert
1963		Maple Heights	Mike Milkovich	Toledo St. Francis DeSales	Gerald Bowsher
1964		Toledo St. Francis DeSales	Richard Leffler	Maple Heights	Mike Milkovich
1965		North Canton	Paul MacDonald	Maple Heights	Mike Milkovich
1966		Maple Heights	Mike Milkovich	Cleveland John Marshall	Gene Gibbons
1967		Maple Heights	Mike Milkovich	Parma Valley Forge	Steve Rudo
1968		Maple Heights	Mike Milkovich	Parma Valley Forge	Steve Rudo
1969		Maple Heights	Mike Milkovich	Bedford	Paul Bogardus
1970		Toledo St. Francis DeSales	Richard Leffler	Maple Heights	Mike Milkovich
1971	A-AA	Columbus DeSales	Robert Triano	Huron	Tom Talbott
	AAA	Maple Heights	Mike Milkovich	Toledo Rogers	Ray Steely
1972	A-AA	Chagrin Falls Kenston	Don Havener	Oregon Cardinal Stritch	Mike Beier
	AAA	Bay Village	Joseph Scalletta	Parma Valley Forge	Steve Rudo
1973	A-AA	Ravenna Southeast	William Steinreide	Oregon Cardinal Stritch	Karl Pankrantz
	AAA	Elyria	Bill Pierson	Akron Garfield	Robert Harvey
1974	A-AA	Columbus DeSales	Robert Triano	Oregon Cardinal Stritch	Karl Pankrantz
	AAA	Maple Heights	Mike Milkovich	North Olmsted	Thomas Peters
1975	A-AA	Medina Highland	Jim Florian	Painesville Harvey	Dale Hlavin
	AAA	Eastlake North	John Matteucci	Maple Heights	Mike Milkovich
1976	A	Summit Station Licking Heights	Ken Ash	Richmond Heights	Mike Papouras
	AA	Mantua Crestwood	Frank DiNapoli	Columbus DeSales	Mike Stanley
	AAA	Cleveland Heights	Larry Hoon	Bay Village Bay	Joe Scaletta
1977	A	Summit Station Licking Heights	Ken Ash	Richmond Heights	Mike Papouras
	AA	Columbus DeSales	Mike Stanley	Columbus Ready	A. R. Trombetti
	AAA	Macedonai Nordonia	Gary Watters	Maple Heights	Mike Milkovich
1978	A	Middlefield Cardinal	Tom Ferry	Richmond Heights	Mike Papouras
	AA	Akron Coventry	Dale Huston	Columbus DeSales	Mike Stanley
	AAA	Lakewood St. Edward	Howard Ferguson	Macedonia Nordonia	Gary Watters
1979	A	Richmond Heights	Mike Papouras	Summit Station Licking Heights	Ken Ash
	AA	Akron Coventry	Dick Miller	Columbus Watterson	Wayne Hiles
	AAA	Lakewood St. Edward	Howard Ferguson	Macedonia Nordonia	Gary Watters
1980	A	Richmond Heights	Mike Papouras	Summit Station Licking Heights	Ken Ash
	AA	Akron Coventry	Dick Miller	Medina Highland	Jim Florian
	AAA	Lakewood St. Edward	Howard Ferguson	Brunswick	Gary Eaton
1981	A	Bluffton	Bill Lodermeier	Summit Station Licking Heights	Lou Vito
	AA	Medina Highland	Jim Florian	Oak Harbor	Hector Gonzales
	AAA	Lakewood St. Edward	Howard Ferguson	Cleveland St. Joseph	John Storey

		Champion	Coach	Runner-up	Coach
1982	A	Columbus Bishop Ready	Bob Stoll	Richmond Heights	Michael Papouras
	AA	St. Paris Graham	Ron McCunn	Swanton	Joe Carone
	AAA	Lakewood St. Edward	Howard Ferguson	North Canton Hoover	Walter Tolarchyk
1983	A	Richmond Heights	Michael Papouras	Columbus Bishop Ready	Bob Stoll
	AA	Bedford Chanel	Ed Govang	Oregon Cardinal Stritch	Tom Talbott
	AAA	Lakewood St. Edward	Howard Ferguson	North Canton Hoover	Walter Tolarchyk
1984	A	Richmond Heights	Mike Papouras	Thompson Ledgemont	Ritch Nasca
	AA	Barnesville	Darrell Davis	Wauseon	Steve Schneider
	AAA	Lakewood St. Edward	Howard Ferguson	Bedford Chanel	Ed Govang
1985	A	Summit Station Licking Heights	Kevin Peck	Thompson Ledgemont	Ritch Nasca
	AA	Oregon Cardinal Stritch	Paul Elzey	Columbus DeSales	David Krend
	AAA	Lakewood St. Edward	Howard Ferguson	North Olmsted	Tom Milkovich
1986	A	Newbury	Cliff Radie	Columbus Grandview Heights	Jim Hein
	AA	Bedford Chanel	Graham Coghill	Columbus Ready	Bob Stoll
	AAA	Lakewood St. Edward	Howard Ferguson	Xenia	Steve Harris
1987	A	Cadiz	John Stephenson	Bridgeport	David LaMotte
	AA	Bedford Chanel	Ed Govang	Twinsburg Chamberlin	David Mariola
	AAA	Lakewood St. Edward	Howard Ferguson	Cleveland St. Ignatius	Mark Avcollie
1988	I	Cleveland St. Ignatius	Mark Avcollie	North Olmsted	Tom Milkovich
	II	Bedford Chanel	Ed Govang	Steubenville	John Craig
	III	Bridgeport	David LaMotte	Columbus Ready	Bob Stoll
1989	I	Lakewood St. Edward	Howard Ferguson	Cleveland St. Joseph	John Storey
	II	Mentor Lake Catholic	Tim Armelli	Chagrin Falls Kenston	Mike Rovtar
	III	Delta	Robin Rayfield	Versailles	Bill Roll
1990	I	Cleveland St. Joseph	John Storey	Stow Walsh Jesuit	Bill Barger
	II	Solon	Tony DiGiovanni	Parma Padua Franciscan	Brian Miluk
	III	Columbus Ready	Mickey Balmert	Wellington	John Sedlick
1991	I	Stow Walsh Jesuit	Bill Barger	Lakewood St. Edward	Greg Urbas
	II	Ravenna Southeast	Ralph Graham	Clyde	Jim Carothers
	III	West Liberty-Salem	Eric Harman	Columbus Ready	Mickey Balmert
1992	I	Lakewood St. Edward	Greg Urbas	Stow Walsh Jesuit	Bill Barger
	II	Uhrichsville Claymont	Eric Toukonen	Medina Buckeye	Jack Nutter
	III	Thompson Ledgemont	Doug Hall	Cadiz	Joel Davia

Wrestling Tournaments, Individuals

FOUR-TIME STATE CHAMPIONS

	Name	High School	Years
1.	Mark Zimmer	Columbus DeSales	1976, 77, 78, 79
2.	Jim Jordan	St. Paris Graham	1979, 80, 81, 82
3.	Jeff Jordan	St. Paris Graham	1980, 81, 82, 83
4.	Erik Burnett	Oberlin	1984, 85, 86, 87
5.	Dan Hanson	Richmond Heights	1984, 85, 86, 87
6.	Ken Ramsey	Lancaster Fisher Catholic	1984, 85
		Columbus Ready	1986, 87

THREE-TIME STATE CHAMPIONS

	Name	High School	Years
1.	John Matteucci	Cleveland West	1946, 47, 48
2.	Bob Marich	Euclid Shore	1947, 48, 49
3.	Richard Bonacci	Cleveland West	1949, 50, 51
4.	James Dregalla	Cleveland John Marshall	1952, 53, 54
5.	Carol Hoppel	Lisbon Beaver	1959, 61, 62
6.	Tom Milkovich	Maple Heights	1967, 68, 69
7.	Jim Hanson	Richmond Heights	1973, 74, 75
8.	Mike DeAnna	Bay Village Bay	1974, 75, 76
9.	Ed Potokar	Richmond Heights	1977, 79, 80
10.	Dan Tussell	Macedonia Nordonia	1978, 79, 80
11.	Mark Falk	Bluffton	1980, 81, 82
12.	Greg Goard	Swanton	1983
		Oak Harbor	1984, 85
13.	Robert Potokar	Richmond Heights	1983, 84, 85
14.	Alan Fried	Lakewood St. Edward	1987, 88, 89
15.	Shawn Nelson	North Royalton	1987, 88, 89
16.	Matt Dernlan	West Liberty-Salem	1989, 90, 91
17.	Dominic DiSabato	Columbus Ready	1989, 90, 91
18.	Luke Fickell	Columbus DeSales	1990, 91, 92

TWO-TIME STATE CHAMPIONS

	Name	High School	Years		Name	High School	Years
1.	Fred Schleicher	Cleveland James Ford Rhodes	1938, 39	40.	Dennis O'Neil	Cleveland Orange	1969, 70
				41.	James Brown	Akron Ellet	1970, 71
2.	George Cherokee	Shadyside	1939, 40	42.	Drew Gundlach	Huron	1970, 71
3.	Bruce Kesselring	Akron East	1939, 40	43.	Don Tomko	Medina Highland	1970, 71
4.	Joe DiCesaro	Cleveland West Tech	1939, 41	44.	Bob Dieli	Columbus Ready	1971, 72
5.	Louis Russo	Cleveland John Hay	1942, 43	45.	Ralph Graham	Chagrin Falls Kenston	1971, 72
6.	Joe Naso	Cleveland West Tech	1943, 44	46.	Tom Bauer	Columbus DeSales	1971, 73
7.	Harry Bostwick	Cleveland West	1944, 45	47.	John Tompkins	Mogadore	1971, 73
8.	Jim Howard	Western Reserve Academy	1944, 45	48.	Shawn Garel	East Cleveland Shaw	1972, 73
				49.	Dave Rodhe	Mantua Crestwood	1972, 73
9.	Jim Roush	Western Reserve Academy	1945, 46	50.	Leroy Kemp	Chardon	1973, 74
10.	Bill Buckingham	Cleveland West	1946, 47	51.	Bill Lewis	Summit Station Licking Hts.	1973, 74
11.	Tom Dubin	Cleveland West Tech	1946, 47				
12.	Bob Bassett	Lakewood	1947, 48	52.	Paul Luther	Oregon Cardinal Stritch	1973, 74
13.	Ian McEwan	Cleveland John Hay	1948, 49	53.	Thom Herold	Columbus DeSales	1974, 75
14.	Steve Kerlin	Bedford	1948, 50	54.	Jeff Sanicky	Mantua Crestwood	1975, 76
15.	Ed Casalicchio	Cleveland John Adams	1949, 50	55.	Phil Anglim	Columbus Watterson	1976, 77
16.	Ralph Giammarino	Cleveland West	1949, 50	56.	Greg Drenik	Wickliffe	1976, 77
17.	Alan Peterson	Cleveland John Marshall	1949, 50	57.	Mike Glass	Jeromesville Hillsdale	1976, 77
				58.	Reggie Johnson	Ashland Crestview	1976, 77
18.	Fred Darienzo	Cleveland West	1950, 51	59.	Mark Lowe	Summit Station Licking Hts.	1976, 77
19.	Pat Palumbo	Maple Heights	1952, 53				
20.	Manuel Paz	Euclid	1952, 53	60.	Bill Walsh	North Olmsted	1976, 77
21.	John Sforzo	Cleveland West Tech	1952, 53	61.	Jerry Burgy	Peninsula Woodridge	1977, 78
22.	Tim Kerlin	Bedford	1953, 54	62.	Joseph Dahlhausen	Newbury	1977, 78
23.	Frank Fiore	Garfield Heights	1954, 55	63.	Vince DiSabato	Columbus Ready	1977, 78
24.	Darryl Hoppel	East Liverpool	1954, 55	64.	Keith Foxx	Akron Coventry	1977, 78
25.	James Kucera	Bedford	1954, 55	65.	Randy Glover	Akron Coventry	1977, 78
26.	Charles Ferrari	Cleveland West	1955, 57	66.	Bill Potts	Akron Coventry	1977, 78
27.	Robert Mantarro	Cleveland South	1956, 57	67.	Mike Stalnaker	Plain City Jonathan Alder	1977, 78
28.	Kenneth Ross	Euclid	1957, 58				
29.	Arthur Hehr	Bridgeport	1958, 59	68.	Chris Coffing	West Chester Lakota Fairfield	1978, 79
30.	Merrill Solowin	Toledo Robert S. Rogers	1959, 60	69.	Joe East	Grove City	1978, 79
				70.	Gus Kallai	Akron Coventry	1978, 79
31.	Robert Douglas	Bridgeport	1959, 61	71.	Randy Jenkins	Macedonai Nordonia Aurora	1978, 79
32.	Jan Maynard	Cleveland South	1962, 63				
33.	Joe Peritore	Maple Heights	1962, 63	72.	Mark Rubish	Columbiana	1978, 79
34.	Ed Cummings	Lyndhurst Charles F. Brush	1963, 64	73.	John Sciarappa	Sandusky St. Mary's Central Catholic	1978, 79
35.	Joe Green	Toledo Scott	1965, 66	74.	Ron Suszek	Richmond Heights	1978, 79
36.	Frank Romano	Maple Heights	1965, 66	75.	Leo DiSabato	Columbus Ready	1979, 80
37.	Greg Wojciechowski	Toledo Whitmer	1967, 68	76.	Joe McFarland	North Olmsted	1979, 80
38.	Ron Angello	Garfield Heights	1969, 70	77.	Mike Potts	Akron Coventry	1979, 80
39.	Cliff Dukes	North Royalton	1969, 70	78.	David Sternberg	Beachwood	1979, 80

The elitists

Ohio's Fastest Pins

Division	Name	High School	Year	Weight	Time
I	Jason Hackett	Lakewood St. Edward	1989	135	14 sec.
II	Tim Moxley	Barnesville	1985	Unl	17 sec.
III/II	Jim Clark	Oberlin	1971	145	13 sec.
III	Rob Sintobin	Delta	1989	189	8 sec.

	Name	High School	Years
79.	Phil Welch	Lakewood St. Edward	1979, 80
80.	Paul Bartolone	Cleveland St. Joseph	1980, 81
81.	Tim Hanson	Richmond Heights	1980, 81
82.	Don Horning	Stow Walsh Jesuit	1980, 81
83.	Jamey Kasser	Summit Station Licking Hts.	1980, 81
84.	Carlos Mincheff	Oak Harbor	1980, 81
85.	William Nye	Orwell Grand Valley	1980, 81
86.	Todd Wyckoff	New London	1980, 81
87.	Ed Young	Norwalk St. Paul	1980, 81
88.	Richard Burton	Medina Highland	1981, 82
89.	Scott Duncan	Marion Pleasant	1981, 82
90.	Greg Elinsky	Lakewood St. Edward	1981, 82
91.	Jim Heffernan	Lakewood St. Edward	1981, 82
92.	Robert Huston	Oak Harbor	1981, 82
93.	Rich Robusto	Stow Walsh Jesuit	1981, 82
94.	Mark Adkins	Richmond Heights	1982, 83
95.	Mark Coleman	Fremont St. Joseph Central Catholic	1982, 83
96.	Mike Davies	Chardon	1982, 83
97.	Ivan Parrish	Caldwell	1982, 83
98.	John Ryba	Bedford Chanel	1982, 83
99.	Brad Gintert	Warren Howland	1983, 84
100.	Jeff Holy	Thompson Ledgemont	1983, 84
101.	Frank McKeon	Thompson Ledgemont	1983, 84
102.	Dan Willaman	North Canton Hoover	1983, 84
103.	Rick Hartman	Cleveland St. Ignatius	1983, 85
104.	Dan Donovan	Bedford Chanel	1984, 85
105.	Tim Moxley	Barnesville	1984, 85
106.	Jeff Strauss	Lakewood St. Edward	1984, 85
107.	Joey Bonaventura	Columbus Grandview Heights	1985, 86

	Name	High School	Years
108.	Monty Dagley	Xenia	1985, 86
109.	Jeff Dernlan	West Liberty-Salem	1985, 86
110.	Mike Funk	Massillon Jackson	1985, 86
111.	Ferd Miller	Oak Harbor	1986, 87
112.	Mike Vargo	Bridgeport	1986, 87
113.	Joe Andrassy	Macedonia Nordonia	1987, 88
114.	Richard Burlenski	Bridgeport	1987, 88
115.	Nick Cianciola	Genoa Area	1987, 88
116.	Michael Coontz	Ravenna Southeast	1987, 88
117.	Steve Dernlan	West Liberty-Salem	1987, 88
118.	Adam DiSabato	Columbus Ready	1987, 88
119.	Rex Holman	Upper Arlington	1987, 88
120.	Tom Neikirk	Middlefield Cardinal	1987, 88
121.	Scott Zapadka	Oregon Stritch	1987, 88
122.	Michael Buddie	Cleveland St. Ignatius	1988, 89
123.	Reed Case	Cadiz	1986, 89
124.	Mario Marinelli	Columbus DeSales	1988, 89
125.	Aaron Moran	Versailles	1988, 89
126.	Dunyasha Yetts	Steubenville	1988, 89
127.	Greg Geovese	Solon	1989, 90
128.	Jim Scavuzzo	Richfield Revere	1989, 90
129.	Dan Carcelli	Cleveland Benedictine	1990, 91
130.	Marty Coontz	Ravenna Southeast	1990, 91
131.	Jermaine Daniels	Huber Heights Wayne	1990, 91
132.	Tim Dernlan	West Liberty-Salem	1990, 91
133.	Markus Mollica	Stow Walsh Jesuit	1990, 91
134.	Tom Nye	Edgerton	1990, 91
135.	Troy Sintobin	Delta	1990, 91
136.	James Smiles	Columbus Ready	1990, 91
137.	Steve St. John	Cleveland Villa Angela- St. Joseph	1990, 91
138.	Willie Wineberg	Fairfield	1991, 92
139.	Clint Musser	Stow Walsh Jesuit	1991, 92
140.	Tony Pariano	Fairview Park Fairview	1991, 92

Mat majors

In the last decade, Lakewood St. Edward took everyone to the mat

In 1974, **Lakewood St. Edward's** varsity wrestlers lost all of their meets. Then **Howard Ferguson** came along and announced that the Eagles would win a state title within three years. Under Ferguson, a wealthy CPA and one-time real estate salesman, the Eagles proceeded to win 10 straight state titles, sent more than 50 wrestlers to Division I colleges and nearly a dozen others to Ivy League schools. In the last 13 years, the St. Edward wrestlers have won an unprecedented 12 state titles and been runner-up once. For six years in a row, they were the nation's number-one high school wrestling program. So much for prophecy.

Ferguson, whose previous coaching experience was at a local YMCA, was a spartan workaholic who believed in outworking the opposition, constantly studying the sport as well as motivation techniques. He installed in his wrestlers what he called "the inner arrogance," and in St Edward's decade of domination, he had at least 15 kids who won 100 matches each. "Be nasty on top," was one of his favorite exhortations.

In 1986, all 15 of the St. Edward seniors won wrestling scholarships, and seven of them were not starters. That was the year St. Edward beat the Maryland state champs, the Delaware state champs, and the nationally number-two-ranked Oklahoma State champs—all in one day, while ESPN filmed the matches. Said Ferguson, "We wrestle our way. We're gonna win no matter what. We don't care who the opponent is. He has no name. He has two arms, two legs, and no face."

Ferguson's successor is **Greg Urbas**, who was runnerup in 1991 before this year's title win. ▶

Ohio Wrestling Tournament Results, 1992

Division I

103—Eddie Jayne (Lakewood St. Edward) dec. Jason Pender (Cincinnati Princeton), 7-2
112—Willie Wineberg (Fairfield) dec. Troy Cameron (Hilliard), 3-2
119—Clint Musser (Stow Walsh Jesuit) dec. Brian Lanese (Lyndhurst Brush), 9-5
125—Kyle Bentley (Parma Heights Valley Forge) dec. Aaron Parks (Toledo St. Francis), 5-3
130—Jonathan Vaughn (Cleveland St. Ignatius) dec. Mike Arnold (Cincinnati St. Xavier), 13-1
135—Peter Nathanson (Shaker Heights) dec. Brad Hollo (Cincinnati St. Xavier), 6-1
140—Roger Chandler (Lakewood St. Edward) pinned Jerry Grammes (Strongsville), 2:50
145—Bill Lacure (North Canton Hoover) dec. Tom Zinkan (Cincinnati Moeller), 8-3
152—Jeff Lawless (Beavercreek) dec. Jason Fickes (Centerville), 9-5
160—Rodrick Franklin (Lorain Southview) dec. Scott Montgomery (Madison), 10-4
171—Mike Auerbach (Bedford) dec. Anthony Gary (Akron Springfield), 6-2
189—Scott Ostholthoff (Cincinnati Moeller) dec. Joe Myers (North Ridgeville), 11-5
Heavyweight—Stephan Terebieniec (Lakewood St. Edward) pinned Jason Wise (Massillon Perry), :18

Division II

103—Brian Santa Maria (Chagrin Falls Kenston) dec. Steve Daugherty (Ravenna), 9-5
112—Shantell Sanders (CAPE) dec. Scott McDaniel (Uhrichsville Claymont), 7-5
119—John Noble (Lebanon) pinned Craig Shaw (Uhrichsville Claymont), 1:02
125—Shawn Enright (Lebanon) pinned Mark Meyers (Milan Edison), 4:59
130—Luke Wimmers (Marysville) dec. Eugene Frankhauser Jr. (Ravenna SE), 11-9
135—Jody Withrow (Wooster Triway) dec. Walt Robertson (Norwalk), 11-3
140—Ryin McDaniel (Uhrichsville Claymont) dec. Keith Strahan (Mantua Crestwood), 7-6
145—Tony Pariano (Fairview Park) dec. Clifford Andres (Clyde), 5-0
152—Chad Kline (Wooster Triway) dec. Clifford Andres (Clyde), 5-0
160—Chad Grether (Macedonia Nordonia) dec. Jeremy Slone (Willard), 3-0
171—James Farley (Medina Buckeye) dec. Rick Tomaro (Broadview Heights Brecksville), 7-3
189—Nick Nutter (Medina Buckeye) dec. Steve Yates (Cleveland Villa Angela-St. Joseph), 7-6
Heavyweight—Luke Fickell (DeSales) pinned Ray Edmonds (Akron Hoban), :54

Division III

103—LeConte Merrell (Mansfield St. Peter) dec. Mark Zeno (Castalia Margaretta), 6-2
112—Jim Boardwine (Streetsboro) dec. Joe Workman (Akron Coventry), 7-2
119—Joe Boardwine (Streetsboro) dec. Steve Walker (Akron Manchester), 9-2
125—Kelly Lipinski (Brookville) dec. Terry Shinkle (Batavia), 6-3
130—Jason Amicon (Ready) dec. Chad Rosin (Sandusky St. Mary's), 15-6
135—Jason Hartman (Wellington) dec. Steve Feckanin (Thompson Ledgemont), 9-6
140—Eric Lippert (Kansas Lakota) dec. Craig Wise (Rootstown), 6-4
145—David Wellmeier (Lima Catholic) dec. Keith Bergman (Versailles), 8-0
152—Scott Sedlick (Wellington) dec. Paul Seim (Dayton Oakwood), 5-3, OT
160—John Gibeaut (Belmont Union) dec. Ralph Conte (Cuyahoga Heights), 3-2
171—Jay Perkins (Beallsville) dec. Mike Dailey (Peninsula Woodridge), 14-8
189—Keith Capizzi (Sandusky St. Mary's) dec. Steve Schumacher (Woodsfield), 9-8
Heavyweight—Steve Pardon (Lincolnview) pinned Tom Hart (Thompson Ledgemont), 1:21

Golf

Champions

		Team		Medalist	
1927		Akron St. Vincent	344	Jim Reston, Dayton Oakwood	77
1928		Cincinnati Hughes	318	Joseph Collins, Cincinnati Hughes	77
1929		Dayton Chaminade	351	John Fisher, Cincinnati Western Hills	80
				Ed Hamant, Dayton Chaminade	80
				R. Wilcox, Piqua	80
				C. Short, Akron West	80
1930		Toledo Central	314	G. Schumacher, Toledo Central	74
1931		Toledo St. John	355	J. Vance, Toledo St. John	83
1932		Columbus North	326	Barney Hunt, Columbus North	77
				Zotkowitz, Dayton Chaminade	77
				Eddie Meister, Shaker Heights	77
1933		Dayton Chaminade	331	Bob Servis, Dayton Oakwood	78
1934		Dayton Fairview	628	Paul Genung, Dayton Fairview	150
1935		Toledo Libbey	655	Bingham, Shaker Heights	155
1936		Dayton Fairview	675	Randolph, Dayton Fairview	158
1937		Columbus Central	644	Jack Kidwell, Columbus Central	152
1938		Worthington	649	McCabe, Franklin	156
1939		Toledo Libbey	652	Bob Hall, Toledo Libbey	155
1940		Toledo DeVilbiss	674	Don Shock, Dayton Fairmont	154
1941		Upper Arlington	658	Pete Sohl, Upper Arlington	151
1942		Sylvania Burnham	688	John Zoller, Hamilton	156
1943		Canton McKinley	660	Pete Dye, Urbana	154
				Marvin Kurjan, Youngstown Rayen	154
1944		Columbus North	665	Jack Carruthers, Upper Arlington	156
1945		Columbus North	639	Tony Blum, Cincinnati Roger Bacon	154
				Merle Moskowitz, Youngstown Rayen	154
1946		Columbus North	680	Clarence Hendrickson, Sandusky	154
1947		Sandusky	680	Leo Biagetti, Sandusky	154
1948		Hamilton	688	Tony Ondrus, Akron Kenmore	156
1949		Reading	668	Tom Matey, Warren Harding	146
1950		Toledo DeVilbiss	627	Fred Jones, Youngstown Rayen	148
				George Frankenfeld, Dayton W. Wright	148
1951		Circleville	666	Pat Schwab, Dayton Fairmont	153
				Dave Moore, Cincinnati Withrow	153
				Fred Jones, Youngstown Rayen	153
1952		Youngstown East	666	Fred Jones, Youngstown Rayen	155
				Fritz Schmidt, Columbus University	155
1953		Columbus Aquinas	653	Bob Shave, Willoughby	158
1954		Columbus Aquinas	622	Bob Shave, Willoughby	148
				Jim Hildebrand, Willoughby	148
1955		Columbus Aquinas	651	Dave Daniels, Bexley	149
1956		Upper Arlington	643	Jack Nicklaus, Upper Arlington	144
1957		Cincinnati St. Xavier	660	Jack Nicklaus, Upper Arlington	148
1958		Shaker Heights	645	Bob Zimmerman, Dayton Fairmont	146
1959		Shaker Heights	640	Earl Weiss, Shaker Heights	151
1960		Upper Arlington	650	*Bob Carson, Columbus Whitehall	153
1961		Kettering Fairmont	661	Bob Littler, Athens	151
1962		Ashland	646	Alex Antonio, Hubbard	148
1963		Kettering Fairmont West	638	Alex Antonio, Hubbard	142
1964		Barberton Norton	635	Ross Bartschy Jr., Upper Arlington	145
1965		Upper Arlington	624	Robert Heisler, Ravenna	146
1966		Ravenna	625	Robert Heisler, Ravenna	145
1967		Shaker Heights	626	*Pete Hummel, Upper Arlington	152
1968		Upper Arlington	652	*Tom Castor, Ashland	153
1969		Upper Arlington	647	Jim Urso, Hamilton Badin	152
1970		Coshocton	634	Kim Miller, Coshocton	149
1971	A	Mogadore	696	Jerry Kennedy, Mogadore	170
	AA	Aurora	631	Kim Heisler, Aurora	146
	AAA	Hubbard	646	Mike Morrow, Stow	152
1972	A	Mogadore	657	Gary Francis, Mogadore	155
	AA	Columbus Watterson	649	Ralph Guarasci, Columbus Watterson	149
	AAA	Upper Arlington	652	Larry Galloway, Upper Arlington	157

Year	Class	Team	Score	Medalist	Score
		Team		*Medalist*	
1973	A	Mogadore	651	Judd Silverman, Ottawa Hills	155
	AA	Columbus Watterson	615	Ralph Guarasci, Columbus Watterson	145
	AAA	Fremont Ross	634	Jim Decker, Fremont Ross	150
1974	A	Sidney Lehman	649	Kart Lampe, Sidney Lehman	158
	AA	Columbus Watterson	620	Ralph Guarasci, Columbus Watterson	145
	AAA	Upper Arlington	664	Dave Leggett, Upper Arlington	153
1974	A	Ottawa Hills	693	Ben Lowenthal, Cincinnati Country Day	167
	AA	Warren J. F. Kennedy	654	Dough Hanzel, Cleveland Orange	153
	AAA	Fairborn Baker	664	John Hamarik, Youngstown Mooney	154
1975	A	Tucsarawas Central Catholic	684	Greg Keatley, Kirtland	161
	AA	Coshocton	651	Mitch Camp, Orrville	153
	AAA	Youngstown Ursuline	654	Ted Moore, Findlay	153
1976	A	Tiffen Calvert	694	*Rick Steiner, Tiffin Calvert	168
	AA	Columbus Watterson	660	Mike McGee, Middletown Madison	158
	AAA	Youngstown Ursuline	653	Rocky Miller, Mt. Vernon	152
1977	A	Gates Mills Hawken	676	Todd McCormack, Gates Mills Hawken	159
	AA	Dublin	650	Tom Walters, Dayton Oakwood	146
	AAA	Upper Arlington	647	Julian Taylor, Youngstown Ursuline	147
1978	A	Gates Mills Hawken	671	Stan Cooke, New London	151
	AA	Columbus Centennial	667	David Learmonth, Columbus Centennial	151
	AAA	Worthington	638	*Julian Taylor, Youngstown Ursuline	151
1979	A	Elmore Woodmore	682	Steve Burner, Elmore Woodmore	155
	AA	Dublin	668	Dan Connelly, Perrysburg	158
	AAA	Fairfield	662	*Jeff Stewart, Wooster	154
1980	A	North Baltimore	692	Jeff Waaland, North Baltimore	161
	AA	Shelby	662	James Elliott, Shelby	157
	AAA	Wooster	675	Ken Saal, Wadsworth	159
1981	A	Elmore Woodmore	671	Jack Pawelkoski, Middletown Fenwick	163
	AA	Dublin	665	David Jeffers, Massillon Tuslaw	156
	AAA	Upper Arlington	636	Chris Westfall, Upper Arlington	148
1982	A	Toledo Ottawa Hills	625	Doug Martin, Van Buren	149
	AA	Coshocton	673	*Kelly Maxwell, Coshocton	157
	AAA	Upper Arlington	648	Dick Connelly, Perrysburg	157
1983	A	Gahanna Columbus Academy	626	Barry Fabyan, Gahanna Columbus Academy	143
	AA	Dublin	671	Tom Carr, Dublin	157
	AAA	Worthington	655	Tom Kies, Lodi Cloverleaf	153
1984	A	Van Buren	649	Per Ola Dahlman, Lynchburg Clay	150
	AA	Canton Central Catholic	670	Barry Fabyan, Columbus Academy (AA)	154
	AAA	Findlay	639	Doug Davis, West Lafayette Ridgewood (AA)	153
				Chip Coman, Worthington (AAA)	153
				Bill Thomas, Ox. Talawanda (AAA)	153
1985	A	Mt. Gilead	617	Chris Oliva, Berlin Cent. Western Reserve	143
	AA	Dayton Oakwood	665	James Caphinger, Eaton (team)	158(S)
				Brian Garman, Warren Champion	150(G)
				Bill Healy, Chesapeake	150(G)
				Ray Montgomery, Burton Berkshire	150(G)
				Steve Mulcahy, Lima Central Catholic	150(G)
				Robert Sowards, Minford	150(G)
				Mark Taylor, Canal Fulton Northwest	150(G)
				Ryan Zahn, Ontario	150(G)
	AAA	Upper Arlington	630	Mike Hubly, Upper Arlington (team)	149(S)
				Brian Bridges, Columbus Whitehall	141(G)
				Steve Stone, Toledo Bowsher	141(G)
1986	A	Zanesville Rosecrans	649	Bob Shubert, Findlay Lib. Benton	150
	AA	Circleville	663	Mark Telerico, Aurora	155
	AAA	Upper Arlington	641	John Hink, Upper Arlington	154
1987	A	South Charleston Southeastern	621	Matt Holtsberry, Lafayette Allen East	146
	AA	Canton Central Catholic	654	Steve Anderson, Circleville	153
	AAA	Toledo St. John's	653	Jerry Hounchell, Troy	152
1988	A	Zanesville Rosecrans	634	Chris Myers, South Charleston Southeastern	144
	AA	Youngstown Mooney	684	Chris Dauk, Richfield Revere	157
	AAA	Fairborn	659	Rob Rittberger, Solon	158
1989	I	Milford	654	Mike Stone, Toledo St. John's	152
	II	Youngstown Mooney	655	Lorin Baber, Tuscarawas Valley	152
	III	Marion Pleasant	614	*Matt Uhl, Marin Pleasant	146
1990	I	Stow Walsh Jesuit	651	Chris Wollman, Parma Normandy	147
	II	Chagrin Falls University School	672	Bunk McMahon, Chagrin Falls University School	156
	III	Van Buren	646	Peter DiSalvo, Versailles	156

		Team			Medalist	
1991	I	Stow Walsh Jesuit	651		Chris Wollman, Parma Normandy	147
	II	Chagrin Falls Univ. School	672		Bunk McMahon, Chagrin Falls	156
	III	Van Buren	646		Peter DiSalvo	156

*Won by playoff
(G) Gray Course
(S) Scarlet Course

Golf Coaches Hall of Fame

1981
George Legge
William Kincaid
Rollie Schultz–Springfield North
Irvine Chlotlos–Granville
Bill Thomas–Upper Arlington
John Harmon–Claymont

1982
George Valentine–Ashland
Phil Allen–Whitehall

1983
John Milhoan–Gallia Academy

1984
Jim Fritzsche–Springfield

1985
Jack Highly–Madison

1986
Marshall Glen–Gahanna-Lincoln
Richard Hadley–Princeton
Jim Rollins–Bethel Tate

1987
Robert Kepler–Ohio State University
Carl Haught–Cadiz

1988
Vernon Hooper–Hillsboro
Dick Wells–Eaton

1989
Dick Hall–Centerville
Tim Tilton–Green Hills
Ken Rockhold–North Royalton
Bill Hammer–John Glenn

1990
John Browder–Strongsville
Tom Reynolds–Findlay

1991
Jim Moyers–Springfield South
Jerry Richards–Trotwood Madison

Top jocks

Jack Nicklaus Recalls The First Time He Broke 70:

"I was 13, working in the drugstore with my father. We slipped away to play nine holes before dinner and I had 35 on the front nine. I begged him to go on. No, he said, Mom had dinner cooking. But if we ate fast and were careful of her feelings, we could be back in 35 minutes. Later, needing an eagle on the last hole for 69, I had a driver and a 2 or a 3-iron and made a long rainbow putt. I think that's when my father decided I had a better future as a golfer than as a stock boy."

At 17, **Jack Nicklaus** was a stocky, 17-year-old Columbus kid who won the International Jaycee Junior Golf Title. It was played in his hometown, and he won it—294-296—by making up a two-stroke deficit and staving off a rigorous challenge by John Konsek.

Cross Country

Championship, Boys

	Champion		Runner-up			Champion		Runner-up	
1928	Lakewood	35.5	Columbus Central	71	1950	Cleveland West	90	Lakewood	138
1929	Lakewood	46	Columbus Central	86	1951	Cleveland Wet Tech.	71	Toledo Waite	119
1930	Salem	35	Columbus East	102					
			Dayton Roosevelt	102	1952	Marion Harding	113	Lakewood	116
1931	Salem	29	Dayton Roosevelt	74	1953	Lakewood	61	Springfield	135
1932	Lakewood	53	Cleveland Lincoln	67	1954	Cleveland John Adams	53	Columbus West	144
1933	Akron East	64.5	Cleveland Lincoln	95	1955	Akron Buchtel	109		
1934	Toledo Scott	39	Akron East	42		Columbus East	109		
1935	Toledo Scott	41	Salem	85	1956	Cleveland East	75	Akron South	118
1936	Toledo Scott	94	Akron East	99	1957	Cleveland West Tech.	84	Akron Buchtel	114
			Akron Garfield	99	1958	Akron North	38	Cleveland West Tech.	56
1937	Akron East	73	Toledo Libbey	80					
1938	Springfield	79	Akron East	88	1959	Cleveland John Adams	123	Parma	125
1939	Akron South	42	Akron North	88	1960	Cleveland John Marshall	58	Akron Buchtel	69
1940	Springfield	62	Akron East	90	1961	Akron Buchtel	53	Lyndhurst Brush	114
1941	Akron North	49	Akron South	66	1962	Amherst Steele	87	Dayton Chaminade	111
1942	NO MEET				1963	Cleveland John Adams	90	Dayton Chaminade	103
1943	Akron North	62	Cleveland John Marshall	79	1964	Cleveland John Marshall	105	Cleveland Heights	149
1944	Cincinnati Western Hills	74	Cleveland West	89	1965	Cleveland St. Joseph	176	Akron Firestone	178
1945	Cleveland West Tech.	105	Cleveland Rhodes	119					
1946	Akron North	66	Cleveland West Tech.	90					
1947	Akron North	67	Akron East	79					
1948	Cleveland West Tech.	84	Cincinnati Central	108					
			Akron East	108					
1949	Cincinnati Central	48	Akron North	106					

CLASS AA

						CLASS A			
1966	Cleveland St. Joseph	57	Cleveland Heights	99	1966	Marion River Valley	113	Kirtland	117
1967	Worthington	100	Cleveland St. Joseph	109	1967	Cortland Lakeview	76	Kent State University School	98
1968	Cleveland St. Joseph	109	Cincinnati Elder	125	1968	Cortland Lakeview	99	Georgetown	101
1969	Cleveland St. Joseph	110	Toledo DeVilbiss	141	1969	Georgetown	127	Kent State University School	168
			Cincinnati Elder	141					

CLASS AAA

	Champion		Runner-up			Champion		Runner-up	
1970	Toledo DeVilbiss	115	Youngstown Austintown-Fitch	140	1980	Kent Roosevelt	44	Bay Village Bay	163
					1981	Kent Roosevelt	91	Amherst Steele	130
1971	Youngstown Austintown-Fitch	79	Sandusky	155	1982	Cincinnati Elder	105	Fairborn	129
1972	Youngstown Austintown-Fitch	112	Upper Arlington	153	1983	West Chester Lakota	120	Stow Walsh Jesuit	127
1973	Cincinnati Elder	111	Uppr Arlington	171	1984	Stow Walsh Jesuit	103	Cincinnati Elder	152
1974	Findlay	103	Youngstown Austintown-Fitch	134	1985	Mentor	104	Shelby	118
1975	Youngstown Austintown Fitch	82	Maple Heights	105		Cincinnati Elder	120	Cincinnati LaSalle	144
1976	Bay Village Bay	102	Lakewood	141		Sylvania Southview	108	Cincinnati Elder	109
1977	Amherst Steele	77	Bay Village Bay	113	1986	Cincinnati Elder	120	Cincinnati LaSalle	144
1978	Cincinnati Colerain	48	Tiffin Columbian	85	1987	Sylvania Southview	108	Cincinnati Elder	109
1979	Lancaster	71	Kent Roosevelt	97	1988	Cincinnati Elder	70	Sylvania Southview	98

CLASS AA

Year	Champion		Runner-up	
1970	Kansas Lakota	84	Chagrin Falls	108
1971	Chagrin Falls	94	Coshocton	103
1972	Chardon	105	Elyria Catholic	115
1973	Elyria Catholic	56	North Robinson Colonel Crawford	115
1974	Elyria Catholic	60	Tipp City Tippecanoe	110
1975	Youngstown Liberty	52	Tipp City Tippecanoe	65
1976	Louisville St. Thomas Aquinas	130	Akron Hoban	166
1977	Elyria Catholic	106	Cinti. Greenhills	122
1978	Elyria Catholic	43	Navarre Fairless	127
1979	Shelby	92	Elyria Catholic	101
1980	Louisville St. Thomas Aquinas	95	Napoleon	96
1981	Louisville St. Thomas Aquinas	79	Chagrin Falls Kenston	126
1982	Oberlin Firelands	121	Parma Hgts. Holy Name	143
1983	Chagrin Falls Kenston	92	Elyria Catholic	110
1984	Bellevue	116	Chagrin Falls Kenston	133
1985	Bellevue	86	Napoleon	105
1986	Cincinnati Greenhills	79	Chagrin Falls Kenston	80
1987	Sandusky Perkins	45	Bellevue	104
1988	Sandusky Perkins	94	Van Wert	138

CLASS A

Year	Champion		Runner-up	
1970	Kent State University School	33	Georgetown	63
1971	Plymouth	70	Georgetown	79
			Kent State University School	79
1972	Cortland Maplewood	92	Caldwell	100
1973	Caldwell	60	Plymouth	71
1974	Plymouth	87	McDonald	97
1975	Defiance Ayersville	99	McDonald	108
1976	West Liberty-Salem	55	Elmore Woodmore	94
1977	West Liberty-Salem	59	Sidney Lehman	135
1978	West Liberty-Salem	35	Cortland Maplewood	89
1979	West Liberty-Salem	41	Cortland Maplewood	89
1980	Sidney Lehman	81	Amanda Clearcreek	104
1981	Lafayette Allen East	88	Toledo Ottawa Hills	96
1982	McDonald	91	Amanda Clearcreek	130
1983	McDonald	94	Caldwell	96
1984	Dayton Christian	79	Caldwell	80
1985	Caldwell	33	Newbury	93
1986	Caldwell	26	Convoy Crestview	111

DIVISION I

Year	Champion		Runner-up	
1989	Cincinnati Elder	72	Sylvania Southview	108
1990	Lancaster	123	Tiffin Columbian	136
1991	Sylvania Southview	95	Cincinnati Elder	113

DIVISION II

Year	Champion		Runner-up	
1989	Sandusky Perkins	71	Swanton	76
1990	Ashtabula Edgewood	101*	Sandusky Perkins	101*
1991	Bay Village Bay	67	Salem	106

*Champion determined in accordance with the National Federation Rules using the better sixth-place finisher.

DIVISION III

Year	Champion		Runner-up	
1989	Caldwell	61	Piketon	89
1990	Caldwell	63	Cortland Maplewood	139
1991	Caldwell	41	Wayne Trace	114

*Champion determined by tie-breaker (6th runner)

The long haul, I

Cross Country Records, Boys

Division	Distance	Record Holder	Time	Year
Division III (Class A)	2 Miles	Dan Zoeller, Tipp City Bethel	9:49.9	1968
	2.5 Miles	Earl Zilles, West Liberty-Salem	12:06.7	1978
	5000 Meters	Bob Burley, New Albany	15:19.3	1982
Division II (Class AA)	2 Miles	Bruce Smith, Martins Ferry	9:33.4	1975
	2.5 Miles	Mitch Bentley, McArthur Vinton	12:03.4	1980
	5000 Meters	Scott Fry, Sandusky Perkins	14:50.2	1985
Division I (Class AAA)	2 Miles	Alan Scharsu, Youngstown Austintown-Fitch	9:15.7	1975
	2.5 Miles	George Nicholas, Dayton Meadowdale	11:36.7	1980
	5000 Meters	Bob Mau, Rocky River	14:58.6	1982

Individual Champions, Boys

In the 1928 through 1930 state tournaments, the distance of the event was 2.5 miles. Beginning in 1931 the distance run was 2.0 miles. This distance was competed through the 1976 season when the distance was increased to 2.5 miles. In 1982, the official distance was increased to 5000 meters (3.1 miles).

For the period of time from 1960 through 1984, the individual qualifiers competed in a separate race from the team qualifiers in the state championship races only. The listing that follows contains the official winners from each race. The winner of the individual qualifiers race is listed first for each year.

1928	Charles Medberry	14:10	Columbus East	1953	Jack Blackburn	10:16.6	Worthington
1929	Harvey Smith	13:18.3	Lakewood	1954	Larry Hamilton	9:56.4	Ashland
1930	Wilford Brantingham	13:11.5	Salem	1955	Jim Russell	10:33.2	Worthington
1931	Harold Horstman	10:21.5	Salem	1956	Ed Butler	10:10.5	Cleveland
1932	Paul Benner	10:38	Newark				John Adams
1933	Paul Benner	10:14	Newark	1957	Alex Fultz	10:24.2	Monroe Lemon
1934	Jim Whitaker	10:00	Kent Roosevelt				Monroe
1935	Wade Campbell	10:24	Fremont	1958	Ray Fleming	9:59.9	Akron North
1936	Paul Roelen	10:08	Salem	1959	Choice Phillip	9:52.0	Cleveland
1937	Graham Sheppard	10:00	Edinburg				John Adams
1938	Sam Cobb	10:12.3	Columbus North	1960	Warren Hand	10:02.0	Dayton Roosevelt
1939	Ray Jordan	9:58.5	Akron South	1960	Mike Gallagher	10:04.1	Toledo Libbey
1940	Elmer McDonnall	10:05	Toledo Waite	1961	Andy Schramm	9:26.4	Cincinnati
1941	Don Rydgig	10:17.1	Akron North				Deer Park
1942	No tournament			1961	Warren Hand	9:51.3	Dayton Roosevelt
1943	Sylvester Stewart	9:53.8	Toledo Waite	1962	James Gilbert	9:39.5	Cleveland
1944	Austin Hutt	10:26	Columbus West				Glenville
1945	John Dewey	10:49.8	Akron North	1962	Alex Jamieson	9:55.9	Lakewood
1946	John Holloman	10:16	Akron East	1963	Ricky Poole	9:51.4	Dayton Jefferson
1947	John Holloman	10:28	Akron East	1963	John Tillman	9:53.5	Akron North
1948	Bob Boxler	10:28.8	Akron East	1964	Charles Starkey	9:47.1	Columbus West
1949	Jackson Wagner	10:18	Akron North	1964	Gary Gold	9:38.8	Cleveland
1950	Ron Truex	10:28.8	Lima Central				John Marshall
1951	George Leith	10:36	Cleveland	1965	Paul Zink	9:42.4	Cleveland West
			West Tech	1965	David Reid	9:31.3	Lakewood
1952	Neil Burson	10:04.5	Toledo Waite				

CLASS AA

1966	Tom Glebremedhim	10:58	Fairview Park Fairview	1966	Charles Starkey	10:29	Columbus West
1966	John Jones	11:05	Marion Elgin	1966	Sid Sink	10:14	Avon
1967	Joe Corry	10:13.9	Zanesville Rosecrans	1967	Reginald McAfee	9:48.3	Cincinnati
							Courier Tech
1967	Dan Boyd	10:22	Kent State University School	1967	Wesley Brock	9:43.7	Toledo Libbey
1968	Dan Zoeller	9:44.9	Tipp City Bethel	1968	Reginald McAfee	9:28.0	Cincinnati
							Courier Tech
1969	Bill Huntington	9:48.3	Orwell Grand Valley	1968	Bill Beaty	9:31.4	Lancaster
1969	Scott Snow	10:03.8	Cortland Lakeview	1969	Bill Beaty	9:45.2	Lancaster
1969	Bruce Melton	10:03.8	Cortland Lakeview	1969	Bill Beaty	9:45.2	Lancaster
1969	Bruce Melton	10:13.4	Crestline	1969	Les Nagy	9:34.7	Niles McKinley

CLASS A			CLASS AA			CLASS AAA		
1970	Ron Leach Covington	10:14.0	1970	Jerry Wenger Zanesfield	9:52.6	1970	Mike Burley Berea	9:44.2
							Jeff Schnell Toledo DeVilbiss	9:40.5
1971	Gary Vippermann Bethel-Tate	10:05	1971	Steve Richards Circleville	9:51.8	1971	Ron Addison Cleveland Rhodes	9:26.9
							Glenn Wilburn Amherst Steele	9:28.3
1972	Ron Dunfee Stewart Federal Hocking	10:07.8	1972	Neil McConnell Hudson	10:00.3	1972	Larry Coy Cleveland John Marshall	9:46
	Ted Rupe Cortland Maplewood	10:03.0		Tom Brumfield Grandview	10:07		Bob Lunn Youngstown Austintown-Fitch	9:45.5
1973	Mike Becraft Georgetown	9:46.4	1973	Mark Kadlec Bedford Chanel	9:49	1973	Mark Hunter Brunswick	9:34
	Dan Cartledge Liberty Center	10:09		Callan Strouss Youngstown Liberty	9:46.0		Peter Kummant Amherst Steele	9:33.0

CLASS A		CLASS AA		CLASS AAA	
1974 Pete Murtaugh Ashland Mapleton	9:53.5	1974 Mark Tapee Columbus Bexley	9:41.0	1974 Rick Music Fairborn Baker	9:34.8
Brian Jonard Caldwell	9:59.7	Bruce Smith Martins Ferry	9:43.6	Peter Kummant Amherst Steele	9:24.7
1975 Fred Myers New Albany	9:58.5	1975 Mark Mellum Pemberville Eastwood	9:44.5	1975 Mike Lacey Westerville South	9:38.1
Bill Ankney Defiance Ayersville	9:46.8	Bruce Smith Martins Ferry	9:33.4	Alan Scharsu Youngstown Austintown-Fitch	9:15.7
1976 Brian Jonard Caldwell	10:07	1976 Jerry Hansen Clyde	9:46.8	1976 Tom Rapp Trotwood-Madison	9:29.6
Fred Myers New Albany	9:56.7	Mike Maynard Cincinnati Greenhills	9:43.5	Alan Scharsu Youngstown Austintown-Fitch	9:19.3
1977 John Locker Lewisburg Twin Valley North	12:21.3	1977 Glen McCaslin Cortland Lakeview	12:17.7	1977 Gerald Vilt Cleveland Rhodes	12:10.7
Doug McDonald Defiance Ayersville	12:34.9	Mike Maynard Cincinnati Greenhills	12:09.9	Alan Scharsu Youngstown Austintown-Fitch	11:46.8
1978 Dean Wood Hicksville	12:40.1	1978 Chuck Bridgman Dayton Chaminade-Julienne	12:05.3	1978 George Nicholas Dayton Meadowdale	11:45.2
Earl Zilles West Liberty-Salem	12:06.7	Joel Marchand Navarre Fairless	12:17.8	John Zishka Lancaster	12:14.3
1979 Jeff Johnson Yellow Springs	12:56.1	1979 Joel Marchand Navarre Fairless	12:11.9	1979 George Nicholas Dayton Meadowdale	12:08.2
Earl Zilles West Liberty-Salem	12:24.4	Mitch Bentley McArthur Vinton County	12:32.2	John Zishka Lancaster	12:12.9
1980 Scott Campbell Ashtabula St. John	12:12.2	1980 Mitch Bentley McArthur Vinton County	12:03.4	1980 George Nicholas Dayton Meadowdale	11:36.7
Tony Thaman Sidney Lehman	12:26.7	George Rodriguez Orgeon Stritch	12:16.1	Clark Haley Lancaster	11:53.3
1981 Dave Richerd Hamler Patrick Henry	12:23	1981 Tom Franek Chagrin Falls Kenston	12:14.7	1981 Bob Mau Rocky River	12:04.8
Dough Lawrence Lafayette Allen East	12:29.4	Ben Weeman Orrville	12:12	Dean Monske Toledo DeVilbiss	11:58
1982 Bob Burley New ALbany	15:19.3	1982 Ben Weeman Orville	15:14.6	1982 Bob Mau Rocky River	14:58.6
Matt Streeter Gates Mills Hawken	15:38.7	Dan Franek Chagrin Falls Kenston	15:33.3	Andy Herr Berea	15:09.8
1983 Scott Mercer Peninsula Woodridge	16:04.5	1983 Tom Schnurr Sandusky St. Marys Central Catholic	15:38.1	1983 Curt Rogers Sandusky	15:41.1
Ken Petty Dayton Christian	15:56.8	Scott Fry Sandusky Perkins	15:31.6	Lowell Terrell Alliance	15:17.3
1984 Bob Henes Peninsula Woodridge	16:14.0	1984 Scott Fry Sandusky Perkins	14:50.2	1984 Mark Croghan Greensburg Green	15:43.8
Tony Carna Caldwell	16:13.9	Troy Jones Coshocton	16:07.4	Matt Linden Parma Normandy	15:52.1
1985 Tony Carna Caldwell	16:01.2	1985 Bob Henes Peninsula Woodridge	15:45.1	1985 Eric Nelson Westerville North	16:00.2
1986 Tony Carna Caldwell	15:44.2	1986 Joe McKown Kansas Lakota	15:31.1	1986 Bob Kennedy Westerville North	15:31.8
1987 Brian Norris Caldwell	15:47.6	1987 Martin Avila Swanton	15:42.2	1987 Bob Kennedy Westerville North	15:03.2
1988 Mondo Tijerina Columbus Grove	16:30.2	1988 Tom Woods Wooster Triway	16:26.0	1988 Dave Briggs Sylvania Southview	16:12.3

DIVISION III		*DIVISION II*		*DIVISION I*	
1989 Stuart Henderson McDonald	15:37.9	1989 Richard Ronald Uhrichsville Claymont	15:47.1	1989 Alan Boos Tiffin Columbian	15:44.4
1990 Brian Hesson, Caldwell	15:35.6	1990 Matt Smith Sandusky Perkins	15:54.9	1990 Darrell Hughes Galloway Westland	15:24.7
1991 Brian Hesson Caldwell	15:30.9	1991 Jason Wertz Canfield	15:45.7	1991 J.J. White Dublin	15:31.4

Cross Country
Championships, Girls

CLASS AAA (two classes)

	CHAMPION		RUNNER-UP	
1978	Upper Arlington	35	Amherst Steele	66
1979	Wadsworth	67	Broadview Hgts. Brecksville	122
			Rocky River	122
1980	Wadsworth	89	Kettering Fairmont East	118
1981	Upper Arlington	60	Broadview Hgts. Brecksville	85

CLASS A-AA (two classes)

1978	Chardon	52	Swanton	58
1979	Chardon	35	Olmsted Falls	85
1980	Olmsted Falls	103	Delaware Olentangy	112
1981	Olmsted Falls	101	Delaware Olentangy	122

CLASS AAA (three classes)

1982	Upper Arlington	50	Lima Shawnee	51
1983	Lima Shawnee	99	Upper Arlington	139
1984	West Chester Lakota	135	Toledo DeVilbiss	148
1985	Upper Arlington	132	Columbus Watterson	149
1986	Upper Arlington	84	Bellevue	109
1987	Bellevue	77	Lakewood	114
1988	North Canton GlenOak	65	Lodi Cloverleaf	105

CLASS AA (three classes)

	CHAMPION		RUNNER-UP	
1982	Delaware Olentangy	79	Olmsted Falls	86
1983	Ravenna Southeast	64	Springfield Northeastern	78
1984	Ravenna Southeast	103	Springfield Northeastern	108
1985	Ravenna Southeast	73	Atwater Waterloo	123
1986	Avon Lake	76	Youngstown Liberty	121
1987	Olmsted Falls	84	Columbus Bexley	104
1988	Avon Lake	50	Cleveland Hgts. Beaumont	56

CLASS A (three classes)

1982	Minster	61	Zanesville Rosecrans	66
1983	Zanesville Rosecrans	45	Lancaster Fisher Catholic	65
1984	Findlay Liberty-Benton	43	Lancaster Fisher Catholic	45
1985	Findlay Liberty-Benton	55	Fort Loramie	103
1986	Findlay Liberty-Benton	49	Minster	72
1987	Sandusky St. Marys	54	Findlay Liberty-Benton	65
1988	Sandusky St. Marys	53	Minster	98

DIVISION I

1989	Worthington	122	Rocky River Magnificat	129
1990	Upper Arlington	89	Amherst Steele	98
1991	Amherst Steele	77	Worthington	88

DIVISION II

1989	Sandusky St. Marys	72	Wickliffe	85
1990	Sandusky St. Marys	85	Minster	123
1991	Chagrin Falls	90	Liberty Benton	120

Individual Champions, Girls

In 1978 when girls competition began in cross country, the distance run was 2.5 miles. In 1982, the official distance was increased to 5000 meters (3.1 miles).

For the races run from 1981 through 1984, the individual qualifiers competed in a separate race from the team qualifiers in the state championship races only. The listing that follows contains the official winners from each race. The winner of the individual qualifiers race is listed first each year.

CLASS AAA
1978 Ann Henderson, Broadview Hgts. Brecksville	13:46.2
1979 Maureen Cogan, Kettering Fairmont East	14:37.8
1980 Sherrie Matthews, Toledo Notre Dame	13:53.5
1980 Sherrie Matthews, Toledo Notre Dame	13:53.5
1980 Sherrie Matthews, Toledo Notre Dame	13:53.5
1981 Tina Cheney, Lima Shawnee	14:01

CLASS A-AA
1978 Mary Jean Wright, Kirtland	14:29.9
1979 Mary Jean Wright, Kirtland	14:19.0
1980 Patty Metzler, North Jackson Jackson-Milton	13:55.1
1981 Patty Metzler, North Jackson Jackson-Milton	13:50.8
1981 C. J. Robinson, Reading	13:33

CLASS A
1982 Patty Metzler North Jackson Jackson-Milton	17:17.8
1982 Susan Nash Zanesville Rosecrans	18:34.4
1983 Maria Newcomer West Liberty-Salem	18:44.4
1983 Susan Nash Zanesville Rosecrans	18:53.05
1984 Shari Coressel Archbold	19:45.1
1984 Micki Bish Findlay Liberty-Benton	19:16.3
1985 Dawn Arrigoni Newbury	19:21.3
1986 Michelle Borgert Kirtland	18:43.1
1987 Michelle Borgert Kirtland	19:00.5
1988 Jana Woehrmyer Minster	19:52.1

CLASS AA
1982 Teresa Dunn Springfield Catholic Central	17:34.5
1982 Michelle Kallikan Olmsted Falls	17:51.2
1983 Michelle Sica Cincinnati Our Lady of Angels	18:01.2
1983 Joanna Dias Ravenna Southeast	18:17.7
1984 Michelle Sica Cincinnati Roger Bacon	18:16.2
1984 Julie Dias Ravenna Southeast	18:00.3
1985 Julie Dias Ravenna Southeast	18:17.9
1986 Kimberly Haluscsak Olmsted Falls	18:47.4
1987 Kim Haluscsak Olmsted Falls	18:27.8
1988 Monica McHenry Cleveland Hgts. Beaumont	19:43.5

CLASS AAA
1982 Kristy Orre Clayton Northmont	17:15.6
1982 Tina Cheney Lima Shawnee	17:28.7
1983 Anne Densmore Elyria	17:26.6
1983 Tina Cheney Lima Shawnee	17:55.5
1984 Kristy Orre Clayton Northmont	18:26.5
1984 Barb Courtade Upper Arlington	18:56.9
1985 Laurie Gomez Youngstown Boardman	18:46.2
1986 Laurie Gomez Youngstown Boardman	18:20.8
1987 Laurie Gomez Youngstown Boardman	17:58.2
1988 Misty Allison Chillicothe	19:32.1

DIVISION II
1989 Michelle Borgert	18:43.5
1990 Rachel Sauder	18:41.7
1991 Brandi Sabino	18:56.2

DIVISION I
1989 India Ford, Euclid	18:33.0
1990 Christina Talkington	18:25.9
1991 Kristen Diehm	18:56

The long haul, II

Cross Country Records, Girls

Class A	2.5 Miles	Patty Metzler, North Jackson-Milton	13:50.0	1981
	5000 Meters	Patty Metzler, North Jackson-Milton	17:17.8	1982
Class AA	2.5 Miles	C. J. Robinson, Reading	13:33.9	1981
	5000 Meters	Teresa Dunn, Springfield Catholic Central	17:43.5	1982
Class AAA	2.5 Miles	Ann Henderson, Broadview Hgts. Brecksville	13:46.2	1978
	5000 Meters	Kristy Orre, Clayton Northmont	17:15.6	1982

Gymnastics

Champions, Boys

The OHSAA conducted a championship tournament in boys gymnastics beginning in 1926 for a period of 12 years through 1937. OHSAA tournaments were discontinued until 1965 when the tournament was resumed. The championship and runner-up teams are listed with the names of coaches. In a few cases, the name of a coach is unknown. Information relative to the coaches will be appreciated.

Champion			Runner-up		
Year School	Coach	Total Points	Year School	Coach	Total Points
1926 Columbus North	M. M. Hagley	439.60	1926 Columbus East	J. A. Stevens	412.00
1927 Columbus North	M. M. Hagley	769.00	1927 Columbus Central	Guy Kesler	742.00
1928 Columbus East	J. A. Stevens	753.20	1928 Columbus North	M. M. Hagley	672.70
1929 Columbus Central	Guy Kesler	756.80	1929 Columbus North	M. M. Hagley	740.40
1930 Columbus Central	Guy Kesler	833.10	1930 Columbus East	J. A. Stevens	778.40
1931 Columbus East	J. A. Stevens	773.30	1931 Columbus Central	Guy Kesler	770.30
1932 Columbus North	M. M. Hagley	721.30	1932 Cleveland East Tech	G. P. Thompson	566.40
1933 Cleveland East Tech	G. P. Thompson	33.00	1933 Columbus North	M. M. Hagley	13.50
1934 Cleveland East Tech	G. P. Thompson	88.00	Columbus East	J. A. Stevens	27.00
			Columbus North	M. M. Hagley	27.00
1935 Cleveland East Tech	Eric Calhoun	45.00	1935 Columbus East	J. A. Stevens	21.00
1936 Cleveland East Tech	G. P. Thompson	53.00	1936 Columbus North	M. M. Hagley	14.00
1937 Cleveland East Tech	G. P. Thompson	41.00	1937 Cleveland John Adams	Allan Owens	18.00
1965 Kettering Fairmont East	Don Powers	45.00	1965 Cuyahoga Falls	Joe Kotys	28.00
1966 Cuyahoga Falls		33.00	1966 Columbus South		26.00
1967 Dayton Belmont	Ed Jones	91.00	1967 Dayton Meadowdale		51.00
1968 Kettering Fairmont East		104.10	1968 St. Clairsville	David McKim	101.775
1969 Kettering Fairmont East	Dick Denny	109.50	1969 St. Clairsville	David McKim	102.30
1970 Miamisburg	Ken Bostelman	146.90	1970 Kettering Fairmont East	Tom Sexton	142.50
1971 Kettering Fairmont East	Tom Sexton	162.55	1971 Miamisburg	Ken Bostelman	162.45
1972 Miamisburg	Ken Bostelman	165.95	1972 Dayton Wayne	Jack Morefield	159.05
1973 Dayton Wayne	Jack Morefield	274.00	1973 Miamisburg	Ken Bostelman	205.00
1974 Franklin	Don Sellman	311.50	1974 Dayton Wayne	Jack Morefield	196.50
1975 Dayton Wayne	Jack Morefield	147.902	1975 Youngstown Boardman	Brian Gallagher	119.701
1976 Dayton Wayne	James Semon	128.433	1976 Miamisburg	Ken Bostelman	127.33
1977 Franklin	Don Sellman	138.99	1977 Cuyahoga Falls	Joe Kotys	136.07
1978 Franklin	Don Sellman	145.88	1978 Youngstown Boardman	Brian Gallagher	136.53
1979 Franklin	Don Sellman	152.28	1979 Worthington	Jerry Baker	145.67
1980 Centerville	Bob Barlow	148.43	1980 Worthington	Jerry Baker	148.22
1981 Miamisburg	Ken Bostelman	158.058	1981 Franklin	Don Sellman	156.408
1982 Franklin	Don Sellman	153.625	1982 Dayton Wayne	Bill Williams	143.758
1983 Miamisburg	John Good	152.308	1983 Franklin	Don Sellman	147.392
1984 Miamisburg	John Good	149.75	1984 Franklin	Don Sellman	147.70
1985 Franklin	Don Sellman	154.55	1985 Columbus Watterson	Tom Scholl	138.50
1986 Franklin	Don Sellman	151.35	1986 Miamisburg	John Good	145.00
1987 Worthington	Rich Aguirre	147.95	1987 Columbus Watterson	Tom Scholl, Dennis McIntyre	140.65
1988 Franklin	Don Sellman	147.60	1988 Miamisburg	John Good	145.25
1989 Franklin	Don Sellman	146.50	1989 Miamisburg	John Good	132.05
1990 Columbus DeSales	Dennis McIntyre	161.35	1990 Miamisburg	John Good	149.90
1991 Columbus DeSales	Dennis McIntyre	164.00	1991 Miamisburg	John Good	143.15
1992 Columbus DeSales	Dennis McIntyre	148.10	1991 Brecksville-Broadview Hts.	Dave Forister	124.85

Gymnastics All-Around Champions

Year	Champion	Points	Year	Champion	Points
1965	Tom Sexton, Kettering Fairmont East	42.80	1979	Chris Kotys, Cuyahoga Falls	51.90
1966	Bruce Trott, Columbus South	47.95	1980	Scott Schuler, Worthington	52.00
1967	Ernest Armstrong, Dayton Belmont	46.15	1981	Dan Bachman, Parma Senior	54.80
1968	Reed Klein, Lyndhurst Brush	42.175	1982	Allan Powers, Miamisburg	53.25
1969	Mike Grimes, Euclid	38.325	1983	Chad Lape, Delaware Olentangy	54.10
1970	Mike Grimes, Euclid	39.85	1984	Chris McKee, Toledo Whitmer	54.50
1971	Doug Griffith, Franklin	46.90	1985	Rick Ijams, Dublin	54.15
1972	David Eby, Dayton Wayne	48.15	1986	Sam Mirto, Youngstown Mooney	53.75
1973	David Eby, Dayton Wayne	50.30	1987	Derek Kish, Doylestown Chippewa	55.25
1974	Mark Fulks, Youngstown Boardman	44.60	1988	Dillon Ashton, Pemberville Eastwood	53.70
1975	Chris Haynam, Youngstown Boardman	47.30	1989	James Knoop, Poland Seminary	55.75
1976	Roland Bischoff, Dayton Wayne	46.70	1990	Drew Durbin, Columbus DeSales	55.60
1977	Chris Kotys, Cuyahoga Falls	45.45	1991	Blaine Wilson, Columbus DeSales	55.70
1978	Douglas Naylor, Franklin	49.35			

Gymnastics Team Champions, Girls

	Champion				Runner-up		
Year	School	Coach	Points	Year	School	Coach	Points
1978	Bay Village Bay	Tony Chiabotti	199.55	1978	Dublin	Barbara Headlee	196.20
1979	Lakewood	Janet LaRocco	202.30	1979	Bay Village Bay	Toni Chiabotti	196.75
1980	Dublin	Connie Montgomery	198.15	1980	Lakewood	Janet LaRocco	197.15
1981	KetteringFairmont West	Linda Burton	198.25	1981	Dublin	Connie Montgomery	191.25
1982	Dublin	Bobbi Montanari	195.25	1982	Centerville	Jim Pignatiello	191.10
1983	Berea	Barb Spatz	200.50	1983	Dublin	Bobbi Montanari	195.00
1984	Dublin	Bobbi Montanari	195.70	1984	Worthington	Marty McLain	191.05
1985	Worthington	Marty McLain	208.80	1985	North Canton GlenOak	Cheryl Christianson	200.60
1986	Worthington	Marty McLain	279.35	1986	Clayton Northmont	Steve Heinrichs	261.60
1987	Worthington	Marty McLain	273.50	1987	Clayton Northmont	Steve Heinrichs	271.55
1988	Worthington	Mindy Fleck	273.15	1988	Cincinnati Turpin	Gail Maundrell	269.65
1989	Worthington	Susan Ford	272.35	1989	North Olmsted	Mike Tatrai	269.25
1990	Rocky River Magnificat	Julie Cleary	140.00	1990	Worthington	Susan Ford	131.70
1991	Rocky River Magnificat	Joe Gura	142.10	1991	Worthington	Susan Ford	133.05
1992	Rocky River Magnificat	Joe Gura	139.30	1992	Upper Arlington	Julie Kayser	139.10

Swimming and Diving
Championships, Boys

Year	Champion	Runner-up	Year	Champion	Runner-up
1928	Lakewood	Cincinnati Withrow	1959	Canton McKinley	Berea
1929	Lakewood	Akron East	1960	Canton McKinley	Lakewood
1930	Cincinnati Hughes	Lakewood	1961	Canton McKinley	Lima Senior
1931	Cleveland YMCA Prep.	Canton McKinley	1962	Lakewood	Upper Arlington
1932	Cleveland Heights	East Cleveland Shaw	1963	Arkon Buchtel	Cleveland Heights
1933	Cleveland Heights	Cincinnati Western Hills	1964	Fairview Park	Akron Buchtel
1934	Cleveland Heights	Shaker Heights	1965	Cleveland Heights	Fairview Park
1935	Cincinnati Western Hills	Akron East	1966	Akron Firestone	Canton McKinley
1936	Fremont Ross	Canton McKinley	1967	Toledo St. Francis DeSales	Akron Firestone
1937	Canton McKinley	Fremont Ross	1968	Toledo St. Francis DeSales	Upper Arlington
1938	Fremont Ross	Canton McKinley	1969	Akron Firestone	Upper Arlington
1939	Canton McKinley and Fremont Ross		1970	Cincinnati St. Xavier	Upper Arlington
1940	Canton McKinley	Fremont Ross	1971	Cincinnati St. Xavier	Upper Arlington
1941	Fremont Ross	Canton McKinley	1972	Cincinnati St. Xavier	Upper Arlington
1942	Fremont Ross	Canton McKinley	1973	Cincinnati St. Xavier	Toledo St. Francis DeSales
1943	Fremont Ross	Lakewood	1974	Cincinnati St. Xavier	Toledo St. Francis DeSales
1944	Findlay	Canton McKinley and Lakewood	1975	Cincinnati St. Xavier	
			1976	Cincinnati St. Xavier	Upper Arlington
1945	Canton McKinley	Cincinnati St. Xavier	1977	Cincinnati St. Xavier	Gates Mills Hawken
1946	Sandusky	Canton McKinley	1978	Cincinnati St. Xavier	Upper Arlington
1947	Cleveland East Tech	Canton McKinley	1979	Cincinnati St. Xavier	Akron Firestone
1948	Cleveland East Tech	Lakewood	1980	Cincinnati St. Xavier	Akron Firestone
1949	Canton McKinley	Fremont Ross	1981	Cincinnati St. Xavier	Akron Firestone
1950	Cincinnati Walnut Hills	Fremont Ross	1982	Akron Firestone	Cincinnati St. Xavier
1951	Canton McKinley	Cincinnati Walnut Hills	1983	Akron Firestone	Cincinnati St. Xavier
1952	Canton McKinley	Fremont Ross	1984	Cincinnati St. Xavier	Upper Arlington
1953	Fremont Ross	Sandusky	1985	Upper Arlington	Cincinnati St. Xavier
1954	Shaker Heights	Cincinnati Walnut Hills and Lakewood	1986	Upper Arlington	Cincinnati Sycamore
			1987	Upper Arlington	Gates Mills Hawken
1955	Cincinnati Walnut Hills	Sandusky	1988	Gates Mills Hawken	North Canton Hoover
1956	Canton McKinley	Sandusky	1989	Gates Mills Hawken	Akron Firestone
1957	Canton McKinley	Upper Arlington	1990	Cincinnati St. Xavier	Gates Mills Hawken
1958	Canton McKinley	Berea	1991	Cincinnati St. Xavier	Hudson
			1992	Cincinnati St. Xavier	Cleveland St. Ignatius

Tournament Swimming/Diving Records, Boys

Event	Record holder	Time	Year	
200 YARDS MEDLEY RELAY	Cincinnati St. Xavier	1:34.14	1991	
	Mike Andrews, Joe Replogle, Jason Davis, Shawn Trokhan			
200 YARDS FREESTYLE	Joe Hudepohl Cincinnati St. Xavier	1:34.96	1991	N
200 YARDS INDIVIDUAL MEDLEY	Mark Rhodenbaugh, Cincinnati Oak Hills	1:48.974	1982	
50 YARDS FREESTYLE	Byron Davis, Gates Mills Hawken	:20.31	1988	
ONE METER DIVING	Randy Chambers, North Canton Hoover	528.35	1978	
100 YARDS BUTTERFLY	David Wilson, Cincinnati Anderson	:49.013	1979	
100 YARDS FREESTYLE	Joe Hudephol, Cincinnati St. Xavier	:43.54	1991	N
500 YARDS FREESTYLE	David Fairbanks, Cincinnati Sycamore	4:26.567	1985	
200 YARDS FREESTYLE RELAY	Cincinnati St. Xavier	1:24.85	1991	
	Joe Hudephol, Jason Davis, Jon Nieberding, Shawn Trokhan			
100 YARDS BACKSTROKE	Mark Rhodenbaugh, Cincinnati Oak Hills	:49.761	1982	
100 YARDS BREASTSTROKE	Glen Mills, Cincinnati Finneytown	:55.442	1980	
400 YARDS FREESTYLE RELAY	Cincinnati St. Xavier	3:05.140	1984	
	Mark Jechura, T. J. Anderson, El-B Bourgraf, George Rathman			

N—NATIONAL RECORD

Swimming and Diving Championships, Girls

Year	Champion	Runner-up	Year	Champion	Runner-up
1977	Worthington Solon		1985	Gates Mills Hawken	Upper Arlington
1978	Worthington	North Canton GlenOak	1986	Gates Mills Hawken	Upper Arlington
1979	Cincinnati Finneytown	Upper Arlington	1987	Gates Mills Hawken	Worthington
1980	Worthington	Upper Arlington	1988	Gates Mills Hawken	Solon
1981	Worthington	Gates Mills Hawken	1989	Worthington	Gates Mills Hawken
1982	Cincinnati Oak Hills and North Canton GlenOak		1990	Gates Mills Hawken	Cincinnati Oak Hills
1983	Toledo St. Ursula Academy	North Canton GlenOak	1991	Cincinnati Ursuline	Cincinnati Oak Hills
1984	Gates Mills Hawken	Toledo St. Ursula Academy	1992	Cincinnati Sycamore	Cincinnati Ursuline

Swimming and Diving Records, Girls

Event	Record holder	Time	Year
200 YARDS MEDLEY RELAY	Cincinnati Oak Hills	1:46.51	1991
	Michelle McCarthy, Cynthia Janssen, Amy Fritsch, Denise McCarthy		
200 YARDS FREESTYLE	Beth Washut, Ashtabula St. John	1:47.652	1981
200 YARDS INDIVIDUAL MEDLEY	Rachel Gustin, Cincinnati Seven Hills	2:03.20	1991
50 YARDS FREESTYLE	Aimee Berzins, Centerville	:22.943	1984
ONE METER DIVING	Nancy Hauck, Sylvania Northview	476.40	1979
100 YARDS BUTTERFLY	Sarah Weis, Sylvania Northview	:55.20	1988
100 YARDS FREESTYLE	Beth Washut, Ashtabula St. John	:49.977	1982
500 YARDS FREESTYLE	Katherine Creighton, Gates Mills Hawken	4:49.49	1988
200 YARDS FREESTYLE RELAY	Cincinnati Ursuline	1:38.74	1991
	Jenni Dahl, Holly Oppelt, Shannon Kieley, Beth Jackson		
100 YARDS BACKSTROKE	Sheri White, Worthington	:56.00	1989
100 YARDS BREASTSTROKE	Kim Rhodenbaugh, Cincinnati Oak Hills	1:02.498	1982
400 YARDS FREESTYLE RELAY	Gates Mills Hawken	3:30.98	1987
	Melissa Burovac, Melanie Valerio, Sarah Dykstra, Katherine Creighton		

Joe Hudepohl, Ohio's only four-time champion, on the state meet: "I just use it like a practice."

Hudepohl: From St. Xavier to Barcelona

In **Joe Hudepohl's** last swim for **Cincinnati St. Xavier High** in early 1992, he led his team to a state title, helped set a state record with the 400-yard relay team, and broke a national prep record—his own—on his 100-yard leg: 43.43. And just before, he tied his own national record in the 50, with a time of 20.01. At the state meet in 1991, Hudepohl set three national records—the 200, 100, and 50-yard freestyle races. He became the first individual to win four state titles, and in a 1991 invitational meet, he beat Matt Biondi.

Then, in early March of 1992, his 1:48.73 in the 200-meter freestyle at the Olympic Swimming Trials in Indiapolis, a come-from-behind win the last few strokes, gained him a berth on the Olypmic Team. The field included four former Olympians and in his heat, Hudepohl became the youngest man to break 1:49. It was not only the best of the 35 competing swimmers but it was the fourth fastest in American history. There was a sign by one fan, carrying a Biblical verse: "John 3:3," and beside him was another fan with another, more secular, message: "Joey 1:47.

Such distinctions were not new to Hudepohl. He was also the youngest ever to break 50 seconds in the 100 freestyle; he was 17 when he did it. The director of information for U.S. Swimming, Jeff Dimond, said, "To have a high school kid this fast is unheard of. It's difficult to put a read on how good he's going to be. He's the most exciting young talent to come along since Matt Biondi."

Hudepohl, the youngest of five children and the son of a Cincinnati tool and die maker, became a swimmer when his mother enrolled him at age 3 at the local YMCA, as she did all the kids. Joe joined the Marlins swim team when he was 11 and by the time he entered St. Xavier, he was already one of the best swimmers in his age group in the country. Despite the trips and the training—the regimen can take between five and six hours a day and may hit 16,000 meters a day, which is 640 lengths of your average YMCA pool—Hudepohl maintains a 96 average in his high school studies and is headed to Stanford.

Said his coach, Jack Simon, "He's the best for his age that there's ever been. "What he's got, he's got naturally. He has an incredible feel for the water..." ◗

Source: Cincinnati Post, Cincinnati Enquirer

Hudepohl vs. the Field

Joe Hudepohl's best time against the best times of selected 200-meter freestyle swimmers

Name	Time	Date	Where	Record
Joe Hudepohl	1.48.70	3/1/1992	Indianapolis prelims	
Giorgio Lamberti	1:46.69	8/15/1989	Bonn, Germany	World
Johnny Weismuller	2:08.00	4/5/1927	Ann Arbor	
Matt Biondi	1:47.72	8/88/1988	Austin, Texas	U.S.
Mark Spitz	1:52.78	8/29/1972	Munich	
Don Schollander	1:54.30	8/30/1968	Long Beach	
Duncan Armstrong	1:47.25	9/19/1988	Seoul	

Tournament Champions, Boys

Year	Class	Singles Champions	Doubles Champions
1920		Conant Ohl, Toledo Scott	Ohl-Waldridge, Toledo Scott
1921		Conant Ohl, Toledo Scott	Ohl-Staley, Toledo Scott
1922		Ed Blockel, Ironton	Dunn-Prall, Youngstown Rayen
1923		Walter Smith, Youngstown Rayen	Westfall-Johnson, Columbus East
1924		Walter Smith, Youngstown Rayen	Bulen-Bradley, Columbus East
1925		Dick Franz, Cincinnati Hughes	Flax-Franz, Cincinnati Hughes
1926		Ellis Flax, Cincinnati Hughes	Flax-Moskowitz, Cincinnati Hughes
1927		Carl Dennison, Youngstown Rayen	Dennison-James, Youngstown Rayen
1928		Carl Dennison, Youngstown Rayen	Brownlee-Moore, Struthers
1929		Nate Ganger, Cleveland East	Ganger-Funk, Cleveland East
1930		Earl Bossong, Cincinnati Western Hills	Bossong-Hines, Cincinnati Western Hills
1931		Bill Chambers, Cincinnati Withrow	Chambers-Meyers, Cincinnati Withrow
1932		Bob Niehousen, Cuyahoga Falls	Schoen-Wishert, Lakewood
1933		Paul Imes, Dayton Steele	Graebner-Slatmeyer, Lakewood
1934		Milt Silberman, East Cleveland Shaw	Graebner-Barthelmy, Lakewood
1935		Paul Graebner, Lakewood	Talbert-Rihm, Cincinnati Hughes
1936		Billy Talbert, Cincinnati Hughes	Amorini-Massman, Cincinnati Purcell
1937		Aldo Amorini, Cincinnati Purcell	Kohl-Brown, Dayton Fairview
1938		Bob Faught, Upper Arlington	Russell-Gorden, Lakewood
1939		Marshall Chambers, Cincinnati Walnut Hills	Russell-Gorden, Lakewood
1940		Marshall Chambers, Cincinnati Walnut Hills	Pickering-Cantwell, Youngstown Rayen
1941		Joe Pickering, Youngstown Rayen	Appel-Thomas, Cincinnati Hughes
1942		Norman Appel, Cincinnati Hughes	Kadar-Bowen, Martins Ferry
1943		Dave Brown, Toledo DeVilbiss	Anderson-Naugle, Wyoming
1944		Jack Pickering, Youngstown Rayen	Brown-Brown, Toledo DeVilbiss
1945		Bob Malaga, Cleveland Latin	Reeb-Schiff, Bexley
1946		Tony Trabert, Cincinnati Walnut Hills	Igel-Collins, Cincinnati St. Xavier
1947		Tony Trabert, Cincinnati Walnut Hills	Igel-Collins, Cincinnati St. Savier
1948		Tony Trabert, Cincinnati Walnut Hills	Gross-Rayen, Cincinnati Elder
1949		John Rauh, Cincinnati Walnut Hills	Rich-Brown, Cincinnati Walnut Hills
1950		John Rauh, Cincinnati Walnut Hills	Rich-Bowling, Cincinnati Walnut Hills
1951		Dick Klitch, Portsmouth	Haring-Reale, Mansfield
1952		Barry McKay, Dayton Oakwood	Hackney-Davidson, Middletown
1953		Barry McKay, Dayton Oakwood	Baron-Garcia, Fremont Ross
1954		Pat Arnold, Middletown	Maffett-Rupp, Middletown
1955		Gunter, Polte, Springfield	Finkleman-Wiley, Middletown
1956		Bill Sprinkle, Cincinnati Walnut Hills	Tenney-Hill, Toledo Ottawa Hills
1957		Jerry Levin, Cincinnati Country Day	Kline-Smith, Mansfield
1958		Jim Tenney, Ottawa Hills	Kline-Smith, Mansfield
1959		Clark Graebner, Lakewood	Guest-Stark, Elyria
1960		Clark Graebner, Lakewood	Beatty-Harrington, Middletown
1961		Clark Graebner, Lakewood	Grunebaum-Griffiths Springfield Shawnee
1962		Tom Mansfield, Upper Arlington	Goode-Burbach, Mansfield
1963		Tom Mansfield, Upper Arlington	Mitchell-Jeffries, Worthington
1964		Bozzy Pierce, Dayton Oakwood	Mitchell-Jeffries, Worthington
1965		Chick Hawley, Cincinnati Princeton	Carpenter-Adams, Upper Arlington
1966		Chuck Parsons, Springfield North	Bright-Leonard, Lima Senior
1967		Robin Fry, Springfield North	Bowen-Stone, Upper Arlington
1968		Robert Binns, Cleveland John Hay	Senich-Senich, Parma
1969		John Peckskamp, Cincinnati Purcell	Burkhart-Buckley, Toledo Ottawa Hills
1970		John Peckskamp, Cincinnati Purcell	Bowen-Lathrop, Upper Arlington
1971	A-AA	Henry Bunis, Cincinnati Country Day	Lanier-Geier, Cincinnati Country Day
	AAA	Rick Slager, Upper Arlington	Patton-Wallace, Upper Arlington
1972	A-AA	Jon Gurian, Bexley	Lanier-Matthews, Cincinnati Country Day
	AAA	Rick Slager, Upper Arlington	Wallace-Hales, Upper Arlington
1973	A-AA	Jon Gurian, Bexley	Carruthers-Zell, Bexley
	AAA	Bob Gardner, Upper Arlington	Brondes-Shaw, Sylvania
1974	A-AA	Mike Carruthers, Bexley	Riedmeyer-Ketcham, Toledo Ottawa Hills
	AAA	Jim Flower, Fremont Ross	Beall-Hadley, Upper Arlington
1975	A-AA	Mike Carruthers, Bexley	Riedmeyer-Ketcham, Toledo Ottawa Hills
	AAA	Erick Iskersky, Toledo St. John's	Learmouth-McLaughlin, Whetstone
1976	A-AA	Chris Cunin, Kirtland	Conlan-Conlan, Warren J. F. Kennedy
	AAA	Erick Iskersky, Toledo St. John's	Kohls-Kohls, Kettering Alter

		Singles Champions	**Doubles Champions**
1977	A-AA	Chris Cunin, Kirtland	Kendle-Kendle, Bellbrook
	AAA	Theodore Kauffman, Toledo Bowsher	Kohls-Kohls, Kettering Alter
1978	A-AA	Barry Conlan, Warren J. F. Kennedy	Schiff-Brady, Bexley
	AAA	Mark Mees, Zanesville	Hendrix-Braun, Upper Arlington
1979	A-AA	Barry Conlan, Warren J. F. Kennedy	Tanguay-Fraley, Elida
	AAA	Mark Mees, Zanesville	Babcox-Littman, Firestone
1980	A-AA	Adam Bottorff, Toledo Ottawa Hills	Sopko-Sopko, Columbus Centennial
	AAA	Adam Abele, Marietta	Redding-Kohls, Kettering Alter
1981	A-AA	Eugene Hagan, Dayton Miami Valley	Raschke-Linden, Sandusky Perkins
	AAA	Mike Massie, Cleveland West Tech	Turner-Ghidotti, Columbus Upper Arlington
1982	A-AA	John Kass, Gahanna Columbus Academy	Mudre-Pangalangan, Columbus St. Francis DeSales
	AAA	Mike Massie, Cleveland West Tech	LaLonde-Auch, Columbus Upper Arlington
1983	A-AA	Jeffrey Scolnick, Cleveland Orange	Pucin-Dockter, Columbus Bishop Watterson
	AAA	Charles Merzbacher, Findlay	Lawton-Lawton, Springfield Greenon
1984	A-AA	Brian Kalbas, Canton Central Catholic	Weisman-Siegel, Columbus Bexley
	AAA	Cliff Riester, Cincinnati Sycamore	Dockter-Pucin, Columbus Watterson
1985	A-AA	Mark Rothchild, Cleveland Orange	Hertzer-Marks, Cleveland Orange
	AAA	Ty Tucker, Zanesville	Ellsworth-Hohiesel, Westerville North
1986	A-AA	David Kass, Bexley	Kibble-Tsibouris, Worthington Christian
	AAA	Greg Seilkop, Centerville	Baldemor-Kronause, Kettering Alter
1987	A-AA	Mark Rothchild, Cleveland Orange	Stern-Sud, Cincinnati Country Day
	AAA	Greg Seilkop, Centerville	England-Moenter, Lima Shawnee
1988	A-AA	Richy Lee, Columbus Academy	Archer-Kibble, Worthington Christian
	AAA	Scott Cuppett, Dayton Stebbins	Sebastian-Whetzel, Upper Arlington
1989	A-AA	Efren Mojica, Youngstown Mooney	Seckel-Stern, Bexley
	AAA	Scott Cuppert, Dayton Stebbins	Leach-Sebastian, Upper Arlington
1990	Div. I	John Amos, Centerville	English-Homorody, Columbus Watterson
	Div. II	Richy Lee, Columbus Academy	Seckel-Stern, Bexley
1991	Div. I	Eric Morton, Beavercreek	Marshall/Goldberg, Cincinnati Sycamore
	Div. II	Jim Thomas, Canton Central Catholic	English/Homorody, Columbus Watterson

Tennis

Tournament Champions, Girls

		Singles Champions	**Doubles Champions**
1976	A-AA	Patti Schiff, Columbus Bexley	Lee Earl-Amy Weiffenbach, Columbus Bexley
	AAA	Julie Quamme, Kettering Fairmont West	Eileen Crotty-Cynthia Scheper, Kettering Alter
1977	A-AA	Patti Schiff, Columbus Bexley	Amy Weiffenbach-Lee Earl, Columbus Bexley
	AAA	Vicki Nelson, Wooster	Tammy Eisel-Amy Schmitz, Ashland
1978	A-AA	Patti Schiff, Columbus Bexley	Amy Weiffenbach-Lee Earl, Columbus Bexley
	AAA	Vicki Nelson, Wooster	Kristi Spangenberg-Cindy Scheper, Centerville
1979	A-AA	Jenny Klitch, Columbus Granview Hgts.	Patty Hammon-Kelly Schumann, Shaker Hgts. Laurel
	AAA	Vicki Nelson, Wooster	Kristi Spangenberg-Cindy Scheper, Centerville
1980	A-AA	Janie Cohodes, Columbus Bexley	Laurie Imes-Kelley Coleman, Toledo Ottawa Hills
	AAA	Beth Herr, Centerville	Jamie Plummer-Renu Dewan, Clayton Northmont
1981	A-AA	Kelly Boyse, Zanesville Rosecrans	Kelly Coleman-Torrey Lott, Toledo Ottawa Hills
	AAA	Beth Herr, Centerville	Angela Farley-Lynne Nabors, Cincinnati Indian Hill
1982	A-AA	Jane Cohodes, Columbus Bexley	Amy Schiff-Marie Ridgeway, Columbus Bexley
	AAA	Joni Urban, Middletown	DeDe Dunkle-Julie Herr, Centerville
1983	A-AA	Kelly Boyse, Zanesville Rosecrans	Marie Ridgeway-Vicki Siegel, Columbus Bexley
	AAA	Liz Alexander, Columbus Upper Arlington	Peri Golden-Jennifer Jones, Columbus Walnut Ridge
1984	A-AA	Tracy Barton, Cincinnati Indian Hill	Aubrey Abbott-Debbie Horton, Cincinnati Indian Hill
	AAA	Jennie Young, Worthington	Julie Herr-DeDe Dunkle, Centerville
1985	A-AA	Andrea Farley, Cincinnati Indian Hill	Aubrey Abbott-Debbie Horton, Cincinnati Indian Hill
	AAA	Ann Grossman, Grove City	Kelly Story-Jennifer Jones, Columbus Walnut Ridge
1986	A-AA	Andrea Farley, Cincinnati Indian Hill	Debbie Horton-Molly Poffenberger, Cincinnati Indian Hill
	AAA	Erica Adams, Toledo Notre Dame Academy	Peri Golden-Kelly Story, Columbus Walnut Ridge
1987	A-AA	Andrea Farley, Cincinnati Indian Hill	Kelly McDonough-Crystal Terry, Cincinnati Madeira
	AAA	Kristin Osmond, Worthington	Denise Mezera-Sheryl Myers, Columbus Watterson
1988	A-AA	Andrea Farley, Cincinnati Indian Hill	Shelby Chesses-Allison Schlonsky, Columbus Hartley
	AAA	Wendy Lyons, Westerville South	Denise Mazera-Sheryl Myers, Columbus Watterson
1990	Div. I	Wendy Lyons, Westerville South	Amy Spiegel-Alison Levy, Cincinnati Sycamore
	Div. II	Sarah Brown, Rocky River	Mandy Krantz-Christie Lacia, Cleveland Orange
1991	Div. I	Melissa Zimpfer, Centerville	Sora Moon-Katherine Rhee, Centerville
	Div. II	Sarah Brown, Rocky River Magnificat	Lisa Barna-Nikki Collier, Cleveland Orange

Volleyball
Champions

Year		Champion	Coach	Runner-up	Coach
1975	A	Frankfort Adena	Marvin Seyfang	Newark Catholic	Kayla Hughes
	AA	Cincinnati Ursuline Academy	Linda Nienhaus	Akron St. Vincent-St. Mary	Mary Jo Kaufmann
	AAA	Stow	Bob MacFarland	Cincinnati Seton	Mary C. Biermann
1976	A	Frankfort Adena	Marvin Seyfang	Milford Center Fairbanks	Patty Pease
	AA	Urbana	Pam Brennig	Columbus Bexley	Sandy Haines
	AAA	Kettering Fairmont West	Frances Eden	Cleveland John Marshall	Linda J. Beebe
1977	A	Milford Center Fairbanks	Patty Pease	Minster	Katie Horstman
	AA	Columbus Bexley	Sandy Haines	Clyde	Nancy Hanger
	AAA	Cincinnati Mother of Mercy	Rose Bauer	Columbus Whitehall-Yearling	Scott Luster
1978	A	Archbold	Char Sharp	Milford Center Fairbanks	Patty Pease
	AA	Cincinnati Madeira	Nadine Wilson	Columbus Bexley	Sandy Haines
	AAA	Kettering Fairmont West	Frances Eden	Columbus Whitehall-Yearling	Scott Luster
1979	A	Newark Catholic	Bill Cooperrider	Archbold	Char Sharp
	AA	Perrysburg	Kathy Freese	Delaware Olentangy	Beth Moore
	AAA	Columbus Whitehall-Yearling	Scott Luster	Cincinnati Mother of Mercy	Rose Koch
1980	A	Newark Catholic	Bill Cooperrider	Archbold	Char Sharp
	AA	Akron Hoban	Mary Howard	Circleville	Joyce O'Brien
	AAA	Cincinnati Mother of Mercy	Rose Koch	Broadview Hgts. Brecksville	Jane Verchio
1981	A	Archbold	Char Sharp	Loudonville	Carolyn Vickers
	AA	Medina Highland	Jill Bouton	Cincinnati Madeira	Nadine Wilson
	AAA	Stow	Bob MacFarland	Perrysburg	Kathy Freese
1982	A	Newark Catholic	Bill Cooperrider	Archbold	Char Sharp
	AA	Columbus DeSales	Kathleen Wiemels	Cincinnati Our Lady of Angels	Caryl Schawe
	AAA	Cincinnati Mother of Mercy	Rose Koch	Canton McKinley Senior	Sue Davis
1983	A	Newark Catholic	Bill Cooperrider	Archbold	Char Sharp
	AA	Springfield Northwestern	Nancy Dutton	Rocky River	Gweynn Hampel
	AAA	Canton McKinley Senior	Sue Davis	Cincinnati Seton	Mary Jett
1984	A	Newark Catholic	Beth Hill	Dola Hardin Northern	Beth Elwood
	AA	Springfield Northwestern	Nancy Dutton	Warsaw River View	Cathy Seipel
	AAA	Cincinnati Seton	Mary Jett	Canton McKinley Senior	Sue Davis
1985	A	St. Henry	DeDe Stoner	Ashland Crestview	Sue Subich
	AA	Fairview Park Fairview	Jill Pompei	Pemberville Eastwood	Kathy Loomis
	AAA	Cincinnati Seton	Mary Jett	Canton McKinley Senior	Sue Davis
1986	A	Canal Winchester	Colleen Ross	Sidney Fairlawn	Wade Wilhelm
	AA	Springfield Northwestern	Nancy Dutton	Granville	Tim Zerull
	AAA	Cincinnati Seton	Mary Ritter	Broadview Hgts. Brecksville	Jane Johnston
1987	A	St. Henry	DeDe Stoner	Peninsula Woodridge	Tina Pollard
	AA	Springfield Northewestern	Nancy Dutton	Akron Hoban	Mary E. Howard
	AAA	Canton McKinley	Sue Davis	Reynoldsburg	Brian Strohm
1988	A	Newark Catholic	Beth Hill	St. Henry	DeDe Stoner
	AA	Fairview Park Fairview	Jill Pompei	Akron Hoban	Mary E. Howard
	AAA	Cincinnati Seton	Mary Ritter	Reynoldsburg	Brian Strohm
1989	A	Newark Catholic	Beth Hill	Ashtabula St. John	David Fowler
	AA	Old Washington Buckeye Trail	Rod Johnson	North Jackson Jackson-Milton	Patrick Keney
	AAA	Reynoldsburg	Brian Strohm	Seton	Mary Ritter
1990	Div. I	Stow	Bob McFarland	Cincinnati Mt. Notre Dame	Sally Knoll
	Div. II	Akron Hoban	Mary Howard	Marion River Valley	Sue Mullins
	Div. III	St. Henry	DeDe Stoner	Old Washington Buckeye Trail	Rod Johnson
	Div. IV	Ft. Recovery	Paula Schritz	Columbus Wehrle	Kris Kern
1991	Div. I	Canton McKinley	Sue Davis	Cincinnati Mother of Mercy	Nancy Hart
	Div. II	Akron Hoban	Mary Howard	SunburyBig Walnut	Ron Lehman
	Div. III	Loudonville	Carolyn Vickers	Fairview Park Fairview	Dana Artman
	Div. IV	West UnityHilltop	Janice Bruner	Centerburg	Kathy Stevens

Softball
Champions

Class		Champion	Coach	Runner-up	Coach
1978	A	Casstown Miami East	Pat Palcic	Jeromesville Hillsdale	Pat Edwards
	AA	Warren Champion	Pat McCutcheon	Springfield Northwestern	Nancy Dutton
	AAA	Akron Springfield	Ray Fowler	Middleburg Hgts. Midpark	Emilie Wiemels
1979	A	Jeromesville Hillsdale	Pat Edwards	Portsmouth Clay	Carol Vice
	AA	Akron Manchester	Cheryl Conway	Germantown Valley View	Dona Layman
	AAA	Akron St. Vincent-St. Mary	Merrylou Windhorst	Dayton Chaminade-Julienne	Tom Tolle
1980	A	Portsmouth Clay	Carol Vice	New Madison Tri-Village	Rick Sheley
	AA	Warren Champion	Pat McCutcheon	Jamestown Greeneview	Fay Sesslar
	AAA	Cuyahoga Falls	Laurel Montgomery	Amelia	Michael Rapp
1981	A	Portsmouth Clay	Carol Vice	Beverly Fort Frye	Becky Strahler
	AA	Kinsman Badger	Barbara Barzak	Warsaw River View	Neatie Burris
	AAA	Tallmadge	Dave Harris	Cincinnati Princeton	Dan Woodruff
1982	A	Archbold	Barbara Short	Lockland	Linda Krause
	AA	Kinsman Badger	Barbara Barzak	Columbus St. Francis DeSales	Kim Benadum
	AAA	Kettering Fairmont East	Jim Zink	Westerville North	Les Randolph
1983	A	Portsmouth Clay	Carol Vice	Mineral Ridge	Brenda Colla
	AA	Akron Hoban	Mary Ann King	Warsaw River View	Neatie Burris
	AAA	Grove City	Ron Hutcheson	Tallmadge	Dave Harris
1984	A	Archbold	Barbara Short	Arcanum	Larry Patrick
	AA	Akron Hoban	Mary Ann King	Richwood North Union	Nancy Rubeck
	AAA	Akron St. Vincent-St. Mary	Merrylou Windhorst	Grove City	Ron Hutcheson
1985	A	Mineral Ridge	Brenda Miele	Archbold	Barbara Short
	AA	Zanesville Maysville	Rob Doss	Brookville	Rebecka Rohrer
	AAA	Hamilton	John Spears	Lakewood	Bob Cochrane
1986	A	Archbold	Barbara Short	Jeromesville Hillsdale	Cathy Applegate
	AA	Akron Hoban	Mary Ann King	Newark Licking Valley	Clint Wright
	AAA	Brunswick	Howard Cook	Massillon Jackson	Jeff Hawkins
1987	A	Strasburg Franklin	Bud Weisgarber	Mineral Ridge	Margaret Deibel
	AA	Akron Hoban	Mary Ann King	Portsmouth West	Kenneth Shupert
	AAA	Tallmadge	Roger Howard	North Canton GlenOak	Debbie Fowler
1988	A	Strasburg Franklin	Bud Weisgarber	Portsmouth Clay	Carol Vice
	AA	Tallmadge	Roger Howard	Portsmouth West	Kenneth Shupert
	AAA	Akron Springfield	Ray Fowler	Sidney	Bryan Deal
1989	A	Strasburg-Franklin	Bud Weisgarber	Versailles	Ron Mescher
	AA	Tallmadge	Roger Howard	Springfield Northwestern	Nancy Dutton
	AAA	Akron Springfield	Ray Fowler	Grove City	Ron Hutcheson
1990	I	Akron Springfield	Ray Fowler	Perrysburg	Mark Hamann
	II	Bucyrus	Jack Hewitt	Tallmadge	Roger Howard
	III	Akron Manchester	Scott Cantrell	Milford Center Fairbanks	Dan Stillings
1991	I	Perrysburg	Mark Hamann	Akron Springfield	Ray Fowler
	II	Akron Hoban	Mary Ann King	Springfield Northwestern	Nancy Dutton
	III	Strasburg-Franklin	Bud Weisgarber	Loudonville	Dave Parker

Fast Pitch State Tournament Records

Records are from the State Semifinals and Championship games since 1978.

TEAM RECORD

MOST RUNS IN ONE GAME BY TWO TEAMS
Div. I Grove City vs. West Carrollton 14-11   1989
Div. II Tallmadge vs. Portsmouth West 16-2   1988
Div. III Archbold vs. Lockland 20-5   1982

MOST RUNS IN ONE GAME BY ONE TEAM
Div. I Cuyahoga Falls 14   1980
Tallmadge 14   1983
Akron St. Vincent-St. Mary 14   1984
Grove City 14   1989
Div. II Tallmadge 16   1988
Div. III Portsmouth Clay 21   1981

MOST RUNS IN ONE INNING BY TWO TEAMS
Div. I Grove City 10, West Carrollton 2   1989
Div. II Tallmadge 8, Shelby 0   1989
Div. III Archbold 11, Lockland 2   1982
Archbold 8, Arcanum 5   1984

MOST RUNS IN ONE INNING BY ONE TEAM
Div. I Grove City 10   1989
Div. II Tallmadge 8   1989
Div. III Archbold 11   1982

MOST INNINGS PLAYED IN GAME
Div. I North Canton GlenOak & Hamilton 11   1987
Div. II Columbus DeSales & Thornville Sheridan 10   1982
Tallmadge & Shelby 10   1989
Div. III Versailles & Strasburg-Franklin 9   1989

MOST HITS IN ONE GAME BY TWO TEAMS
Div. I West Carrollton & Grove City 24   1989
Div. II Springfield Northwestern & Portsmouth West 23   1989
Div. III Portsmouth Clay 19, Archbold 9   1980

MOST HITS IN ONE GAME BY ONE TEAM
Div. I Akron Springfield 19   1989
Div. II Akron Manchester 16   1979
Div. III Portsmouth Clay 19   1980
Strasburg Franklin 19   1989

INDIVIDUAL RECORDS

MOST HITS BY INDIVIDUAL, ONE GAME
Div. I Kim Knots, Akron Springfield 3   1978
Michelle Brodeur, Akron St. Vincent-St. Mary 3   1979
Becky Bailey, Tallmadge 3   1981
Stacy Lovelace, Westerville North 3   1982
Kathy Thornton, Tallmadge 3   1983
Melissa Casino, Akron St. Vincent-St. Mary 3   1984
Rhonda King, Westerville North 3   1985
Missey Smith, Tallmadge 3   1987
Marci Raymondi, Massillon Perry 3   1988
Div. II Sharon McFarland, Warren Champion 4   1980
Kim George, Zanesville Maysville 4   1985

Patty Barrett, Massillon Jackson 4   1986
Div. III Kelly Porter, Portsmouth Clay 4   1980
Dawn George, New Madison Tri-Village 4   1980
Diann Wright, Beverly Ft. Frye 4   1981
Dana Patrone, Mineral Ridge 4   1983

MOST TWO BASE HITS
Div. I Kathy Thornton, Tallmadge 2   1983
Carla Brookbank, Akron Springfield 2   1989
Div. II Several with 1
Div. III Chris Rutledge, Pioneer North Central 2   1983

MOST THREE BASE HITS
Div. I Becky Bailey, Tallmadge 2   1981
Div. II Christi Hill, Jamestown Greeneview 2   1980
Kim George, Zanesville Marysville 2   1985
Div. III Several with 1

MOST HOME RUNS
Div. I-II-III Several with 1.

MOST STOLEN BASES
Div. I Melissa Casino, Akron St. Vincent-St. Mary 3   1984
Molly Wagner, Akron St. Vincent-ST. Mary 3   1984
Div. II Shelly Poff, Tallmadge 3   1989
Div. III Susan Grau, Lockland 4   1982

MOST RBIS
Div. I Pam Mayes, Akron Springfield 6   1989
Div. II Gina Casalinova, Akron Hoban 4   1983
Lynn DeLuca, Tallmadge 4   1988
Div. III Lori Ward, Strasburg-Franklin 5   1987
Michelle Phillabaum, Strasburg-Franklin 5   1989

MOST STRIKE OUTS
Div. I Molly Wagner, Akron St. Vincent-St. Mary 12   1984
Div. II Danette Vance, Akron Manchester 14   1979
Div. III Lisa Frederick, Akron Manchester 17   1990

NO HIT, NO RUN GAME BY PITCHER
Tami Schlicher, Springfield Northwestern (vs. Columbus Hartley 5-0)   1978
Susie Hardy, Jeromesville Hillsdale (vs. Old Washington Buckeye Trail 18-0)   1979
Sara Starling, Kinsman Badger (vs. St. Marys Memorial 5-0)   1981
Sara Starling, Kinsman Badger (vs. Columbus Briggs 7-0)   1982
Julie Croft, Mineral Ridge (vs. Hamilton New Miami 8-0)   1983
Molly Wagner, Akron St. Vincent-St. Mary (vs. Kettering Fairmont 14-0)   1984
Tammy Spidell, Strasburg-Franklin (vs. Mineral Ridge 9-0)   1987
Lisa Frederick, Akron Manchester (vs. Milford Center Fairbanks 7-0)   1990

Field Hockey

Champions

	Champion	Coach	Runner-up	Coach
1979	Kettering Fairmont West	Martha Sinkhorn	Shaker Heights	Linda Betley
1980	Kettering Fairmont West	Martha Sinkhorn	Kettering Fairmont East	Barbara Rausch
1981	Kent Roosevelt	Emma Owen	Hudson	Patricia Hackenburg
1982	Kettering Fairmont West	Wendy Devine	Hudson	Patricia Hackenburg
1983	Kettering Fairmont	Wendy Devine	Hudson	Patricia Hackenburg
1984	Hudson	Patricia Hackenburg	Columbus Bexley	Laura Hebert
1985	Kettering Fairmont	Wendy Devine	Hudson	Patricia Laflin
1986	Hudson	Connie Walton	Kettering Fairmont	Wendy Devine
1987	Columbus School for Girls	Sharon Salzer	Shaker Heights	Linda Betley
1988	Worthington High School	Kim Willis	Kent Roosevelt	Barb Meloy
1989	Kettering Fairmont	Christine Eby	Hudson	Kim Willis
1990	Kettering Fairmont	Christine Eby	Columbus Upper Arlington	Margie Soteriades
1991	Shaker Heights	Linda Betley	Hudson	Connie Walton

Ice Hockey

Champions

	Champions		Runner-up			Champion		Runner-up	
1978	Findlay	8	Bowling Green	7	1986	Lakewood St. Edward	6	Cleveland Heights	5
1979	Centerville	6	Shaker Heights	3	1987	Cleveland Heights	4	Lakewood	3
1980	Bowling Green	5	Toledo Central Catholic	2				St. Edward (2 OT)	
1981	Shaker Heights	10	Kent Roosevelt	4	1988	Parma Padua Franciscan	4	Toledo St. Francis	2
1982	Kent Roosevelt	4	Sylvania Northview	3				DeSales	
1983	Findlay	6	Bowling Green	4	1989	Parma Padua Franciscan	5	Garfield Heights Trinity	1
1984	Bowling Green	10	Toledo Whitmer	3	1990	Lakewood St. Edward	9	Sylvania Northview	1
1985	Lakewood St. Edward	1	North Olmsted	0	1991	Bowling Green	2	Parma Padua	1
								Franciscan	
					1992	Lakewood St. Edward	1	Bowling Green	0(3OT)

Ohio State University Football, The Record

Year	Record	Pct.	Coach	Year	Record	Pct.	Coach
1890	1-3-0	.250	A. S. Lilley, J. Ryder	1933	7-1-0	.875	Sam S. Willaman
1891	2-2-0	.500	Alexander S. Lilley	1934	7-1-0	.875	Francis A. Schmidt
1892	5-2-0	.714	Jack Ryder	1935	7-1-0	.875	Francis A. Schmidt
1893	4-5-0	.444	Jack Ryder	1936	5-3-0	.625	Francis A. Schmidt
1894	6-5-0	.545	Jack Ryder	1937	6-2-0	.750	Francis A. Schmidt
1895	4-4-2	.500	Jack Ryder	1938	4-3-1	.563	Francis A. Schmidt
1896	5-5-1	.500	Charles A. Hickey	1939	6-2-0	.750	Francis A. Schmidt
1897	1-7-1	.167	David F. Edwards	1940	4-4-0	.500	Francis A. Schmidt
1898	3-5-0	.375	Jack Ryder	1941	6-1-1	.813	Paul E. Brown
1899	9-0-1	.950	John B. C. Eckstorm	1942	9-1-0	.900	Paul E. Brown
1900	8-1-1	.850	John B. C. Eckstorm	1943	3-6-0	.333	Paul E. Brown
1901	5-3-1	.611	John B. C. Eckstorm	1944	9-0-0	1.000	Carroll C. Widdoes
1902	6-2-2	.700	Perry Hale	1945	7-2-0	.778	Carroll C. Widdoes
1903	8-3-0	.727	Perry Hale	1946	4-3-2	.555	Paul O. Bixler
1904	6-5-0	.545	E. R. Sweetland	1947	2-6-1	.278	Wesley E. Fesler
1905	8-2-2	.818	E. R. Sweetland	1948	6-3-0	.667	Wesley E. Fesler
1906	8-1-0	.889	A. E. Herrnstein	1949	7-1-2	.800	Wesley E. Fesler
1907	7-2-1	.750	A. E. Herrnstein	1950	6-3-0	.667	Wesley E. Fesler
1908	6-4-0	.600	A. E. Herrnstein	1951	4-3-2	.555	W. W. Hayes
1909	7-3-0	.700	A. E. Herrnstein	1952	6-3-0	.667	W. W. Hayes
1910	6-1-3	.750	Howard Jones	1953	6-3-0	.667	W. W. Hayes
1911	5-3-2	.600	Harry Vaughn	1954	10-0-0	1.000	W. W. Hayes
1912	6-3-0	.667	John R. Richards	1955	7-2-0	.778	W. W. Hayes
1913	4-2-1	.643	John W. Wilce	1956	6-3-0	.667	W. W. Hayes
1914	5-2-0	.714	John W. Wilce	1957	9-1-0	.900	W. W. Hayes
1915	5-1-1	.786	John W. Wilce	1958	6-1-2	.778	W. W. Hayes
1916	7-0-0	1.000	John W. Wilce	1959	3-5-1	.389	W. W. Hayes
1917	8-0-1	.944	John W. Wilce	1960	7-2-0	.778	W. W. Hayes
1918	3-3-0	.500	John W. Wilce	1961	8-0-1	.944	W. W. Hayes
1919	6-1-0	.857	John W. Wilce	1962	6-3-0	.667	W. W. Hayes
1920	7-1-0	.875	John W. Wilce	1963	5-3-1	.611	W. W. Hayes
1921	5-2-0	.714	John W. Wilce	1964	7-2-0	.778	W. W. Hayes
1922	3-4-0	.429	John W. Wilce	1965	7-2-0	.778	W. W. Hayes
1923	3-4-1	.438	John W. Wilce	1966	4-5-0	.444	W. W. Hayes
1924	2-3-3	.438	John W. Wilce	1967	6-3-0	.667	W. W. Hayes
1925	4-3-1	.563	John W. Wilce	1968	10-0-0	1.000	W. W. Hayes
1926	7-1-0	.875	John W. Wilce	1969	8-1-0	.889	W. W. Hayes
1927	4-4-0	.500	John W. Wilce	1970	9-1-0	.900	W. W. Hayes
1928	5-2-1	.688	John W. Wilce	1971	6-4-0	.600	W. W. Hayes
1929	4-3-1	.563	Sam S. Willaman	1972	9-2-0	.818	W. W. Hayes
1930	5-2-1	.688	Sam S. Willaman	1973	10-0-1	.954	W. W. Hayes
1931	6-3-0	.667	Sam S. Willaman	1974	10-2-0	.833	W. W. Hayes
1932	4-1-3	.688	Sam S. Willaman	1975	11-1-0	.917	W. W. Hayes

Year	Record	Pct.	Coach	Year	Record	Pct.	Coach
1976	9-2-1	.791	W. W. Hayes	1985	9-3-0	.750	Earle Bruce
1977	9-3-0	.750	W. W. Hayes	1986	10-3-0	.769	Earle Bruce
1978	7-4-1	.625	W. W. Hayes	1987	6-4-1	.591	Earle Bruce
1979	11-1-0	.917	Earle Bruce	1988	4-6-1	.409	John Cooper
1980	9-3-0	.750	Earle Bruce	1989	8-4-0	.667	John Cooper
1981	9-3-0	.750	Earle Bruce	1990	7-4-1	.625	John Cooper
1982	9-3-0	.750	Earle Bruce	1991	8-4-0	.667	John Cooper
1983	9-3-0	.750	Earle Bruce				
1984	9-3-0	.750	Earle Bruce	**Totals**	**626-253-50**	**.701**	

Ohio State Bowl Scores

Year	Bowl				Year	Bowl			
1921	Rose Bowl	OSU	0	California 28	1980	Rose Bowl	OSU 16	So. Cal	17
1950	Rose Bowl	OSU	17	California 14	1980	Fiesta Bowl	OSU 19	Penn State	31
1955	Rose Bowl	OSU	20	So. Cal 7	1981	Liberty Bowl	OSU 31	Navy	28
1958	Rose Bowl	OSU	10	Oregon 7	1982	Holiday Bowl	OSU 47	BYU	17
1969	Rose Bowl	OSU	27	So. Cal 16	1984	Fiesta Bowl	OSU 28	Pittsburgh	23
1971	Rose Bowl	OSU	17	Stanford 27	1985	Rose Bowl	OSU 17	So. Cal	20
1973	Rose Bowl	OSU	17	So. Cal 42	1985	Citrus Bowl	OSU 10	BYU	7
1974	Rose Bowl	OSU	42	So. Cal 21	1987	Cotton Bowl	OSU 28	Texas A&M	12
1975	Rose Bowl	OSU	17	So. Cal 18	1989	Hall of Fame Bowl	OSU 14	Auburn	31
1976	Rose Bowl	OSU	10	UCLA 23	1990	Liberty Bowl	OSU 11	Air Force	23
1977	Orange Bowl	OSU	27	Colorado 10	1991	Hall of Fame Bowl	OSU 17	Syracuse	24
1978	Sugar Bowl	OSU	6	Alabama 35					
1978	Gator Bowl	OSU	15	Clemson 17					

Overall—Won 11, Lost 11
Rose Bowl—Won 5, Lost 7

The OSU marching band has not had a woodwind present for over a half a century. That's because in 1934 Professor Eugene J. Weigel declared that only the brass instruments could properly noise up a football stadium, thus the clarinets, saxaphones, flutes, "and other wimp instruments" were banished. The Buckeye band was often referred to as "ten musical drummers and 110 frustrated plumbers."

Source: Ben Kline, Dayton Dayton News

OSU, The Coaches

Coach	Years	Record	Pct.	Coach	Years	Record	Pct.
Alexander S. Lilley	1890-1891	3-2-0	.600	Sam S. Willaman	1929-1933	26-10-5	.695
Jack Ryder	1892-1895			Francis A. Schmidt	1934-1940	39-16-1	.705
	1898	22-24-2	.479	Paul E. Brown	1941-1943	18-8-1	.685
Charles A. Hickey	1896	5-5-1	.500	Carroll C. Widdoes	1944-1945	16-2-0	.889
David F. Edwards	1897						
		1-7-1	.167	Paul O. Bixler	1946	4-3-2	.556
John B. Eckstorm	1899-1901	22-4-3	.810	Wesley E. Fesler	1947-1950	21-13-3	.608
Perry Hale	1902-1903	14-5-2	.714	W. W. "Woody" Hayes	1951-1978	205-61-10	.761
E. R. Sweetland	1904-1905	14-7-2	.652	Earle Bruce	1979-1987	81-26-1	.755
A. E. Herrnstein	1906-1909	28-10-1	.731	John Cooper	1988-1991	27-18-2	.596
Howard Jones	1910	6-1-3	.750				
Harry Vaughn	1911	5-3-2	.600	***All-Time Record***	***102***	***641-261-51***	***.699***
John R. Richards	1912	6-3-0	.667				
John W. Wilce	1913-1928	78-33-9	.688				

OSU, Big Ten Standings

(Since OSU Entered Conference in 1913)

Year	Team	Record		Year	Team	Record		Year	Team	Record
1913	Chicago	7-0-0		1939	Ohio State	5-1-0			Purdue	6-1-0
1914	Illinois	6-0-0		1940	Minnesota	6-0-0		1968	Ohio State	7-0-0
1915	Minnesota	3-0-1		1941	Minnesota	5-0-0		1969	Ohio State	6-1-0
1916	Ohio State	4-0-0		1942	Ohio State	5-1-0			Michigan	6-1-0
1917	Ohio State	4-0-0		1943	Michigan	6-0-0		1970	Ohio State	7-0-0
1918	Illinos	4-0-0			Purdue	6-0-0		1971	Michigan	8-0-0
	Michigan	2-0-0		1944	Ohio State	6-0-0		1972	Ohio State	7-1-0
	Purdue	1-0-0		1945	Indiana	5-0-1			Michigan	7-1-0
1919	Illinois	6-1-0		1946	Illinois	6-1-0		1973	Ohio State	7-0-1
1920	Ohio State	5-0-0		1947	Michigan	6-0-0			Michigan	7-0-1
1921	Iowa	5-0-0		1948	Michigan	6-0-0		1974	Ohio State	7-1-0
1922	Iowa								Michigan	7-1-0
		5-0-0		1949	Ohio State	4-1-1		1975	Ohio State	8-0-0
	Michigan	4-0-0			Michigan	4-1-1		1976	Ohio State	7-1-0
1923	Illinois	5-0-0		1950	Michigan	4-1-1			Michigan	7-1-0
	Michigan	4-0-0		1951	Illinois	5-0-1		1977	Ohio State	7-1-0
1924	Chicago	3-0-3		1952	Purdue	4-1-1			Michigan	7-1-0
1925	Michigan	5-1-0			Wisconsin	4-1-1		1978	Michigan	7-1-0
1926	Michigan	5-0-0		1953	Illinois	5-1-0			Michigan State	7-1-0
	Northwestern	5-0-0			Michigan	5-1-0		1979	Ohio State	8-0-0
1927	Illinois	5-0-0		1954	Ohio State	7-0-0		1980	Michigan	8-0-0
1928	Illinois	4-1-0		1955	Ohio State	6-0-0		1981	Ohio State	6-2-0
1929	Purdue	5-0-0		1956	Iowa	5-1-0			Iowa	6-2-0
1930	Michigan	5-0-0		1957	Ohio State	7-0-0		1982	Michigan	8-1-0
	Northwestern	5-0-0		1958	Iowa	5-1-0		1983	Illinois	9-0-0
1931	Michigan	5-1-0		1959	Wisconsin	5-2-0		1984	Ohio State	7-2-0
	Northwestern	5-1-0		1960	Minnesota	5-1-0		1985	Iowa	7-1-0
	Purdue	5-1-0			Iowa	5-1-0		1986	Ohio State	7-1-0
1932	Michigan	6-0-0		1961	Ohio State	6-0-0			Michigan	7-1-0
1933	Michigan	5-0-1		1962	Wisconsin	6-1-0		1987	Michigan State	7-0-1
1934	Minnesota	5-0-0		1963	Illinois	5-1-1		1988	Michigan	7-0-1
1935	Ohio State	5-0-0		1964	Michigan	6-1-0		1989	Michigan	8-0-0
	Minnesota	5-0-0		1965	Michigan State	7-0-0		1990	Illinois	6-2-0
1936	Northwestern	6-0-0		1966	Michigan State	7-0-0			Iowa	6-2-0
1937	Minnesota	5-0-0		1967	Indiana	6-1-0			Michigan	6-2-0
1938	Minnesota	4-1-0			Minnesota	6-1-0			Michigan State	6-2-0
								1991	Michigan	8-0-0

Francis Schmidt's mindset was to "always think lateral." He had more than 350 plays, and kept dreaming up more. Because of his one-sided scores, writers called him "Close the Gates of Mercy" Schmidt.

The Coach Who Put Ohio State on the National Map

Football, as an institution, is not noted for its turn toward irony but one of the more ironic moments in all of sports must be that the coach who first put Columbus, Ohio, on the football map was a loud, salty, ex-bayonet instructor who loved wide-open razzle-dazzle football. His name was **Francis Schmidt**, and he came to Ohio State in 1934, a time that by today's dictates seems so long ago as to be paleolithic. But Schmidt, with his restless mind for innovation, paved the way for the game that was to come, even if Wayne Woodrow himself would have blanched at Schmidt's play-calling. And while OSU football had been respectable since **Chic Harley** had first given it national notoriety, the Buckeyes had not won a conference title in fifteen years.

Schmidt's offense included a formation that resembled today's I-formation, and his high scoring contests drew for the first time intense national recognition to the Buckeyes. Schmidt himself favored bow ties and looked like a properous businessman. But he was always thinking football, doodling plays in notebooks and on tablecloths. A visitor in Schmidt's office noted that the calender had none of the days torn off and when he examined it he discovered there was a different play diagrammed on back of each of the 365 sheets. Schmidt had so many plays that his 1936 quarterback, **Tippy Dye**, carried cards in his helmet. On one play his helmet was knocked off and the playing field was littered with Schmidt's cards. One story illustrating his single-mindedness had Schmidt at a service station working in his hoisted car while the oil was being changed, then absent-mindedly stepping out into the grease pit. He was volatile, swore like a stevedore, and trusted no one.

In 1934, his first team missed an unbeaten season and the conference title by one point—at Illinois. In 1935, the year the Bucks shared the Big Ten title, they played Notre Dame in a game that many thought would be the game for the national championship. The Bucks took a 13-0 halftime lead and Grantland Rice said in the press box that it was the greatest display of football he had ever seen. But the Irish came back and, with time running out, scored on a sensational pass to win 18-13. Said star halfback **Dick Heekin** later, "I met some guy in my neighborhood who told me his wife had a miscarriage after that game, as if it was my fault..." Sportswriters would later call the game the greatest game ever played.

Sportswriters called the Bucks "the Scarlet Scourge" because of the one-sided—85-7, 76-0, 60-0—scores. After seven seasons, he had won 39, lost 16 and tied one. He had also shut out Michigan three times in a row.

As late as the 1939 season, OSU led the nation in total offense, had five shutouts in eight games, and won the Big Ten title. But Schmidt's habits as a loner and his lack of organization led to his departure. His uninhibited offense had perplexed his opponents for years and his teams had been so entertaining that the fans filled the stadium in unprecedented numbers—Schmidt's teams, for the first time, brought 50,000 people to the stadium, an increase of 36 per cent during the Depression. Today, he would have consistently been in the eye of the media. Ahead of his time, colorful, yet prey to his own difficulties, Schmidt brought abiding national attention to the Buckeye campus. After him, the program would never be the same. ◗

Points
Game—30 by Pete Johnson vs. North Carolina, 1975
30 by Keith Byars vs. Illinois, 1984
Season—156 by Pete Johnson, 1975
Career—348 by Pete Johnson, 1973-76

Touchdowns
Game—5 by Pete Johnson vs. North Carolina, 1975
5 by Keith Byars vs. Illinois, 1984
Season—26 by Pete Johnson, 1975
Career—58 by Pete Johnson, 1973-76

Field Goals
Game—5 by Bob Atha vs. Indiana, 1981
Season—18 by Vlade Janakievski, 1979
18 by Pat O'Morrow, 1988
Career—41 by Vlade Janakievski, 1977-80

Points After Touchdown Attempts (Kicks)
Game—10 by Vic Janowicz vs. Iowa, 1950
Season—55 by Blair Conway, 1973
Career—184 by Rich Spangler, 1982-85

Points After Touchdown Made
Game—10 by Vic Janowicz vs. Iowa, 1950
Season—53 by Rich Spangler, 1983
Career—177 by Rich Spangler, 1982-85

Yards Rushing
Game—274 by Keith Byars vs. Illinos, 1984
Season—1,764 by Keith Byars, 1984
Career—5,589 by Archie Griffin, 1972-75

Rushing Attempts
Game—44 by Harold Henson at Northwestern, 1972
Season—336 by Keith Byars, 1984
Career—924 by Archie Griffin, 1972-75

Pass Attempts
Game—52 by Art Schlichter vs. Florida State, 1981
Season—350 by Art Schlichter, 1981
Career—951 by Art Schlichter, 1978-81

Punt Return Yards
Game—170 by Neal Colzie vs. Michigan State, 1973
Season—679 by Neal Colzie, 1973
Career—895 by Garcia Lane, 1980-83

Kickoff Returns
Game—5 by Karl Sturtz vs. Southern Methodist, 1950

Pass Completions
Game—31 by Art Schlichter vs. Florida State, 1981
Season—183 by Art Schlichter, 1981
Career—497 by Art Schlichter, 1978-81

Yards Passing
Game—458 by Art Schlichter vs. Florida State, 1981
Season—2,551 by Art Schlichter, 1981
Career—7,547 by Art Schlichter, 1978-81

Touchdown Passes
Game—5 by John Borton vs. Washington State, 1952
Season—19 by Jim Karsatos, 1985
Career—50 by Art Schlichter, 1978-81

Pass Receptions
Game—13 by Gary Williams vs. Florida State, 1981
Season—69 by Cris Carter, 1986
Career—168 by Cris Carter, 1984-86

Yards Receiving
Game—220 by Gary Williams vs. Florida State, 1981
Season—1,127 by Cris Carter, 1986
Career—2,792 by Gary Williams, 1979-82

Touchdowns Receiving
Game—4 by Bob Grimes vs. Washington State, 1952
Season—11 by Cris Carter, 1986
Career—27 by Cris Carter, 1984-86

Total Offense
Game—412 by Art Schlichter vs. Florida State, 1981
Season—2,509 by Art Schlichter, 1981
Career—8,850 by Art Schlichter, 1978-81

Punt Returns
Game—8 by Neal Colzie vs. Michigan State, 1973
Season—40 by Neal Colzie, 1973
40 by Garcia Lane, 1982
Career—89 by Garcia Lane, 1980-83

Total Tackles
Game-29 by Chris Spielman vs. Mich. 10-19 (solo-assist), 1986
29 by Tom Cousineau vs. Penn State, 9-20 (solo-assist), 1978
Season—211 by Tom Cousineau, 101-110 (solo-assist), 1978
Career—572 by Marcus Marek, 256-316 (solo-assist), 1979-82

Hot tickets

OSU football priority list for Ohio Stadium's 86,000 seats:

1.	Students	25,000
2.	Faculty and staff	15,000
3.	19+ year season ticket-holders	15,000
4.	Major OSU donors	15,000
5.	Single game tickets for alumni association members	7,600
6.	Fans of visiting teams	4,000
7.	Ex-OSU football players	2,000
8.	Certain perennial OSU football supporters	1,500
9.	Elected public officials	900
10.	Everybody else	0

Miscellaneous Individual Records
5 by Howard Cassady vs. Illinois, 1953
5 by Tim Spencer vs. Florida State, 1981
5 by Carlos Snow vs. Pittsburgh, 1988
Season—24 by Jamie Holland, 1986
Career—42 by Howard Cassady, 1952-55
Kickoff Return Yards
Game—213 by Carlos Snow vs. Pittsburgh, 1988
Season—513 by Carlos Snow, 1988
Career—1380 by Carlos Snow, 1988-91
Punts
Game—21 by Vic Janowicz vs. Michigan, 1950
Season—65 by Tom Orosz, 1980
Career—162 by Tom Orosz, 1977-80
Punting Yards
Game—685 by Vic Janowicz vs. Michigan, 1950
Season—2,653 by Tom Orosz, 1980
Career—6,838 by Tom Skladany, 1973-76
Punting Average
Game—57.3 by Fred Morrison at Wisconsin, 1949
Season—47.1 by Tom Tupa, 1984
Career—44.7 by Tom Tupa, 1984-87
Pass Interceptions
Game—3 by Arnie Chonko vs. Indiana, 1964
3 by Bruce Ruhl vs. Wisconsin, 1974
3 by Craig Cassady vs. Michigan State, 1975
3 by Fred Bruney vs. Michigan, 1952
Season—9 by Mike Sensibaugh, 1969
9 by Craig Cassady, 1975
Career—22 by Mike Sensibaugh, 1968-70
Solo Tackles
Game—16 by Tom Cousineau vs. Southern
Methodist, 1978
Season—105 by Chris Spielman, 1986
Career—283 by Chris Spielman, 1984-87
Assisted Tackles
Game—20 by Tom Cousineau vs. Penn State, 1978
Season—110 by Tom Cousineau, 1978
Career—316 by Marcus Marek, 1979-82

Most consecutive extra points made—52, Matt Frantz,
Most consecutive passes completed—12,
Bill Mrukowski vs. UCLA (9) and Illinois (3), 1961
12, Jim Karsatos vs. Wisconsin, 1985
Most consecutive games 100 yards or more rushing—31,
(Regular Season) Archie Griffin, 1973, 1974, 1975
21, (Includes Bowl) Archie Griffin, 1973, 1974
Most consecutive games catching a pass—48,
Gary Williams, 1979-82
Most consecutive games 200 or more yards passing—3,
Most consecutive games 100 or more yards passing—17,
Art Schlichter (Final 5 games in 1980 and all
12 games in 1981)

Longest Plays by Ohio State
Longest Rushing Play
89 yards by Gene Fekete vs. Pittsburgh, 11-7-42 (TD)
Longest Passing Play
86 yards by Art Schlichter to Calvin Murray vs.
Washington State, 9-22-79 (TD)
Longest Field Goal
59 yards by Tom Skladany at Illinois, 11-8-75
Longest Punt
87 yards by Karl Edwards at Illinois, 10-15-83
Longest Punt Return
87 yards by Robert Demmel vs. Iowa, 19-28-50 (TD)
Longest Kickoff Return
103 yards by Dean Sensanbaugher at Great Lakes,
10-9-43, (TD)
Longest Pass Interception
100 yards by David Brown at Purdue, 10-18-86 (TD)

OSU, Team Records

Points
Game—128 vs. Oberlin, 1916
Season—437 in 1974
Touchdowns
Game—19 vs. Oberlin, 1916
Season—59 in 1974
Extra Points
Game-14 vs. Oberlin, 1916
Season—56 in 1974
First Downs
Game—39 vs. Drake, 1935
Season—276 in 1974
Plays from Scrimmage
Game—101 vs. T.C.U., 1969; Illinois, 1969
Season—938 in 1981
Times Carried from Scrimmage
Game—86 vs. Illinois, 1943
Season—734 in 1974
Pass Attempts
Game—52 vs. Florida State (31 comp.), 1981
Season—371 (193 comp.), in 1981
Pass Completions
Game—31 vs. Florida State (52 att.), 1981
Season—193 (371 att.), in 1981
Best Completion Percentage (15 or more passes)
Game—.857 (18 of 21) vs. Washington State,
1952Season—.606 (185 of 306), in 1985

Rushing Yards
Game—517 vs. Illinois, 1962; Illinois, 1974
Season—4,199 in 1974
Passing Yards
Game—458 vs. Florida State, 1981
Season—2,699 in 1981, 12 games
Total Offense
Game—715 vs. Utah, 1986
Season—5,252 in 1974
Most Punts
Game—21 vs. Michigan, 1950
Season—71 in 1951

Miscellaneous Team Records
Most consecutive wins without ties—22 (1967-69)
Most consecutive conference wins—17
(1954-56, 1967-69 and 1974-1976)
Most consecutive losses—5 (1890-91 and 1897)
Most consecutive wins in Ohio Stadium—24 (1972-75)
Most yardage punting, one game—685 vs. Michigan, 1950
Most average yardage punting, one season—47.1, 1984
(45 punts)
Most yards penalized, two teams, one game—
250 vs. Illinois, 1980 (OSU 134, Illinois 116)

Ohio Staters in the College Football Hall of Fame

Players

Chic Harley, HB
All-American 1916-17, '19
Gaylord Stinchcomb, HB
All-American 1920
Wes Fesler, E
All-American 1928-30
Gomer Jones, C
All-American 1935
Gust Zarnas, G
All-American 1937

Bill Willis, T
All-American 1944
Les Horvath, QB
All-American 1945-46
Warren Amling, G-T
All-American 1945-46
Jim Daniell, T
All-Big Ten 1949
Vic Janowicz, HB
All-American 1950

Howard Cassady, HB
All-American 1954-55
Jim Parker, G
All-American 1955-56
Aurealius Thomas, G
All-American 1957
Jim Stillwagon
All-American 1969-70
Archie Griffin, TB
All-American 1973-74-75

Coaches

Howard Jones, 1910
John Wilce, 1913-28
Francis Schmidt, 1934-40
Ernie Godfrey, 1929-61
(Assistant Coach)

W. W. "Woody" Hayes, 1951-78
Sid Gillman, 1941
(Assistant Coach)
Doyt Perry, 1951-54
(Assistant Coach)

Three-Time All-American Selections
Chic Harley, Running Back—1916, 1917, 1919
Wesley Fesler, End—1928, 1929, 1930
Archie Griffin, Tailback—1973, 1974, 1975
Tom Skladany, Punter-Kicker—1974, 1975, 1976

John Hicks, Offensive Tackle—1972, 1973
Warren Amling, Guard/Tackle—1945, 1946
Randy Gradishar, Linebacker—1972, 1973
Howard Cassady, Running Back—1954, 1955
Van DeCree, Defensive End—1973, 1974
Jim Parker, Guard—1955, 1956

Two-Time All-American Selections
Iolas Huffman, Guard/Tackler—1920, 1921
Jack Tatum, Defensive Back—1969, 1970
Edwin Hess, Guard—1925, 1926
Jim Stillwagon, Middle Guard—1969, 1970
Merle Wendt, End—1934, 1935

Chris Ward, Offensive Tackle—1976, 1977
Jim Houston, End—1958, 1959
Tom Cousineau, Linebacker—1977, 1978
Bob Ferguson, Fullback—1960, 1961
Chris Spielman, Linebacker—1986, 1987
Ike Kelley, Linebacker—1964, 1965

Immortal Chic

*Chic Harley
After a stint in
World War I,
Harley returned to
make All
American a third
time.*

The East Side Kid Who Invented OSU Football

Chic Harley was the original OSU All-American, the unlikely-looking local kid who launched the Buckeye football program into prominence. Harley was an East High export, a quiet chap who, at 145 pounds and a scant 5-7, looked more like, one writer noted, a member of the debate team. But not on the field where he was an all-purpose wunderkind. He was fearless, innovative, stylish, and could run, pass, punt, dropkick. He was also won varsity letters in three other sports. He was the Archie Griffin of his day, OSU's first superstar, and he made All-American teams for two straight years. He was, in fact, OSU's first All-American. Then the war came along, and Harley enlisted. In 1918, without Harley, OSU resumed its earlier mediocrity. But in 1919, Harley was back, unimpaired by absence. He made All-American a third time. During his tenure, OSU had lost one game but what the school had really gained was national prominence. In three brief seasons, Chic Harley had plastered OSU's name across the national front pages. He was called "The Immortal Chic," and for years, on his birthday, he received hundreds of cards. In Columbus, people still say he was the man who invented OSU football. ▶

Robert Smith: after a turbulent year, the storybook saga is set to continue. OSU's most dramatic freshman back since Archie Griffin resumes his gridiron career.

Mr. Smith Goes to Columbus

When **Robert Smith** left Cleveland's **Euclid High** and became—as a freshman—Ohio State's starting varsity tailback, he was accustomed to the glare of attention. As a high school junior, he ran for 1,564 yards and 21 touchdowns and won Ohio's first Mr. Football Award. As a senior, he upped the college ante on himself by rushing for 2,322 yards, 35 touchdowns, and his second Mr. Football Award. In a three-year varsity career, he had gained 5,318 yards and scored 71 touchdowns, capping it all off by being named the nation's outstanding high school player.

To support such lofty athletic credentials, Smith never slowed down. On Buckeye Stadium turf in 1990 he promptly ran for another 1,126 yards. He led the team with eight rushing touchdowns, went over 100 yards five times, and led the Big Ten with a 6.4 yards-per-carry average, as well as finishing second in the Big Ten in all-purpose yardage—135.6. In addition, Smith broke OSU's freshman rushing record of 867 yards, set almost twenty years before by Archie Griffin, the most-lauded runner in Ohio college history; this made Smith only the 26th freshman in major college history to gain 1,000 yards in a season.

Smith was an academic star as well; he chose OSU not for football but medicine. He scored 1,200 on his Scholastic Aptitude Test. When he first visited OSU, he wasn't interested in seeing the weight room; he wanted to see the med school and the library. "Football," he said, "is a means to an end; it's my vehicle to a college education." Smith was well on his way to giving the great assembly of Robert Smiths everywhere a permanent icon. But before the 1991 season, there was trouble in Buckeye paradise: Smith quit the team.

Amid a blizzard of headlines from the national media down to Ohio's crossroads dailies, it seemed the storied career of Robert Smith would have, at the least, a change of venue. The cause of Smith's resignation centered, ultimately, on a personality clash with Elliot Uzelac, the Bucks' new assistant head coach and offensive coordinator, described politely as "a Type-A personality with a reputation for toughness." One of Smith's contentions was that Uzelac pressured him to miss classes so he could attend practice or meetings. The Uzelac side said that Smith was too serious about academics, and had no sense of humor.

Uzelac responded by undergoing an emergency angioplasty; Smith by staying on to run track and ponder a transfer to the west coast. But in early 1992, Uzelac resigned—under pressure—and Smith was set to return to football. This came after a meeting between Smith, Uzelac, and head coach John Cooper, in which the three seemingly reached an accord. Then, according to the Plain Dealer, Cooper left the room and Uzelac again confronted Smith.

Said Smith, looking toward the autumn, "I'm not a perfect student. I'm not a perfect athlete and I'm not a perfect gentleman." As a freshman, though, he was close, on the field and in the classroom. And no matter how headstrong, his populist clash with Uzelac showed the same kind of courage he had already demonstrated to the Big Ten. Stay tuned for the rest of the story. ▶

Mr. Heisman

Archie Griffin became an OSU freshman sensation in his second college game. He had been in class for only three days when his 239 yards vs. UNC broke a 1945 school record.

Heisman Trophy winners from Ohio

Year	Player	School	Hometown
1942	Frank Sinkwich	Georgia Tech	Youngstown
1944	Les Horvath	Ohio State	Parma
1950	Vic Janowicz	Ohio State	Elyria
1951	Dick Kazmaier	Princeton	Maumee
1955	Howard Cassady	Ohio State	Columbus
1963	Roger Staubach	Navy	Cincinnati
1974	Archie Griffin	Ohio State	Columbus
1975	Archie Griffin	Ohio State	Columbus
1991	Desmond Howard	Michigan	Cleveland

Rara Avis

Ohioan **Dick Kazmaier**, who won the Heisman Trophy in 1951 while playing for Princeton, was one of the last of the great single-wing tailbacks. In the single wing formation, the multipurpose tailback was the object of everyone's disaffections and, thus, took a beating. Said Sports Illustrated, "Indeed, it's probably the vulnerability of the single-wing tailback, a rare bird who must be as good at passing as running, that has been most responsible for the demise of the formation." Kazmaier, upon graduation, said he knew that he had become outdated. "I was 5-11 and between 170 and 175 pounds, and off the field I looked pretty much like everybody else...Now, though, you have players who seem to have been bred to play just one position, who develop muscles just for that use. I don't know how a tailback could survive today."

Unsinkable Sinkwich

Frank Sinkwich, the 1942 Heisman winner from Georgia, was a schoolboy halfback from Youngstown, Ohio, the first player from the Southeastern Conference—and Ohio—to win the trophy. He led Georgia to an 11-1 record, including a 9-0 win over UCLA in the Rose Bowl, then became an All-Pro with the Detroit Lions.

On the Record, OSU's Best

Archie Griffin, a bandy-legged little Columbus tailback, was the first and only player to win the Heisman twice. By the time Griffin's senior year rolled around, he was a shoo-in: he'd led Ohio State to an unbeaten season, and become the first college player to rush for more than 5,000 yards. He'd also gained 6,003 all-purpose yards for another record, and set yet another NCAA mark with his 31-game streak of 100-yard-plus games. OSU was 40-5-1 during Griffin's regime, and in a record four Rose Bowls. The question was, could Griffin make it in professional ball. Answered his coach, Woody Hayes: "Well, he may not be as big as they like, but he's as brave as they like."

A Glue-fingered Cleveland Kid Snowballs the Heisman Voting

In the fall of 1991, the little Cleveland receiver, **Desmond Howard**, was the second-biggest winner in Heisman Trophy history. He beat Casey Weldon of Florida State by 1,574 points, a total surpassed only by O.J. Simpson in 1968. This avalanche of votes was provoked by Howard's circus catches and kick returns, which broke nearly every major receiving and scoring record in the annals of the University of Michigan.

At **Cleveland St. Joseph**, where he and his Michigan quarterback, **Elvis Grbac**, first teamed up, Howard was the featured tailback and defensive back, gaining 1,499 yards his senior season while scoring 17 touchdowns. Grbac, meanwhile, averaged about a dozen passes a game, and he and Howard hooked up only one time for a score. Before he had finished his junior season at Michigan, however, he and Grbac had tied the NCAA record for scoring passes by one duo—30—and the Heisman was merely a formality.

While Howard and Grbac did not presage an electrifying pass-and-catch combination in Cleveland, they did presage success; they beat ten regular-season opponents, then beat St. Edward in their first playoff game before losing to Boardman in three overtimes, a game Howard opened by returning the kickoff 92 yards for a touchdown.

His defining moment at Michigan may have been "The Catch," the sensational fourth-and-one, 25-yard, full-stretch reception of Grbac's lob into the corner of the end zone that enabled Michigan to beat Notre Dame for the first time in five years. It was a catch so impossibly athletic that even Notre Dame fans stood up and cheered. He had scored four touchdowns in Michigan's opener against Boston College, but this was the catch that paved the way to his Heisman. He averaged 159 all-purpose yards a game, and set several NCAA records, including most consecutive regular season games with at least one touchdown reception—10. In nine of Michigan's games, Howard scored at least twice and averaged 17.5 yards every time he touched the ball. Wrote Sports Illustrated: "There is an eloquence to Howard's play, a sense that it pleases his entire body, from his eyes to the bottoms of his cleats, to simply catch a football before 100,000 people on a Saturday afternoon."

In Cleveland, Howard was the son of a tool and die maker who worked overtime in order to send Howard to a private Catholic school and give him a chance at earning good college board scores and an athletic scholarship. Howard's nickname is "Magic," because when he was 11 and playing in a East Side recreational league basketball tournament, he came within two points of outscoring the other team by himself. "To work at something until it looks easy defines my relationship to the word `magic,'" he says.

In high school, Desmond didn't attend his senior prom because he had a track meet the next day. By the time he got to Michigan, he was so startled by the plethora of talent, he lined up with the defensive backs, thinking he and his 4.3 speed had a better chance there. But Bo Schembechler had spotted him. When somebody asked Schembechler what he was going to do when his leading receiver, John Kolestar, graduated, Bo said, "I've got this crafty little devil, Desmond Howard." The rest, as we know it, is history. ▶

Ohio college bowl game results*

Tangerine Bowl
Orlando, Florida

1962	Houston 49, Miami(Ohio) 21
1968	Richmond 49, Ohio University 42
1969	*Toledo* 56, Davidson 33
1970	*Toledo* 40, William and Mary 12
1971	*Toledo* 28, Richmond 3
1972	Tampa 21, Kent State 18
1973	*Miami*(Ohio) 16, Florida 7
1974	*Miami*(Ohio) 21, Georgia 10
1975	*Miami*(Ohio) 20, South Carolina 7

Sun Bowl
El Paso, Texas

1941	*Western Reserve University* 26, Arizona State 13
1947	*Cincinnati* 18, Virginia Tech 6
1948	*Miami* 13, Texas Tech 12
1951	West Texas State 14, Cincinnati 13
1963	West Texas State 15, Ohio University 14

Glass Bowl
Toledo, Ohio

1946	*Toledo* 21, Bates College 12
1947	*Toledo* 20, New Hampshire 14
1948	*Toledo* 27, Oklahoma City 14
1949	*Cincinnati* 33, Toledo 13

Refrigerator Bowl
Evansville, Indiana

1954	Delaware 19, Kent State 7

Salad Bowl
Tempe, Arizona

1949	*Xavier* 33, Arizona State 21
1951	*Miami*(Ohio) 34, Arizona State 21

Grantland Rice Bowl
Mufreesboro, Tennessee

1964	Middle Tennessee State 20, Muskingum 0
1966	Tennessee A&I State 34, Muskingum 7
1968	Louisiana Tech 33, University of Akron 13

*(See Ohio State, page 91)

1962 *Wittenberg*
1964 *Wittenberg*
    (mythical small-college champions, Washington TD Club)

Stagg Bowl
Columbus, Ohio

1969 **Wittenberg** 27, William Jewell 21
    (the first Amos Alonzo Stagg Bowl)
1970 **Capital** 34, Luther College 21
1971 Samford 20, Ohio Wesleyan 10
    (Game declared no contest because NCAA found Samford guilty of using ineligible players)
1972 **Heidelberg** 24, Ft. Valley Georgia State 16

Mercy Bowl
Los Angeles, California

1961 Fresno State 36, **Bowling Green** 6
    (The Mercy Bowl was a one-time-only game with proceeds going to the victims of the plane crash in Toledo that took the lives of 16 California Polytechnic Institute football players after a 1960 game at BGSU.)

California Bowl
Fresno, California

1981 *Toledo* 27, San Jose State 25
1982 Fresno State 29, *Bowling Green* 28
1984 NV-Las Vegas 30, *Toledo* 13
    (Toledo won later by forfeit)
1985 Fresno State 51, *Bowling Green* 7
1986 San Jose State 37, Miami(Ohio) 7
1991 **Bowling Green** 28, Fresno State 21

National Championships

1942 *Ohio State* (AP)
1954 *Ohio State* (AP) (Won Rose Bowl)
1957 *Ohio State* (UP) (Won Rose Bowl)
1968 *Ohio State* (AP) (Won Rose Bowl)
1973 *Wittenberg* (NCAA Division III)
1975 *Wittenberg* (NCAA Division III)
    (Runnerup, 1978, 1979)
1976 (Akron, NCAA Division II runnerup)
1978 *Baldwin-Wallace* (NCAA Division III)
1979 *Findlay*, NAIA Division II
    (Runnerup, 1978)
1979 (Youngstown State, NCAA Division II runnerup)
1980 (Wilmington, NAIA Division II runnerup)
1980 *Dayton* (NCAA Division III)
    (Runnerup 1981, 1987, 1991)
1983 (Central State, NCAA Division II runnerup)
1989 *Dayton* (NCAA Division III)
1990 *Central State* (NAIA Division I)
    (Runnerup, 1991)
1991 *Youngstown State* (NCAA Division I-AA)

"HECKUVA FOOTBALL SEASON, HUH, HARRIET?...HARRIET?..."

Football

University of Cincinnati, The Record

Year	Record	Year	Record	Year	Record	Year	Record
1885	1-0-1	1922	1-7-1	**Sun Bowl**		1972	2-9-0
1886	2-0-0	1923	6-3-0	UC 18, Virginia Tech 6		1973	4-7-0
1887	1-0-0	1924	2-6-1			1974	7-4-0
1888	1-0-1	1925	4-5-0	1947	7-3-0	1975	6-5-0
1889	1-1-0	1926	3-5-1	1948	3-6-1	1976	9-2-0
1890	2-1-1	1927	2-5-2			1977	5-4-2
1891	4-2-1	1928	1-8-0	1949	7-4-0	1978	5-6-0
1892	1-2-0	1929	4-4-1			1979	2-9-0
1893	0-6-0	1930	5-4-0	**Glass Bowl**		1980	2-9-0
1894	3-3-0	1931	5-4-0	UC 33, Toledo 13		1981	6-5-0
1895	3-3-0	1932	7-2-0			1982	6-5-0
1896	4-3-1	1933	7-2-0	1950	8-4-0	1983	4-6-1
1897	9-1-1	1934	6-2-1			1984	2-9-0
1898	5-1-3	1935	7-2-0	**Sun Bowl**		1985	5-6-0
1899	5-2-0	1936	1-5-3	West Texas State 14, UC 13		1986	5-6-0
1900	3-4-1	1937	0-10-0			1987	4-7-0
1901	1-3-1	1938	4-5-0	1951	10-1-0	1988	3-8-0
1902	4-2-2	1939	4-3-2	1952	8-1-1	1989	1-9-1
1903	1-8-0	1940	5-3-1	1953	9-1-0	1990	1-10-0
1904	7-1-0	1941	6-3-0	1954	8-2-0	1991	4-7
1905	4-3-0	1942	8-2-0	1955	1-6-2		
1906	0-7-2	1943	None	1956	4-5-0		
1907	None	1944	None	1957	5-4-1		
1908	1-4-1	1945	4-4-0	1958	6-2-2		
1909	4-3-1	1946	9-2-0	1959	5-4-1		
1910	6-3-0			1960	4-6-0		
1911	6-2-1			1961	3-7-0		
1912	3-4-1			1962	2-8-0		
1913	5-3-1			1963	6-4-0		
1914	6-3-0			1964	8-2-0		
1915	4-5-0			1965	5-5-0		
1916	0-8-1			1966	3-7-0		
1917	0-6-0			1967	3-6-0		
1918	3-0-2			1968	5-4-1		
1919	3-4-1			1969	4-6-0		
1920	4-5-0			1970	7-4-0		
1921	2-6-0			1971	7-4-0		

UC, The Coaches

Coach	Seasons	W-L-T	Percent	Coach	Seasons	W-L-T	Percent
No coach	1888-93	9-12-3	.438	George Babcock	1927-30	12-21-3	.375
W. Durant Berry	1894-95	6-6-0	.500	Dana King	1931-34	25-10-1	.708
William Reynolds	1896	4-3-1	.562	Russ Cohen	1935-37	8-11-3	.432
Tom Fennel	1897	9-1-1	.864	W. Woodward	1937	0-6-0	.000
Frank Cavanagh	1898	5-1-3	.722	Joe Meyer	1938-42	27-16-3	.620
Dan Reed	1899-00	8-6-1	.567	Ray Nolting	1945-48	23-15-1	.603
Henry Pratt	1901	1-3-1	.300	Sid Gillman	1949-54	50-13-1	.789
Anthony Chez	1902-03	5-10-2	.353	George Blackburn	1955-60	25-27-6	.483
Amos Foster	1904-05	11-4-0	.733	Chuck Studley	1961-66	27-33-0	.450
William Foley	1906	0-7-2	.111	Homer Rice	1967-68	8-10-1	.447
Ralph Onott	1907-08	1-4-1	.250	Ray Callahan	1969-72	20-23-0	.465
Robert Burch	1909-11	16-8-2	.654	Tony Mason	1973-76	26-18-0	.591
Lowell Dana	1912-13	8-7-2	.529	Ralph Staub	1977-80	14-28-2	.341
George Little	1914-15	10-8-0	.556	Mike Gottfried	1981-82	12-10-0	.545
Ion Cortright	1916	0-8-1	.056	Watson Brown	1983	4-6-1	.409
Frank Marty	1917	0-6-0	.000	Dave Currey	1984-88	19-36-0	.345
Boyd Chambers	1918-21	12-15-3	.450	Tim Murphy	1989-	6-26-1	.182
George McLaren	1922-26	16-26-3	.389				

UC, The Statistics

1. Most passes completed, game—56, Greg Cook vs. Ohio, 1968
2. Most passing yards, game—554, Greg Cook vs. Ohio, 1968
3. Most passing yards, season—3,272, Greg Cook, 1968 (led nation)
4. Longest passing play—95 yards, Greg Cook to Tom Rossley, vs. Louisville, 1968 (TD)
5. Most yards rushing, game—267, Clem Turner vs. Kansas State, 1966
6. Most yards, career—4,242, Reggie Taylor, 1983-86
7. Most passes caught, game—13, Tom Rossley vs. Wichita State, 1968
8. Most passes caught, career—111, Roosevelt Mukes, 1985-88
9. Most receiving yards, game—254, Tom Rossley vs. Louisville, 1968
10. Best average per reception, career—21.9, Jim O'Brien, 1967-69
11. Most points scored, game—25, Jim O'Brien vs. Tampa, 1968
12. Highest punting average, career—42.5, Mike Connell, 1974-77
13. Longest kickoff return—99 yards, Keith Jenkins vs. Houston, 1975 (TD)
14. Most points scored, game—67 vs. Virginia Military, 1953

High-tech Gillman

Gillman: He took the fields of Ohio and stretched them. "If you want to ring the cash register," he said, "you have to pass."

Training in Ohio, Sid Gillman Revolutionized the Passing Game

Sid Gillman, the innovator of the modern pro passing game, was also the man who established Miami as "the Cradle of Coaches," as well as reviving the football fortunes of the University of Cincinnati. He's still the winningest Bearcat coach; from 1949-1954, he went 50-13-1 before leaving Ohio for the San Diego Chargers where his offenses overhauled the still-young pro game. Gillman, regarded as the premier student of technical football, began his Ohio career as a good defensive end at OSU, then stayed on as an assistant.

He served another assistant stint at Denison before becoming head coach at both Miami and UC. Gillman taught offense to Vince Lombardi, and no less an authority than ex-San Francisco coach Bill Walsh credits Gillman with the innovations that changed the passing game—notably option blocking, spreading the field, filling all the passing lanes, and hitting the receivers on the break. Some say every major-college pass offense, and most of the pro ones, are derived from Gillman's system. ▶

There has been
but one Ohio
college product
to start at
quarterback in
the Super
Bowl—*Ron
Jawarski* of
*Youngstown
State,* who
started for the
Philadelphia
Eagles in 1980.

Football

Youngstown State University, The Record

Year	Record		Year	Record		Year	Record		Year	Record
1938	4-50		1960	6-2-0		1978	10-2-0		1988	4-7-0
1939	4-50		1961	4-4-1		*NCAA Division II Playoffs*			1989	9-4-0
1940	7-1-1		1962	6-3-0		YSU 21, Nebraska-Omaha 14			*NCAA Division I-AA Playoffs*	
1941	7-0-1		1963	5-4-1		Eastern Illinois 26, YSU 22			YSU 28, Eastern Kentucky 24	
1942	6-3-0		1964	6-1-2					Furman 42, YSU 23	
1943	None		1965	6-2-0		1979	11-2-0			
1944	None		1966	5-3-1		*NCAA Division II Playoffs*			1990	11-1-0
1945	None		1967	4-5-0		YSU 50, South Dakota State 7			*NCAA Division I-AA Playoffs*	
1946	7-1-0		1968	3-6-0		YSU 52, Alabama A&M 0			Central Florida 20, YSU 17	
1947	8-2-0		1969	2-6-0		Delaware 38, YSU 21				
1948	4-3-2		1970	0-9-0					1991	12-3
1949	4-3-1		1971	2-6-0		1980	2-8-1		*NCAA Division I-AA Playoffs*	
1950	3-5-0		1972	4-4-1		1981	7-4-0		YSU 17, Villanova 16	
1951	2-6-1		1973	4-6-0		1982	6-5-0		YSU 30, Nevada-Reno 28	
1952	4-3-1					1983	4-7-0		YSU 10, Samford 0	
1953	7-1-0		1974	8-2-0		1984	7-4-0		YSU 25, Marshall 17 (Finals)	
1954	7-2-0		*NCAA Division II Playoffs*			1985	5-6-0		NCAA Division I-AA	
1955	4-5-0		Delaware 35, YSU 14			1986	2-9-0		Champions	
1956	4-4-0									
1957	3-6-0		1975	5-4-0		1987	8-4-0			
1958	4-4-0		1976	4-6-0		*NCAA Division I-AA Playoffs*				
1959	5-4-1		1977	7-3-0		Northern Iowa 31, YSU 28				

YSU, The Coaches

Name	Years	W-L	Percent
Dwight "Dike" Beede	1938-1972	147-118-14	.552
Rey Dempsey	1973-74	12-8-0	.600
Bill Narduzzi	1975-85	68-51-1	.571
Jim Tressel	1986-	46-28-0	.622

"MOM, NOW THAT THE SEASON'S OVER, CAN WE CHANGE DAD'S CHANNEL?"

*Dike Beede: "We've
never picked any
patsies. You can't
become tough
without playing
tough people."*

At Youngstown, Dike Beede and His Wife Sewed up Football's First Penalty Flag

The penalty flag, like so many other inauspicious beginnings, began with little note in a 1941 game between **Youngstown College** and Oklahoma City. Coach **Dike Beede** had been grousing about the horn. Before the penalty flag, football referees blew a horn. If it happened to be a rousing game, no one in the stands could hear the horn.

So Dike asked his wife to get out her sewing kit, and she sewed four triangles of red cloth from her daughter's Halloween costume together with four triangles of white cloth from an old bed sheet, weighted a corner with curtain weights and there it was: the first penalty flag in existence.

Before the game, played at Rayen High School Stadium, Dike handed his homemade flags to the officials and asked a favor.

"Irma can't hear the horns in the stands," he said. "If you fellows would drop one of these flags whenever there's a penalty, I think we'll have a better game."

The flags flew, Youngstown College won the game, and three of the officials promptly tossed the flags.

The head lineman, a man named Jack McPhee, kept his. "I'm a Scotsman," he said later. "I never throw anything away. In 1943, or perhaps it was 1944—McPhee cannot remember—he tossed Irma's flag on a key play between Ohio State and Iowa. The game was in Columbus and the Big Ten commissioner was there. By the next weekend, the whole conference had adopted the flag. By 1948, the NFL was using it. Jack McPhee's original ended up in the College Hall of Fame at Kings Island, next to a plaque with Dike's name on it.

For nearly four decades, Dike Beede's name was synonymous with Youngstown football. He coached without a conference, a stadium, or fulltime assistants. He coached for ten years before he was a full-time employee at the college—he began for $1 a year and part-time insurance benefits. He recruited local boys because he liked the steel mill kids for their toughness, but also because they had to live at home—Youngstown College didn't have a dorm.

Wrote Bob Trebilcock, "He wasn't a flashy coach; he wasn't a profane man. His sense of decorum was such that he covered his mouth when he chewed tobacco." He promised his players an education, and he taught them sportsmanship as well. When he handed out a scholarship, it was never revoked, and he was just as likely to give one to the manager. He brought a bushel of apples on the bus for every trip and even today the locals say the fruit trees along Route 7 from Columbiana to Youngstown were planted by Dike's boys.

When he retired, he was still teaching one of the courses he loved—forestry. In 1957 he was named both the Small College Coach of the Year and the Ohio Tree Farmer of the Year. He began at Youngstown in 1926, the youngest college coach in the game—he was 23—and he finished 40 years later as the oldest active coach in the game and a 175-146-20 record. In 1982, Youngstown State University dedicated Stambaugh Stadium. It was named for a benefactor. The field was named for Dike. "For over forty years, the Youngstown Penquins were on the road," the dedication speaker said. "Today, they came home." ▶

University of Dayton, The Record

Year	Record	Year	Record	Year	Record	Year	Record
1923	4-5	1941	7-3	1958	2-8	1976	4-7
1924	7-3	1941	7-3	1959	3-7	1977	8-3
1925	7-2	1942	8-2	1960	1-9	1978	9-2-1
1926	8-2	1943	None	1961	2-8	1979	8-2-1
1927	6-3	1944	None	1962	2-8	1980	14-0
1928	6-3	1945	None	1963	1-7-2	1981	12-2
1929	4-5	1946	6-3	1964	3-7	1982	6-4
1930	4-3-2	1947	6-3	1965	1-8-1	1983	7-3
1931	5-3-2	1948	7-2-1	1966	8-2	1984	10-1
1932	9-2	1949	6-3	1967	6-3-1	1985	7-3
1933	7-2-1	1950	4-6	1968	5-5	1986	10-1
1934	4-3-1	1951	7-2	1969	3-7	1987	11-3
1935	4-4-1	1952	6-5	1970	5-4-1	1988	9-2
1936	4-5	1953	3-5-1	1971	5-6	1989	13-0-1
1937	7-2	1954	5-5	1972	4-6-1	1990	11-1
1938	7-2	1955	3-6-1	1973	5-5-1	1991	13-1
1939	4-4-1	1956	4-6	1974	3-8		
1940	6-3-1	1957	6-3-1	1975	5-6		

UD, winningest coaches

Coach	Years	W-L	Percent
Rick Carter	1977-80	39-7-2	.833
Mike Kelly	1981-present	96-20-1	.825
Harry Baujan	1923-46	124-64-8	.653
Joe Gavin	1947-53	39-26-2	.597
John McVey	1965-72	36-41-4	.469

UD, the statistics

1. Most passes completed, game—29, Tom Vosberg vs. Toledo, 1974 (Division I);
   18, Dan Sharley vs. John Carroll, 1990 (Division III)
2. Most passing yards, game—318, Tom Vosberg vs. Toledo, 1974 (Division I);
   306, Dan Sharley vs. John Carroll, 1990 (Division III)
3. Most passing yards, season—1,914, Tom Vosberg, 1974 (Division I);
   1,633, Dan Sharley, 1990 (Division III)
4. Most passing yards, career—3,688, B.J. Dailey, 1974-77 (Division I and III);
   3,229, Dan Sharley, 1987-90 (Division III); and 2,896, Ken Polke, 1970-73 (Division I)
5. Most yards rushing, game—236, Gary Kosins vs. Akron, 1970 (Division I);
   234, Dave Jones vs. Wayne State, 1987 (Division III)
6. Most yards, career—2,940, Sylvester Monroe, 1975-78 (includes Division I);
   2,812, Gary Kosins, 1969-71 (Division I);
   2,684, Dave Jones, 1984-87 (Division III)
7. Most passes caught, game—10, Larry Nickels vs. East Carolina, 1972 (Division I);
   9, Joe D. Clark vs. Villanova, 1977 (Division III)
8. Most passes caught, career—109, Tim Eubank, 1985-88 (Division I);
   99, Larry Nickels, 1972-75 (Division I)
9. Most receiving yards, game—223, Al Laubenthal vs. John Carroll, 1980 (Division III);
   186, Larry Nickels vs. East Carolina (Division I)
10. Best average per reception, career—21.1, Al Laubenthal, 1977-80 (Division III);
    119.5, Kelvin Kirk, 1972-75 (Division I)
11. Most points scored, game—30, Richard Punch vs. Aquinas, 1916;
    Gary Kosins vs. Xavier, 1970;
    Kevin Hofacre vs. John Carroll, 1989
12. Highest punting average, career—39.6, Dan Quinn, 1970-71 (Division I);
    35.7; Jack Cameron, 1987-90 (Division III)
13. Longest kickoff return—98 (TD), Bobby Recker vs. Xavier, 1950 (Division I);
    92 (TD), Gradlin Pruitt vs. Otterbein, 1978 (Division III)
14. Most points scored, game—326, Mike Duvic, 1986-89 (Division III);
    246, Gary Kosins, 1969-71 (Division I)

That Championship Decade

The Dayton Flyers went 13-1 in 1991, captured their third consecutive undefeated regular season, earned a sixth consecutive playoff berth, and made it to the NCAA Division III Championship game for the fifth time since 1980. Though the Flyers lost to the Ithaca Bombers in the Amos Alonzo Stagg Bowl, head coach Mike Kelly won his 100th game, became the school's all-time leader in winning percentage (11 years, 109-21-1, .836), and moved up to seventh in collegiate winning percentage in all divisions, all-time.

UD Playoff Records, 1980-1991

1980
First round—Dayton 34, Baldwin-Wallace 0
Second round—Dayton 28, Widener 24
National Championship
Stagg Bowl—Dayton 63, Ithaca 0

1981
First round—Dayton 19, Augustana 7
Second round—Dayton 38, Lawrence 0
National Championship
Stagg Bowl—Widener 17, Dayton 10

1984
First round—Augustana 14, Dayton 13

1986
First round—Mount Union 42, Dayton 36

1987
First round—Dayton 52, Capital 28
Second round—Dayton 38, Augustana 36
Third round—Dayton 34, Central Iowa 0
National Championship
Stagg Bowl—Wagner 19, Dayton 3

1988
First round—Wittenberg 35, Dayton 28 (2OT)

1989
First round—Dayton 35, John Carroll 10
Second round—Dayton 28, Millikin 16
Third round—Dayton 28, St. John's 0
National Championship
Stagg Bowl—Dayton 17, Union 7

1990
First round—Dayton 24, Augustana 14
Second round—Allegheny 31, Dayton 23

1991
First round—Dayton 27, Baldwin-Wallace 10
Second round—Dayton 28, Allegheny 25 (OT)
Third round—Dayton 19, St. John's 7
National Championship
Stagg Bowl—Ithaca 34, Dayton 20

Coach Joe: At the helm of the top-ranked predominately black school in America over the last five years

Unheralded Central State: One of the Nation's Sterling Football Powers

To find Coach **Billy Joe**, one must know **Central State University's** gymnasium, for his office is almost underneath the basketball court, a great old court festooned with the titles the sports program has won—1968 NAIA basketball national champions, undefeated national basketball champions in 1964-65, national girls' track championship in 1991 and, of course, Billy Joe's national football title in 1990. The office is in one corner of the building, across from hardware-laden trophy cases, and the office itself is almost a museum, photographs and trophies and plaques of all sizes and weight.

Billy Joe, after sterling careers on every level from sandlot to the pros, was backfield coach for the Eagles. He got a Super Bowl ring there, but it was no big deal; he already had one—he played on Weeb Ewbank's great Jets team, the Namath-quarterbacked team that put the AFL on the map by upsetting a young Don Shula and his Baltimore Colts.

Billy Joe wanted to be a head coach. He would rather be a head coach almost anywhere, rather than even a top assistant. "I am creative and innovative and I want this applied to the game. A head coach may or may not listen. He may even implement some of the things. But, as head coach, *I* listen to me..."

"We have to be successful with one ethnic group," says Coach Joe. "Now consider what that means. Suppose Notre Dame could play only Irish kids. Or USC could play only Italians. It's tough being competitive with only one ethnic group."

But for Billy Joe, it's only so tough. Consider that his program has been in the national playoffs every year since he arrived, that one of those teams—the 1990 team—was national NAIA Division I champions, and two others played for it, the 1983 team losing to North Dakota State,

and the 1991 team losing to Central Arkansas in the waning seconds. Two players from the 1990 team—cornerback **Vince Buck** and offensive lineman **Erik Williams** were high draft picks by New Orleans and Dallas. Mighty Grambling and the legendary Eddie Robinson has never beaten Coach Joe's teams, nay, has never beaten CSU. These days, it is virtually impossible to get a game with Grambling.

Billy Joe comes out of a physicalness that preordained a playing career: even in high school, he was extraordinarily big and athletic. He was a 235-pound running back in high school, and bigger than that in college.

Billy Joe went to Villanova where he became a 60' shotputter and the star running back on a team that won back-to-back bowl games. He was the MVP of the 1961 Sun Bowl, and the most valuable back the next year in the Liberty Bowl. With the 1963 Broncos in the old American League he was the rookie of the year, and went on to play with the Bills, Dolphins, and Jets. That year with the Jets, he tied a pro record by scoring three touchdowns in one quarter, against the Patriots.

It is not something he thinks a lot about these days, the past, because he is inclined to live in the present. And because the work seems so important. "I don't give it that much thought. I am concerned with impacting people's lives now. There's a crisis now among young Afro-American males. Playing and coaching have both been great. But they aren't, in and of themselves, important enough. Winning games isn't important enough. I have to make an impact. If scores weren't kept at all, I'd still like the game. Of course, I work real hard to win..." ▶

"WHERE WILL IT END, BERNARD? WHERE WILL IT ALL END?"

Football

Ohio College Coach of Year

Year	Coach	University	Year	Coach	University
1952	Ara Parseghian	Miami	1973	Bill Mallory	Miami
1953	Carroll Widdoes	Ohio	1974	Dick Crum	Miami
1954	Paul Hoememan	Heidelberg	1975	Dick Crum	Miami
1955	Ed Sherman	Muskingum	1976	Jim Dennison	Akron
1956	Doyt Perry	Bowling Green	1977	Lee Tressel	Baldwin-Wallace
1957	Bill Edwards	Wittenberg	1978	Bill Narduzzi	Youngstown State
1958	Trevor Rees	Kent State	1979	Earle Bruce	Ohio State
1959	Doyt Perry	Bowling Green	1980	Lee Tressel	Baldwin-Wallace
1960	Bill Hess	Ohio	1981	Chuck Stobart	Toledo
1961	Lee Tressel	Baldwin-Wallace	1982	Bob Packard	Baldwin-Wallace
1962	Bill Edwards	Wittenberg	1983	Billy Joe	Central State
1963	Keith Piper	Denison	1984	Dan Simrell	Toledo
1964	Ed Sherman	Muskingum	1985	Denny Stotz	Bowling Green
1966	Glenn "Bo" Schembechler	Miami	1986	Larry Kehres	Mount Union
1967	Frank Lauterbur	Toledo	1987	Mike Kelly	Dayton
1968	Bill Hess	Ohio	1988	Ron Murphy	Wittenberg
1969	Frank Lauterbur	Toledo	1989	Jim Tressel	Youngstown State
1970	Gene Slaughter	Capital	1990	Jim Tressel	Youngstown State
1971	Jack Murphy	Toledo	1991	Jim Tressel	Youngstown State
1972	Don James	Kent State			

Results of the 1991 College Football Coach of the Year Award voting (first-place votes in parenthesis)

Coach	School	Votes
Jim Tressel	Youngstown State (10)	56
Gary Blackney	Bowling Green (12)	54
Bob Packard	Baldwin-Wallace (3)	20
Mike Kelly	Dayton	13
Richard Strahm	Findlay (1)	4
Billy Joe	Central State	2
John Cooper	Ohio State	1
Tom Kaczkowski	Ohio Northern	1
Carlin Carpenter	Bluffton	1
Tim Murphy	Cincinnati	1

Source: Columbus Dispatch

A good man's worth

Football coaches, State-supported Colleges

John Cooper, OSU, $110,400
Gerry Faust, Akron, $89,000
Tim Murphy, Cincinnati, $78,000
Billy Joe, Central State (head coach and AD), $77,175
Pete Cordelli, Kent State, $75,000
Tom Lichtenberg, Ohio University, $75,000
Randy Walker, Miami, $74,200
Gary Blackney, Bowling Green, $72,000
Gary Pinkel, Toledo, $69,304
Jim Tressel, Youngstown State, $65,000
William L. Young, OSU assistant, $61,800
Gene A. Huey, OSU assistant, $52,200
Robert M. Junko, Akron assistant, $52,000
Robert Turner, OSU assistant, $50,760
Ronald A. Hudson, OSU assistant, $50,040

Other Coaches and administrators

James Jones, OSU AD, $101,160
Rick Taylor, Cincinnati AD, $98,280
Al Bohl, Toledo AD, $86,395
Harry Weinbrecht, Shawnee State AD (and volleyball coach), $45,655
Randy Ayers, OSU basketball, $81,120
Bob Huggins, Cincinnati basketball, $80,000
Michael Boyd, Cleveland State basketball, $70,000
Jim McDonald, Kent State basketball, $70,000
Joseph Wright, Miami basketball, $65,000
Ralph Underhill, Wright State basketball, $65,000
Jim Larranaga, Bowling Greenbasketball, $62,246
Jay Eck, Toledo basketball, $61,846
Nancy Darsch, OSU women's basketball, $53,640
Shelley Patterson, Ohio University women's basketball assistant, $28,500
Robin Smith, Shawnee State women's basketball, head, part-time, $6,000
Jeremiah York, Bowling Green hockey (assistant AD), $72,967
George Gwozdecky, Miami hockey, $34,610
Terrence Flanagan, Bowling Green hockey assistant, $34,345
Lillian Fesperman, Miami field hockey, $34,225
James D. Brown, OSU golf, $53,160
Bob Cooley, Ohio University golf, $9,056
Scott Hammond, Ohio University swimming, $43,339
James Stone, OSU volleyball, $38,400
Chris Miner, Ohio University softball, $33,427
Duane Theiss, OSU baseball assistant, $21,360
Jim Schmitz, Cincinnati baseball, $20,000
Gerald Lackey, Cincinnati women's basketball assistant, $14,000
Patrick Cherry, OSU rifle, $3,510
Charlotte Remenyik, OSU fencing, men and women, $38,640

Source: Columbus Dispatch

Basketball

Ohio State University, The Record

Year	Won	Lost	Pct.	Pts.	Opp. Pts.	Coach	Year	Won	Lost	Pct.	Pts.	Opp. Pts.	Coach
1899	12	4	.750	282	96		1945	x15	5	.750	1073	859	Harold G. Olsen
1900	8	4	.667	234	128		*1946	x16	5	.762	1051	917	Harold G. Olsen
1901	1	3	.250	47	50		1947	7	13	.350	987	1050	William H. H. Dye
1902			*No Intercollegiate Basketball*				1948	10	10	.500	1163	1129	William H. H. Dye
1903	5	2	.714	259	101	D. C. Huddleson	1949	14	7	.667	1280	1172	William H. H. Dye
1904	10	4	.714	669	334	D. C. Huddleson	*1950	x22	4	.846	1697	1469	William H. H. Dye
1905	12	2	.857	566	247		1951	6	16	.273	1399	1525	Floyd S. Stahl
1906	9	1	.900	289	163		1952	8	14	.364	1382	1525	Floyd S. Stahl
1907	7	5	.593	392	275		1953	10	12	.454	1557	1594	Floyd S. Stahl
1908	5	6	.454	401	261		1954	11	11	.500	1727	1700	Floyd S. Stahl
1909	11	1	.909	428	242	Thomas Kibler	1955	10	12	.455	1684	1759	Floyd S. Stahl
1910	11	1	.909	460	230	Thomas Kibler	1956	16	6	.728	1849	1698	Floyd S. Stahl
1911	7	2	.778	305	202		1957	14	8	.636	1682	1576	Floyd S. Stahl
1912	7	5	.583	368	254	Lynn W. St. John	1958	9	13	.409	1595	1629	Floyd S. Stahl
1913	13	7	.632	540	452	Lynn W. St. John	1959	11	11	.500	1781	1769	Fred R. Taylor
1914	11	4	.733	402	321	Lynn W. St. John	*1960	x25	3	.893	2532	1953	Fred R. Taylor
1915	7	10	.412	359	363	Lynn W. St. John	*1961	x27	1	.964	2838	1840	Fred R. Taylor
1916	9	13	.409	499	554	Lynn W. St. John	*1962	x26	2	.928	2344	1855	Fred R. Taylor
1917	15	11	.577	697	599	Lynn W. St. John	**1963	20	4	.833	1883	1682	Fred R. Taylor
1918	12	7	.632	582	503	Lynn W. St. John	**1964	16	8	.667	1985	1865	Fred R. Taylor
1919	7	12	.369	475	525	Lynn W. St. John	1965	12	12	.500	1921	1981	Fred R. Taylor
1920	17	10	.630	801	690	George Trautman	1966	11	13	.458	1861	1923	Fred R. Taylor
1921	4	13	.235	422	553	George Trautman	1967	13	11	.542	1838	1898	Fred R. Taylor
1922	8	10	.444	438	494	George Trautman	**1968	x21	8	.724	2386	2135	Fred R. Taylor
1923	4	11	.267	365	499	Harold G. Olsen	1969	17	7	.708	1956	1841	Fred R. Taylor
1924	12	5	.706	544	429	Harold G. Olsen	1970	17	7	.708	2114	1955	Fred R. Taylor
*1925	14	2	.875	517	381	Harold G. Olsen	*1971	x20	6	.769	2107	1922	Fred R. Taylor
1926	10	7	.588	486	432	Harold G. Olsen	1972	18	6	.750	1781	1624	Fred R. Taylor
1927	11	6	.647	521	453	Harold G. Olsen	1973	14	10	.583	1900	1798	Fred R. Taylor
1928	5	12	.294	487	616	Harold G. Olsen	1974	9	15	.375	1716	1732	Fred R. Taylor
1929	9	8	.529	530	523	Harold G. Olsen	1975	14	14	.500	2228	2173	Fred R. Taylor
1930	4	11	.267	355	442	Harold G. Olsen	1976	6	20	.231	1931	2083	Fred R. Taylor
1931	4	13	.235	418	464	Harold G. Olsen	1977	11	16	.407	1825	1984	Eldon Miller
1932	9	9	.500	515	498	Harold G. Olsen	1978	16	11	.593	2163	2069	Eldon Miller
**1933	17	3	.850	724	525	Harold G. Olsen	1979	+19	12	.613	2323	2248	Eldon Miller
1934	8	12	.400	611	651	Harold G. Olsen	1980	x21	8	.724	2090	1867	Eldon Miller
1935	13	6	.684	624	577	Harold G. Olsen	1981	14	13	.519	1922	1903	Eldon Miller
1936	12	8	.600	654	590	Harold G. Olsen	1982	x21	10	.677	1929	1874	Eldon Miller
1937	13	7	.650	644	630	Harold G. Olsen	1983	x20	10	.667	2219	2097	Eldon Miller
1938	12	8	.600	767	701	Harold G. Olsen	1984	+15	14	.517	1952	1925	Eldon Miller
*1939	x16	7	.676	999	908	Harold G. Olsen	1985	x20	10	.677	2320	2190	Eldon Miller
1940	13	7	.650	828	749	Harold G. Olsen	1986	+19	14	.576	2482	2386	Eldon Miller
1941	10	10	.500	855	851	Harold G. Olsen	1987	x20	13	.606	2802	2572	Gary Williams
1942	6	14	.300	836	969	Harold G. Olsen	1988	+20	13	.606	2505	2473	Gary Williams
1943	8	9	.471	758	792	Harold G. Olsen	1989	+19	15	.559	2579	2720	Gary Williams
*1944	x14	7	.667	1153	1004	Harold G. Olsen	1990	x17	13	.567	2268	2206	Randy Ayers
							**1991	x27	4	.871	2624	2123	Randy Ayers
							*1992	x26	6	.813	2579	2137	Randy Ayers

*Big Ten Champion
**Co-Champion
x NCAA Tournament
+NIT

Post-Season Tournaments

Over the years, Ohio State has appeared in 17 NCAA tournaments, including the very first one in 1939 when OSU finished as runner-up. The Buckeyes, who have made it to the Final Four eight times and appeared in four championship games, have an overall tournament record of 26-15.

1939
OSU 64, Wake Forest 52
OSU 53, Villanova 36
National Finals
Oregon 46, OSU 33*

1944
OSU 57, Temple 47
Dartmouth 60, OSU 53*

1945
OSU 45, Kentucky 37
New York U. 70, OSU 65 (OT)*

1946
OSU 46, Harvard 38
North Carolina 60, OSU 57
OSU 63, California 45*

1950
C.C.N.Y. 56, OSU 55
OSU 72, Holy Cross 52

1960
OSU 98, W. Kentucky 79
OSU 86, Georgia Tech 69
OSU 76, New York U. 54
National Finals
OSU 75, California 55*

1961
OSU 56, Louisville 55
OSU 87, Kentucky 74
OSU 95, St. Joseph's 69
National Finals
Cincinnati 70, OSU 65 (OT)*

1962
OSU 93, W. Kentucky 73
OSU 74, Kentucky 64
OSU 84, Wake Forest 68
National Finals
Cincinnati 71, OSU 59*

1968
OSU 79, E. Tennessee 72
OSU 82, Kentucky 81
North Carolina 80, OSU 66
OSU 89, Houston 85*

1971
OSU 60, Marquette 59
W. Kentucky 81, OSU 78 (OT)

1980
OSU 89, Arizona State 75
U.C.L.A. 72, OSU 68

1982
James Madison 55, OSU 48

1983
OSU 79, Syracuse 74
North Carolina 64, OSU 51

1985
OSU 75, Iowa State 64
Louisiana Tech 79, OSU 67

1987
OSU 91, Kentucky 77
Georgetown 82, OSU 79

1990
OSU 84, Providence 83 (OT)
UNLV 76, OSU 65

1991
OSU 97, Towson State 86
OSU 65, Georgia Tech 61
St. John's 91, OSU 74

1992
OSU 83, Mississippi Valley State 56
OSU 78, Connecticut 55
OSU 80, UNC 73
Michigan 75, OSU 71 (OT)

*Final Four

National Invitation Tournament

1979
OSU 80, St. Joseph's 66
OSU 79, Maryland 72
OSU 55, Indiana 64
OSU 86, Alabama 96

1984
OSU 57, Xavier 60 (OT)

1986
OSU 65, Ohio Univ. 62
OSU 71, Texas 65
OSU 79, BYU 68
OSU 79, La. Tech 66
Championship
OSU 73, Wyoming 63

1988
OSU 86, Old Dominion 73
OSU 86, Cleveland State 80
OSU 68, New Mexico 65
OSU 64, Colorado State 62
Championship
OSU 67, Connecticut 72

1989
OSU 81, Akron 70
OSU 85, Nebraska 74
OSU 80, St. John's 83 (OT)
Totals: Won 13, Lost 5

Ohio State Players and Coaches in the Basketball Hall of Fame

L. W. St. John	Coach	1912-19
Neil Johnston	Player	1947-48
Harold Olsen	Coach	1923-46
John Havlicek	Player	1960-62
Fred Taylor	Coach	1959-76
Jerry Lucas	Player	1960-62

OSU All-Americans

Player	Position	Year
Johnny Miner	Forward	1925
Jimmy Hull	Forward	1939
Dick Schnittker	Forward	1950
Robin Freeman	Guard	1955-56
Frank Howard	Forward	1957
Paul Ebert	Center	1954
Larry Siegfried	Guard	1961
John Havlicek	Forward	1962
Gary Bradds	Center	1963-64
Kelvin Ransy	Guard	1980

OSU, The Coaches

Coach	Years	Won	Lost	Pct.
D. C. Huddleson	1903-1904	15	6	.714
Thomas Kibler	1909-1910	22	2	.917
Lynn W. St. John	1912-1919	79	69	.534
George M. Trautman	1920-1922	29	33	.468
Harold G. Olsen	1923-1946	255	192	.570
William H. H. Dye	1947-1950	53	34	.609
Floyd S. Stahl	1951-1958	84	92	.477
Fred R. Taylor	1959-1976	297	158	.653
Eldon Miller	1977-1986	176	118	.599
Gary Williams	1987-1989	59	41	.590
Randy Ayers	1990-1991	44	17	.721

OSU, Individual Records

Most Points
Game—49, Gary Bradds vs. Illinois, 2-10-64
Season—958, Dennis Hopson, 1987, 33 games
Career—2,096, Dennis Hopson, 1984-87, 125 games
Best Scoring Average
Season—32.9, Robin Freeman, 1956, 723 points, 22 games
Career—28.0, Robin Freeman, 1954-56,
57 games, 1,597 points
Most Field Goals Made
Game—20, Gary Bradds vs. Purdue, 1-25-64
Season—338, Dennis Hopson, 1987, 33 games
Career—834, Herb Williams, 1978-81
Best Field Goal Percentage (min. 8 attempts)
Game—1.000, John Havlicek at Michigan,
2-4-61, 9 FGM, 9 FGA
Season—.637, Jerry Lucas, 1960, 283 FGM, 444 FGA
Career—.624, Jerry Lucas, 1960-62, 776 FGM, 1,243 FGA
Most Free Throws Made
Game—18, Gary Bradds at Michigan State, 1-27-64
Season—215, Dennis Hopson, 1987, 33 games
Career—438, Jerry Lucas, 1960-62
Best Free Throw Percentage (min. 13 attempts)
Game—1.000, Larry Siegfried vs. Purdue, 3-7-59,
16 FTM, 16 FTA
Season—.900, Jody Finney, 1969, 99 FTM, 110 FTA
Career—.862, Jody Finney, 1968-70, 250 FTM, 290 FTA
Most Rebounds
Game—32, Frank Howard vs. Brigham Young, 1-29-56
Season—499, Jerry Lucas, 1962, 28 games
Career—1,411, Jerry Lucas, 1960-62

Most Assists
Game—14, Curtis Wilson at Purdue, 1-7-88
Season—188, Curtis Wilson, 1988
Career—516, Kelvin Ransey, 1977-80
Best Rebounding Average
Season—17.8, Jerry Lucas, 1962, 28 games, 499 rebounds
Career—17.2, Jerry Lucas, 1960-62, 82 games, 1,411 rebounds
Most Blocked Shots
Game—9, Brad Sellers vs. Louisiana Tech
at New York, 3-24-86
Season—97, Brad Sellers, 1986
Career—328, Herb Williams, 1978-81
Most Steals
Game 8—, Troy Taylor vs. St. Joseph's at
Santa Clara, CA, 12-29-83
Season—74, Curtis Wilson, 1987
Career—204, Jay Burson, 1986-89
Most Games Played
Career—133, Jerry Francis, 1986-89, 126 started
Most Three-point Field Goals Made
Game—9, Jay Burson vs. Florida at New York, 12-27-88
Season—67, Dennis Hopson, 1987
Career—67, Dennis Hopson, 1987
Best Three-point Field Goal Percentage (min. 5 attempts)
Game—.800, James Bradley at Northwestern,
2-18-89, 4 FGM, 5 FGA
Season—.553, Larry Huggins, 1983, 21 FGM, 38 FGA
Career—.553, Larry Huggins, 1983, 21 FGM, 38 FGA

Buckeyes Play Championship Season But Miss Final Championship

The headlines read: "Buckeyes Can't Find Miracle Against Michigan." In the Southeast Regional NCAA Final, **Ohio State** lost a late four-point lead to Michigan's disdainful freshmen, then went into overtime where the Fabulous Frosh upset the Bucks, 75-71. In OSU's last Final Eight appearance, in 1971 against Western Kentucky, the Bucks had also lost in overtime. This loss was particularly painful, especially since OSU had beaten Michigan twice in the regular season. It brought back memories of the 1962 NCAA final when Cincinnati upset OSU for the second straight year.

The key OSU shot came with 3:40 left in regulation, a three-pointer from 12 feet out by **Chris Jent** that nicked the front rim. OSU had gone on a 13-2 run and was up, 61-57, and the concensus was that this was the valedictory shot. "If I hit that three," said Jent, "we put the game away. They would have been done...They just gave us so many opportunities to win and we couldn't get the job done."

Wrote Plain Dealer columnist Bill Livingston, "In overtime, the Buckeyes had nothing but their great hearts left. Michigan, bigger, more talented, backing up their mouths with their arms and legs, ran away from OSU in the five extra minutes that should have never been played."

The overbearing court insolence of the Michigan freshmen paid off, as they pushed the Bucks out of their set. **Jimmy Jackson**, while scoring 20 points, was only 9-21 and committed a career-high nine turnovers. "We were like a team that hasn't been here before," he said. "We didn't execute. If you don't execute in a big game, that's when you lose..."

Indeed, the news courtside after the first two games of the Southeast Regional when OSU beat Mississippi Valley State and Connecticut, was that the Buckeyes could win without Jackson. He was a commanding presence, yet still missed 29 of 39 field goal attempts. Against UNC, Jackson was again sub-par, going 8-for-17 and 18 points. It was Dayton guard **Jamie Skelton** who filled the void, coming off the bench and scoring five of his 14 points in the last 2:16. Teammate **Lawrence Funderburke**, the big 6-9 sophomore, had 21 points and seven rebounds, countering UNC's big man, the 7-foot Eric Montross, who had 21 points and 12 rebounds. Funderburke held the first-half fort, so that Skelton and Jackson could rally in the second half. OSU shot only 36 percent in the first half, and Funderburke's play kept OSU in the game. The final was 80-73, but closer than the points indicated.

It was still an extraordinary season for OSU, winning its first outright Big Ten title since 1971, and spending most of the season ranked in the top ten. The bad news is that the Bucks lose five seniors and perhaps Jackson, who could go to the NBA. The seniors—**Jamaal Brown**, Chris Jent, **Bill Robinson**, **Steve Hall**, and **Mark Baker**—were all recruited by Coach **Randy Ayers** when he was Gary Williams' assistant. Ayers has another good class of recruits coming in, and **Antonio Watson**, a 6-7 forward from Columbus Eastmoor who sat out the season because of failure to meet Proposition 48 requirements, will be eligible. The new group includes Ohio's two-time Mr. Basketball, **Greg Simpson** of Lima, Upper Arlington's **Nate Wilbourne**, a 6-11 center; **Charles "Killer" Macon**, a 6-7 forward who has been called the best prep basketball player in Indiana; and another Hoosier, **Gerald Eaker**, a 6-11 center. ▶

115

OSU, Team Records

		Team/Site	Date		
Most Points Scored, Ohio State	Pts.		Date		
	116	Delaware State/Columbus	11-28-90		
Most Points Scored, Opponents	Pts		Date		
	122	Indiana/Columbus	2-2-59		
Most Field Goals Made, Ohio State	FGM	Team/Site	Date	FGA	Pct.
	50	Delaware/Columbus	1-11-60	86	.581
Most Field Goals Made, Opponents	FGM	Team/Site	Date	FGA	Pct.
	50	Indiana/Columbus	2-2-59	79	.633
Most Field Goals Attempted, Ohio State	FGA	Team/Site	Date	FGM	Pct.
	103	Miami (FL)/Miami	12-21-53	44	.427
Most Field Goals Attempted, Opponents	FGA	Team/Site	Date	FGM	Pct.
	103	Illinois/Champaign	1-20-54	24	.233
Best Field Goal Percentage, Ohio State	Pct.	Team/Site	Date	FGM	FGA
	.723	Minnesota/Minneapolis	1-22-81	34	47
Best Field Goal Percentage, Opponents	Pct.	Team/Site	Date	FGM	FGA
	.696	Indiana/Bloomington	3-12-83	32	46
Most Free Throws Made, Ohio State	FTM	Team/Site	Date	FTA	Pct.
	38	Washington State/Columbus	12-21-68	45	.844
Most Free Throws Made, Opponents	FTM	Team/Site	Date	FTA	Pct.
	40	Indiana/Bloomington	3-5-55	56	.714
	40	Michigan State/East Lansing	3-24-83	45	.889
Most Free Throws Attempted, Ohio State	FTA	Team/Site	Date	FTM	Pct.
	56	Wisconsin/Madison	2-20-56	25	.446
Most Free Throws Attempted, Opponents	FTA	Team/Site	Date	FTM	Pct.
	56	Indiana/Bloomington	3-5-55	40	.714
Best Free Throw Percentage, Ohio State	Pct.	Team/Site	Date	FTA	FTM
	1.0	Iowa/Columbus	2-2-85	2	2
Best Free Throw Percentage, Opponents	Pct.	Team/Site	Date	FTA	FTM
	1.0	Minnesota/Columbus	1-19-74	21	21
Most Rebounds, Ohio State	REB	Team/Site	Date		
	75	Seton Hall/New York	12-27-60		
Most Rebounds, Opponents	REB	Team/Site	Date		
	85	Michigan State/East Lansing	1-19-59		
Most Personal Fouls, Ohio State	PF	Team/Site	Date		
	40	Purdue/Columbus	3-5-81		
Most Personal Fouls, Opponents	PF	Team/Site	Date		
	35	Michigan/Ann Arbor	1-27-68		
Most Assists, Ohio State	AST	Team/Site	Date		
	31	Michigan State/East Lansing	1-6-75		
Most Assists, Opponents	AST	Team/Site	Date		
	31	Indiana/Honolulu	12-28-74		
Most Blocked Shots, Ohio State	BLK	Team/Site	Date		
	15	Iowa/Columbus	2-23-80		
Most Blocked Shots, Opponents	BLK	Team/Site	Date		
	12	Florida/Gainesville	12-16-87		
Most Steals, Ohio State	ST	Team/Site	Date		
	20	Siena/Columbus	12-4-86		
Most Steals, Opponents	ST	Team/Site	Date		
	17	Arizona State/Tempe	12-20-80		
	17	Missouri-St. Louis/Columbus	11-28-87		
Most 3-Pt. Field Goals Made, Ohio State	FGM	Team/Site	Date	FGA	Pct.
	11	Florida/New York	12-27-88	18	.611
Most 3-Pt. Field Goals Made, Opponents	FGM	Team/Site	Date	FGA	Pct.
	11	Western Michigan/Columbus	12-2-87	15	.733
Best 3-Pt. Field Goals Pct., Ohio State	Pct.	Team/Site	Date	FGM	FGA
	1.0	Purdue/Columbus	3-5-83	3	3
Best 3-Pt. Field Goals Pct., Opponents	Pct.	Team/Site	Date	FGM	FGA
	.875	Illinois/Champaign	1-27-90	7	8
Most Overall Wins in a Season	27		1961		
	27		1991		
Most Regular Season Wins	25		1991		
Most Big Ten Wins	15		1991		
Most Games with OSU Score Over 100	7		1991		

Note: All-time non-collegiate points scored by Ohio State was 134 vs. North High in Columbus during the 1903-04 season.

Jimmy Jackson spent his OSU career as the team's focal point, this past season leading the conference in scoring with 22.5 points, and OSU in rebounding, 6.9 a game.

Jimmy Jackson: At the Top, and Counting

After *Jimmy Jackson's* cold hand in the NCAA Tournament, fans were leaving the boat, of course, but the cognoscenti were still carrying on the debate: How wide does Jim Jackson's talent range—is he the best since Clark Kellog, or could he possibly be the best since Jerry Lucas? And with OSU's stellar crop of young recruits, could he and teammate **Lawrence Funderburke** keep the Buckeyes at the top of the cage ladder? Indeed, the more appropriate question was: would he return for his senior season, as he indicated he'd prefer, or enter the NBA ranks early?

Part of the Buckeye's lategoing difficulties stemmed from the fact that as one writer put it, "they were known as the Jackson Five, a basketball team of one star and four backup singers." While Jackson struggled in the tournament, the backups—particularly Funderburke—began to emerge.

But even such a stern critic as ex-Buckeye Bobby Knight has called Jackson "marvelous." This, after Jackson, in what has been called "the greatest game ever played in St. John Arena," helped beat Indiana in double overtime in February of 1991. It was teammate **Treg Lee's** shot that won the game, 97-95, but the sophomore Jackson set it up, in a combination of split-second moves and positionings toward the basket that demonstrated his great court sense.

After being the Big Ten Freshman of the Year, followed by being the Big Ten Player of the Year as a sophomore, as well as All-American, Jackson will be a cinch to make the All-American team three years in a row should he decide to play his senior year.

A prep star at **Toledo Macomber**, Jackson was first a football player and there are those who thought his early skills as a tight end would have made him a collegiate All-American. But as a freshman on the Macomber basketball team, he was team leader playing with four seniors. Before he left Toledo, Jackson had won two Mr. Basketball awards and Macomber had won the state championship.

The reason, says Buckeye coach **Randy Ayers**, is Jackson's work ethic. There are still Toledo folks who recall seeing Jackson running across the bridges with weights wrapped around his ankles, or running the hills at Ottawa Park with his boots on, in the snow. It was routine for Jackson to shoot 1,000 jump shots a day. Jackson was gifted with a classic basketball player's physique—he's 6-6, 220 pounds, muscular, but with "soft" hands—a legacy from his family. His father and uncle were both tall, both All-City prep players in Toledo on a team that went to the state finals. Those who know, however, say it is Jackson's work ethic that has made him a contender for national player of the year. Says Ed Scrutchins, director of athletics for the Toledo Public Schools, "Somebody is giving you a crock of crap if they are taking credit for Jimmy being Jimmy. He is mostly Jimmy-taught. He watches, observes, works. He taught himself."

Ayers noted that Jackson needed just nine games to adjust to college basketball. Most players need at least a year. Thus almost from the time Jackson set foot in St. John Arena, he has been the Buckeye's leading scorer. But Jackson controls the game in ways other than scoring. He's a point guard who can get up court against pressure defenses, and then he can drop back as a number two guard and shoot from the three-point line. He can also be a small forward. Wrote one sportswriter, "He has a blue-collar approach that rolls straight out of his hometown of Toledo, Ohio." ▶

In March of 1958, **Xavier** was the first Ohio college team to win a National Invitation Basketball Tournament. Xavier did it by beating a neighbor from up the road, **Dayton**. The score was 78-74, and Xavier's **Hank Stein** was the tournament's MVP. When The Muskies got to Madison Square Garden seeded No. 12, no one had ever heard of them. Only two fans saw them off at the airport—but over 10,000 welcomed them back.

Source: Cincinnati Post

Basketball

Xavier University, The Record

1919-20	0-1	1954-55	13-13	1963-64	16-10	1985-86	25-5
1920-21	2-1			1964-65	11-15	**NCAA Tournament**	
1921-22	2-3	1955-56	17-11	1965-66	13-13	Xavier 80, Alabama 97	
1922-23	2-0	**NIT Tournament**		1966-67	13-13		
1923-24	12-4	Xavier 84, St. Louis 80		1967-68	10-16	1986-87	19-13
1924-25	6-7	Xavier 68, Dayton 72		1968-69	10-16	**NCAA Tournament**	
1925-26	10-8			1969-70	5-20	Xavier 70, Missouri 69	
1926-27	11-3	1956-57	20-8	1970-71	9-17	Xavier 60, Duke 65	
1927-28	8-1	**NIT Tournament**		1971-72	12-14		
1928-29	9-6	Xavier 85 Seton Hall 79		1972-73	3-23	1987-88	26-4
1929-30	8-8	Xavier 81, Bradley 116		1973-74	8-18	**NCAA Tournament**	
1030-31	10-3			1974-75	11-15	Xavier 72, Kansas 85	
1931-32	10-3	1957-58	19-11	1975-76	14-12		
1932-33	5-3	**NIT Tournament**		1976-77	10-17	1988-89	21-12
1933-34	9-1	Xavier 95, Niagara 86		1977-78	13-14	**NCAA Tournament**	
1934-35	14-4	Xavier 72, Bradley 62		1978-79	14-13	Xavier 87, Michigan 92	
1935-36	8-7	Xavier 72, St. Bonaventure 53		1979-80	8-18		
1936-37	7-7	Xavier 78, Dayton (Finals,		1980-81	12-16	1989-90	28-5
1937-38	10-9	OT) 74		1981-82	8-20	**NCAA Tournament**	
1938-39	13-7	NIT Champions				Xavier 87, Kansas State 79	
1939-40	7-16			1982-83	22-8	Xavier 74, Georgetown 71	
1940-41	13-9	1958-59	12-13	**NCAA Tournament**		Xavier 89, Texas 102	
1941-42	10-8	1959-60	17-9	Xavier 75, Alcorn St. 81			
1942-43	6-10					1990-91	22-10
1943-44	None	1960-61	17-10	1983-84	22-11	**NCAA Tournament**	
1944-45	None	**NCAA Tournament**		**NIT Tournament**		Xavier 89, Nebraska 84	
1945-46	3-16	Xavier 66, Morehead 71		Xavier 60, Ohio State (OT)		Xavier 50, Connecticut 66	
1946-47	8-17			57			
1947-48	24-8	1961-62	14-12	Xavier 58, Nebraska 57		Totals	852-728
1948-49	16-10			Xavier 62, Michigan 63		Percentage	.539
1949-50	12-16	1962-63	12-16				
1950-51	16-10	**National Catholic Tourn.**		1984-85	16-13		
1951-52	10-14	Xavier 80, Creighton 67					
1952-53	11-12	Xavier 89, St. Bonaventure					
1953-54	18-12	(finals) 75					

Xavier, The Coaches

Name	Seasons	Games	W-L	Percent
Pete Gillen	6(1985-91)	190	141-49	.747
Joe Meyer	13(1920-33)	145	95-50	.655
Jim McCafferty	6(1957-63)	162	91-71	.562
Ned Wulk	6(1951-57)	159	89-70	.560
Lew Hirt	5(1946-51)	137	76-61	.555
Clem Crowe	10(1933-43)	175	97-78	,554
Don Ruberg	4(1963-67)	104	53-51	.51l0
Bob Staak	6(1979-85)	174	88-86	.506
Tay Baker	6(1973-79)	159	70-89	.440
George Krajack	4(1967-71)	103	34-69	.330
Dick Campbell	2(1971-73)	52	15-37	.288
Ed Burns	1(1945-46)	19	3-16	.158
Harry Gilligan	1(1919-20)	1	0-1	.000

Pete, repeat

Almost overnight, it seemed, Pete Gillen came from nowhere and suddenly little-known Xavier was out of its midwestern shadows and into the bright lights of NCAA play.

The news in Cincinnati: Xavier —and Habit—Will Return

The big basketball news in Cincinnat in the winter of 1992 was that **Pete Gillen** and his **Xavier** Musketeers were NOT going to the NCAA Tournament. In Gillen's first six seasons, he steered Xavier into the NCAA Tournament six times. Only one other coach had ever done that—West Virginia's Fred Schaus (1955-1960). Thus Gillen had walked where such illuminaries as Bobby Knight and Dean Smith had not. The good news at the end of this uncharacteristic season was that Gillen's team was a young team and everybody would be coming back to repair the damage.

Before Gillen came to Xavier, its finest basketball moment was in 1958 when the Musketeers entered the NIT Tournament as bottom seed and ended by upsetting the then-powerful Dayton Flyers. The program had been a-building under Gillen's predecessor **Bob Staak**, and under Gillen, in his first job as head coach, it flew. In the 1990 NCAAs, Xavier was the surprise team, upsetting Kansas State, then—unimagineably—boffing superpower Georgetown to get into the third round against the University of Texas. When Gillen began the 1991-1992 season, he had a 141-49 record—a near 75 per cent winning ratio. He ranked fifth among the active Division I coaches in winning percentage.

Gillen's charm, however, does not come solely from his won-loss record; he's a former English major who knows the difference between a press and a participle, and with his East Coast background—Brooklyn Prep, Fairfield University—he carries a standing order of one-liners and aphorisms. On coaching, he might say, "Coaches are like fiddlers on the roof, if you'll allow me to be a little theatrical. It's shaky at best. You can be playing a pretty good tune but all of a sudden you could be in the drainage bin with leaves all around your neck." On finally ending a losing streak at Dayton, he said, "We haven't won at Dayton since before the Russian Revolution. Rasputin was in junior high school."

He was a walk-on at Fairfield University, the prototypical scrappy little guard. He earned a scholarship his junior year but his highest moment came when he coached his dorm's intramural team. "I was doing with them what I couldn't do myself on the court," he said.

Gillen paid his assistant dues with Rollie Massimino at Villanova, and with Digger Phelps at Notre Dame. It was big news in Cincinnati when, in 1991, Gillen turned down the head coaching job at Notre Dame. The sporting press had, as one writer observed, "all but passed the hat for his farewell watch," and when Gillen said "no," it was the surprise of the season.

Said John Fleischman" "In coaching, teethmarks are an occupational hazard. Pete Gillen doesn't think he did anything rash or irrational or even remarkable in refusing Notre Dame. He doesn't think he has worked any miracles at Xavier. Given the corruption he sees undermining college basketball today and his own belief in the imperfectability of human nature, Gillen regards disaster as always likely in the long run...In the short run, he plays to win."

Thus, consider the 1991-1992 season an aberration, the man who refers to himself as "Harvey Sweatsocks" will be back, knocking on the NCAA portals again. ▶

College basketball's *first instant replay* occurred at the University of Dayton Arena during 1984's first round play between Morehead State and North Carolina A&T. Official Mickey Crowley asked ESPN announcers to help determine which Aggie player would shoot from the foul line by rerunning the play. The Aggies won 69-68, and the NCAA enacted the "Crowley Rule," banning instant replay.

Xavier, The Statistics

1. Most points, game—Steve Thomas, 50, vs. Detroit, 1964
2. Most points, career—Byron Larkin, 2,696, 1984-88
3. Highest point average, season—Steve Thomas, 30, 1963-64
4. Most rebounds, game—Bob Pelkington, 31, vs. St. Francis, 1964
5. Most rebounds, career—Tyrone Hill, 1,380, 1986-90
6. Highest rebound average, season—Bob Pelkington, 21.8, 1963-64 (led nation)
7. Most assists, game—Keith Walker, 18, vs. Detroit, 1980
8. Most steals, game—Jamal Walker, 8, vs. Fordham, 1991
9. Most blocks, game—Dave Payton (1978) and Aaron Williams (1990), 7
10. Highest free throw percentage, game—Steve Thomas, 16-16 vs. Canisius, 1964
11. Most personal fouls, season—Aaron Williams, 115, 1990-91
12. Team points, game—125 vs. Florida International, 1988

Basketball

University of Dayton, The Record

1903-04	5-1	1950-51	27-5	1956-57	19-9	1965-66	23-6
1904-05	6-1	**NIT Tournament**		**NIT Tournament**		**NCAA Tournament**	
1905-06	7-2	UD 77, Lawrence Tech 71		Dayton 79, St. Peter's 71		UD 58, Miami 51	
1906-07	14-0	UD 74, Arizona 68		Temple 77, Dayton 66		Kentucky 86, UD 79 (Second	
1907-08	10-3	UD 69, St. John's 62 (OT)				round)	
1908-09	12-2	Brigham Young 62, UD 43		1957-58	25-4	Western Kentucky 82,	
1909-10	5-6	(Final)		**NIT Tournament**		Dayton 68 (Consolation)	
1910-11	10-0			Dayton 74, Fordham 70			
1911-12	13-0	1951-52	28-5	Dayton 80, St. John's 56		1966-67	25-6
1912-13	11-0	**NIT Tournament**		Xavier 78, Dayton 74		**NCAA Tournament**	
1913-14	5-4	Dayton 81, New York U. 66		(OT)(Final)		Dayton 69, Western	
1914-15	4-4	Dayton 68, St. Louis 58				Kentucky, 67 (OT)	
1915-16	11-2	Dayton 69, St. Bonaventure		1958-59	14-12	Dayton 53, Tennessee 52	
1916-17	8-3	62				(Second round)	
1917-18	2-4	LaSalle 75, Dayton 64 (Final)		1959-60	21-7	Dayton 71, Virginia Tech 66	
1918-19	3-4			**NIT Tournament**		(OT)(Regional finals)	
1919-20	5-8	**NCAA Tournament**		Dayton 72, Temple 51		Dayton 76, North Carolina	
1920-21	6-16	Illinois 80, Dayton 61 (First		Bradley 78, Dayton 64		62 (Semi-finals)	
1921-22	6-8	round)				UCLA 79, Dayton 64 (Finals)	
1922-23	9-7	Dayton 77, Princeton 61		1960-61	20-9		
1923-24	3-5	(Second round)		**NIT Tournament**		1967-68	21-9
1924-25	9-11			Dayton 62, Temple 60		**NIT Tournament**	
1925-26	7-8	1952-53	16-13	St. Louis 67, Dayton 60		Dayton 87, West Virginia 68	
1926-27	10-9			Holy Cross 85, Dayton 76		Dayton 61, Fordham 60	
1927-28	11-5	1953-54	25-7			Dayton 76, Notre Dame 74	
1928-29	9-10	**NIT Tournament**		1961-62	24-6	Dayton 61, Kansas 48 (Final)	
1929-30	4-14	Dayton 90, Manhattan 79		**NIT Tournament**		NIT Championship	
1930-31	2-15	Niagara 77, Dayton 74		Dayton 79, Wichita 71			
1931-32	3-12			Dayton 94, Houston 77		1968-69	20-7
1932-33	7-7	1954-55	25-4	Dayton 98, Loyola (Chicago)		**NCAA Tournament**	
1933-34	9-7	**NIT Tournament**		82		Colorado State 52, Dayton	
1934-35	4-11	Dayton 97, St. Louis 81		Dayton 73, St. John's 67		50	
1935-36	3-13	Dayton 79, St. Francis 73		(Final)			
1936-37	7-12	(OT)		NIT Championship		1969-70	19-8
1937-38	6-11	Duquesne 70, Dayton 58				**NCAA Tournament**	
1938-39	2-12	(Final)		1962-63	16-10	Houston 71, Dayton 64	
1939-40	4-17			1963-64	15-10		
1940-41	9-14	1955-56	25-4			1970-71	18-9
1941-42	12-6	**NIT Tournament**		1964-65	22-7	**NIT Tournament**	
1942-43	9-8	Dayton 72, Xavier 68		**NCAA Tournament**		Duke 68, UD 60	
1943-44	None	Dayton 89, St. Francis 58		Michigan 98, Dayton 71			
1944-45	None	Louisville 93, Dayton 80		(Second round)		1971-72	13-13
1945-46	3-13	(Final)		Dayton 75, DePaul 69		1972-73	13-13
1946-47	4-17			(Consolation)			
1947-48	12-14						
1948-49	16-14						
1949-50	24-8						

1973-74	20-9

NCAA Tournament
Dayton 88, Los Angeles St. 80
UCLA 11, Dayton 100 (3 OT)(Second round)
New Mexico 66, Dayton 61 (Consolation)

1974-75	10-16
1975-76	14-13
1976-77	16-11

1977-78	19-10

NIT Tournament
Dayton 108, Fairfield 93
Georgetown 71, Dayton 62

1978-79	19-10

NIT Tournament
Dayton 105, Holy Cross 81
Purdue 84, Dayton 70

1979-80	13-14

1980-81	18-11

NIT Tournament
Dayton 66, Fordham 65 (2 OT)
Purdue 50, Dayton 46

1981-82	21-9

NIT Tournament
Dayton 76, Connecticut 75 (OT)
Dayton 61, Illinois 58
Oklahoma 91, Dayton 82

1982-83	18-10

1983-84	21-11

NCAA Tournament
Dayton 74, LSU 66
Dayton 89, Oklahoma 85 (Second round)
Dayton 64, Washington 58 (Regional West)
Georgetown 61, Dayton 49 (Regional Finals West)

1984-85	19-10

NCAA Tournament
Villanova 51, Dayton 49

1985-86	17-13

NIT Tournament
McNeese State 86, Dayton 75

1986-87	13-15
1987-88	13-18
1988-89	12-17

1989-90	22-10

NCAA Tournament
Dayton 88, Illinois 86
Arkansas 86, Dayton 84 (Second round Midwest)

1990-91	14-15

Totals	*1,120-753*
Percentage	*.598*

UD, The Coaches

Name	Seasons	W-L	Percent
Father William O'Malley	1909-11	15-6	.714
Harry Solimano	1911-14, 1919-20	34-12	.739
Al Mahrt	1913-15, 1918-19	9-12	.429
Alfred McCray	1915-17	19-5	.791
Dutch Thiele	1920-21	6-16	.273
William Sherry	1921-22	6-8	.429
Van Hill	1922-23	9-7	.563
Harry Baujan	1923-28	46-38	.548
George Fitzgerald	1928-29	9-10	.474
Bill Belanich	1929-33	16-48	.250
Louis Tschudi	1933-35	13-18	.419
Joe Holsinger	1935-39	18-48	.273
James Carter	1939-43, 1945-47	41-75	.353
Tom Blackburn	1947-64	352-141	.714
Don Donoher	1964-89	437-275	.614
Jim O'Brien	1989-	36-25	.590

UD, The Statistics

1. Most points, game—Donald Smith, 52, vs. Loyola, 1973
2. Most points, career—Roosevelt Chapman, 2,233, 1980-84
3. Highest point average, season—Henry Finkel, 25.3, 1964-65
4. Most rebounds, game—Garry Roggenburk, 32, vs. Miami(OH), 1959
5. Most rebounds, career—John Horan, 1,341, 1951-55
6. Highest rebound average, season—Don May, 16.7, 1966-67
7. Most assists, game—Negele Knight, 15, vs. Xavier, 1990
8. Most steals, game—Jack Zimmerman, 9, vs. Seton Hall, 1977
9. Most blocks, game—Erv Giddings, 6, vs. Youngstown State, 1977
10. Highest free throw percentage, game—Henry Finkel, 15-15, vs. Canisius, 1965
11. Most personal fouls, season—Don Meineke, 140, 1951-52
12. Team points, game—124 vs. Portland, 1967

One of the great all-time college shooters, Bevo Francis made second-team All-America his freshman year, then went on to score 3,272 points in only two seasons of play.

Assorted Ohio National Basketball Records

NCAA overtime record: seven, **Cincinnati** over Bradley, 75-73, December 21, 1881

Most points scored in a NCAA tournament regional game: 56, by **Oscar Robertson**, Cincinnati, vs. Arkansas in the 1958 Midwest regional

Most points scored in an NCAA tournament game: 61, by Austin Carr of Notre Dame, in 112-82 win over **Ohio**, first round, March 7, 1970

First time the majority of players in the NCAA title game are black: 1963, when Loyola (four) plays **Cincinnati** (three). Loyola wins in overtime, 60-58.

Longest college basketball game: **Cincinnati** over Bradley, 75-73, seven overtimes. The game began on December 21, 1981, and ended on December 22.

NCAA Division II Men's all-time individual leader: **Bevo Francis**, 113 points, Rio Grande vs. Hillsdale, 1954.

Division II season scoring average: 46.5 points, **Bevo Francis**, Rio Grande, 1954.

Division I record for highest overall free-throw percentage during the 1980s: **Ohio State**, 74.61.

Largest margin of victory for an NBA team: **Cleveland Cavaliers'** 68-point spread in a 148–80 win over the Miami Heat, 1991. ▶

The Rio Grande Story

Bevo Francis once scored 116 points in a game—three more than his enduring 38-year-old record—but the NCAA disallowed it because **Rio Grande College** was playing a junior college. Bevo was only a freshman, and he averaged 50.1 points a game and the NCAA didn't allow that, either.

Next year, though, Coach **Newt Oliver** scheduled Wake Forest, Villanova, Miami, Butler, Providence, and the like—and played some of them in Madison Square Garden. Bevo hit 113 that year, and averaged 46.5, and both still stand as Division II records. He was 6-9 and had a fadeaway jump shot "that was so soft it would sit on the rim until it fell in," said one writer.

Rio Grande not only scheduled the competition, it beat them. The little college from nowhere took Villanova into overtime and beat Provi-

dence the next night. It also beat Creighton and Wake Forest. Rio Grande beat Wake Forest in the final seconds, 67-65, on Francis's soft shot at the top of the key. The fans, said Oliver, "sounded like 100 women at a bargain sale of summer shoes." The night Francis scored 113 against Hillsdale, he was 37-42 free throws. The team finished 21-7.

Francis was a poor Wellsville kid whose scholarship consisted of $75 a month for groceries and $35 for a furnished apartment. He also had a campus job that paid fifty cents an hour. He was married, and after two seasons, he quit school. He played awhile in the pros but never liked the travel and soon came home. He was tired of basketball. Said his coach, Oliver, "He was the greatest shooter I ever saw." ▶

University of Cincinnati, The Record

1901-02	0-1	1947-48	17-7	1960-61	27-3	1970-71	14-12
1902-03	4-4	1948-49	23-5	**NCAA Tournament**		1971-72	17-9
1903-04	4-5	1949-50	20-6	UC 78, Texas Tech 56		1972-73	17-9
1904-05	6-3			UC 69, Kansas 64 (Midwest			
1905-06	2-0	1950-51	18-4	regional)		1973-74	19-8
1906-07	7-2	**NIT Tournament**		UC 82, Utah 67		**NIT Tournament**	
1907-08	9-0	St. Bonaventure 70, UC 67		UC 70, Ohio State 65		Boston College 63, UC 62	
1908-09	6-4	(OT)		(OT)(Finals)			
1909-10	3-2			NCAA National Champion-		1974-75	23-6
1910-11	3-6	1951-52	11-16	ship		**NCAA Tournament**	
1911-12	2-9	1952-53	11-13			UC 87, Texas A&M 79	
1912-13	4-7	1953-54	11-10	1961-62	29-2	Louisville 78, UC 63	
1913-14	2-8			**NCAA Tournament**		UC 95, Notre Dame 87	
1914-15	3-8	1954-55	21-8	UC 66, Creighton 46			
1915-16	1-9	**NIT Tournament**		UC 73, Colorado 46		1975-76	25-6
1916-17	3-8	UC 85, Niagara 83 (2 OT)		(Midwest regional)		**NCAA Tournament**	
1917-18	2-6	Duquesne 65, UC 51		UC 72, UCLA 70		Notre Dame 79, UC 78	
1918-19	3-11	UC 96, St. Francis 91		UC 71, Ohio State 59 (Finals)			
1919-20	5-9			NCAA National Champion-		1976-77	25-5
1920-21	10-11	1955-56	17-7	ship		**NCAA Tournament**	
1921-22	15-8					Marquette 66, UC 51	
1922-23	13-9	1956-57	15-9	1962-63	26-2		
1923-24	11-8	**NIT Tournament**		**NCAA Tournament**		1977-78	17-10
1924-25	5-14	St. Bonaventure 90, UC 72		UC 73, Texas 68		1978-79	13-14
1925-26	17-2			UC 67, Colorado 60		1979-80	13-15
1926-27	13-5	1957-58	25-3	(Midwest regional)		1980-81	16-13
1927-28	14-4	**NCAA Tournament**		UC 80, Oregon State 46		1981-82	15-12
1928-29	13-4	Kansas State 83, UC 80 (OT)		Loyola (Ill.) 60, UC 58		1982-83	11-17
1929-30	14-4	UC 97, Arkansas 62		(OT)(Finals)		1983-84	3-25
1930-31	2-15					1984-85	17-14
1931-32	4-11	1958-59	26-4	1963-64	17-9	1985-86	12-16
1932-33	9-9	**NCAA Tournament**		1964-65	14-12	1986-87	12-16
1933-34	12-7	UC 77, Texas Christian 73				1987-88	15-12
1934-35	16-3	UC 85, Kansas State 75		1965-66	21-7	1988-89	15-12
1935-36	10-7	(Midwest regional)		**NCAA Tournament**		1989-90	20-14
1936-37	9-10	California 64, UC 58		Texas-El Paso 78, UC 76 (OT)			
1937-38	6-11	UC 98, Louisville 85		Southern Methodist 89, UC		1990-91	18-12
1938-39	12-5			84		**NIT Tournament**	
1939-40	8-9	1959-60	28-2	1966-67	17-9	UC 82, Ball State 55	
1940-41	6-12	**NCAA Tournament**		1967-68	18-8	Oklahoma 89, UC 81 (OT)	
1941-42	10-10	UC 99, Depaul 59		1968-69	17-9		
1942-43	9-10	UC 82, Kansas 71 (Midwest				1991-92	29-5
1943-44	6-5	regional)		1969-70	21-6	**NCAA Tournament**	
1944-45	8-9	California 77, UC 69		**NIT Tournament**		UC 85, Delaware 47	
1945-46	8-13	UC 95, New York U. 71		Army 72, UC 67		UC 77, Michigan State 65	
1946-47	17-9					UC 69, UTEP 67	
						UC 88, Memphis State 57	
						Michigan 76, UC 72	

Totals   **1168-754**
Percentage   **.608**

Oscar Robertson was such a dominant figure in basketball that when he went from UC to the NBA, his assists record—9,887—wasn't broken for 17 years. Magic Johnson finally did it last year. Johnson popularized the triple-double stat—double figures in points, rebounds, and assists—but it was Robertson who invented it. Back in 1961, for instance, Robertson averaged a triple double for the entire season: 30.8 points, 12.4 rebounds, and 11.3 assists.

UC, The Coaches

Name	Seasons	W-L	Percent
Henry S. Pratt	1901-02	0-1	.000
Anthony W. Chez	1902-04	8-9	.471
Amos Foster	1904-09	30-9	.769
C.A. Schroetter	1909-10	3-2	.600
Russ Easton	1910-14	11-30	.268
George Little	1914-16	4-17	.190
Ion Cortright	1916-17	3-8	.273
Whitelaw Morrison	1917-18	2-6	.250
Boyd Chambers	1918-28	106-81	.567
Frank Rice	1928-32	33-34	.493
John Halliday	1932-33	9-8	.529
Tay Brown	1933-37	47-27	.635
Walter Van Winklw	1937-39	18-16	.529
Clark Ballard	1939-42	24-31	.436
Bob Ruess	1942-44	15-15	.500
Ray Farnham	1944-46	16-22	.421
John Wiethe	1946-52	106-47	.693
George Smith	1952-60	154-56	.733
Ed Jucker	1960-65	113-28	.801
Tay Baker	1965-72	125-60	.676
Gale Catlett	1972-78	126-44	.741
Ed Badger	1978-83	68-71	.489
Tony Yates	1983-89	70-100	.412
Bob Huggins	1989-	38-26	.584

UC, The Statistics

1. Most points, game—Oscar Robertson, 62, vs. North Texas State, 1959-60
2. Most points, career—Oscar Robertson, 2,973, 1958-60
3. Highest point average, season—Oscar Robertson, 35.1, 1957-58
4. Most rebounds, game—Connie Dierking, 33, vs. Loyola (La.), 1956-57
5. Most rebounds, career—Oscar Robertson, 1,338, 1958-60
6. Highest rebound average, season—Connie Dierking, 18.8, 1956-57
7. Most assists, game—Eddie Lee, 15, vs. Seton Hall, 1978-79
8. Most steals, game—Brian Williams, 6, vs. Kent State, 1976-77
9. Most blocks, game—Rick Roberson, 10, vs. Bradley, 1966-67
10. Highest free throw percentage, game—Oscar Robertson, 14-14, vs. Xavier, 1957-58
11. Most personal fouls, season—Keith Starks, 128, 1989-90
12. Team points, game—127, vs. North Texas State, 1957-58

Bob Huggins, a three-time All-Ohio player in high school, learned the sport by playing for his father. He began the 1990-91 season ranked 24th among all active college coaches with a winning percentage of .678–206-98.

Cincinnati Bearcats: The 1992 NCAA Cinderella Team

The 1992 NCAA dream died hard in Cincinnati, but die it did, precisely as the oddsmakers had predicted. The River City upstarts, having not seen such bright lights since the glory days of the early 1960s when UC teams made the Final Four five straight years, came within a sliver of getting into the title game. But Michigan's hearty freshmen and their height advantage controlled the rebounding and wore down the seven-point lead a gallant UC held with 15 minutes left. Final: 76-72.

The game was appropriately summed up by writer Tim Sullivan: "In the midst of a mismatch, in a game that might easily have been a blowout, the little club from Clifton scratched and scraped and scared the living twlight out of Michigan's Fab Five..."

The Bearcats created 12 turnovers and eight steals in the first half, leading 41-38. But in the second half, the superior Michigan size began to tell. The 'Cats caused only five turnovers the second half, and could never adequately stop the Wolverines inside. Still, with 1:57 to go, **Nicky Van Excel's** 22-foot three-pointer made it 70-67. Unfortunately, that was as close as it would be.

UC's season was still a triumph of teamwork—there were five newcomers in a nine-man rotation—coaching agility, perseverance, and good fortune. The Bearcats came through their field by strong wins, but also by way of upsets to the higher seeds. They were out of a new conference, as well. Said one analyst, "The Great Midwest sounds like a railroad."

The team leader was take-charge 6-3 guard **Anthony Buford**, who followed coach **Bob Huggins** to UC from Akron. Huggins recruited Buford in Flint, Michigan, by shooting baskets with him in a driveway. He was joined by starting center, 6-10 **Corie**

Blount, a junior college transfer, **Terry Nelson, Herb Jones, Erik Martin,** Van Excel, et al., seven juco transfers in all. This brought media "whispers" that UC had an outlaw program, rumors dispelled by the players' backgrounds and demeanor on and off the court.

Throughout the tournament, Huggins wore the same double-breasted brown suit, which he promised to Arnies Bar and Grill fpr an auction. He also wore the same courtside characteristic, which was, usually, apoplectic. Buford recalled Huggins at Akron smashing stools and breaking chalkboards, and the equipment manager cleared the dressing room of breakables before halftime. Said Buford, "I've seen him break three Rolex watches." Said Huggins, "There was a guy in Akron who used to get them for me for $20 a pop."

Huggins, a coach's son from Gnadenhutton, Ohio, had brought UC basketball back to national attention, something it had little familiarity with since **Ed Jucker** won the national title in 1961 and 1962—upsets over OSU, the only times teams from the same state played for the national title—then lost it to Loyola of Chicago in overtime in 1963. And before Jucker, George Smith's teams went 7-3 in the NCAAs, finishing second and fourth in the nation. It was Smith who coached one of the game's great basketball legends, **Oscar Robertson**, who was then the dominant figure in the college game. He averaged 32.6 points a game in 1958, and 33.7 the next year, then went on to a brilliant professional career. The Big O was such a dominant figure that no other Bearcat has come within 1,000 points of his scoring total—**Roger McLendon's** career 1,789 (1985-88) is closest to Robertson's 2,973. ▶

Wright State University, The Record

1970-71	7-17	WSU 69, Northern Michigan 70	WSU 92, District of Columbia 73 (Finals)	1986-87	20-8
1971-72	9-14			1987-88	16-11
1972-73	17-5	WSU 96, Indiana State-Evansville 89	NCAA Division II National Championship	1988-89	17-11
1973-74	17-8			1989-90	21-7
1974-75	15-10			1990-91	19-9
1975-76	20-8	**1981-82** 22-7	**1983-84** 19-9		
1976-77	11-16	**NCAA Division II Tournament**		**Totals**	**392-182**
1977-78	14-13		**1984-85** 22-7	**Percentage**	**.617**
1978-79	20-8	WSU 71, Kentucky Wesleyan 76 (OT)	**NCAA Tournament** WSU 61, Lewis 53		
1979-80	25-3	WSU 87, Bellarmine 86 (2OT)	WSU 72, Kentucky Wesleyan 84		

1979-80   25-3
NCAA Division II Tournament
WSU 75, Northern Michigan 66
WSU 68, St. Joseph's 73

1980-81   25-4
NCAA Division II Tournament
WSU 96, Kentucky Wesleyan 76

1982-83   28-4
NCAA Division II Tournament
WSU 69, Kentucky Wesleyan 67
WSU 73, Bloomsburg State 53
WSU 57, Cal State-Bakersfield 50

1985-86   28-3
NCAA Tournament
WSU 94, Kentucky Wesleyan 84
WSU 77, SIU-Edwardsville 73
WSU 75, Cheyney 78

Wright State Coaches

Name	Seasons	W-L	Percent
John Ross	1970-75	65-54	.546
Marcus Jackson	1975-77	45-37	.548
Ralph Underhill	1978-	282-91	.756

Wright State, The Statistics

1. Most points, game—Mark Vest, 43, vs. Marycrest, 1984
2. Most points, career—Bob Schaefer, 1,634, 1975-79
3. Highest point average, season—Rodney Benson, 21.9, 1980-81
4. Most rebounds, season—Rondey Robinson, 299, 1988-89
5. Most rebounds, career—Jim Minch, 784, 1970-74
6. Most rebounds, game—Sean Hammonds, 21, vs. Chicago State
7. Most assists, game—Lenny Lyons, 15, vs. Kentucky Wesleyan, and vs. Kentucky State, 1986
8. Most steals, season—Rick Martin, 103, 1974-75
9. Most free throws, game—Bob Schaefer, 13, vs. Wittenberg, 1977
10. Highest free throw percentage, game—Eddie Crowe, 12-12, St. Joseph's, 1978
11. Most personal fouls, season—Grant Marion, 111, 1985-86
12. Team points, game—133, vs. Northeastern Illinois, 1979

Basketball

Cleveland State, The Record

1965-66	4-14	1979-80	18-8	1986-87	25-8	1988-89	18-10
1966-67	8-13	1980-81	18-9	*NIT Tournament*		1989-90	15-13
1967-68	7-15	1981-82	17-10	CSU 92, Tenn-Chattanooga		1990-91	12-16
1968-69	12-14	1982-83	8-20	73			
1970-71	5-20	1983-84	14-16	CSU 77, Illinois State 79		*Totals*	*(as CSU)*
1971-72	8-18	1984-85	21-8				*321-338*
1972-73	9-14			1987-88	22-8	*Percentage*	*.487*
1973-74	6-20	1985-86	29-4	*NIT Tournament*			
1974-75	13-11	*NCAA Tournament*		CSU 89, Illinois State 83			*(overall)*
1975-76	6-19	CSU 83, Indiana 79		CSU 80, OSU 86			*488-723*
1976-77	11-16	CSU 75, St. Joseph's 69				*Percentage*	*.403*
1977-78	12-13	CSU 70, Navy 71					
1978-79	15-10						

Cleveland State, The Statistics

1. Most points, game—49, Frank Edwards vs. Xavier, 1981
2. Most points, career—2,256, Ken McFadden, 1985-89
3. Most points, season—708, Ken McFadden, 1986-87(soph)
4. Most rebounds, game—30, Weldon Kytle vs. Malone, 1965
5. Most rebounds, career—1,241, Weldon Kytle, 1961-65
6. Highest rebound average, season—18.5, Weldon Kytle, 1962-63
7. Most assists, game—16, Ken McFadden vs. Northern Iowa, 1989
8. Most steals, game—12, Kenny Robertson vs. Wagner, 1988
9. Best field goal percentage, career—.661 (323 of 489), Brian Parker, 1988-90
10. Most free throws, game—19, Mike Campbell vs. Buffalo State, 1967
11. Most personal fouls, team, season—722, 1987-88
12. Team points, game—135, vs. Clarion, 1986

Humble origins

Weldon Kytle, after nearly three decades, still holds a lion's share of CSU records. He is fifth on the scoring list, with 1,408 points.

How Cleveland State Came to be Called Cleveland State

Cleveland State's basketball history began in 1929 when little **Fenn College** played its first game, losing to Hiram College, 27-18. For the next 36 years, except for two years during World War II, the Fenn Foxes played on a variety of courts, from YMCAs and high school gyms to the Cleveland Arena. They came in as winners, and went out the same way—the Foxes were .500 or better in each of their first and last three seasons—but there were only two winning seasons in the intervening 28 years. A half-dozen varsity records established by Fenn players and teams survive, however—**Weldon Kytle**, for example, still holds the top five single-game rebounding records—and three of the university's 20 leading scorers are Foxes, even though the Vikings play nearly twice as many games in a career. The Fenn era ended with the 1964-65 season, when all Fenn records were carried over and lettermen were recognized as CSU monogram winners.

Source: Cleveland State University basketball media guide, 1991-92

Ohio Basketball, 1992

University of Akron basketball

Mid-Continent Conference (men)
North Star Conference (women)

	W	L	Pct.	Coach
Men				
Season	16	12	.571	Coleman Crawford
Conf.	10	6	.625	
Women				
Season	6	22	.214	Lisa Fitch
Conf.	3	9	.250	

Titles
Men: None
Women: None

Records Set
Men: Mark Albert, set two MCC records for three-point field goals this season. The first was for most in a single game (Akron defeating Wright State, 89-86 in 2OT, Feb. 8, 1992) in which he had eleven. The second was for most in a single season: 110 out of 256 attempts (averaging 3.9 per game). At the end of the regular season, Albert was also second in NCAA records for most 3 pt. goals in a season. This may change, however, by the end of this year's tournament.

Women: Angela Harris was named to the second All-North Star Conference Team for '92.

Bowling Green State University basketball

Mid-American Conference

	W	L	Pct.	Coach
Men				
Season	14	15	.483	Jim Larranaga
Conf.	8	8	.500	
Women				
Season	24	5	.827	Jaci Clark
Conf.	14	2	.875	

Titles
Men: None
Women: None

Records Set
Men: None
Women: None

Cleveland State University basketball

Mid-Continent Conference
North Star Conference

	W	L	Pct.	Coach
Men				
Season	16	13	.552	Mike Boyd
Conf.	7	9	.438	
Women				
Season	8	21	.276	Loretta Hummeldorf
Conf.	4	8	.333	

Titles
Men: None
Women: None

Records Set
Men: None
Women: In 1992, the women's team broke the North Star Conference record for free throws attempted in a season with 899.

University of Dayton basketball

Midwestern Collegiate Conference

	W	L	Pct.	Coach
Men				
Season	15	16	.484	Jim O'Brien
Conf.	5	5	.500	
Women				
Season	10	18	.357	Sue Ramsey
Conf.	4	8	.333	

Titles
Men: None
Women: None

Records Set
Men: None
Women: None

Kent State University basketball

Mid-American Conference

	W	L	Pct.	Coach
Men				
Season	9	19	.321	Jim McDonald
Conf.	6	10	.375	
Women				
Season	18	12	.600	Bob Lindsay
Conf.	10	6	.625	

Titles
Men: None
Women: Kent State women were runners-up for the MAC Tournament Championship after losing to Toledo, 78-57, in the final game (March 14, 1992).

Records Set
Men: None
Women: None

Ohio University basketball

Mid-American Conference

	W	L	Pct.	Coach
Men				
Season	18	10	.643	Larry Hunter
Conf.	10	6	.625	
Women				
Season	11	17	.393	Marsha Reall
Conf.	5	11	.312	

Titles
Men: None
Women: None

Records Set
Men: None
Women: None

Miami University basketball

Mid-American Conference

	W	L	Pct.	Coach
Men				
Season	23	8	.742	Joby Wright
Conf.	13	3	.813	
Women				
Season	14	14	.500	Linda Wunder
Conf.	9	7	.562	

Titles
Men: In 1992 Miami won both the MAC League and Tournament (by defeating Ball State, 58-57) champion in basketball.

In 1992 Miami participated in the NCAA playoffs but was knocked out of the first round by North Carolina (68-63).
Women: None

Records Set
Men: Mike Williams set a new MAC record for field goal percentage in a season (.693).
Women: None

University of Toledo basketball

Mid-American Conference

	W	L	Pct.	Coach
Men				
Season	7	20	.259	Larry Gipson
Conf.	3	13	.188	
Women				
Season	26	6	.812	Bill Fennelly
Conf.	15	1	.937	

Titles
Men: None
Women: The TU women were MAC Regular Season and Tournament Champions in 1992. They defeated Kent State in the final tournament game 78-57, March 14, 1992.

They also went to the NCAA Women's Tournament in which they won the 1st round at Providence (74-64, 3/18/92) and lost the second round to Maryland (60-73, 3/21/92).

Records Set
Men: None
Women: None

Wright State University basketball

Mid-Continent Conference (men)
North Star Conference (women)

	W	L	Pct.	Coach
Men				
Season	15	13	.536	Ralph Underhill
Conf.	9	7	.562	
Women				
Season	8	20	.286	Terry Hall
Conf.	5	7	.417	

Titles
Men: None
Women: None

Records Set
Men: None
Women: None

Xavier University basketball

Midwestern Collegiate Conference (men)
North Star Conference (women)

	W	L	Pct.	Coach
Men				
Season	15	12	.556	Pete Gillen
Conf.	7	3	.700	
Women				
Season	19	10	.655	Mark Ehlen
Conf.	9	3	.750	

Titles
Men: None
Women:Xavier was the North Star Conference regular
season champion in 1992 and runner-up for tourna-
ment champion after losing the final game to Notre
Dame (59-54). Xavier Women also recorded the
university's best overall record basketball (19/10) and
North Star Conference record (9/3).

Records Set
Men: None
Women:None (other than the school record of most
wins in a season)

Youngstown State University basketball

Independent*

	W	L	Pct.	Coach
Men	6	22	.214	John Stroia
Women	19	9	.678	Ed DiGregorio

Titles
Men: None
Women: None

Records Set

Men: None
Women: None

*1992 will be Youngstown State's last season as an
independent. They will become part of the Mid-
Continent/North Star conference next year.

OSU Track

Indoor Records

Event	Record	Athlete(s)	Date
55-Meter Hurdles	7.24	Dan Oliver	2/10/79
		Alvin Taylor	1979
55-Meter Dash	6.15	George Nicholas	3/10/84
200-Meter Dash	21.40	Aaron Payne	2/2/91
300-Meter Dash	33.80	Zoraba Ross	1987
400-Meter Dash	46.66	Butch Reynolds	2/28/86
440-Yard Dash	46.57	Butch Reynolds	1987
500-Meter Dash	1:00.86	Butch Reynolds	1987
600-Yard Run	1:06.87	Butch Reynolds	1987
600-Meter Run	1:18.07	Keeon Gregory	1988
800-Meter Run	1:49.23	Mike Anderson	2/2/85
1,000-Meter Run	2:26.04	Mark Croghan	1/26/91
1,500-Meter Run	3:46.59	Glenn Klassa	3/9/85
One-Mile Run	4:02.10	Glenn Klassa	1985
3,000-Meter Run	8:01.60	Mark Croghan	1/26/91
5,000-Meter Run	14:14.07	Mark Croghan	2/24/90
High Jump	7-3 1/2	Mark Cannon	2/22/91
Long Jump	26-3	Joe Greene	3/10/90
Triple Jump	55 1/4	Joe Greene	3/11/89
Pole Vault	16-10 3/4	Paul Huzyak	2/10/90
Shot Put	70-1 3/4	Kevin Akins	2/13/82
4 x 400-Meter Relay	3:06.71	Green, Gregory, Ross, Reynolds	3/8/86
(oversized)	3:10.22	Green, Gregory, Ross, Reynolds	3/8/86
4 x 800-Meter Relay	7:31.6	Simko, Rider, Buckhannon, Crane	1979
Sprint Medley Relay	3:29.64	Scruggs, Broughton, Baseer, Anderson	1983
Distance Medley Relay	9:51.7	Anderson, Baseer, Golias, Hatch	2/4/84
One-Mile Relay	3:09.32	Reed, Gregory, Ross, Reynolds	1987

Outdoor Records

Event	Record	Athlete	Date
110-Meter Hurdles	13.62	Dan Oliver	1979
400-Meter Hurdles	49.2	Glenn Davis	1958
100-Meter Dash	10.2	Jesse Owens	1936
200-Meter Dash	20.46	Butch Reynolds	1987
400-Meter Dash	44.10	Butch Reynolds	1987
800-Meter Run	1:46.60	Scott Rider	1982
1,500-Meter Run	3:37.5	Tom Byers	1974
One-Mile Run	4:00.1	Tom Byers	1974
3,000-Meter Stplchs.	8:10.69	Mark Croghan	7/17/91
5,000-Meter Run	13:49.0	Steve Crane	1979
10,000-Meter Run	29:57.6	Robin Smith	4/10/76
High Jump	7-2 1/2	Mark Cannon	4/21/91
Long Jump	27-7 1/4	Joe Greene	1989
Triple Jump	55-4 3/4	Joe Greene	6/16/89
Pole Vault	16-11 1/2	Paul Huzyak	4/13/91
Shot Put	69-9 1/2	Kevin Akins	1982
Discus	178-3	Kevin Akins	5/8/82
Javelin	203-2	John Butya	1973
Decathlon	7,456 pts	Ray Hupp	1971
4 x 100-Meter Relay	39.93	Reed, Holland, Banks, Reynolds	5/23/86
4 x 200-Meter Relay	1:24.01	Hughes, Ross, Gregory, Reynolds	1987
4 x 400-Meter Relay	3:02.32	Gregory, Reed, Ross, Reynolds	1987
4 x 800-Meter Relay	7:26.66	Gregory, Ross, Langer, Klassa	4/5/86
4 x 1,500-Meter Relay	15:58.1	Mounts, Smith, Glidewell, Hurd	1976
Spring Medley Relay	3:19.81	Hansel, Oller, Anderson, Rider	1982
Distance Medley Relay	9:43.0	Baseer, Anderson, Golias, Klassa	1984

All OSU Indoor Performers, Men

(with personal bests)

Event	Name	Mark	Year
50-Yard Hurdles	Glenn Davis	6.1	1958
60-Yard Hurdles	Robert Wright	7.3	1943
55-Meter Hurdles (FAT)	Dan Oliver	7.24	1979
55-Meter Hurdles (Hand-Timed)	Dan Oliver	7.1	1979
70-Yard Hurdles	Jim Barber	8.3	1970
55-Meter Dash	George Nicholas	6.15	1984
60-Yard Dash (FAT)	Kelly Reed	6.16	1986
60-Yard Dash (Hand-Timed)	Jerry Hill	6.0	1969
300-Yard Dash	Jim Harris	30.4	1970
300-Meter Dash	Zoraba Ross	33.80	1987
400-Meter Dash	Harry Reynolds	46.66	1986
440-Yard Dash	Harry Reynolds	46.57	1987
500-Meter Dash	Harry Reynolds	60.56	1987
600-Yard Run	Harry Reynolds	1:06.87	1987
600-Meter Run	Keeon Gregory	1:18.07	1988
800-Meter Run	Mike Anderson	1:49.23	1985
880-Yard Run	Scott Rider	1:50.89	1982
1,000-Yard Run	Tom Byers	2:06.6	1974
1,000-Meter Run	Mark Croghan	2:26.04	1991
1,500-Meter Run	Glenn Klassa	3:46.59	1985
One-Mile Run	Glenn Klassa	4:02.10	1985
3,000-Meter Run	Mark Croghan	8:01.60	1991
Two-Mile Run	Steve Crane	8:47.0	1978
Three-Mile Run	Steve Crane	13:44.2	1979
5,000- Meter Run	Mark Croghan	14:14.07	1990
High Jump	Mark Cannon	7-3 1/4	1991
Long Jump	Joe Greene	26-3	1990
Triple Jump	Joe Greene	55-0 1/4	1989
Pole Vault	Paul Huzyak	16-10 3/4	1990
Shot Put	Kevin Akins	70-1 3/4	1982
One-Mile Relay	Reed, Gregory Ross, Reynolds	3:09.32	1987
4 x 400-Meter Relay	Reed, Gregory, Ross, Reynolds	3:10.47	1986

All-time OSU Outdoor Performers, Men

(with personal bests)

Event	Name	Mark	Year
110-Meter Hurdles	Dan Oliver	13.62	1979
400-Meter Hurdles	Glenn Davis	49.2	1958
100-Meter Dash	Jesse Owens	10.20	1936
200-Meter Dash	Harry Reynolds	20.46	1987
400-Meter Dash	Harry Reynolds	44.10	1987
800-Meter Run	Scott Rider	1:46.60	1982
1,500-Meter Run	Tom Byers	3:37.50	1974
3,000-Meter Steeplechase	Mark Croghan	8:10.69	1991
5,000-Meter Run	Steve Crane	13:49.00	1979
10,000-Meter Run	Robin Smith	29:57.60	1976
High Jump	Mark Cannon	7-2 1/2	1991
Long Jump	Joe Greene	27-7 1/4	1989
Triple Jump	Joe Greene	55-1 1/4	1989
Pole Vault	Paul Huzyak	16-11 1/2	1991
Shot Put	Kevin Akins	69-9 1/2	1982
Discus	Kevin Akins	178-3	1982
4 x 100-Meter Relay	Reed, Holland, Banks, Reynolds	39.93	1986
4 x 400-Meter Relay	Reed, Gregory, Ross, Reynolds	3:02.32	1987
Javelin	Tim Schmidt	175-4 3/4	1991

In Cleveland, when Jesse Owens went out for track, his coach took him to a race track one day after a loss and gave him a lecture on perseverance while making him watch the faces of winning horses. Owens was seldom beaten again.

The OSU track star, Jesse Owens, gives the world a lesson

In the 1936 Berlin Olympics, the skinny black kid from Ohio State fouled twice in the qualifying attempts for the broad jump. Once more and he'd be out. His opponent was Luz Long, the tall, muscular, blue-eyed, sandy-haired German—Hitler's quintessential Aryan.

The kid felt someone touch his shoulder. "What has taken your goat, Jazze Owenz?" a voice asked. It was Luz Long. "Jump from behind the takeoff board," Long said, and he put a towel down to mark the place. **Jesse Owens** took Long's generosity and qualified with a record jump.

In the finals, Long took the lead, and Owens jumped farther. Long's second jump beat that. Owens' was better by half an inch. Long's third set an Olympic record, and Owens hugged him. Then Owens jumped. He jumped farther than anyone had ever jumped. And when he came down, he heard Long shouting his name. The Germans, in spite of Hitler calling Owens and his black teammates "America's black auxiliaries," were cheering, too: "Jazze Owenz! Jazze Owenz! Jazze Owenz!

It may have been the finest moment in Olympic history: the blond German and the black son of an illiterate Alabama sharecropper embracing. It was one of the tiny human moments that belie the institutional force of politics, and the world had been watching.

The world went on, however, and James Cleveland Owens, although he was perhaps the most famous man in America, came home to back doors and the rear of buses. The most famous man in America had only two job offers. One was as a Cleveland playground instructor for $28 a week, and the other was racing a horse in a 100-yard dash.

Owens perserved, though. Perseverance was the only trait a lot of blacks had in Owens' time. His family was so poor the kids decorated their Christmas tree with socks, and ate meat only three times a year.

Although he was offered scholarships all over the country, he came to OSU, which didn't give track scholarships, and worked his way through as a night elevator operator.

As an OSU student in 1935, Owens—with a back injury—beat or equaled six world records, all within 45 minutes in a Big Ten meet in Ann Arbor. In his time, he set a 60-yard dash record record that lasted 40 years, and a long jump that lasted 25. His 100-meter record is still the OSU school record, and it was set 56 years ago. His Berlin times in the 100 and 200 meter dashes would have won Olympic medals as recently as the 1960s. And he is one of only two men to win four gold medals in the Olympic track and field events.

It is true Jesse Owens had rhythm. But it was perseverance that got him through. It may have been perseverance tinged with naivete—there seemed to be that side to him—and it was always perseverance without bitterness. He overcame illness, poverty, failure, even a charge of income tax evasion (a result, again, of naivete). He always believed his mother, who told him, "What you puts in is exactly what you gets out."

He was a black man who voted Republican, a believer. He made a living as "a respectable Negro," earning as much as $100,000 a year in public relations and the lecture circuit, and along the way and amid the sometimes curious turns of his life, he was always an American symbol.

He was an amalgam of timing, prowess—and determination. The first two were largely gifts. The third belonged to him alone. "Life—the inner life—is the true Olympics," he said in his biography. ▶

OSU NCAA Outdoor Champions

1921	Gaylord Stinchcomb	Long Jump
1925	Ray Bunker	Hammer Throw
1926	George Guthrie	120-Yard High Hurdles
1929	George Simpson	100-Yard Dash, 200-Yard Dash
	Dick Rockaway	120-Yard High Hurdles
	Peter Rasmus	Discus
1930	George Simpson	220-Yard Dash
1931	Jack Keller	220-Yard Low Hurdles, 120-Yard High Hurdles
1932	Jack Keller	220-Yard Low Hurdles
1935	Jesse Owens	Long Jump, 100-Yard Dash
		200-Yard Dash, 200-Yard Low Hurdles
1936	Jesse Owens	Long Jump, 100-Meter Dash
		200-Meter Dash, 200-Yard Low Hurdles
	Dave Albritton	High Jump
	Mel Walker	High Jump
	Charles Beetham	800-Meter Run
1937	Dave Albritton	High Jump
1938	Dave Albritton	High Jump
1941	Robert Wright	120-Yard High Hurdles,220-Yard Low Hurdles
1942	Dallas Dupre	Long Jump
	Robert Wright	120-Yard High Hurdles, 200-Yard Low Hurdles
1944	Ralph Tyler	Long Jump
	John Schmidt	Pole Vault
1947	William Clifford	880-Yard Run
1948	Mal Whitfield	800-Meter Run
1949	Mal Whitfield	880-Yard Run
1958	Glenn Davis	440-Yard Run
1971	Ray Hupp	Decathlon
1987	Harry Reynolds	400-Meter Dash
1988	Joe Greene	Triple Jump
1989	Joe Greene	Long Jump
1990	Mark Croghan	3000-Meter Steeplechase
1991	Mark Croghan	3,000-Meter Steeplechase

All-time OSU Indoor Performers, Women

(with personal bests)

55-Meter/60-Yard Hurdles
Stephanie Hightower — 7.47 — 1980

55-Meter Dash
Bridgette Tate — 6.85 — 1989

200-Meter Dash
Bridgette Tate — 23.65 — 1985

400-Meter Dash
Diane Dixon — 53.16 — 1983

600-Meter Run
Lorrie Oldham — 1:32.13 — 1980

800-Meter Run
Carmen Yiamouyiannis — 2:11.45 — 1984

1,000-Meter Run
Carolyn Moore — 2:54.94 — 1987

1,500-Meter Run
Maureen Cogan — 4:25.14 — 1984

One-Mile Run
Maureen Cogan — 4:45.11 — 1984

3,000-Meter Run
Maureen Cogan — 9:18.92 — 1984

5,000-Meter Run
Maureen Cogan — 16:23.00 — 1986

High Jump
Barbara Kester — 5-11 — 1989

Long Jump
Theresa Diggs — 20-4 — 1988

Triple Jump
Monique Hayes — 40-6 — 1991

Shot Put
Susan Matz — 50-6 3/4 — 1990

Pentathlon
Joyce Finley — 3,625 pts. — 1991

All-time OSU Outdoor Performers, Women

(with personal bests)

100-Meter High Hurdles

Stephanie Hightower	12.90	1980

400-Meter Low Hurdles

Arnita Green	57.79	1991

100-Meter Dash

Bridgette Tate	11.54	1988

200-Meter Dash

Bridgette Tate	23.03	1987

400-Meter Dash

Diane Dixon	52.63	1983

800-Meter Run

Tonja Stewart	2:09.10	1987

1,500-Meter Run

Kathryn Monard	4:24.89	1986

3,000-Meter Run

Maureen Cogan	9:14.40	1984

5,000-Meter Run

Maureen Cogan	15:57.51	1985

10,000-Meter Run

Beth Sheridan	34:05.60	1980

High Jump

Inge-Lise Christensen	5-11	1981

Long Jump

Theresa Diggs	20-11 3/4	1988

Triple Jump

Kimberly Tyler	41-4 1/4	1991

Shot Put

Elizabeth Bunge	50-1	1986

Discus

Nadine Cox	166-4	1983

Javelin

Joyce Finley	106-4	1991

Heptathlon

Joyce Finley	4,822 pts.	1991

Ohio State Women's Indoor National Championships

1980	AIAW (at Missouri)	Team: 13th/41; 41 points
	Stephanie Hightower	1st 60-Meter Hurdles
		4th 60-Meter Dash

Ohio State Women's Outdoor National Championships, Women

1979	AIAW (at Michigan State)	Team: 20th/55; 10 points
	Stephanie Hightower	1st 100-Meter Hurdles
1980	AIAW (at Oregon)	Team: 18th/51; 10 points
	Stephanie Hightower	1st 100-Meter Hurdles

Baseball

OSU, The Coaches

Years	Coach	Overall W-L-T	Pct.	Big Ten W-L-T	Pct.	Titles
1901-02	Jack Reed	15-11-0	.625			
1903	C.W. Dickerson	9-5-1	.633			
1913-28	L.W. St. John	191-99-8	.654	77-52-3	.595	2
1929-32	Wayne Wright	37-26-1	.586	15-19-0	.441	0
1933-38, 47-50	Floyd Stahl	128-109-1	.540	53-56-0	.486	0
1939-44	Fred Mackey	78-60-0	.565	25-33-0	.431	1
1945-46	Lowell Wrigley	18-26-1	.411	7-13-0	.200	0
1951-75	Marty Karow	478-343-16	.571	203-148-1	.578	5
1976-87	Dick Finn	310-262-5	.542	92-99-0	.482	0
1988-	Bob Todd	151-97-1	.608	68-44-0	.607	1
108-Year Totals		1415-1038-34	.576	540-464-4	.538	9

OSU, The Record

BATTING AVERAGE
Robby Cobb - .363 (233-641) (1980-83)

AT BATS
Jay Semke - 670 (1986-89)

HITS
Robby Cobb - 233 (1980-83)

STOLEN BASES
Bo Rein - 49 (1965-67)

WINS
Tom Schwarber - 28 (1987-91)

INNINGS PITCHED
Tom Schwarber - 295 (1987-91)

FEWEST HITS ALLOWED
(175 or more innings)
Joe Sadelfield - 124 (1967-1969)

DOUBLES
Robby Cobb - 48 (1980-83)

TRIPLES
Scott Meadows - 11 (1985-88)

HOME RUNS
Jeff King - 37 (1981-84)

FEWEST BASE-0N-BALLS ALLOWED
(175 or more innings)
Dick Boggs - 75 (1966-68)

STRIKEOUTS
Steve Arlin - 294 (1965-66)

FEWEST RUNS ALLOWED
(175 or more innings)
Steve Arlin - 70 (1965-66)

RUNS SCORED
Robby Cobb - 183 (1980-83)

RUNS BATTED IN
Eric Pfaff - 163 (1982-85
Jeff King - 163 (1981-84)

BASE-ON-BALLS
Greg Mohler - 136 (1981-84

FEWEST EARNED RUNS
(175 or more innings)
Steve Arlin - 55 (1965-55)

EARNED RUN AVERAGE
(175 or more innings)
Steve Arlin - 2.01 (1965-55)

WIN-LOSS PERCENTAGE
(10 or more wins)
Steve Arlin - .889 (24-3) (1965-66)

Miscellaneous Records

Hitting Streak:
23 games, Jay Semke, games 13-35, 1987
21 games, Keith Klodnick, games 1-21, 1991

Consecutive Times Reached Base:
13, John Prosenjak, 1934 (3 walks, 5 hits, 1 walk, 4 hits in three games)

Strikeouts - One Game:
20, Steve Arlin (Washington State, 1965, 15 innings)
18, Bill Gable (Kent State, 1963, 7 innings)

Strikeouts - Nine Innings:
17, Bill Cunningham (Illinois, 1985)

Innings Pitched - One Game:
16, Steve Arlin (Michigan, 1965)

OSU No Hitters:
Dave Mumaw, 4-23-89, vs. Indiana (7 innings), OSU 2-0
Bill Cunningham and Jeff Aurentz, 4-13-82, vs. Bowling Green (8 innings), OSU 4-1
Kerry Sabo, 4-16-80, vs. Cleveland State (7 innings), OSU 12-0
Joe Sparma, 5-18-63, vs. Michigan (7 innings), OSU 3-0
Gene Rogers, 5-23-59, vs. Purdue (7 innings), OSU 6-0
Bill Soter and Ron Disher, 4-2-55, vs. Pitt (7 innings), OSU 8-1

NCAA Baseball Championship

1965	Championship Game	Arizona State 2, OSU 1
1966	Championship Game	OSU 8, Oklahoma State 2

Team play

Other OSU Sports: The NCAA Championship Teams

Men's **golf**—1946, 1979
Men's **gymnastics**—1985
Men's **Swimming and Diving**—1943, 1945, 1946, 1947, 1949, 1950, 1952, 1954, 1955, 1956, 1962
Men's **Track and Field**—1929 (outdoor)

OSU's run of national swimming titles is because of the legendary Mike Peppe, whose novel training techniques, inspired recruiting, and total obsession with his port brought the school an unmatched string of wins, titles, and records. Peppe took swimming away from the east coast schools, winning the NCAA championship 11 times. OSU was the first college team to win the National AAU championships, and he won six indoor and four outdoor titles before AAU competition was dropped in 1956. That was the year Peppe's divers won first, second, third, and fourth places in the NCAA diving championships. They also represented the entire U.S. springboard Olympic team that year and won the gold, the silver, and fourth place. From 1931-1963, Peppe's kids won 312 individual championships. His divers won 101 of a possible 113 national diving titles, and his athletes accounted for 137 major titles. Five of them earned Olympic gold medals, and his program is yet unmatched by Division I challengers. ▶

Mid-American Conference
Champions, Men

	Football	Cross Country	Wrestling	Swimming
1992			Miami	Eastern Michigan
1991	Bowling Green	Eastern Michigan	Miami	Eastern Michigan
1990	Central Michigan	Eastern Michigan	Kent	Eastern Michigan
1989	Ball State	Central Michigan	Kent	Eastern Michigan
1988	Western Michigan	Central Michigan	Kent	Eastern Michigan
1987	Eastern Michigan	Ball State	Central Michigan	Eastern Michigan
1986	Miami	Eastern Michigan	Central Michigan	Eastern Michigan
1985	Bowling Green	Miami	Northern Illinois	Eastern Michigan
1984	Toledo	Miami	Miami	Eastern Michigan
1983	Northern Illinois	Miami	Toledo	Eastern Michigan
1982	Bowling Green	None Held	Kent	Eastern Michigan
1981	Toledo	Miami	Kent	Eastern Michigan
1980	Central Michigan	Western Michigan	Kent	Eastern Michigan
1979	Central Michigan	Western Michigan	Kent	Kent
1978	Ball State	Miami	Kent	Eastern Michigan
1977	Miami	Western Michigan	Kent	Kent
1976	Ball State	Western Michigan	Ohio	Kent
1975	Miami	Ball State	Ohio	Miami
1974	Miami	Eastern Michigan	Ohio	Kent
1973	Miami	Eastern Michigan	Ohio	Kent
1972	Kent	Miami	Ohio	Kent
1971	Toledo	Miami	Ohio	Ohio
1970	Toledo	Western Michigan	Ohio	Ohio
1969	Toledo	Bowling Green	Toledo	Ohio
1968	Ohio	Western Michigan	Miami	Miami
1967	Toledo & Ohio	Miami	Miami	Miami
1966	Miami & W. Michigan	Western Michigan	Bowling Green	Ohio
1965	Bowling Green & Miami	Miami	Miami	Ohio
1964	Bowling Green	Ohio	Miami	Western Michigan
1963	Ohio	Western Michigan	Toledo	Western Michigan
1962	Bowling Green	Ohio	Toledo	Bowling Green
1961	Bowling Green	Western Michigan	Miami	Ohio
1960	Ohio	Western Michigan	Bowling Green	Bowling Green
1959	Bowling Green	Western Michigan	Bowling Green	Bowling Green
1958	Miami	Western Michigan	Kent	Bowling Green
1957	Miami	Western Michigan	Ohio	Bowling Green
1956	Bowling Green	Miami	Ohio	Bowling Green
1955	Miami	Miami	Ohio	Miami
1954	Miami	Miami	Toledo	Ohio
1953	Ohio	Miami	Toledo	Ohio
1952	Cincinnati	Miami	Toledo	
1951	Cincinnati	Miami		
1950	Miami	Miami		
1949	Cincinnati	Miami		
1948	Miami	Western Michigan		
1947	Cincinnati	Miami		

	Basketball	Baseball	Track	Tennis	Golf
1992	Miami				
1991	Eastern Michigan	Ohio	Eastern Michigan	Ball State	Miami
1990	Ball State	Central Michigan	Eastern Michigan	Ball State	Miami
1989	Ball State	Western Michigan	Eastern Michigan	Miami & Ball State	Miami
1988	Eastern Michigan	Central Michigan	Eastern Michigan	Ball State	Miami
1987	Central Michigan	Central Michigan	Eastern Michigan	Ball State	Miami
1986	Miami	Central Michigan	Eastern Michigan	Ball State	Ball State
1985	Ohio	Central Michigan	Western Michigan	Ball State	Northern Illinois
1984	Miami	Central Michigan	Eastern Michigan	Ball State	Kent
1983	Bowling Green	Ohio, Western Michigan	Eastern Michigan	Miami	Bowling Green
1982	Ball State	Ohio, Western Michigan	Eastern Michigan	Miami	Ball State
1981	Ball State, Bowling Green, Northern Illinois, Toledo, Western Michigan	Central Michigan	Miami	Western Michigan	Miami
1980	Toledo	Central Michigan	Western Michigan	Miami	Ohio
1979	Toledo & Central Michigan	Miami	Miami	Miami	Ohio
1978	Miami	Eastern Michigan	Eastern Michigan	Miami	Bowling Green
1977	Central Michigan & Miami	Central Michigan	Eastern Michigan	Miami	Kent
1976	Western Michigan	Eastern Michigan	Western Michigan	Miami	Northern Illinois
1975	Central Michigan	Eastern Michigan	Kent	Miami	Ball State
1974	Ohio	Miami	Eastern Michigan	Miami	Miami
1973	Miami	Miami	Kent	Toledo	Bowling Green
1972	Ohio & Toledo	Bowling Green	Bowling Green	Miami	Bowling Green
1971	Miami	Ohio	Western Michigan	Toledo	Ohio
1970	Ohio	Ohio	Western Michigan	Toledo	Miami
1969	Miami	Ohio	Western Michigan	Toledo	Ohio
1968	Bowling Green	Ohio	Western Michigan	Toledo	Kent
1967	Toledo	Western Michigan	Miami	Toledo	Ohio
1966	Miami	Western Michigan	Western Michigan	Toledo	Marshall
1965	Ohio & Miami	Ohio	Western Michigan	Western Michigan	Ohio
1964	Ohio	Kent & Ohio	Western Michigan	Bowling Green & Miami	Ohio & Toledo
1963	Bowling Green	Western Michigan	Western Michigan	Western Michigan	Ohio
1962	Bowling Green	Western Michigan	Western Michigan	Western Michigan	Marshall
1961	Ohio	Western Michigan	Western Michigan	Western Michigan	Ohio
1960	Ohio	Ohio	Western Michigan	Western Michigan	Ohio
1959	Bowling Green & Miami	Western Michigan & Ohio	Western Michigan	Western Michigan	Ohio
1958	Miami	Western Michigan	Western Michigan	Western Michigan	Ohio
1957	Miami	Western Michigan	Miami	Western Michigan	Ohio
1956	Marshall	Ohio	Miami	W. Michigan & Miami	Bowling Green
1955	Miami	Western Michigan	Miami	Western Michigan	Ohio
1954	Toledo	Ohio	Miami	Western Michigan	Kent & Ohio
1953	Miami	Ohio	Miami	Miami	Ohio
1952	Miami & Western Michigan	Western Michigan	Miami	Western Michigan	Ohio
1951	Cincinnati	Western Michigan	Miami	Cincinnati	Ohio
1950	Cincinnati	Western Michigan	Miami	Western Michigan	Miami
1949	Cincinnati	Western Michigan	Miami	Cincinnati	West. Michigan
1948	Cincinnati	Ohio	Miami	Cincinnati	Miami
1947	Cincinnati & Butler	Wayne State	Cincinnati	Wayne State	

All-Time MAC Champions/Men

	FB	CC	BKB	WR	SW	BAB	TR	TE	GO	TOTAL
Ball State	2	2	3 (1)	0	0	0	0	6 (1)	3	16 (2)
Bowling Green	8 (1)	1	6 (2)	3	6	1	1	1 (1)	5	32 (4)
Central Michigan	2	1	4 (2)	2	0	8	0	0	0	17 (2)
Eastern Michigan	1	3	1	0	11	4	10	0	0	30
Kent	1	0	0	9	6	1(1)	2	0	4 (1)	23 (2)
Miami	13 (2)	18	15 (4)	6	4	3	13	14 (3)	8	94 (9)
Ohio	5 (1)	2	8 (2)	10	8	13(3)	0	0	18 (2)	64 (8)
Toledo	6 (1)	0	5 (3)	7	0	0	0	7	1 (1)	26 (5)
Western Michigan	2 (1)	14	3 (2)	0	2	15(2)	16	15 (2)	1	68 (7)

(Shared Championships)

The Reese Trophy

The Mid-American Conference's Reese Trophy is emblematic of excellence and is awarded annually to the member institution compiling the best record in the nine men's MAC sports. Points are given on a 9-8-7-6-5-4-3-2-1 basis. The winning school receives a replica of the original trophy, which was retired by Ohio in 1970 after three straight wins.

The Mid-American Conference has rewarded all-sports supremacy since 1957-58. The trophy was named the Reese Trophy in 1964, following the retirement of the late Dr. David E. Reese, a Dayton dentist and official who served the conference as commissioner for 17 years from 1947-64.

Beginning with the 1982-83 season, the system for compiling Reese Trophy points changed. The MAC sponsors nine men's sports championships. Each member of the MAC is required to compete in football, basketball and baseball, and participate in a total of six men's sports. When compiling Reese Trophy points, the top six sports per institution are to be counted, but three of the six must be football, basketball and baseball.

Reese Trophy Winners

Year	Winner	(Championships)	Points
1991	Eastern Michigan	(bkb, tr, cc, sw)	45.5
1990	Ball State	(bkb, te)	45
1989	Ball State	(bkb, te)	44
1988	Eastern Michigan	(fb, bkb, sw, tr)	52
1987	Miami	(fb, go)	45
1986	Miami	(cc, bkb)	56
1985	Miami	(cc)	49.5
1984	Miami	(cc, bkb, wr)	52
1983	Miami	(te)	52
1982	Miami	(cc, te)	68
1981	Western Michigan	(cc, te, bkb)	71
1980	Miami	(te)	67.5
1979	Miami	(cc, bab, tr, te)	70.5
1978	Miami	(fb, bkb, te)	76
1977	Miami	(bkb, te)	64.5
1976	Miami	(fb, te)	64
1975	Miami	(fb, sw, te)	66
1974	Miami	(fb, bab, te, go)	76.5
1973	Miami	(cc, bkb, bab)	57.5
1972	Bowling Green	(bab, go)	38
1971	Ohio	(sw, wr, bab, go)	44.5
1970	Ohio	(bkb, sw, wr, bab)	42
1969	Ohio	(fb, sw, bab, go)	56.5
1968	Ohio	(bab)	46.5
1967	Miami	(wr, sw, tr)	49.5
1966	Miami	(cc, bkb)	48
1965	Ohio	(cc, bab, go)	45.5
1964	Ohio	(fb, bkb, go)	51.5
1963	Ohio	(cc, go)	49
1962	Western Michigan	(cc, bab, tr, te)	52.5
1961	Ohio	(fb, bkb, sw, go)	47
1960	Ohio	(bkb, bab, go)	47
1959	Bowling Green	(wr, sw)	49.5
1958	Miami	(fb, bkb)	44

Miami Redskins Add to Legend With Near Upset of UNC in '92 NCAA Tournament

The Miami Redskins, at 23-7 the 1991-92 champions of the Mid-American Conference and headed into the NCAA Tournament to face the University of North Carolina, were not new to high places. In 1978, for instance, Miami finished 19-9 and hit defending national champion Marquette in the first round of the NCAA, pulling off a stunning overtime upset, 84-81.

In the winter of 1992, under second-year coach and former Bobby Knight assistant Joby Wright, Miami won the Mid-American Conference—and the conference tournament—with its man-to-man defense and even-handed offense that featured a lineup that usually didn't even start its scoring leader. David Scott, the 6-7 senior forward and twice all-MAC, averaged a point every 82 seconds over his last three years—a 15-point average—yet until his senior season he had made only two career starts. Scott was arguably the Redskins' top player but he prospered in coming off the bench, where he revved up the offense and became the NCAA's leading scorer for a sixth man (17.4 ppg).

Early in the season, after blow-outs against Ohio State and the University of Cincinnati, the mercurial Wright made his team practice in the wee morning hours after returning to Oxford. One sportswriter said Wright was "schooled in tempest by basketball's stormy master," and noted that his was the dominant basketball personality in the MAC. Wright was the captain and scoring leader of Bobby Knight's first Indiana team, in 1972, had a pro tour, and returned to be a Knight assistant, an appreciation for Knight-time defense already a staple of his cage persona. His coaching tactics, indebted to Knight or not, seemed to work.

Thus the Redskins were not in awe of the Tar Heels, who had reached the NCAA Sweet 16 in 11 straight years. And they took the game to North Carolina, playing them, in Wright's phrase, "head-up tough." The Tar Heels shot 39 per cent from the floor, when they usually shoot 50 per cent. The Redskins led for seven straight minutes in the second half and they stuffed star guard Hubert Davis, UNC's leading scorer, who was two-for-17.

Then with 32.4 seconds on the game clock, UNC with a 64-63 lead, the ball came back to Miami. Jamie Mercurio lobbed a long inbounds pass to John McKenna in the lane in front of the goal, and McKenna passed to Scott, who was breaking toward the goal, only one man, a sub, between him and the goal. UNC's George Lynch, however, swiped the pass, and that was it. The game ended at 68-63. Said McKenna, "I read Scott breaking toward the ball. I saw him open and I threw it. If I had it to do over again, I wouldn't have thrown the same pass." Said Scott, "The ball was basically in my hands. The next thing I knew, somebody had come from behind me. I never saw him coming."

The Redskins never really arrested the power play of 7-foot center Eric Montross, who wore Miami down in the final minutes, particularly at close range, but as one headline later read: "Miami Madness nearly puts a chill in the Tar Heels." Once again, the Redskins had played at the top levels of the game, and they had come frightfully close to adding to the Miami legends of storybook sport upsets. ▶

Mid-American Conference
Champions, Women

	Volleyball	Field Hockey	Cross Country
1991	Bowling Green	Kent	Ohio
1990	Miami	Central Michigan	Ohio
1989	Bowling Green	Ball State	Ohio & Central Michigan
1988	Western Michigan	Kent	Ohio
1987	Western Michigan	Ohio	Ohio
1986	Western Michigan	Ball State	Western Michigan
1985	Western Michigan	Ball State	Western Michigan
1984	Western Michigan	Ball State	Western Michigan
1983	Western Michigan	Ball State	Bowling Green
1982	Western Michigan	Miami & Ohio	Bowling Green
1981	Miami		Bowling Green
1980	Miami		Bowling Green

	Basketball	Gymnastics	Swimming
1991	Toledo	Central Michigan	Ohio
1990	Miami	Central Michigan	Ohio
1989	Bowling Green	Kent	Ohio
1988	Bowling Green	Kent	Miami
1987	Bowling Green	Western Michigan	Miami
1986	Ohio	Western Michigan	Miami
1985	Central Michigan	Bowling Green	Miami
1984	Central Michigan	Kent	Miami
1983	Miami	Bowling Green	Miami
1982	Miami	Bowling Green	Miami
1981	Kent	Kent	Bowling Green

	Softball	Tennis	Track
1991	Central Michigan	Miami	Eastern Michigan
1990	Kent	Western Michigan	Eastern Michigan
1989	Toledo	Miami	Eastern Michigan
1988	Bowling Green	Miami	Eastern Michigan
1987	Central Michigan	Miami	Eastern Michigan
1986	Central Michigan	Miami	Miami
1985	Toledo	Miami	Western Michigan
1984	Western Michigan	Miami & Western Michigan	Ohio
1983	Central Michigan	Miami	Ohio
1982	Central Michigan	Miami	Eastern Michigan
1981		Miami	Bowling Green

The Jacoby Trophy

The Mid-American Conference began sponsoring championships in women's sports in 1981. A new trophy, which is called the Jacoby Trophy, was added for the 1982-83 season with the trophy being presented annually to the MAC school compiling the best record in the nine women's conference sports.

Points are figured on a 9-8-7-6-5-4-3-2-1 basis. Since not all nine MAC schools have all nine sports, a system similar to the Reese Trophy procedure is used in compiling totals for the Jacoby Trophy. Each member of the MAC is required to participate in at least six of the nine women's sports, and must participate in basketball, volleyball and softball. When compiling Jacoby Trophy points, a school must count the three required sports plus three of the six optional sports.

The Jacoby Trophy is named in honor of Fred Jacoby, who served as Commissioner of the MAC from 1971-82. It was during Jacoby's tenure that the women's programs were brought into the MAC structure.

Former Jacoby Trophy Winners

Year	Winner	(Championships)	Points	Runner-Up	(Championshsips)	Points
1991	Central Michigan	(sb, gym)	47	Miami	(te)	42.5
1990	Central Michigan	(fh, gym)	43.5	Eastern Michigan	(tr)	41.5
1989	Kent	(fh, gym)	40	Western Michigan	(none)	39.5
1988	Bowling Green	(bkb, sb)	49	Eastern Michigan	(tr)	39
1987	Western Michigan	(vb, xc, gym)	49	Central Michigan	(sb)	41.5
1986	Western Michigan	(vb, xc, gym)	50.5	Bowling Green	(none)	46
1985	Western Michigan	(vb, xc, tr)	52.5	Bowling Green	(gym)	47
				Central Michigan	(bkb, sb)	47
1984	Western Michigan	(vb, sb, tn)	51.5	Central Michigan	(bkb, sb)	46
1983	Miami	(sw, vb, bkb, tn, sb)	52	Bowling Green	(cc, gym)	46

Weeb Ewbank: the Miami grad who became the only coach to win championships in both the NFL and the AFL

Miami University: America's factory of coaches

"Filing down Route 73," wrote Miami University alumnus David Hyde, "the football migrants stumble into this seam by the thousands each August after battling with road maps and memories for some semblance of direction. The national audience tends toward confusion, too..."

The kids still wear sweatshirts that say, "Miami is in Ohio, dammit," and as a disgruntled athletic director used to say, "We were Miami University in Oxford, Ohio, while the other one was an Indian reservation." The irony is that, until fairly recently, it was Oxford that had the football program as well, especially in the four decades between World War II and the early 1980s. Miami earned its reputation by becoming the "Cradle of Coaches," sending out a wave of weighty tacticians who learned the craft as "Oxford scholars" and went on to head some of the most successful programs in America. Among them were such stalwarts as **Earl (Red) Blaik, Paul Brown, Sid Gillman, Woody Hayes, Weeb Ewbank, Bo Schembechler, John Pont, Ara Parseghian, Paul Dietzel, Bill Arnsparger, Bill Mallory, Carmen Cozza,** and **Dick Crum.**

In its enlightened decades, Miami went to seven bowl games, losing only twice. And along the way, the Redskins had more than their share of big wins, including consecutive upset bowl wins over Florida, Georgia, and South Carolina in the mid-1970s, as well as a 1986 upset of 8th-ranked LSU, coached by former Miami grad Arnsparger. Sports Illustrated called it the upset of the 1986 season. "The players always regarded us as `Little Miami Who,'" said **Bob Hitchens,** an All-American on the 1972 team. In 1959, the coaches of three of the top four teams in America, according to AP ratings, were Miami grads: number one LSU, Paul Dietzel, '48; number three Army, Red Blaik, '18; and number four Northwestern, Ara Parseghian, '49. In the pro ranks that autumn, the old Western and Eastern Leagues were topped by the Browns of Paul Brown, `30, and the Colts of Weeb Ewbank, `28.

Ewbank went out of Miami and coached in two of the most dramatic pro games in the history of the sport. The first was the Colts' 23-17 overtime against the Giants in 1958, watched by millions of television viewers just as the game was gaining asendency. Its ascent was complete a decade later when Ewbank, now coach of the upstart NY Jets, met his old Colts team in Super Bowl III and, with his brash quarterback, Joe Namath, engineered a stunning 16-7 upset that set league parity.

When Miami upset undefeated Purdue in 1962, the Akron Beacon-Journal commented on the term "Little Miami" and editorialized that "a more descriptive term for Purdue's conquerors would be `Old Miami,' as it was sixty years old when Purdue was founded..." And a New York writer said, "Far from being a football factory, Miami of Ohio is an idyll of the healthiest traditions of American campus life, where a lack of over-emphasis produces a more well-rounded man."

One of the biggest Ohio rivalries, no matter the record, is still the Miami-Cincinnati game—the oldest football rivalry west of the Alleghenies, played since 1893. ◗

Ohio Athletic Conference

Profile

The Ohio Athletic Conference is the third oldest existing collegiate conference. Founded in 1902, the OAC is pre-dated only by the Michigan Intercollegiate Athletic Association (1888) and the Big Ten (1895).

The OAC sponsors championships in 20 sports, 11 men's and nine women's. The conference has sponsored championships in football since 1902. Women's championships were added in 1984.

The present conference membership consists of 10 private liberal arts colleges in Ohio. The enrollments at the 10 schools range from 1000 to 3600. All of the schools were founded in the 19th century and have long and outstanding academic reputations. While maintaining these high academic standards, Ohio Conference athletic teams and athletes have enjoyed a great deal of success on a regional and national level. The athletic competition is viewed not as an end in itself, but as an extension of the educational programs.

All-Sports Champions, Men

Year	All-Sports Champion	Championships Won
1990-91	Mount Union	Cross Country, Football, Track
1989-90	Baldwin-Wallace	None
1988-89	Wittenberg	Football*%, Basketball*, Tennis, Golf
1987-88	Mount Union	Cross Country, Wrestling, Track
1986-87	Mount Union	Football, Soccer, Wrestling, Track
1985-86	Wittenberg	Tennis, Golf
1984-85	Wittenberg	Soccer, Basketball, Tennis, Golf
1983-84	Denison	Tennis, Lacrosse
1982-83	Ohio Wesleyan	None
1981-82	Ohio Northern	Baseball
1980-81	Wittenberg	Golf
1979-80	Ohio Wesleyan	Soccer
1978-79	Wittenberg	Basketball+, Football
1977-78	Wooster	Basketball*, Soccer
1976-77	Ohio Wesleyan	Soccer, Tennis
1975-76	Wittenberg	Basketball*
1974-75	Mount Union	Cross Country, Soccer, Track#
1973-74	Mount Union	Wrestling, Track@#
1972-73	Balwin-Wallace	Wrestling
1971-72	Baldwin-Wallace	Wrestling, Track@#
1970-71	Wooster	Basketball*, Soccer
1969-70	Wittenberg	Football, Wrestling
1968-69	Baldwin-Wallace	Basketball*, Football, Track#
1967-68	Denison	Basketball*+, Golf, Tennis, Wrestling
1966-67	Baldwin-Wallace	Basketball+
1965-66	Wittenberg	Baseball, Tennis
1964-65	Akron	Basketball*+, Track#
1963-64	Akron	Cross Country, Basketball+
1962-63	Akron	Cross Country, Track#
1961-62	Ohio Wesleyan	Basketball*, Tennis
1960-61	Ohio Wesleyan	Baseball, Tennis

*Regular Season Champion +Tournament Champion
@Indoor Track Champion #Outdoor Track Champion

All-Sports Champions, Women

Year	All-Sports Champion	Championships Won
1990-91	Mount Union	Cross Country
1989-90	Muskingum	Volleyball, Softball
1988-89	Muskingum	Volleyball%, Basketball, Softball
1987-88	Ohio Northern	Volleyball, Basketball
1986-87	Ohio Northern	Volleyball%, Basketball%, Softball
1985-86	Muskingum	Softball, Outdoor Track
1984-85	Ohio Northern	Volleyball, Softball

%Co-champions

Football Champions

Year	Team	Record	Year	Team	Record	Year	Team	Record
1991	Mt. Union	10-1-0	1955	Muskingum	7-0-0	1927	Miami	7-1-0
1990	Mt. Union	11-1-0	1954	Heidelberg	5-0-1		Muskingum	7-1-0
1989	John Carroll	7-1-0	1953	Ohio Wesleyan	7-0-0	1926	Muskingum	7-0-0
1988	Wittenberg	7-1-0	1952	Heidelberg	5-1-0	1925	Ohio Wesleyan	5-0-0
	Baldwin-Wallace	7-1-0	1951	Ohio Wesleyan	6-0-0	1924	Oberlin	8-0-0
1987	Capital	6-1-1	1950	Muskingum	6-0-0	1923	Wooster	8-0-0
1986	Mount Union	8-0-0	1949	Muskingum	7-0-0	1922	Ohio Wesleyan	7-0-0
1985	Mount Union	8-0-0	1948	Heidelberg	7-0-0	1921	Miami	7-0-0
1984	Baldwin-Wallace	8-0-0	1947	Denison	6-0-0	1920	Wooster	8-0-0
1971	Ohio Wesleyan	6-0-0	1946	Otterbein	5-0-0	1919	Wooster	8-0-0
1970	Vacated		1945	Oberlin	4-0-0	1918	Wittenberg	4-0-0
1969	Wittenberg	4-0-0	1944	Conference inactive		1917	Miami	5-0-1
1968	Baldwin-Wallace	4-0-0	1943	Conference inactive		1916	Miami	5-0-1
1967	Ohio Wesleyan	6-0-0	1942	Ohio Northern	5-0-1	1915	Western Reserve	6-1-0
1966	Muskingum	6-0-0	1941	Case	4-0-0	1914	Denison	5-1-0
	Wittenberg	4-0-0	1940	Wittenberg	7-0-0	1913	Oberlin	5-0-1
1965	Muskingum	7-0-0	1939	Muskingum	7-0-0	1912	Ohio State	5-0-0
1964	Wittenberg	7-0-0	1938	John Carroll	4-0-1	1911	Oberlin	4-0-1
1963	Wittenberg	6-0-1	1937	Baldwin-Wallace	4-0-0	1910	Oberlin	3-0-1
1962	Wittenberg	6-0-0	1936	Marietta	4-0-0	1909	Oberlin	4-0-1
1961	Wittenberg	6-0-0	1935	Baldwin-Wallace	8-0-0	1908	Western Reserve	6-1-0
1960	Muskingum	7-0-0	1934	Wooster	8-0-0	1907	Western Reserve	5-1-0
1959	Heidelberg	5-1-0	1933	Dayton	3-0-1	1906	Ohio State	3-0-0
	Wooster	5-1-0	1932	Case	6-0-0	1905	Case	3-0-1
1958	Wittenberg	6-0-0	1931	Muskingum	4-0-0	1904	Case	4-1-0
1957	Denison	6-1-0	1930	Muskingum	3-0-1	1903	Case	5-0-0
	Wittenberg	6-1-0	1929	Muskingum	5-0-0	1902	Case	5-0-0
1956	Heidelberg	5-1-0	1928	Heidelberg	6-0-1			

Home of champions

Wittenberg University: number one in your program

Football
Winningest football program in NCAA Division III—524 wins
Five national championships—1962, 1964, 1969, 1973, 1975; runners-up in 1978 and 1979
More first team All-Americans—16—than any other Division III program
35 winning seasons since 1955—a NCAA record
Nation's winningest college football team of the 1960s—79-9-1
Nation's best defensive team of the 1970s—9.4 points per game
OAC champion 15 times

Basketball
Winningest basketball program in NCAA Division III history—a 35-year overall record of 742-197 and a .790 percentage
National champions in 1977 and 1961; runner-up in 1983, 1976, and 1963; third in 1987 and 1980
More first team All-Americans—seven—than any other Division III program
35 consecutive years without a losing season
Average of 21 wins per season for past 35 years
22 OAC or NCAC regular season titles

Basketball Champions

Year	Team	Record	Year	Team	Record	Year	Team	Record
1991-92	Otterbein	27-4		Wittenberg	10-2	1947-48	Wooster	14-2
1990-91	Otterbein	29-2	1971-72	Wittenberg	10-2	1946-47	Capital	16-2#
1989-90	Otterbein	15-3	1970-71	Wooster	12-0	1945-46	Wittenberg	13-2#
1988-89	Wittenberg	15-1	1969-70	Capital	13-0		Akron	19-5#
1987-88	Ohio Northern	13-3	1968-69	Baldwin-Wallace	11-2	1944-45	Akron	21-2#
1986-87	Otterbein	14-2		Wittenberg	11-2	1943-44	Denison	18-2#
1985-86	Otterbein	16-0	1967-68	Baldwin-Wallace	11-2	1942-43	Mount Union	9-5
1984-85	Wittenberg	14-2		Denison	11-2	1941-42	Mount Union	11-1
	Otterbein	14-2	1966-67	Wittenberg	12-1	1940-41	Muskingum	11-7#
1983-84	Capital	11-2	1965-66	Akron	11-2	1939-40	Wooster	14-0
1982-83	Capital	11-2		Mount Union	11-2	1938-39	Wooster	15-0
1981-82	Ohio Northern	11-2	1964-65	Akron	12-2	1937-38	Wittenberg	19-7#
1980-81	Otterbein	12-1		Wittenberg	12-2	1936-37	Muskingum	14-2#
	Wittenberg	12-1	1963-64	Wittenberg	13-1	1935-36	Marietta	8-1
1979-80	Wittenberg	13-0	1962-63	Wittenberg	14-0	1934-35	Baldwin-Wallace	11-5#
1978-79	Baldwin-Wallance	13-0	1961-62	Ohio Wesleyan	15-1	1933-34	Akron	15-1#
*1977-78	Wooster (North)	10-2	1960-61	Wittenberg	10-0	1932-33	Otterbein	12-0
	Wittenberg (South)	10-2	1959-60	Wittenberg	12-0	1931-32	Mount Union	12-0
*1976-77	Wooster (North)	10-2	1958-59	Wittenberg	13-1	1930-31	Mount Union	12-2
	Wittenberg (South)	10-2	1957-58	Akron	20-6#	1929-30	Wooster	11-2
*1975-76	Ohio Northern(North)	9-3	1956-57	Capital	14-61#	1928-29	Mount Union	11-1
	Otterbein (South)	10-2	1955-56	Akron	18-6#	1927-28	Ohio Wesleyan	16-5#
	Wittenberg (South)	10-2	1954-55	Marietta	11-0	1926-27	Muskingum	19-2#
1974-75	Marietta	11-2	1953-54	Marietta	11-0	1925-26	Mount Union	10-0
1973-74	Muskingum	10-2	1952-53	Akron	17-7#		Muskingum	10-0
	Wittenberg	10-2	1951-52	Wooster	10-0	1924-25	Mount Union	13-1
1972-73	Capital	10-2	1950-51	Muskingtum	20-3#	1923-24	Mount Union	12-1
	Muskingum	10-2	1949-50	Oberlin	8-1	#Overall Record		
	Otterbein	10-2	1948-49	Ohio Wesleyan	13-3	*Seasons of Divisional Play		

Basketball Tournament Champions, Men

Year	Team	Year	Team	Year	Team
1992	Otterbein	1980	Ohio Northern	1968	Denison
1991	Otterbein	1979	Wittenberg	1967	Baldwin-Wallace
1990	Muskingum	1978	Otterbein	1966	Akron
1989	Otterbein	1977	Muskingum	1965	Akron
1988	Muskingum	1976	Oberlin	1964	Akron
1987	Wittenberg	1975	Wittenberg	1963	Wittenberg
1986	Otterbein	1974	Wittenberg	1962	Wittenberg
1985	Wittenberg	1973	Wooster	1961	Wittenberg
1984	Capital	1972	Wittenberg	1960	Wittenberg
1983	Wittenberg	1971	Capital	1959	Akron
1982	Wittenberg	1970	Oberlin	(1992 Tournament championship:	
1981	Wittenberg	1969	Wittenberg	Otterbein 88, Baldwin-Wallace 76)	

Basketball Regular Season Champions, Women

Year	Team	Record	Year	Team	Record
1991-92	Capitol	29-2	1987-88	Ohio Northern	15-1
1990-91	Capital	24-3	1986-87	Capital & Ohio Northern	14-2
1989-90	Heidelberg	15-3	1985-86	Capital	15-0
1988-89	Muskingum	16-0	1984-85	Capital	16-0

Basketball Tournament Champions, Women

1992	Capital	1988	Ohio Northern
1991	Muskingum	1987	Capital
1990	Heidelberg	1986	Ohio Northern
1989	Muskingum	1985	Muskingum

Baseball Playoff Champions

Year	Champion	Year	Champion	Year	Champion
1991	Marietta	1975	Marietta	1964	Mount Union
1990	Marietta	1974	Ohio Northern	1963	Wittenberg
1989	Otterbein	1973	Marietta	1962	Hiram
1988	Marietta	1972	Marietta	1961	Ohio Wesleyan
1987	Marietta	1971	Marietta	1960	Wittenberg
1986	Marietta	1970	Marietta & Mount	1959	Wittenberg
1985	Baldwin-Wallace		Union Game tied at	1958	Ohio Wesleyan
1984	Marietta		2 when halted	1957	Wittenberg
1983	Ohio Northern		by rain	1956	Marietta
1982	Ohio Northern	1969	Ohio Wesleyan	1955	Wittenberg
1981	Marietta		OAC Baseball Champions	1954	Akron
1980	Marietta	1968	Wittenberg	1953	Records Incomplete
1979	Marietta	1967	Hiram	1952	Muskingum
1978	Marietta	1966	Wittenberg	1951	Records Incomplete
1977	Marietta	1965	Ohio Wesleyan	1950	Records Incomplete
1976	Ohio Northern			1949	Ohio Northern

Outdoor Track & Field Champions, Men

1991	Mount Union	1960	Wooster	1930	Oberlin
1990	Otterbein	1959	Ohio Wesleyan	1929	Oberlin
1989	Mount Union	1958	Ohio Wesleyan	1928	Ohio Wesleyan
1988	Mount Union	1957	Ohio Wesleyan	1927	Ohio Wesleyan
1987	Mount Union	1956	Oberlin	1926	Miami
1986	Mount Union	1955	Denison	1925	Ohio Wesleyan
1985	Mount Union	1954	Ohio Wesleyan	1924	Ohio Wesleyan
1984	Mount Union	1953	Wooster	1923	Ohio Wesleyan
1983	Mount Union	1952	Ohio Wesleyan	1922	Oberlin
1982	Baldwin-Wallace	1951	Ohio Wesleyan	1921	Ohio Wesleyan
1981	Baldwin-Wallace	1950	Oberlin	1920	Ohio State
1980	Baldwin-Wallace	1949	Oberlin	1919	Ohio State
1979	Baldwin-Wallace	1948	Baldwin-Wallace	1918	Ohio State
1978	Mount Union	1947	Baldwin-Wallace	1917	Ohio State
1977	Baldwin-Wallace	1946	Baldwin-Wallace	1916	Ohio State
1976	Baldwin-Wallace	1945	Baldwin-Wallace	1915	Ohio State
1975	Mount Union	1944	No Meet Held	1914	Ohio State
1974	Mount Union	1943	Baldwin-Wallace	1913	Ohio State
1973	Mount Union	1942	Oberlin	1912	Ohio State
1972	Baldwin-Wallace	1941	Denison	1911	Ohio State
1971	Mount Union	1940	Oberlin	1910	Oberlin
1970	Baldwin-Wallace	1939	Toledo	1909	Ohio State
1969	Baldwin-Wallace	1938	Oberlin	1908	Ohio State
1968	Mount Union	1937	Oberlin	1907	Ohio State
1967	Mount Union	1936	Oberlin	1906	Ohio State
1966	Akron	1935	Oberlin	1905	Ohio State
1965	Akron	1934	Wooster	1904	Oberlin
1964	Mount Union	1933	Denison	1903	Oberlin
1963	Akron	1932	Oberlin		
1962	Akron	1931	Oberlin		
1961	Akron				

A **John Carroll** sophomore, **Joe Turi** from University School, became JC's first national swimming champion. In March, he won the 100-yard breaststroke at the NCAA Division III Championships. Time: 56.94, second-fastest time in Division III history, and only the third time the 57-second mark has been broken. **Jay Gindin** of **Case Western Reserve** (NCAC) won the national 200-yard butterfly title with a 1:50.53.

Indoor Track & Field Champions, Men

Year	Champion	Year	Champion	Year	Champion
1992	Mount Union	1978	Mount Union	1964	Mount Union
1991	Mount Union	1977	Baldwin-Wallace	1963	Mount Union
1990	Mount Union	1976	Baldwin-Wallace	1962	Baldwin-Wallace
1989	Mount Union	1975	Baldwin-Wallace	1961	Wooster
1988	Mount Union	1974	Mount Union	1960	Capital
1987	Mount Union	1973	Mount Union	1959	Ohio Wesleyan
1986	Mount Union	1972	Baldwin-Wallace	1958	Ohio Wesleyan
1985	Mount Union	1971	Baldwin-Wallace	1957	Ohio Wesleyan
1984	Mount Union	1970	Baldwin-Wallace	1956	Denison
1983	Mount Union	1969	Mount Union	1955	Ohio Wesleyan
1982	Mount Union	1968	Mount Union	1954	Ohio Wesleyan
1981	Baldwin-Wallace	1967	Mount Union	1953	Denison
1980	Baldwin-Wallace	1966	Mount Union	1952	Denison
1979	Baldwin-Wallace	1965	Mount Union	1951	Ohio Wesleyan

Outdoor Track & Field Champions, Women

Year	Champion	Year	Champion
1991	Baldwin-Wallace	1987	Muskingum
1990	Baldwin-Wallace	1986	Muskingum
1989	Baldwin-Wallace	1985	Muskingum
1988	Baldwin-Wallace		

Indoor Track & Field Team Champions, Women

Year	Champion	Year	Champion
1992	Baldwin-Wallace	1989	Baldwin-Wallace
1991	Baldwin-Wallace	1988	Baldwin-Wallace
1990	Baldwin-Wallace	1987	Muskingum
		1986	Mount Union

Swimming Champions, Men

Year	Champion	Year	Champion	Year	Champion
1992	John Carroll	1969	Kenyon	1950	Oberlin
1991	John Carroll	1968	Kenyon	1949	Oberlin
1990	John Carroll	1967	Kenyon	1948	Kenyon
1985-89*		1966	Kenyon	1947	Oberlin
1984	Kenyon	1965	Kenyon	1946	Oberlin
1983	Kenyon	1964	Kenyon	1945	Oberlin
1982	Kenyon	1963	Kenyon	1944	Oberlin
1981	Kenyon	1962	Kenyon	1943	Kenyon
1980	Kenyon	1961	Kenyon	1942	Oberlin
1979	Kenyon	1960	Kenyon	1941	Kenyon
1978	Kenyon	1959	Kenyon	1940	Kenyon
1977	Kenyon	1958	Kenyon	1939	Kenyon
1976	Kenyon	1957	Kenyon	1938	Kenyon
1975	Kenyon	1956	Kenyon	1937	Case
1974	Kenyon	1955	Kenyon		
1973	Kenyon	1954	Kenyon		
1972	Kenyon	1953	Wooster		
1971	Kenyon	1952	Oberlin		
1970	Kenyon	1951	Oberlin		

*In these years, the OAC did not sponsor a championship in men's swimming due to the low number of schools participating in the sport.

Swimming Champions, Women

Year	Team Champion
1992	John Carooll
1991	John Carroll
1990	John Carroll

Wrestling Champions

1992	John Carroll	1979	Muskingum	1966	Baldwin-Wallace
1991	John Carroll	1978	Ohio Northern	1965	Baldwin-Wallace
1990	Mount Union	1977	Ohio Northern	1964	Hiram
1989	Mount Union	1976	Ohio Northern	1963	Baldwin-Wallace
1988	Mount Union	1975	Ohio Northern	1962	Hiram
1987	Mount Union	1974	Mount Union	1961	Hiram
1986	Mount Union	1973	Baldwin-Wallace	1960	Hiram
1985	Mount Union	1972	Baldwin-Wallace	1959	Hiram
1984	Capital	1971	Baldwin-Wallace	1958	Akron
1983	Capital	1970	Wittenberg		Oberlin
1982	Capital	1969	Denison	1957	Oberlin
1981	Ohio Northern	1968	Denison	1956	Oberlin
1980	Ohio Northern	1967	Hiram	1955	Akron
				1954	Akron

Tennis Champions, Men

1991	Ohio Northern	1971	Ohio Wesleyan	1952	Kenyon
1990	John Carroll	1970	Kenyon	1951	Kenyon
1989	Wittenberg	1969	Oberlin	1949	Kenyon
1988	Wittenberg	1968	Denison		Oberlin
1987	Wittenberg	1967	Denison	1948	Oberlin
1986	Wittenberg	1966	Wittenberg	1947	John Carroll
1985	Wittenberg	1965	Ohio Wesleyan		Oberlin
1984	Denison	1964	Wittenberg		Toledo
1983	Denison	1963	Denison	1946	Kenyon
1982	Denison	1962	Ohio Wesleyan	1945	No Meet
1981	Denison	1961	Ohio Wesleyan	1944	No Meet
1980	Denison	1960	Ohio Wesleyan	1943	Otterbein
1979	Denison	1959	Kenyon	1942	Kenyon
1978	Ohio Wesleyan	1958	Ohio Wesleyan	1941	Kenyon
1977	Ohio Wesleyan	1957	Denison	1940	Kenyon
1976	Ohio Wesleyan	1956	Denison	1939	Kenyon
1975	Ohio Wesleyan	1955	Denison	1938	Kenyon
1974	Ohio Wesleyan	1954	Denison		
1973	Ohio Wesleyan	1953	Kenyon		
1972	Wittenberg		Ohio Wesleyan		

Tennis Champions, Women

1991	John Carroll	1987	Wittenberg
1990	Hiram	1986	Otterbein
1989	Wittenberg	1985	Wittenberg
1988	Wittenberg		

Soccer Champions, Men

Year	Team (Overall Record)	OAC Record	Year	Team (Overall Record)	OAC Record
1991	Hiram (11-4-3)	8-1-0	1984	Marietta (12-3-1)	6-2-0
	John Carroll (15-1-0)	8-1-0		Mount Union (11-5-0)	6-2-0
1990	Hiram (14-3-1)	8-0-1		Wittenberg (8-8-1)	6-2-0
1989	Hiram (11-4-2)	8-1-0	1974	Mount Union (12-1-0)	8-0-0
	Capital (12-4)	8-1-0	1973	Ohio Wesleyan (8-4-2)	7-1-1
1988	Otterbein (10-8)	7-1-0	1972	Wooster (8-3-1)	6-0-0
1987	Otterbein (10-7-1)	6-1-1	1971	Ohio Wesleyan (9-0-2)	8-0-1
	Capital (8-5-3)	6-1-1	1970	Wooster (10-1-1)	8-0-0
1986	Mount Union (8-6-2)	7-0-1	1969	Wooster (7-5-1)	7-0-0
1985	Otterbein (10-5-2)	7-0-1			

Conference Game Results, 1975-83

1983	Mount Union 1, Denison 0	1978	Wooster 1, Wittenberg 0
1982	Wooster 1, Ohio Wesleyan 0	1977	Wooster 2, Ohio Wesleyan 1 (OT)
1981	Ohio Wesleyan 2, Kenyon 1	1976	Ohio Wesleyan 2, Wooster 1
1980	Ohio Wesleyan 1, Wooster 0	1975	Ohio Wesleyan 1, Wooster 0
1979	Ohio Wesleyan 2, Oberlin 1 (3 OT)		

Soccer Champions, Women

1991	Heidelberg	1989	Marietta
1990	Heidelberg	1988	Mount Union

Big guns

All-Time National Wins, Division III Basketball

School	National rank	Wins
Wittenberg	1	1,190
Wooster	3	1,059
Muskingum	9	978
Ohio Wesleyan	13	962
Mount Union	14	953

Cross Country Champions, Men

1991	Mount Union	1965	Akron	1939	Oberlin
1990	Mount Union	1964	Mount Union	1938	Wooster
1989	Otterbein	1963	Akron	1937	Oberlin
1988	Otterbein	1962	Akron	1936	Oberlin
1987	Mount Union	1961	Muskingum	1935	Oberlin
1986	Otterbein	1960	Oberlin	1934	Oberlin
1985	Mount Union	1959	Oberlin	1933	Wooster
1984	Mount Union	1958	Ohio Wesleyan	1932	Oberlin
1983	Baldwin-Wallace	1957	Ohio Wesleyan	1931	Oberlin
1982	Baldwin-Wallace	1956	Ohio Wesleyan	1930	Oberlin
1981	Baldwin-Wallace	1955	Oberlin	1929	Oberlin
1980	Otterbein	1954	No Meet	1928	Muskingum
1979	Baldwin-Wallace	1953	Oberlin	1927	Muskingum
1978	Mount Union	1952	Oberlin	1926	Miami
1977	Mount Union	1951	Wooster	1925	Oberlin
1976	Mount Union	1950	Oberlin	1924	Ohio Wesleyan
1975	Mount Union	1949	Oberlin	1923	Oberlin
1974	Mount Union	1948	Oberlin	1922	Ohio Wesleyan
1973	Baldwin-Wallace	1947	Case	1921	Ohio State
1972	Denison	1946	Oberlin	1920	Ohio State
1971	Mount Union	1945	No Meet	1919	Ohio State
1970	Mount Union	1944	No Meet	1918	Cincinnati
1969	Mount Union	1943	No Meet	1917	Ohio State
1968	Mount Union	1942	Bowling Green	1916	Ohio State
1967	Mount Union	1941	Oberlin	1915	Ohio State
1966	Mount Union	1940	Oberlin	1914	Ohio State

Cross Country Individual Champions

1991	Steve Stobart, (OTT)	1965	Turner (WITT)	1939	Gil Dodds (Ashland
1990	Jeff Powles, (MTU)	1964	George Wetherbee (AK)	1938	Gil Dodds (Ashland)
1989	Bob Boggs (OTT)	1963	Campbell (AK)	1937	Good (OBE)
1988	Bob Boggs (OTT)	1962	Russell (B-W)	1936	Bob Cheqwidden (WOO)
1987	Todd Callahan (MTU)	1961	Keller (OBE)	1935	Bob Cheqwidden (WOO)
1986	Marcel Stephens (MTU)	1960	Kelker (Hiram)	1934	Manlove (OBE)
1985	Scott Alpeter (OTT)	1959	Craig Taylor (WOO)	1933	Frank Knotsen (WOO)
1984	Craig Polman (MTU)	1958	John Gutnecht (OWU)	1932	Frank Knotsen (WOO)
1983	Marty Healy (B-W)	1957	John Gutnecht (OWU)	1931	Records Incomplete
1982	Mark Burns (OTT)	1956	John Gutnecht (OWU)	1930	Records Incomplete
1981	John Timmins (OWU)	1955	John Gutnecht (OWU)	1929	Service (OBE)
1980	Jeff Kneice (OTT)	1954	No Meet	1928	John Moreley (WOO)
1979	Victor Smith (MTU)	1953	John Miller (OBE)	1927	Anderson (ONU)
1978	Mike Becraft (ONU)	1952	Loveh (AK)	1926	Weaver Emery (Miami)
1977	Mike Becraft (ONU)	1951	Dave Allison (WOO)	1925	Weaver Emery (Miami)
1976	Larry Coy (B-W)	1950	Dave Allison (WOO)	1924	Whitey Helms (OWU)
1975	Rich Kempe (MTU)	1949	Phil Thomas (OBE)	1923	Whitey Helms (OWU)
1974	Bob Lunn (MTU)	1948	Jim Swomley (OWU)	1922	Kale (OWU)
1973	Al Smith (OBE)	1947	Phil Thomas (OBE)	1921	Cranz (OSU)
1972	Tim King (MTU)	1946	Phil Thomas (OBE)	1920	Guerney (OSU)
1971	Tim King (MTU)	1945	No Meet	1919	Mittendorf (CINCY)
1970	Mark Hunter (MTU)	1944	No Meet	1918	Milhope (CINCY)
1969	Bruce Ronald (MTU)	1943	No Meet	1917	Roach (OSU)
1968	John Rudisill (DEN)	1942	George McDonald (BG)	1916	Fall (OBE)
1967	Milt Gess (MTU)	1941	Record Incomplete	1915	Ferguson (OSU)
1966	Doug Ford (MTU)	1940	Gil Dodds (Ashland)	1914	Nevin (OSU)

Cross Country Champions, Women

	Team		Individual
1991	Mount Union	1991	Patti Russell, Mount Union
1990	Mount Union	1990	Harriett Geiger, Muskingum
1989	Baldwin-Wallace	1989	Becky Nichols, Mount Union
1988	Baldwin-Wallace	1988	Lisa Winans, Baldwin-Wallace
1987	Baldwin-Wallace	1987	Martha Dora, Baldwin-Wallace
1986	Baldwin-Wallace & Mount Union	1986	Carolyn Donoghue, Otterbein
1985	Wittenberg	1985	Tina Cronin, Mount Union

Golf Champions

1991	Hedelberg	1972	Ohio Wesleyan	1953	Mount Union
	Hiram	1971	Ohio Wesleyan	1952	Ohio Wesleyan
1990	John Carroll	1970	Ohio Wesleyan	1951	Denison
1989	Wittenberg	1969	Ohio Wesleyan		Ohio Wesleyan
1988	Wittenberg	1968	Denison	1950	Kent State
1987	Muskingum	1967	Denison	1949	Denison
1986	Wittenberg	1966	Denison	1948	Denison
1985	Wittenberg	1965	Kenyon	1947	Kenyon
1984	Ohio Wesleyan	1964	Denison	1946	No Meet
1983	Capital	1963	Denison	1945	No Meet
1982	Wittenberg	1962	Denison	1944	No Meet
1981	Wittenberg	1961	Akron	1943	No Meet
1980	Capital	1960	Denison	1942	Oberlin
1979	Ohio Wesleyan	1959	Denison	1941	Toledo
1978	Muskingum	1958	Akron	1940	Toledo
1977	Wooster		Wooster	1939	Toledo
1976	Wooster	1957	Akron	1938	Denison
1975	Wooster	1956	Denison	1937	Oberlin
1974	Wittenberg	1955	Ohio Wesleyan	1936	Oberlin
1973	Wooster	1954	Wooster		

Golf Medalists

Year	Player (School)	Holes	Total	Year	Player (School)	Holes	Total
1991	Todd Studnick	36	152				
1990	Dan Nichols (Baldwin-Wallace)	36	158	1974	Doug Doer (Kenyon)	54	217
1989	Ricky Lyons (Wittenberg)	36	152	1973	Gary Welshhans (Wooster)	36	154
1988	Doug Houser (Wittenberg)	36	153	1972	Ben Smeltzer (Ohio Wesleyan)	36	153
1987	Greg Emrick (Muskingum)	36	151	1971	Gary Lipski (Hiram)	36	149
1986	Scott Copeland (Wittenberg)	54	230	1970	Don Kepple (Denison)	36	151
1985	Tom Parrine (Mount Union)	54	222	1969	Henry Fitzgerald (OWU)	36	148
1984	Jim Kincaid (Wittenberg)	54	224	1968	Steve Bartlett (Kenyon)	36	142
1983	Bill Stebelton (Capital)	54	217	1967	Steve Bartlett (Kenyon)	18	75
1982	Bill Thomas (Denison)	54	224	1966	Bob Logan(Wittenberg)	36	148
1981	Tom Atchison (Wittenberg)	54	228	1965	Perry Hudson (Kenyon)	36	145
1980	Ken Weixel (Capital)	54	221	1964	McKinnon (Mount Union)	36	142
1979	Mike McBroom (Ohio Wesleyan)	54	220	1963	Rake (Marietta)	36	149
1978	Greg Nye (Wooster)	54	228	1962	Pultz (Denison)	36	143
1977	Greg Nye (Wooster)	54	223	1961	Stevenson (Akron)	36	153
1976	Doug Doer (Kenyon)	54	220	1960	Jim Logue (Wittenberg)	36	143
1975	Mike Schneider (Wooster)	54	224	1959	Dale Hill (Denison)	36	157

Softball Champions

1991	Capital	1987	Ohio Northern
1990	Muskingum	1986	Muskingum
1989	Muskingum	1985	Ohio Northern
1988	Muskingum		

Volleyball Champions

1991	Ohio Northern	1987	Ohio Northern
1990	Ohio Northern	1986	Ohio Northern & Heidelberg
1989	Muskingum		(Co-Champions)
1988	Muskingum & Ohio Northern	1985	Ohio Northern
	(Co-Champions)	1984	Ohio Northern

Unsinkable Kenyon

Coach Steen: *"There's something about him that makes people swim fast."* Missi Nelson, Kenyon NCAA champion

Kenyon: America's Best Small-college Swimming Program

At tiny, unlikely Gambier, Kenyon conjures images of an island of academic intelligentsia, not high-powered athletics, yet here in central Ohio the twain have not only met, they have merged. In 1991, the men's team won its 12th consecutive NCAA Division III national championship—no other team in the country, regardless of size, has won more. The women, meanwhile, have won eight titles.

The school itself has won conference titles for the last 38 years, and the individual honors are almost past the counting. Jim Born (Kenyon '86) won 17 NCAA swimming titles, second only to Olympic champion Pablo Morales. Patty Abt (Kenyon '87) won 23 NCAA titles—the most ever by anyone. Since 1976, Jim Steen has coached more than 100 All-American swimmers, who, among them, earned nearly a thousand All-American designations.

The women's team began with Steen in 1976, as a club sport. In 1977, they won the Ohio State Small College Meet, and every state or conference championship since. They won their first NCAA championship in 1984, and every won of those since, along with more than 90 All-American certificates, 30 NCAA records, and 60 NCAA individual and relay titles. In slightly over a decade, they have dominated the sport unlike any other team in any sport.

Said writer Mark Shelton, "At a college like Kenyon, this all seems something more than incongruous. Kenyon is an assertively high-toned, militantly liberal-arts, quintessentially eggheaded place, draped in social history and overgrown with ivy." In competition, though, Kenyon wins against Division II schools and can beat some Division I programs. "Kenyon makes its meets with the big Division I schools interesting and competitive, which in terms of pure athleticism is a staggering accomplishment," writes Shelton. "They fare far better swimming against Ohio State than the Division III football champs would do lining up in Ohio Stadium. And the swimmers manage to do it at a place with a long history of nonconformism and free-thinking and cultural arts, all the while being assimilated into the life of the college themselves." ▶

North Coast Athletic Conference
Champions

Baseball
1991	Wooster
1990	Wooster
1989	Ohio Wesleyan
1988	Wooster
1987	Wooster
1986	Ohio Wesleyan
1985	Allegheny, Wooster

Men's Basketball
1991	Wittenberg
1990	Wittenberg
1989	Allegheny, Wooster
1988	Allegheny, Ohio Wesleyan
1987	Ohio Wesleyan
1986	Allegheny, Ohio Wesleyan
1985	Ohio Wesleyan

Women's Basketball
1991	Wittenberg
1990	Wooster
1989	Allegheny
1988	Allegheny
1987	Allegheny
1986	Allegheny
1985	Allegheny, Wooster

Men's Cross Country
1991	Denison
1990	Denison
1989	Wooster
1988	Case Reserve
1987	Wooster
1986	Case Reserve
1985	Case Reserve
1984	Allegheny

Women's Cross Country
1991	Allegheny
1990	Allegheny
1989	Allegheny
1988	Allegheny
1987	Wooster
1986	Allegheny
1985	Allegheny
1984	Oberlin

Field Hockey
1991	Ohio Wesleyan
1990	Ohio Wesleyan
1989	Ohio Wesleyan
1988	Ohio Wesleyan
1987	Ohio Wesleyan
1986	Denison, Wooster
1985	Denison
1984	Denison

Football
1991	Allegheny
1990	Allegheny
1989	Kenyon, Ohio Wesleyan
1988	Allegheny
1987	Allegheny
1986	Denison
1985	Denison
1984	Case Reserve

Golf
1991	Allegheny
1990	Ohio Wesleyan
1989	Ohio Wesleyan
1988	Ohio Wesleyan
1987	Ohio Wesleyan
1986	Allegheny
1985	Wooster

Men's Lacrosse
1991	Ohio Wesleyan
1990	Ohio Wesleyan
1989	Ohio Wesleyan
1988	Ohio Wesleyan
1987	Ohio Wesleyan
1986	Denison
1985	Denison

Women's Lacrosse
1991	Denison
1990	Denison
1989	Denison
1988	Denison
1987	Denison
1986	Denison
1985	Denison

Men's Soccer
1991	Ohio Wesleyan
1990	Allegheny
1989	Wooster
1988	Ohio Wesleyan
1987	Ohio Wesleyan
1986	Ohio Wesleyan
1985	Denison
1984	Ohio Wesleyan

Women's Soccer
1991	Wooster
1990	Ohio Wesleyan, Wooster
1989	Allegheny, Ohio Wesleyan
1988	Allegheny
1987	Allegheny
1986	Allegheny
1985	Allegheny
1984	Denison

Men's Swimming
1991	Kenyon
1990	Kenyon
1989	Kenyon
1988	Kenyon
1987	Kenyon
1986	Kenyon
1985	Kenyon

Women's Swimming
1991	Kenyon
1990	Kenyon
1989	Kenyon
1988	Kenyon
1987	Kenyon
1986	Kenyon
1985	Kenyon

Men's Tennis
1991	Kenyon
1990	Wooster
1989	Denison, Kenyon, Wooster
1988	Denison
1987	Denison
1986	Denison
1985	Denison, Wooster

Women's Tennis
1991	Kenyon
1990	Kenyon
1989	Kenyon
1988	Kenyon
1987	Kenyon
1986	Kenyon
1985	Allegheny

Men's Indoor Track
1991	Denison
1990	Ohio Wesleyan
1989	Ohio Wesleyan
1988	Wooster
1987	Denison
1986	Denison
1985	Denison

Women's Indoor Track
1991	Ohio Wesleyan
1990	Ohio Wesleyan
1989	Ohio Wesleyan
1988	Wooster
1987	Allegheny
1986	Wooster
1985	Ohio Wesleyan

Men's Outdoor Track
1991	Denison
1990	Ohio Wesleyan
1989	Denison
1988	Denison
1987	Denison
1986	Denison
1985	Denison

Women's Outdoor Track
1991	Ohio Wesleyan
1990	Allegheny
1989	Ohio Wesleyan
1988	Wooster
1987	Wooster
1986	Wooster
1985	Wooster

Volleyball
1991	Allegheny
1990	Allegheny
1989	Allegheny
1988	Allegheny
1987	Kenyon
1986	Kenyon
1985	Allegheny
1984	Wooster

*Denison gets a leg
up on its modern
competition by
using an offense
that went out with
the detachable
collar. But if Keith
Piper's single-wing
is a dinasaur, then
it, like the coach
himself, is
remarkably agile.*

At Denison, Keith Piper Keeps the Single Wing Alive and Well

It comes as no surprise in ardently historical Granville, the home of **Denison University**, that the brand of football is historical as well. It is so historical, actually, that it might qualify the Big Red's stadium for inclusion on the National Register of Historical Places. For the Denison Stadium is probably the last remaining place in America that one can watch a bona fide single wing football team plying its glorious trade. The last major college to use the single wing was Princeton, which gave it up in 1969. But up until nearly 1950, it was football's dominant offense. **Keith Piper**, a Civil War buff who has been coaching Denison forever—since 1954, which constitutes forever in a world that cannot even recall the single wing—likes the formation because it's ideal, he says, for utilizing slower, smaller players and, "because opponents only see it once a year, you take them by surprise."

The essence of the single wing is that there's no back directly under center; the tailback usually lines up about five yards behind, the fullback beside him. The remaining back—the wingback—lines up just outside the tight end. While anyone can receive the hike, at Denison it is usually the tailback, who runs, hand off, passes, or punts. The quarterback seldom sees the ball, and after calling the signals from off to one side, is usually the lead blocker. Piper refers to him as "a retarded guard."

Any of the backs may spin, reverse, hand off, fake, run, block, pass, or receive, and the unbalanced line uses double-team and trap blocking. "Part of it is my age," says Piper, who was an All-Ohio single wing center at Baldwin-Wallace College and near 200 victories, the winningest active college coach in Ohio. "I remember all the great single wing teams and names, and I had a good time playing it myself. I remember watching Massillon High play the single wing in 1932. Paul Brown was the coach. They had a kid named Pokey Blunt and he ran a reverse one time and there wasn't an opponenet left standing on the field. It was fantastic. I always wanted a team that looked like that..."

Piper originally used the formation when he had an All-American tailback named **Tony Hall**, a transfer from OSU who later became a Dayton congressman, and in 1978 he had a little tailback, **Clay Sampson**, who set an Ohio Athletic Conference record by rushing 54 times. "We're no good without a tailback," says Piper.

In addition to Piper and the single wing, the Big Red has residual notoriety because **Woody Hayes** both played and coached at Denison. As a coach, he had two undefeated seasons. There was one other Denison coach of particular note, one **Dr. Walter J. Livingston**, 1911-1926, who wore a brown derby to each game and flung it into the stands if he won. In all, the doctor lost 75 derbies. There is good evidence that Livingston's 1912 team favored the forward pass well before fashion, and used it to beat Wittenberg 68-0.

At any rate, Keith Piper, in his stubborn vigil, has history on his side. "The smell of mouldy leather in the locker room, wintergreen, cod-liver oil—we had to bring our own teaspoon so the coach could give us three spoonsful of cod-liver oil after every practice—that, to me, is football," he says. "There's a flavor there I try to bring out." ▶

the Top Feats in Ohio Sports History

1. **Jesse Owens**, Cleveland resident, wins four gold medals at the 1936 Olympics.

2. Cincinnati Reds player-manager **Pete Rose** in 1985 breaks Ty Cobb's major-league hit record.

3. **Archie Griffin**, Ohio State tailback, wins back-to-back Heisman trophies, in 1974 and 1975.

4. **Cincinnati Reds** sweep Oakland Athletics in the 1990 World Series.

5. **Jack Nicklaus** of Columbus in 1986 wins his sixth Masters.

6. **Johnny VanderMeer**, Cincinnati Reds pitcher, throws two consecutive no-hitters in 1938.

7. **Cleveland Browns** win the National Football League championship in 1950, their first year in the league.

8. **Cincinnati Reds** sweep New York Yankees in 1976 World Series.

9. **Ohio State** wins 1954 and 1968 national championships.

10. **Ohio State**, with **Jerry Lucas** and **John Havlicek**, wins 1960 NCAA basketball championship.

11. **University of Cincinnati**, with **Oscar Robertson**, wins back-to-back NCAA national basketball championships in 1961 and 1962.

12. **Frank Robinson**, named in 1975 by the Cleveland Indians, becomes major leagues' first black manager.

13. The 1954 **Cleveland Indians** win American League pennant, and a league record 111 games.

14. **Cleveland Browns** upset Baltimore 27-0 and win 1964 NFL title.

15. **Cleveland Indians** beat Brooklyn Dodgers to win the 1920 World Series.

16. **Cleveland** stops Joe DiMaggio's 56-game hitting streak in 1941.

17. **Cleveland** wins one-game American League playoff against the Boston Red Sox, then beat Boston Braves in World Series.

18. **Bob Feller** pitches opening day no-hitter in 1940, against Detroit Tigers.

19. **Paul Brown** fired as coach of the Cleveland Browns after 1962 season; returns with new franchise in 1968 at Cincinnati.

20. **Cleveland Cavaliers** beat Washington in first round of 1976 playoffs before losing to Boston in the "Miracle of Richfield."

21. **University of Toledo** wins 35 straight football games from 1969 to 1971, second-longest streak in college history.

22. **Ray (Boom Boom) Mancini** of Youngstown wins world lightweight boxing title in 1982.

23. **Bowling Green** wins NCAA national hockey championship in 1984.

24. **Carry Back**, trained by Cleveland's **Jack Price**, wins 1961 Kentucky Derby.

25. **St. Ignatius** of Cleveland is named national high school football champion of 1989 by USA Today.

*Source: The feats were chosen by 175 Ohio sports writers and sportscasters for the video, **Great Moments in Ohio Sports**, reprinted courtesy the Ohio Lottery Commission and Media Drop-In Productions*

Kosar and the Browns: A Gritty, Blue-Collar Gridiron Match

When Bernie Kosar left the Miami Hurricanes after only two seasons and came back home to Cleveland in 1985, there had not been a quarterback so suited to a franchise since Joe Willie Namath adopted Broadway. Kosar was a Broadman kid, a three-sport star in high school who passed for 2,222 yards and 19 TDs his senior year, and grew up watching Brian Sipe and dreaming about playing for the Browns himself. "He was," said Bill Livingston, "a one-man reaffirmation of Cleveland as a major-league town." He was the superstar who not only wanted to play in Cleveland, said Livingston, he wouldn't play anywhere else. He was a perfect match for the gritty blue-collar demeanor of the Browns' fans.

Kosar navigated the Browns into post-season play his first five years, which included four division titles. He owned the NFL's lowest all-time interception percentage (2.62 in 1991) while being the youngest starting quarterback during his first three seasons. After six years, he held 16 club all-time passing records.

Even his downstate rivals, the Cincinnati Bengals, admired him. Said Bengal linebacker Reggie Williams, "You sort of marvel at his awkwardness." Kosar did appear awkward, gangly, slow of foot, with that sideways stance under center and his half-cocked, sidearm throws. But after all was said and done, Kosar left the opposition awkward. "Kosar," said one writer, "is the master water-torture quarterback." Said a Bengal cornerback: "He throws to places you can't get to." Sam Wyche called it "manipulating the ball around." Kosar might not have Boomer Esaison's arm strength, but he was patient, and exceedingly smart.

In 1989, when the fans began to pick at him and he was playing with a hurt elbow behind a makeshift offensive line, he demonstrated the ultimate class: he uncomplainingly showed up for work, exhibiting his classical patience and—after being benched in the last quarter of the last home game, against Cincinnati—he beat Minnesota by driving his teammates 51 yards in the final three and a half minutes, then—in overtime—flinging a 39-yard fingertip strike to Reggie Langhorne for the win. Even in the unsettled, building seasons of 1990 and 1991, Kosar was looking like The Franchise again.

As a high school senior in his hometown of Broadman, the suburb of Youngstown—only an hour from the Browns' stadium—Kosar was the best quarterback in Ohio. The critics came out early, dissecting his heterodox throwing motion. "Yeah," someone said, finally, "but the one thing that Bernie's always known how to do perfectly is beat you." He did, too. At whatever sport. Basketball, one-on-one. Darts. Poker. He once took on a group of other NFL quarterbacks at throwing a football through a tire. He was five-for-five, and no one else was close.

When Miami University came courting, their people rated Kosar one of the three best QBs in America. The story was that Bernie signed with Miami because when Miami's coach, Howard Schnellenberger, walked up on the Kosar's porch, the Kosar's cocker spaniel didn't bark at him.

In Kosar's two seasons at Miami, he set 22 records, and in his first season took Miami to the national championship. Miami upset Nebraska that year in the Orange Bowl, 31-30. Kosar hasn't taken Cleveland all the way yet but his stock is undiminished. Said Art Modell: "I fully expect Bernie Kosar to be the best quarterback I ever had, or ever will have..." ▶

Top dawg, I

The **Browns** have made the NFL playoffs 22 times in its 41-year franchise history. Only the LA Rams and the NY Giants have done as well. Since 1950, the Browns have won more games than any other club—338-222-10.

Source: Cleveland Browns media guide, 1991

Football

Cleveland Browns, The Record

All-American Conference
1946   12-2
Championship: New York   W 14-9
1947   12-1-1
Championship: New York   W 14-3
1948   14-0
Championship: Buffalo   W 49-7
1949   9-1-2
Playoff: Buffalo   W 31-2
Championship: San Francisco   W 21-7

National Football League
1950   10-2
Playoff: NY Giants, W 8-3
Championship: Los Angeles, W 30-28

1951   11-1
Championship: Los Angeles, L 24-17

1952   8-4
Championship: Detroit, L 17-7

1953   11-1
Championship: Detroit, L 17-16

1954   9-3
Championship: Detroit, W 56-10

1955   9-2-1
Championship: Los Angeles, W 38-14

1956   5-7

1957   9-2-1
Championship: Detroit, L 59-14

1958   9-3

Playoff: NY Giants, L 10-0

1959   7-5
1960   8-3-1
1961   8-5-1
1962   7-6-1
1963   10-4

1964   10-3-1
Championship: Baltimore, W 27-0

1965   11-3
Championship: Green Bay, L 23-12

1966   9-5

1967   9-5
Playoff: Dallas, L 52-14

1968   10-4
Playoff: Dallas, W 31-20
Championship: Baltimore, L 34-0

1969   10-3-1
Playoff: Dallas, W 38-14
Championship: Minnesota, L 27-7

1970   7-7

1971   9-5
Playoff: Baltimore, L 20-3

1972   10-4
Playoff: Miami, L 20-14

1973   7-5-2
1974   4-10
1975   3-11

1976   9-5
1977   6-8
1978   8-8
1979   9-7

1980   11-5
Playoff: Oakland, L 14-12

1981   5-11

1982   4-5
Playoff: Raiders, L 27-10

1983   9-7
1984   5-11

1985   8-8
Playoffs: Miami, L 24-21

1986   12-4
AFC Playoffs: NY Jets, W 23-20 (2OT)
AFC Championship: Denver, L 38-33

1987   10-5
AFC Playoffs: Indianapolis W 38-21
AFC Championship: Denver, L 38-33

1988   10-6
AFC Wildcard: Houston, L 24-23

1989   9-6-1
AFC Playoffs: Buffalo, W 34-30
AFC Championship: Denver, L 37-21

1990   3-13
1991   6-10

Browns, The Coaches

Coach	Years	Record	Percent	Coach	Years	Record	Percent
Paul Brown	1946-1962	167-53-8	.759	Marty Schottenheimer	1984-1988	46-31-0	.597
Blanton Collier	1963-1970	79-38-2	.675	Bud Carson	1989-1990	12-14-1	.444
Nick Skorich	1971-1974	30-26-2	.536	Jim Shofner	1990	1-7	.125
Forrest Gregg	1975-1977	18-23-0	.439	Bill Belichick	1991-	6-10	.375
Dick Modzelewski	1977*	0-1-0	.000	*One game only	Includes playoff games		
Sam Rutigliano	1978-1984	47-51-0	.480				

Browns, Individual Records

Service

Most Seasons
Career   17   Lou Groza   (1950-59, 61-67)

Most Consecutive Seasons
Career   14   Doug Dieken   (1971-84)

Most Games
Career   216   Lou Groza   (1950-59, 61-67)

Most Consecutive Games
203   Doug Dieken   (1971-84)

Most Consecutive Starts
194   Doug Dieken   (1971-84)

Scoring

Most Total Points
Career   1,349   Lou Groza
(1950-59, 61-67), 641 PAT, 234 FG, 1 TD
Season   126   Jim Brown   (1965)
Game   36   Dub Jones   (11-25-51 vs. Chi. Brs.), 6 TD

Most Points, Rookie Season
75   Jeff Jaeger   (1987)

Most Consecutive Games Scoring
107   Lou Groza   (1950) 9 (1959) 2

Most Touchdowns by a Rookie
11   Dub Jones   (1950)

Most Touchdowns
Career   126   Jim Brown   (1957-65)
Season   21   Jim Brown   (1965)
Game   6   Dub Jones   (11-25-51 vs. Chi. Brs.)

Most Seasons, 100 or More Points
3   Jim Brown   (1958, 62, 65)

Most Consecutive Games Scoring Touchdowns
10   Jim Brown   (1965)

Most Points After Touchdown
Career   641   Lou Groza   (1950-59, 61-67)
Season   51   Lou Groza   (1966)
Game   8   Lou Groza   (12-6-53 vs. N.Y.)

Most Consecutive PATs Made
138   Lou Groza   (1963-66)

Most PATs Attempted
Career   658   Lou Groza   (1950-59, 61-67)
Season   52   Lou Groza   (1966)
Game   8   Lou Groza (12-6-53 vs. N.Y.)

Most Field Goals Attempted
Career   405   Lou Groza   (1950-59, 61-67)
Season   33   Lou Groza   (1952, 64)
Game   7   Don Cockroft   (10-19-75 vs. Den.)

Most Field Goals
Career   234   Lou Groza   (1950-59, 61-67)
Season   24   Matt Bahr   (1984)
Game   5   Don Cockroft   (10-19-75 vs. Den.)

Longest Field Goal
60 yds.   Steve Cox   (10-21-84 vs. Cin.)

Most Consecutive Games Field Goals Made
14   Lou Groza   (1950) 10 (1951) 4

Most Consecutive Field Goals Made
16   Don Cockroft   (1974) 11 (1975) 5

Highest Field Goal Percentage
Career   74.1   Matt Bahr   (1981-89), 143-193
Season   88.5   Lou Groza   (1953), 23-26

Rushing

Most Rushing Attempts
Career   2,359   Jim Brown   (1957-65)
Season   305   Jim Brown   (1961)
Game   37   Jim Brown   (10-4-59 vs. Chi. Cards)

Most Yards Rushing
Career   12,312   Jim Brown   (1957-65)
Season   1,863   Jim Brown   (1963)
Game   237   Jim Brown   (11-24-57 vs. L.A.)

Most Seasons, 1,000 Or More Rushing
7   Jim Brown   (1958-61, 63-65)

Longest Rushing Plays
90 yds.   Bobby Mitchell   (11-15-59 vs. Wash.) TD

Most Games, 100 Or More Yards Rushing
Career   58   Jim Brown   (1957-65)
Season   9   Jim Brown   (1958, 1963)

Most Consecutive 100-Yard Rushing Games
6   Jim Brown   (1958)

Most Touchdowns Rushing

Career	106	Jim Brown	(1957-65)
Season	17	Jim Brown	(1958, 65)
Game	5	Jim Brown	(11-1-59 vs. Balt.)

Most Consecutive Games Touchdowns Rushing

	9	Leroy Kelly	(1968)

Best Rushing Average

Career	5.22	Jim Brown	(1957-65), 2,359-12,312
Season	6.40	Jim Brown	(1963), 291-1863
Game	17.09	Marion Motley	(10-29-50 vs. Pin.), 11-188

Passing

Most Passing Attempts

Career	3,439	Brian Sipe	(1974-83)
Season	567	Brian Sipe	(1981)
Game	57	Brian Sipe	(9-7-81 vs. S.D.)

Most Passes Completed

Career	1,944	Brian Sipe (1974-83)
Season	337	Brian Sipe (1980)
Game	33	Brian Sipe (12-5-82 vs. S.D.)

Most Consecutive Completions

	16	Bernie Kosar
		(10-29-89 vs. Hou. through 11-5-89 at T.B.)

Most Yards Passing

Career	23,713	Brian Sipe	(1974-83)
Season	4,132	Brian Sipe	(1980)
Game	444	Brian Sipe	(10-25-81 vs. Balt.)

Longest Pass Plays

	97 yds.	Bernie Kosar
		(10-23-89 vs. Chi. Brs.) to W. Slaughter, TD

Most Touchdown Passes

Career	154	Brian Sipe	(1974-83)
Season	30	Brian Sipe	(1980)
Game	5	Frank Ryan	(12-12-64 vs. N.Y.)

Most Consecutive Games TD Passes

	23	Frank Ryan	(1965) 1 (1967) 8

Most Passes Had Intercepted

Career	149	Brian Sipe	(1974-83)
Season	26	Brian Sipe	(1979), 535 atts.
Game	6	Brian Sipe	(11-22-81 vs. Pitt.), 39 atts.

Most Consecutive Attempts None Intercepted

	208	Milt Plum	(1959-60)

Lowest Interception Rate

Career	2.48	Bernie Kosar	(1985-91), 71 of 2,857
Season	1.80	Bernie Kosar	(1991), 9 of 494

Highest Passing Percentage

Career	58.3	Bernie Kosar	(1985-91), 2,857-1,671
Season	64.7	Otto Graham	(1953), 258-167
Game	82.1	Brian Sipe	(10-24-76 vs. S.D.), 28-23

Pass Receiving

Most Receptions

Career	662	Ozzie Newsome	(1978-1990)
Season	89	Ozzie Newsome	(1984)
Game	14	Ozzie Newsome	(10-14-84 vs. N.Y.J.)

Most Receptions By a Rookie

	54	Eric Metcalf	(1989)

Most Consecutive Games Receptions

	150	Ozzie Newsome	(1979) 9 (1989) 7

Most Yards Receiving

Career	7,980	Ozzie Newsome	(1978-90)
Season	1,236	Webster Slaughter	(1989)
Game	191	Ozzie Newsome	(10-14-84 vs. N.Y.J.), 14

Most Seasons, 50 Or More Receptions

	6	Ozzie Newsome	(1979-81, 83-85)

Longest Reception

	97 yds.	Webster Slaughter
		(10-23-89 vs. Chi.) from B. Kosar—TD

Most Touchdowns Receiving

Career	70	Gary Collins	(1962-71)
Season	13	Gary Collins	(1963)
Game	3	MacSpeedie	(11-25-51 vs. Chi. Brs.)
	3	Darrell Brewster	(12-6-53 vs. N.Y.)
	3	Ray Renfro	(11-22-59 vs. Pitt.)
	3	Gary Collins	(10-20-63 vs. Phil.)
	3	Reggie Rucker	(9-12-76 vs. N.Y.J.)
	3	Larry Poole	(11-13-77 vs. Pitt.)
	3	Calvin Hill	(11-19-78 vs. Balt.)

Most Consecutive Games TD Receptions

	7	Gary Collins	(1963) 2 (1964) 5

Best Receiving Average

Career	19.6	Ray Renfro	(1952-63), 281
Season	28.1	Clarence Weathers	(1985), 16-449
Game	46.0	Webster Slaughter	
			(10-29-89 vs. Hou.), 4-184

Most Games, 100 Or More Yards Receiving

Career	15	Webster Slaughter	(1986-91)
Season	4	Gary Collins	(1965)

Interceptions

Most Interceptions

Career	45	Thom Darden	(1972-74, 76-81)
Season	10	Thom Darden	(1978)
Game	3	Tommy James	(11-15-50 vs. Chi. Cards)
	3	Tommy James	(11-1-53 vs. Wash.)
	3	Bobby Franklin	(12-11-60 bs. Chi. Brs.)
	3	Bernie Parrish	(12-3-61 bs. Dall.)
	3	Ross Fichtner	(10-23-66 vs. Dall.)
	3	Ron Bolton	(11-27-77 vs. L.A.)
	3	Hanford Dixon	(11-19-82 vs. Pitt.)
	3	Frank Minnifield	(11-22-87 at Hou.)

Most Yards Interceptions Returned

Career	820	Thom Darden	(1972-74, 76-81)
Season	238	Bernie Parrish	(1960)
Game	115	Bernie Parrish	(12-11-60 vs. Chi. Brs.), 2

Longest Interception Return, Yards

	92	Bernie Parrish	(12-11-60 vs. Chi. Brs.), TD

Most Touchdowns on Interceptions

Career	5	Warren Lahr	(1950-59)
Season	2	Warren Lahr	(1950, 51)
	2	Ken Konz	(1954)
	2	Bobby Franklin	(1960)
	2	Jim Houston	(1967)
	2	Thane Gash	(1989)
Game	2	Bobby Franklin	(12-11-60 vs. Chi. Brs.)

Highest Average Gain on Interceptions

Career	21.7	Oliver Davis	(1977-80), 11
Season	39.7	Bernie Parrish	(1960), 6
Game	57.5	Bernie Parrish	(12-11-60 vs. Chi. Brs.), 2

Most Consecutive Games Interceptions

7	Ben Davis	(1968)

Fumbles

Most Fumbles

Career	62	Brian Sipe	(1974-83)
Season	16	Paul McDonald	(1984)
Game	4	Otto Graham	(10-25-53 vs. N.Y.)
	4	Ken Brown	(10-8-72 vs. K.C.)
	4	Paul McDonald	(12-20-81 vs. Sea.)

Most Opponents' Fumbles Recovered

Career	19	Len Ford	(1950-57)
Season	5	Len Ford	(1954)
Game	2	Accomplished 20 times; last time by Clinton Burrell	(12-26-82 vs. Hou.)

Most Touchdowns, Career (Opponent Recovered)

	2	Vince Costello	(1957-66)
	2	Walter Johnson	(1965-76)
	2	David Grayson	(1987-90)

Longest Opponents' Fumble Return

89	Don Paul	(11-10-57 vs. Pitt.), TD

Punting

Most Punts

Career	651	Don Cockroft	(1968-80)
Season	97	Bryan Wagner	(1989)
Game	12	Horace Gillom	(12-3-50 vs. Phil.)
	12	Bryan Wagner	(11-19-89 vs. K.C.)

Highest Average Yardage Punting

Career	43.8	Horace Gillom	(1950-56), 385
Season	46.7	Gary Collins	(1965), 65
Game	54.8	Horace Gillom	(11-28-54 vs. N.Y.), 4

Longest Punts

80 yds.	Horace Gillom	(11-28-54 vs. N.Y.)

Most Punt Returns

Career	161	Gerald McNeil	(1986-89)
Season	49	Gerald McNeil	(1989)
Game	7	Chet Hanulak	(11-7-54 vs. Wash.)
	7	Dino Hall	(10-25-81 vs. Balt.)
	7	Gerald McNeil	(10-12-86 vs. K.C.)
	7	Gerald McNeil	(11-16-86 vs. L.A. Raiders)
	7	Gerald McNeil	(11-19-89 vs. K.C.)

Most Yards, Punt Returns

Career	1,545	Gerald McNeil	(1986-89)
Season	496	Gerald McNeil	(1989)
Game	109	Leroy Kelly	(11-28-65 vs. Pitt.), 4

Longest Punt Returns

84 yds.	Gerald McNeil	(9-28-86 vs. Det.), TD

Best Average, Punt Returns

Career	11.8	Greg Pruitt	(1973-81), 56
Game	27.7	Bobby Mitchell	(10-8-61 vs. Wash.), 3

Most Touchdowns, Punt Returns

Career	3	Bobby Mitchell	(1958-61)
	3	Leroy Kelly	(1964-73)
Season	2	Leroy Kelly	(1965)
Game	1	Accomplished 13 times; last time by Gerald McNeil (9-28-86 vs. Det.)	

Kickoff Returns

Most Kickoff Returns

Career	151	Dino Hall	(1979-83)
Season	52	Eric Metcalf	(1990)
Game	9	Dino Hall	(10-7-79 vs. Pitt.)

Most Yards, Kickoff Returns

Career	3,185	Dino Hall	(1979-83)
Season	1,052	Eric Metcalf	(1990)
Game	172	Dino Hall	(10-7-79 vs. Pitt.)

Longest Kickoff Returns

104 yds.	Carl Ward	(11-26-67 vs. Wash.), TD

Best Average, Kickoff Returns

Career	26.3	Greg Pruitt	(1973-81), 58
Game	48.3	Gerald McNeil	(10-5-86 at Pitt.), 3

Most Touchdowns, Kickoff Returns

Career	3	Bobby Mitchell	(1958-61)
Season	2	Eric Metcalf	(1990)
Game	1	Accomplished 10 times; last time by Eric Metcalf (12-9-90 at Hou.)	

Combined Net Yards Gained

Attempts

Career	2,658	Jim Brown	(1957-65)
Season	354	Jim Brown	(1961)
Game	39	Jim Brown	(10-4-59 vs. Chi. Cards)
	39	Mike Pruitt	(12-3-81 vs. Hou.)

Combined Yardage

Career	15,459	Jim Brown	(1957-65)
Season	2,131	Jim Brown	(1963)
Game	313	Jim Brown	(11-19-61 vs. Phil.)

Average Gain

Career	8.84	Bobby Mitchell	(1958-61), 669-5,916
Season	9.27	Eric Metcalf	(1990), 189-1,752
Game	14.95	Leroy Kelly	(12-4-66 vs. N.Y.), 20-299

QB Sacks

Most Sacks

Career	69	Jerry Sherk	(1970-81)
Season	14-1/2	Bill Glass	(1965)
Game	4	Jerry Sherk	(11-14-76 vs. Phil.)
	4	Mack Mitchell	(11-20-77 vs. N.Y.G.)

Most Consecutive Games at Least One Sack

	7	Bill Glass	(1966)

Most Sack Yards

Career	547	Jerry Sherk	(1970-81)
Season	125-1/2	Reggie Camp	(1984)
Game	39	Reggie Camp	(11-25-84 vs. Hou.)

Most By Rookie

Season	8	Mack Mitchell	(1975)
Game	3	Chip Banks	(9-12-82 vs. Sea.)

Browns, Career Statistics

Rushing

	Player	Years	Carries	Yards	Avg.
1.	Jim Brown	1957-65	2,359	12,312	5.2
2.	Leroy Kelly	1964-73	1,727	7,274	4.2
3.	Mike Pruitt	1976-84	1,593	6,540	4.1
4.	Greg Pruitt	1973-81	1,158	5,496	4.7
5.	Kevin Mack	1985-91	1,112	4,547	4.1
6.	Ernie Green	1962-68	668	3,204	4.8
7.	Earnest Byner	1984-88	672	2,713	4.0
8.	Bobby Mitchell	1958-61	423	2,297	5.4
9.	Cleo Miller	1975-82	546	2,286	4.2
10.	Bo Scott	1969-74	554	2,124	3.8

Receiving

	Player	Years	Recep.	Yards	Avg.	TDs
1.	Ozzie Newsome, TE	1978-90	662	7,980	12.1	47
2.	Ray Renfro, RB/WR	1952-63	281	5,508	19.6	50
3.	Gary Collins, WR	1962-71	331	5,299	16.0	70
4.	Paul Warfield, WR	1964-69, 76-77	271	5,210	19.2	52
5.	Reggie Rucker, WR	1975-81	310	4,953	15.9	32
6.	Webster Slaughter, WR	1986-91	305	4,834	15.8	27
7.	Dave Logan, WR	1976-83	262	4,247	16.2	24
8.	Milt Morin, TE	1966-75	271	4,208	15.5	16
9.	Brian Brennan, WR	1984-91	315	4,148	13.2	19
10.	Dante Lavelli, WR	1950-56	244	3,908	16.0	33

*Does not include AAFC statistics.

Passing

	Player	Years	Atts.	Comp.	Yards	TDs	INTs	RTG
1.	Milt Plum	1957-61	1,083	627	8,917	66	39	89.9
2.	Bernie Kosar	1985-91	2,857	1,671	19,937	103	71	81.6
3.	Frank Ryan	1962-68	1,755	907	13,361	134	88	81.4
4.	Otto Graham	1950-55	*1,565	872	13,499	88	94	78.2
5.	Brian Sipe	1974-83	3,439	1,944	23,713	154	149	74.8
6.	Bill Nelsen	1968-72	1,314	689	9,725	71	71	72.1
7.	Mike Phipps	1970-76	1,317	633	7,700	40	81	51.0

*Does not include AAFC statistics.
Only players with 1,000 or more attempts.

Point makers

Top seasons of scoring, Browns

1. Jim Brown, 1965, 21 TDs, 126 points
2. Leroy Kelly, 1968, 20 TDs, 120 points
3. Lou Groza, 1964, 49 PAT, 115 points
4. Jim Brown, 1962, 18 TDs, 108 [points
5. Jim Brown, 1958, 18 TDs, 108 points
6. Lou Groza, 1953, 39 PAT, 23 FG,108 points
7. Matt Bahr, 1988, 32 PAT, 34 FG, 104 points
8. Matt Bahr, 1983, 38 PAT, 21 FG, 101 points

Source: Browns media guide

father Football: Paul Brown, 1908-1991

Born: September 7, 1908, Norwalk, Ohio. Died: August 5, 1991, Cincinnati

1924: Graduates from Massillon High at 16 after an oversized prep career as an undersized quarterback. His first high school letter was as a freshman pole vaulter.

1930: Graduates with bachelor of arts from Miami University in Oxford, Ohio, after transferring from Ohio State where he is not allowed to try out for football because of his size. He becomes Miami's quarterback and punter. Hired as head coach at Severn Prep School in Maryland; loses one game in two years.

1932: Hired as head coach at Massillon High, inheriting a team that has just gone 2-6-2, he wins six state championships and four mythical national titles in nine years. His Tigers once scored 50 points against Kent State in a scrimmage before Kent called the game.

1940: Massillon unscored upon until last game when Canton McKinley gets six points. Season: Massillon 477, Opponents 6.

1941: Hired as head coach at Ohio State; wins school's first national title the following year.

1943: Inducted into Navy and stationed at the Great Lakes Naval Center near Chicago; appointed head football coach where he first coaches a Canton fullback named Marion Motley. They upset Notre Dame 39-7.

1946: Hired as coach and general manager of the Cleveland Browns in the new All-American Conference, which would rival the NFL. The conference lasts four years; each year the Browns are the champions. Brown's assembly of that original team is considered the greatest talent roundup in the history of pro sports.

1950: Browns win NFL championship first year in league, going 10-2 and beating the Los Angeles Rams 30-28 in the title game, on a Lou Groza field goal. The Browns win titles in 1950, 1954, and 1955, and play for the NFL title seven of the Browns first eight years.

1962: Brown fired by new owner Art Modell, who bought team in 1961. Brown's last team goes 7-6-1. A communications gap between Brown and Modell, and between Brown and his players, are major points of contention. Brown has been in Cleveland 17 seasons, and only once has he lost more games than he has won.

1967: Begins the Cincinnati Bengals, an American Football League expansion team. He is also inducted into the Pro Football Hall of Fame.

1968: Cincinnati scores upset victories over Denver and Buffalo in its first two home games; finishes season at 3-11. Brown is head coach, general manager, and part owner. "I'm living again," he says.

1969: Cincinnati opens season 3-0, finishes 4-9-1 as Brown is named AFL Coach of the Year.

1970: On August 29, 57,112 fans—a record Cincinnati sports crowd—come to Riverfront to watch Brown's first coaching outing against his old team. A gangly quarterback named Sam Wyche leads the upstart Bengals to a 31-24 exhibition win over the Browns, who featured seven All-NFL players.

1970: Cincinnati wins last seven games to go 8-6 and captures division title in Bengals' third season of play. No team had ever come so far so quickly.

1973: Cincinnati goes 10-4; wins second AFC Central title.

1975: Cincinnati goes 11-3 and earns wild-card playoff spot; loses in first round for third time.

1976: Brown retires as head coach, January 1. His .609 winning percentage is fourth; his 170 wins in 21 NFL seasons are seventh.

1981: Cincinnati ends regular season at 12-4 and loses 26-21 to San Francisco in Super Bowl XVI. Brown is named NFL Executive of Year.

1988: Cincinnati again ends regular season at 12-4, and is beaten in Super Bowl XXIII 20-16 by San Francisco, on a brilliant last-minute drive by Joe Montana. Brown again named NFL Executive of Year.

1989: Brown is presented the National Football Foundation and Hall of Fame's Gold Medal. The medal is the highest individual award presented by the foundation.

1991: Brown is inducted into Ohio State University Hall of Fame.

Innovations, by Brown

Forty-yard times
Intelligence tests for players
Practice routines, position coaches, year round coaches
Game film, printed playbooks, classroom study
Play-calling from the sidelines, the messenger guard
Breaking the color line in pro football
Keeping players and coaches in a hotel the night before a game
Developing precise pass routes
The draw play
Face bars on helmets

The Record

Years	Team	W-L-T	Percent
High School			
1930-31	Severn Prep	16-1-1	.941
1932-40	Massillon	80-8-2	.900
College			
1941-43	Ohio State	18-8-1	.685
Military			
1944-45	Great Lakes	15-5-2	.727
Professional			
1946-62	Cleveland	167-54-8	.747
1968-75	Cincinnati	55-59-1	.483
41 years	6 teams	351-135-15	.716

Football

Cincinnati Bengals, The Record

Regular Season Results
Won 174, Lost 181, Tied 1

Year	Record	Year	Record	Year	Record	Year	Record
1968	3-11-0	1975	11-3-0	1982	7-2-0	1989	8-8-0
1969	4-9-1	1976	10-4-0	1983	7-9-0	1990	9-7-0
1970	8-6-0	1977	8-6-0	1984	8-8-0	1991	3-13-0
1971	4-10-0	1978	4-12-0	1985	7-9-0		
1972	8-6-0	1979	4-12-0	1986	10-6-0		
1973	10-4-0	1980	6-10-0	1987	4-11-0		
1974	7-7-0	1981	12-4-0	1988	12-4-0		

Playoff Results

Bengals		Opp.
	1970	
	AFC Divisional Playoff	
0	at Baltimore	17
	1975	
	AFC Divisional Playoff	
28	at Oakland	31
	1981	
	AFC Champsionship Game	
27	San Diego	7
	1982	
	AFC Playoff Game	
17	New York Jets	44

Bengals		Opp.
	1988	
	AFC Championship Game	
21	Buffalo	10
	1973	
	AFC Divisional Playoff	
16	at Miami	34
	1981	
	AFC Divisional Playoff	
28	Buffalo	21
	1981	
	Super Bowl XVI	
21	San Franciso	26
	at Pontiac, Mich.	

Bengals		Opp.
	1988	
	AFC Divisional Playoff	
21	Seatlle	13
	1988	
	Super Bowl XXIII	
16	San Francisco at Miami	20
	1990	
	AFC Divisional Playoff	
20	at Los Angeles	10

Bengals, The Coaches

(Regular Season)

Season	Coach	Record	Pct.	Season	Coach	Record	Pct.
1968	Paul Brown	3-11-0	.214	1984	Sam Wyche	8-8-0	.500
1969	Paul Brown	4-9-1	.308	1985	Sam Wyche	7-9-0	.438
1970**	Paul Brown	8-6-0	.571	1986	Sam Wyche	10-6-0	.625
1971	Paul Brown	4-10-0	.286	1987	Sam Wyche	4-11-0	.267
1972	Paul Brown	8-6-0	.576	1988****	Sam Wyche	12-4-0	.667
1973**	Paul Brown	10-4-0	.714	1989	Sam Wyche	8-8-0	.500
1974	Paul Brown	7-7-0	.500	1990**	Sam Wyche	9-7-0	.563
1975*	Paul Brown	11-3-0	.786	1991	Sam Wyche	3-13-0	.188
1976	Bill Johnson	10-4-0	.714				
1977	Bill Johnson	8-6-0	.571				
1978	Bill Johnson	0-5-0	.000				
	Homer Rice	4-7-0	.572				
1979	Homer Rice	4-12-0	.250				
1980	Forrest Gregg	6-10-0	.267				
1981****	Forrest Gregg	12-4-0	.750				
1982*	Forrest Gregg	7-2-0	.778				
1983	Forrest Gregg	7-9-0	.437				

*AFC Wild Card Playoff Team
**AFC Central Division Champion
***AFC Champion
****AFC Super Bowl Tournament Team

Bengals, Individual Records

(Regular Season)

Scoring

Total Points Scored

Career	875	Jim Breech		1980-
Season	120	Jim Breech		1985
Game	24	Larry Kinnebrew, Oct. 28, 1984 at Houston		

Total Touchdowns

Career	70	Pete Johnson	1977-83
Season	16	Pete Johnson	1981
Game	4	Larry Kinnebrew, Oct. 28, 1984 at Houston	

Rushing Touchdowns

Career	64	Pete Johnson	1977-83
Season	15	Ickey Woods	1988
Game	3	Paul Robinson, Nov. 17, 1968 at Miami	

Reception Touchdowns

Career	53	Isaac Curtis	1973-84
Season	10	Isaac Curtis	1974
Game	3	Bob Trumpy, Nov. 9, 1969 at Houston	

Touchdowns by Return, Etc.

Career	13	Lemar Parrish	1970-78
Season	3	Lemar Parrish	1970
Game	2	Lemar Perrish, Nov. 8, 1970 at Buffalo	

Points After Touchdown

Career	377	Jim Breech	1980-
Season	56	Jim Breech	1988
Game	8	Jim Breech, Oct. 29, 1989 vs. Tampa Bay	

Field Goals
Total Field Goals

Career	166	Jim Breech	1980-
Season	27	Horst Muhlmann	1972
Game	5	Horst Muhlmann, Nov. 8, 1970 at Buffalo	

Field Goal Percentage

Career	70.3	Jim Breech (166-236)	1980-
Season	86.0	Jim Breech (12/14)	1989

Longest Field Goals

55	Chris Bahr, Sept. 23, 1979 vs. Houston

Rushing

Rushing Attempts

Career	1402	Pete Johnson	1977-83
Season	274	Pete Johnson	1981
Game	38	Pete Johnson, Dec. 4, 1983 at Pittsburgh	

Rushing Yardage

Career	5,421	Pete Johnson	1977-83
Season	1,230	James Brooks	1989
Game	163	James Brooks, Dec. 7, 1986 at New England	

Longest Rushing Plays

87	Paul Robinson, Oct. 27, 1968 at Oakland (TD)

Passing

Passing Attempts

Career	4,475	Ken Anderson	1971-86
Season	479	Ken Anderson	1981
Game	56	Ken Anderon, Dec. 20, 1982 at San Diego	

Pass Completions

Career	2,654	Ken Anderson	1971-86
Season	300	Ken Anderson	1981
Game	40	Ken Anderson, Dec. 20, 1982 at San Diego	

Note: Bengal records are through the 1990 season.

Passing Yards

Career	32,838	Ken Anderson	1971-86
Season	3,959	Boomer Esiason	1986
Game	447	Ken Anderson, Nov. 17, 1975 vs. Buffalo	

Longest Pass Completions

94 Ken Anderson to Billy Brooks, Nov. 13, 1977 at Minnesota (TD)

Passes for Touchdowns

Career	197	Ken Anderson	1971-86
Season	29	Ken Anderson	1981
Game	5	Boomer Esiason, Oct. 29, 1989 vs. Tampa Bay	

Passes Had Intercepted

Career	160	Ken Anderson	1971-86
Season	22	Ken Anderson	1978
Game	5	Boomer Esiason, Oct. 16, 1988 at New England	

Pass Receiving

Total Receptions

Career	420	Isaac Curtis	1973-84
Season	71	Dan Ross	1981
Game	11	Tim McGee, Nov. 19, 1989 vs. Detroit	

Reception Yardage

Career	7,106	Isaac Curtis	1973-84
Season	1,273	Eddie Brown	1988
Game	216	Eddie Brown, Nov. 16, 1988 vs. Pittsburgh	

Average Yards Per Reception

Career	18.4	Tim McGee	1986
Season	26.8	Billy Brooks (8/214)	1979

Punting

Total Punts

Career	698	Pat McInally	1976-85
Season	91	Pat McInally	1978
Game	10	Dale Livingston, Oct. 6, 1968 at Denver	

Punt Yardage

Career	29,307	Pat McInally	1976-85
Season	3,919	Pat McInally	1978
Game	483	Dave Lewis, Sept. 26, 1971 at Pittsburgh	

Longest Punts

Game	67	Pat McInally, Sept. 18, 1977 vs. Cleveland	

Average Yards Per Punt

Career	43.8	Dave Lewis (284/12446)	1970-73

Kickoff Returns

Total Returns

Career	97	Bernard Jackson	1972-76
Season	55	David (Deacon) Turner	1979
Game	7	David (Deacon) Turner, Sept. 30, 1979 at Dallas	

Kickoff Return Yardage

Career	2,355	Bernard Jackson	1972-76
Season	1,149	David (Deacon) Turner	1979
Game	192	Stanford Jennings, Nov. 13, 1988 at Kansas City	

Longest Kickoff Returns

Game	98	Stanford Jennings, Nov. 13, 1988 vs. Kansas City (TD)	

Punt Returns

Total Returns

Career	130	Lemar Parrish	1970-78
Season	32	Vaughn Lusby	1979
Game	7	Tony Davis, Nov. 27, 1977 vs. New York Giants	

Punt Return Yardage

Career	1,201	Lemar Parrish	1970-78
Season	376	Mike Martin	1984
Game	106	Tommy Casanova, Oct. 8, 1972 vs. Denver	

Longest Punt Returns

Game	90	Lemar Parrish, Oct. 6, 1974 vs. Washington (TD)	

Pass Interceptions

Number Interceptions

Career	65	Ken Riley	1969-83
Season	9	Ken Riley	1976
Game	3	David Fulcher	
	3	Lemar Parrish, Dec. 17, 1972 at Houston	
	3	Ken Riley, Dec. 12, 1976 at New York Jets	
	3	Louis Breeden, Dec. 14, 1980 at Chicago	
	3	Ken Riley, Nov. 28, 1982 vs. Los Angeles Raiders	

Interception Return Yardage

Career	596	Ken Riley	1969-83
Season	167	Ray Griffin	1979

Longest Interception Returns

Game	102	Louis Breeden at San Diego, 1981	

Safeties Scored

Career	3	Reggie Williams (1980, 1982, 1983)	

*Last accomplished by team Oct. 23, 1988 vs. Houston

Bengals All-Time Statistics

Rushing

Player	Att.	Yds.	Avg.	LG	TD
1. James Brooks, RB 1984-90	1,192	5,876	4.9	65	76
2. Pete Johnson, RB 1977-83	1,402	5,421	3.9	65	64
3. Essex Johnson, RB 1968-75	676	3,070	4.5	86t	18
4. Boobie Clark, RB 1973-78	780	2,978	3.8	26	25
5. Archie Griffin, RB 1976-83	692	2,808	4.1	77t	7
6. Charles Alexander, RB 1979-85	748	2,635	3.5	37	13
7. Larry Kinnebrew, RB 1983-88	632	2,587	4.1	52	36
8. Paul Robinson, RB 1968-72	617	2,441	4.0	87t	19
9. Ken Anderson, QB 1971-86	397	2,200	5.6	43	20
10. Jesse Phillips, RB 1968-72	424	1,860	4.4	83	8

Receiving

Player	No.	Yds.	Avg.	LG	TD
1. Isaac Curtis, WR 1973-84	420	7,106	16.9	85	53
2. Cris Collinsworth, WR 1981-88	417	6,698	16.1	74	36
3. Eddie Brown, WR 1985-90	304	5,307	17.4	86	38
4. Bob Trumpy, TE 1968-77	298	4,630	15.5	80	35
5. Dan Ross, TE 1979-83	263	3,204	12.2	38	16
6. Rodney Holman, TE 1982-90	261	3,618	13.9	73	30
7. James Brooks, RB 1984-90	250	2,664	10.7	57	28
8. Archie Griffin, RB 1976-83	192	1,607	8.4	52	7
9. Tim McGee, WR 1986-90	187	3,318	17.7	78	17
10. Pete Johnson, RB 1977-83	186	1,430	7.7	34	6

Scoring

Player	TDR	TDP	TDRt	PAT/PAT	FG/FG	SAF	Pts.
1. Jim Breech, K 1980-90	0	0	0	459/481	201/284	0	2,062
2. Horst Muhlmann, K 1969-74	0	0	0	189/195	120/187	0	549
3. Pete Johnson, RB 1977-83	64	6	0	—	—	0	420
4. James Brooks, RB 1984-90	35	29	0	—	—	0	362
5. Isaac Curtis, WR 1973-84	0	53	0	—	—	0	318
6. Chris Bahr, K 1976-79	0	0	0	130/139	62/105	0	316
7. Larry Kinnebrew, RB 1983-87	36	3	0	—	—	0	234
8. Eddie Brown, WR 1985-90	0	38	0	—	—	0	228
9. Cris Collinsworth, WR 1981-88	0	36	0	—	—	0	216
10. Bob Trumpy, TE 1968-77	0	35	0	—	—	0	210

Passing

Player	Att.	Com.	Pct.	Yds.	TDS	Pct.	Int	Pct	Avg.	Rating
1. Greg Cook, QB 1969-74	200	107	53.5	1,865	15	7.5	11	5.5	9.33	87.7
2. Boomer Esiason, QB 1984-90	2,687	1,520	56.6	21,381	150	5.6	88	3.6	8.00	85.8
3. Eric Wilhelm, QB	75	42	56.0	542	4	5.3	2	2.7	7.2	85.5
4. Sam Wyche, QB 1968-70	220	115	52.3	1,743	12	5.5	8	3.6	7.92	82.0
5. Ken Anderson, QB 1971-86	4,475	2,654	59.3	32,838	197	4.4	160	3.6	7.34	81.9
6. Turk Schonert, QB 1980-85, 87-88	350	216	62.1	2,765	7	2.0	12	3.4	7.87	79.3
7. Virgil Carter, QB 1970-73	582	328	56.4	3,850	22	3.8	20	3.4	6.62	75.2
8. Dewey Warren, QB 1968	80	47	58.8	506	1	1.3	4	5.0	6.32	60.9
9. Jon Stofa, QB 1968-69	177	85	48.0	896	5	2.8	5	2.8	5.06	60.8
10. Jack Thompson, QB 1979-82	370	175	47.3	2,072	13	3.5	19	5.1	5.6	55.3

* As of March 11, 1992, all-time stats that included results of the 1991 season were unavailable from the Bengals. The stats listed here run through the end of the 1990 season

Hit man

Cincinnati Bengal All-Pro offensive tackle **Anthony Munoz,** who has played nearly 20 games a season for 12 years, has taken an estimated 13,000 professional hits.

Source: Cincinnati Post

Football

Ohioans in Pro Hall of Fame

Name	Hometown	Position	Size	Team(s)
Cliff Battles	Akron	halfback	6-1, 201	Boston Braves, Boston Redskins, Washington Redskins(1932-37)
Paul Brown	Norwalk	coach		Cleveland Browns(1946-62)
Joe Carr	Columbus	administrator		NFL(1921-39)
Larry Csonka	Stowe	fullback	6-3, 235	Miami Dolphins, New York Giants(1968-79)
Len Dawson	Alliance	quarterback	6-0, 190	Pittsburgh Steelers, Browns, Dallas Texans, Kansas City Chiefs(1957-75)
Lou Groza	Martins Ferry	tackle, kicker	6-3, 250	Browns(1946-67)
Wilbur (Pete) Henry	Mansfield	tackle	6-0, 250	Canton Bulldogs, Giants, Pottsville Maroons(1920-28)
Clark Hinkle	Toronto	fullback	5-11, 201	Green Bay Packers(1932-41)
Jack Lambert	Mantua	linebacker	6-4, 220	Steelers(1974-84)
Dante Lavelli	Hudson	end	6-0, 199	Browns(1946-56)
George McAfee	Ironton	halfback	6-0, 177	Chicago Bears(1940-1950)
August (Mike) Michalske	Cleveland	guard	6-0, 209	New York Yankees, Packers(1926-37)
Alan Page	Canton	tackle	6-4, 225	Minnesota Vikings, Bears(1967-81)
Roger Staubach	Cincinnati	quarterback	6-3, 202	Dallas Cowboys(1969-79)
Paul Warfield	Warren	receiver	6-0, 188	Browns, Dolphins(1964-77)
Bill Willis	Columbus	middle guard	6-2, 215	Browns(1946-53)

Jack the ripper

Portage County's Jack Lambert Evolved into Pro Football's Best Middle Linebacker

Jack Lambert, who came out of Mantua, Ohio, and through **Kent State**, went on to become the NFL's last great middle linebacker, a nine-time Pro Bowler whose defensive play helped the Pittsburgh Steelers win four Super Bowls.

He was tall and skinny, with a slightly maniacal appearance on the football field because of his missing bridgework and intimidating glare. But while he was considered too light, he was the only rookie to break into the Steelers' 1974 lineup and for a decade was the team's leading tackler.

He was a Mantua farm boy recruited mostly by Mid-American Conference schools and told by pro scouts he'd never play in the NFL. But he became the last piece of the puzzle that gave Pittsburgh its fabled Steel Curtain defense and its four trips to the Super Bowl. Twice, Lambert was named Defensive Player of the Year (1976 and 1979), and he was Pittsburgh's defensive captain for eight years. The traits that made him a great linebacker were speed—he ran a 4.6 forty—football savvy, and an almost supernatural intensity. Once, teammate Joe Greene said, "Jack Lambert, he's so mean that he don't even like himself." Weight, always the rap against him, was certainly not part of the equation; his playing weight was about 218. "I give away 20 pounds every time I step on the field," said Lambert, "so I have to be 20 pounds more aggressive." Said Steelers' linebacker, Jack Ham: "What set him apart was his ability to play the pass. He was the best, most complete middle linebacker to ever play the game." Lambert was elected to the Pro Football Hall of Fame in 1990, on his first try. ▶

Football

Boomer Esiason, *Bengal quarterback, $3,000,000*
Bernie Kosar, *Browns quarterback, $2,329,000 (average)*
Michael Dean Perry, *Browns Pro Bowl lineman, $1,400,000*
Anthony Munoz, *Bengal Pro Bowl offensive tackle, $900,000*
    Kirk Scrafford, *Munoz' backup, $93,500*
Average salary, Bengal starters—$661,500
Average Salary, Browns starters—$611,500
Largest fine for NFL coach, ex-Bengal coach **Sam Wyche**, *$27,800, for*
    violating league media relations policy for third time (1990)
In 1991, the Browns had the second highest payroll in the NFL—
    $28,348,750—or $4,724,791 per win
Franchise value: **Cleveland Browns**, *$145 million*
    Cincinnati Bengals, *$125 million*

Baseball

Barry Larkin, *Cincinnati Reds shortstop, $5,500,000*
($1.5 million signing bonus, base of $4 million; if Larkin plays the entire
    schedule, $3,512 per inning)
Chris Sabo, *Cincinnati Reds third baseman, $1,275,000*
Tom Browning, *Cincinnati Reds pitcher, $2,650,000*
Franchise value: **Cincinnati Reds**, *$102.3 million*
    Cleveland Indians, *$75 million*
Cincinnati Reds estimated 1991 profit, $13.4 million

Other

Average salary, **Cleveland Crunch** *of the Major Soccer League, $33,000*
    and change
Highest paid pro basketball player, Cleveland Cavaliers' **John Williams**,
    $4 million signing bonus, $1 million in salary

Source: Football, NFL Players Association; Baseball, AP from player and management sources

In 1992, it will cost a family of four an average of $72.28 to attend a **Reds** *game—lowest average in the majors. The Reds have the lowest average ticket price, $7.20, and the only $1 hot dog.* **The Indians** *have the second-lowest average ticket price, $7.70. The major league average is $9.41. The average cost is based on four tickets, four hot dogs, four soft drinks, two beers, two baseball caps, two programs, and parking.*

Source: Team Marketing Report

Cleveland Indians Records, 1901-1991

Year	Position	W	L	GB	Pct.	Manager
1901	Seventh	54	82	28 1/2	.397	James R. McAleer
1902	Fifth	69	67	14	.507	William R. Armour
1903	Third	77	63	15	.550	William R. Armour
1904	Fourth	86	65	7 1/2	.570	Armour—Napoleon Lajoie
1905	Fifth	76	78	19	.494	Napoleon Lajoie
1906	Third	89	64	5	.582	Napoleon Lajoie
1907	Fourth	85	67	8	.559	Napoleon Lajoie
1908	Second	90	64	1/2	.584	Napoleon Lajoie
1909	Sixth	71	82	27 1/2	.464	Lajoie—James McGuire
1910	Fifth	71	81	32	.467	James McGuire
1911	Third	80	73	22	.523	McGuire—George Stovall
1912	Fifth	75	78	30 1/2	.490	Harry Davis—J. L. Birmingham
1913	Third	86	66	9.1/2	.566	J. L. Birmingham
1914	Eighth	51	102	48 1/2	.333	J. L. Birmingham
1915	Seventh	57	95	44 1/2	.375	Birmingham—Lee Fohl
1916	Sixth	77	77	14	.500	Lee Fohl
1917	Third	88	66	12	.571	Lee Fohl
1918	Second (a)	73	56	2 1/2	.566	Lee Fohl
1919	Second	84	55	3 1/2	.604	Fohl—Tris Speaker
1920	First	98	56	—	.636	Tris Speaker
1921	Second	94	60	4 1/2	.610	Tris Speaker
1922	Fourth	78	76	16	.507	Tris Speaker
1923	Third	82	71	16 1/2	.536	Tris Speaker
1924	Sixth	67	86	24 1/2	.438	Tris Speaker
1925	Sixth	70	84	27 1/2	.455	Tris Speaker
1926	Second	88	66	3	.571	Tris Speaker
1927	Sixth	66	86	43 1/2	.431	Jack McAllister
1928	Seventh	62	92	39	.403	Roger Peckinpaugh
1929	Third	81	71	24	.533	Roger Peckinpaugh
1930	Fourth	81	73	21	.526	Roger Peckinpaugh
1931	Fourth	78	76	30	.506	Roger Peckinpaugh
1932	Fourth	87	65	19	.572	Roger Peckinpaugh
1933	Fourth	75	76	23 1/2	.497	Peckinpaugh—Walter Johnson
1934	Third	85	69	16	.552	Walter Johnson
1935	Third	82	71	12	.536	Johnson—Steve O'Neill
1936	Fifth	80	74	22 1/2	.519	Steve O'Neill
1937	Fourth	83	71	19	.539	Steve O'Neill
1938	Third	86	66	13	.566	Oscar Vitt
1939	Third	87	67	20 1/2	.565	Oscar Vitt
1940	Second	89	65	1	.578	Oscar Vitt
1941	Fourth (b)	75	79	26	.487	Roger Peckinpaugh
1942	Fourth	75	79	28	.487	Lou Boudreau
1943	Third	82	71	15 1/2	.536	Lou Boudreau
1944	Fifth (c)	72	82	17	.468	Lou Boudreau
1945	Fifth	73	72	11	.503	Lou Boudreau
1946	Sixth	68	86	36	.442	Lou Boudreau

Year	Position	W	L	GB	Pct.	Manager
1947	Fourth	80	74	17	.519	Lou Boudreau
1948	First	97	58	—	.626	Lou Boudreau
1949	Third	89	65	8	.578	Lou Boudreau
1950	Fourth	92	62	6	.597	Lou Boudreau
1951	Second	93	61	5	.604	Al Lopez
1952	Second	93	61	2	.604	Al Lopez
1953	Second	92	62	8 1/2	.597	Al Lopez
1954	First	111	43	—	.721	Al Lopez
1955	Second	93	61	3	.604	Al Lopez
1956	Second	88	66	9	.571	Al Lopez
1957	Sixth	76	77	21 1/2	.497	Kerby Farrell
1958	Fourth	77	76	14 1/2	.503	Bobby Bragan—Joe Gordon
1959	Second	89	65	5	.578	Joe Gordon
1960	Fourth	76	78	21	.494	Gordon—Jimmie Dykes
1961	Fifth	78	83	30 1/2	.484	Jimmie Dykes
1962	Sixth	80	82	16	.494	Mel McGaha
1963	Fifth (d)	79	83	25 1/2	.488	Birdie Tebbetts
1964	Sixth (e)	79	83	20	.488	Birdie Tebbetts
1965	Fifth	87	75	15	.537	Birdie Tebbetts
1966	Fifth	81	81	17	.500	Tebbetts—George Strickland
1967	Eighth	75	87	17	.463	Joe Adcock
1968	Third	86	75	16 1/2	.534	Alvin Dark
1969	Sixth	62	99	46 1/2	.385	Alvin Dark
1970	Fifth	76	86	32	.469	Alvin Dark
1971	Sixth	60	102	43	.370	Dark—John Lipon
1972	Fifth	72	84	14	.462	Ken Aspromonte
1973	Sixth	71	91	26	.438	Ken Aspromonte
1974	Fourth	77	85	14	.475	Ken Aspromonte
1975	Fourth	79	80	15 1/2	.497	Frank Robinson
1976	Fourth	81	78	16	.509	Frank Robinson
1977	Fifth	71	90	28 1/2	.441	Robinson—Jeff Torborg
1978	Sixth	69	90	29	.434	Jeff Torborg
1979	Sixth	81	80	22	.503	Torborg—Dave Garcia
1980	Sixth	79	81	23	.494	Dave Garcia
1981	Sixth	52	51	7	.505	Dave Garcia
1982	Sixth (f)	78	84	17	.481	Dave Garcia
1983	Seventh	70	92	28	.432	Mike Ferraro—Pat Corrales
1984	Sixth	75	87	29 1/2	.463	Pat Corrales
1985	Seventh	60	102	39 1/2	.370	Pat Corrales
1986	Fifth	84	78	11 1/2	.519	Pat Corrales
1987	Seventh	61	101	37	.377	Corrales—Doc Edwards
1988	Sixth	78	84	11	.481	Doc Edwards
1989	Sixth	73	89	16	.451	Edwards—John Hart
1990	Fourth	77	85	11	.475	John McNamara
1991	Seventh	57	105	34	.352	Mike Hargrove
Totals		7119	6930		.507	

Finishes: First–3; Second–12; Third–14; Fourth–18; Fifth–15; Sixth–20; Seventh–6; Eighth–2
Highest Percentage: .721 in 1954 (American League record)
Lowest Percentage: .333 in 1914
(a)   Short season because of World War I
        Two games forfeited on Labor Day
(b)   Tied with Detroit for fourth
(c)   Tied with Philadelphia for fifth
(d)   Tied with Detroit for fifth
(e)   Tied with Minnesota for sixth
(f)   Tied with Toronto for sixth

The big show

Indians in the World Series

1920—Indians beat Brooklyn Dodgers, best-of-nine, 5-2

1948—Indians beat Boston Braves, best-of-seven, 4-2

1954—Indians lose to New York Giants, best of seven, 0-4

Baseball

Indians, Team Records

Individual Batting/Game

Most at-bats .... 11, Johnny Burnett, July 10, 1932
Most runs .... 5, many players, last done by Joe Carter, Sept. 6, 1986
Most hits .... 6, many players, last done by Jorge Orta, June 15, 1980
Most hits, extra inning game .... 9, John Burnett, July 10, 1932
Most hits, two consecutive games .... 11, John Burnett, July 9 (2) & July 10 (9), 1932
Most consecutive hits .... 11, Tris Speaker, 1920
Most one base hits, extra inning game .... 7, John Burnett, July 10, 1932
Most doubles, game .... 4, many times, last done by Vic Wertz, Sept. 26, 1956
Most consecutive doubles, game .... 4, Lou Boudreau, July 10, 1946
Vic Wertz, Sept. 26, 1956
Most triples .... 3, many players, last done by Ben Chapman, July 3, 1939
Most triples with bases filled .... 2, Duane Kuiper, July 27, 1978
Most total bases, game .... 16, Rocky Colavito, June 10, 1959
Most extra base hits, game .... 5, Lou Boudreau, July 14, 1946
(4 doubles and 1 home run)
Most time, two hits, one inning .... 2, John Hodapp, July 24, 1928
Most consecutive extra base hits .... 7, Elmer Smith, Sept. 4 and 5, 1921
(two games) (3 doubles and 4 home runs)
Most extra bases on long hits .... 16, Rocky Colavito, June 10, 1959
Most RBI, game .... 8, Earl Averill, July 12, 1930; Sept. 17, 1930
8, Pat Seery, July 13, 1945
8, Bill Glynn, July 5, 1954
Most RBI, two consecutive games .... 11, Earl Averill, Sept. 17, 1930 (doubleheader)
Most bases on balls, game .... 6, Andre Thornton, May 2, 1984
Most strikeouts, game .... 5, Larry Doby, April 25, 1948
Rick Manning, May 15, 1977
Most strikeouts, two consecutive games .... 8, Pedro Ramos, August 19 and 23, 1963
Most stolen bases, game .... 5, Alex Cole, August 1, 1990
Most sacrifice bunts, game .... 4, Ray Chapman, August 31, 1919
(c)
Felix Fermin, August 22, 1989 .... (c)
Two doubles, one inning .... Duane Kuiper, August 30, 1982
Home run and triple, one inning .... Earl Averill, July 6, 1937
Bruce Campbell, May 2, 1938
Home run and double, one inning .... Many times, last done by Gorman Thomas, Sept. 3, 1983
Most total bases, inning .... 7, Earl Averill, July 6, 1937
7, Bruce Campbell, May 2, 1938
Most extra base hits, inning .... 2, many players, last done by Gorman Thomas, Sept. 3, 1983
Most RBI, inning .... 4, many times, last done by Mitch Webster, August 10, 1990
Most RBI, one inning .... 4, many times, last done by Albert Belle, July 24, 1989
Most bases on balls, inning .... 2, many times, last done by Alex Cole and Jerry Browne, Oct. 2, 1990

Individual Home Runs

Most, game .... 4, Rocky Colavito, June 10, 1959 (consecutive)
Most, two games .... 5, Joe Carter, July 18 (2), July 19 (3), 1989
Most, designated hitter .... 31, Andre Thornton, 1982
Most, three or more in a game, season .... 2, Joe Carter, June 24, July 19, 1989
Most, three or more in a game, career .... 4, Joe Carter, 1989 (2), 1987, 1986
Most, both sides of the plate, same game .... Tony Bernazard, July 1, 1986
Most grand slams, two consecutive games .... 2, Jim Busby, July 5 & 6, 1956
Most season (LH) .... 42, Hal Trosky, 1936
Most season (RH) .... 43, Al Rosen, 1953
Most season (switch hitter) .... 17, Tony Bernazard, 1986
Most season, Rookie .... 37, Al Rosen, 1950
Most, home .... 30, Hal Trosky, 1936
Most, road .... 23, Rocky Colavito, 1959
Most, one month .... 13, Hal Trosky, July, 1937
13, Rocky Colavito, August, 1958
Most grand slams, season .... 4, Al Rosen, 1959
Most pinch hit, season .... 3, Ron Kittle, 1987
3, Ted Uhlaender, 1970
Most consecutive pinch-hit home runs .... 2, Gary Alexander, July 5 & 6, 1980
Most season 20 or more .... 7, Larry Doby
Most consecutive seasons, 20 or more .... 7, Larry Doby, 1949-55
Home run first plate appearance .... Earl Averill, April 16, 1929

Jay Bell, Sept. 29, 1986
Most home runs, first two major league games .... 2, Earl Averill, April 16 & 17, 1929
(c) Ties Major League Record

Individual Batting/Season

Category	Record	Player	Year
Highest batting average (season)	408	Joe Jackson	1911
Highest slugging pct.	644	Hal Trosky	1936
Most games	163	Leon Wagner	1964
Most at bats (LH)	653	Mickey Rocco	1944
Most at bats (RH)	663	Joe Carter	1986
Most hits	233	Joe Jackson	1911
Most hits and walks	311	Tris Speaker	1920, 1923
Most singles	172	Charley Jamieson	1923
Most doubles	64	George Burns	1926
Most triples	26	Joe Jackson	1912(a)
Most long hits	96	Hal Trosky	1936
Most total bases	405	Hal Trosky	1936
Most RBI (LH)	162	Hal Trosky	1936
Most RBI (RH)	145	Al Rosen	1953
Most RBI (switch-hitter)	80	Roy Cullenbine	1944
Most GWRBI	15	Andre Thornton	1982
Most runs	140	Earl Averill	1931
Most bases on balls (LH)	111	Mike Hargrove	1980
Most bases on balls (RH)	109	Andre Thornton	1982
Most strikeouts (LH)	121	Larry Doby	1953
	121	Leon Wagner	1964
Most strikeouts (RH)	166	Cory Snyder	1987
Fewest strikeouts	4	Joe Sewell	1925
		Joe Sewell	1929(b)
Most sacrifice hits (including sacrifice flies)	67	Ray Chapman	1917(b)
Most sacrifice hits (no sacrifice flies)	46	Billy Bradley	1907
Most sacrifice flies	12	Vic Power	1961
Most hit by pitcher	17	Minnie Minoso	1959
Most stolen bases	61	MiguelDilone	1980
Most caught stealing	23	Bobby Bonds	1979
Most grounded in double play	28	JulioFranco	1986
Fewest grounded into double play	3	Jose Cardenal	1968
	3	Cory Snyder	1987
Most consecutive games batted safely	29	Bill Bradley	1902
Most consecutive games, one or more RBI	9	Al Rosen (18)	1954
Most pinch hits	19	Bob Hale	1960
Most consecutive pinch hits	5	Bob Hale	1960

(a)   Ties American League Record
(b)   Major League Record

Individual Batting/Lifetime

Record		Player
Highest batting avergage	375	Joe Jackson
Highest slugging pct.	551	Hal Trosky
Most seasons	15	Terry Turner
Most games	1,617	Terry Turner
Most consecutive games	1,103	Joe Sewell
Most at bats	6,037	Nap Lajoie
Most runs	1,154	Earl Averill
Most hits	2,051	Nap Lajoie
Most singles	1,516	Nap Lajoie
Most doubles	486	Tris Speaker
Most triples	121	Earl Averill
Most home runs	226	Earl Averill
Most grand slam home runs	9	Al Rosen
Most extra base hits	724	Earl Averill
Most total bases	3,201	Earl Averill
Most RBI	1,085	Earl Averill
Most bases on balls	726	Earl Averill
Most strikeouts	805	Larry Doby
Most stolen bases	254	Terry Turner

Joe Sewell, the Cleveland Indian shortstop during the 1920s, was the most difficult batter to strike out in the history of the game. In his fourteen seasons, he went to bat 7,132 times and struck out only 114 times. No other player has even come close to his 62.6 ratio.

Source: The Great All-Time Baseball Record Book, Macmillan

Top All-Time Tribe Hitting Streaks

Player	Year	No. of Games	Player	Year	No. of Games
Bill Bradley	1902	29	Julio Franco	1988	22
Joe Jackson	1911	28	Nap Lajoie	1904	21
Hal Trosky	1936	28	Odell Hale	1936	21
Dale Mitchell	1953	27	Dale Mitchell	1948	21
Harry Bay	1902	26	Larry Doby	1951	21
Charlie Jamieson	1923	23	Dale Mitchell	1953	21
Tris Speaker	1923	23	Joe Carter	1986	21
Dale Mitchell	1951	23	Julio Franco	1988	21
Ray Fosse	1970	23	Earl Averill	1936	20
Mike Hargrove	1980	23	Roy Weatherly	1936	20
John Hodapp	1929	22	Joe Vosmik	1936	20
Dale Mitchell	1947	22	Al Rosen	1953	20
Al Smith	1956	22	Vic Power	1960	20
John Romano	1961	22			

Individual Pitching/Game

Most innings pitched .... 19, Stan Coveleski, May 14, 1918
Most hits allowed .... 23, Charles Baxter, April 28, 1901
Most bases on balls .... 11, Gus Dorner, May 23, 1903
Most home runs, inning .... 4, Cal McLish, May 27, 1957
Most strikeouts, game .... 18, Bob Feller, Oct. 2, 1938
Most strikeouts, extra inning game .... 19, Luis Tiant, July 3, 1968
Most strikeouts, inning .... 4, Guy Morton, June 11, 1916
.... 4, Lee Strange, September 2, 1964
.... 4, Mike Paxton, July 21, 1978
Most consecutive strikeouts .... 6, Bob Feller, Oct. 2, 1938 vs. Detroit
Most strikeouts, two consecutive games (RHP) .... 32, Luis Tiant, June 29 (13) and July 3 (19), 1968
Most strikeouts, two consecutive games (LHP) .... 30, Sam McDowell, May 1 (16) and May 6 (14), 1968
Most strikeouts, three consecutive games .... 41, Luis Tiant, June 23 (9), June 29 (13), July 3 (19), 1968
Most hit batter, inning .... 3, Bud Black, July 8, 1988, fourth inning(c)
Most balks, inning .... 3, Milburn Shoffner, May 12, 1930
(c)Ties Major League Record

Individual Pitching/Lifetime

Record		Player
Most games won	266	Bob Feller
Most years winning 20 or more games	7	Bob Lemon
Most defeats	186	Mel Harder
Most games started	484	Bob Feller
Most completed games	279	Bob Feller
Most innings pitched	3,828	Bob Feller
Most no-hit games	3	Bob Feller
Most one-hit games	12	Bob Feller
Most seasons	20	Mel Harder
Most games	582	Mel Harder
Most bases on balls	1,764	Bob Feller
Most strikeouts	2,581	Bob Feller
Most shutouts	46	Bob Feller
Most saves	121	Doug Jones

Individual Pitching/Season

Record		Player	Year
Most games (LHP)	76	Sid Monge	1979
Most games (RHP)	66	Doug Jones	1990
Most games started	44	George Uhle	1923
Most complete games	36	Bob Feller	1946
Most innings pitched	371	Bob Feller	1946
Most wins (LHP)	23	Vean Gregg	1911
Most wins (RHP)	31	Jim Bagby, Sr.	1920
Most consecutive wins	15	Johnny Allen	1937
	15	Gaylord Perry	1974
Most wins, relief	12	Sid Monge	1979
Most losses	22	Pete Dowling	1901
Most consecutive losses	13	Guy Morton	1914
Most losses, relief	10	Jim Kern	1977-78
	10	Dan Spillner	1982
	10	Doug Jones	1989
Most saves (LHP)	21	Dave LaRoche	1976

Most saves (RHP)	43	Doug Jones	1990
Most consecutive saves	15	Doug Jones	1988
(in 15 consecutive appearances)			
Most games finished	64	Doug Jones	1990
Most shutouts	10	Bob Feller	1946
	10	Bob Lemon	1948
Most shutout losses	7	Bob Feller	1946
Most consecutive shutouts	4	Luis Tiant	1968
Most consecutive shutout innings	41	Luis Tiant	1968
Most consecutive hitless innings	22.1	Dennis Eckersley	1977
Most strikeouts (LHP)	325	Sam McDowell	1965
Most strikeouts (RHP)	348	Bob Feller	1946
Most bases on balls	208	Bob Feller	1936(b)
Most wild pitches	18	Sam McDowel	1967
Most hit batsmen	20	Otto Hess	1906
Most balks	8	Tom Candiotti	1989
Most hits allowed	328	George Uhle	1923
Most runs allowed	167	George Uhle	1923
Most earned runs allowed	150	George Uhle	1923
Most home runs allowed	37	Luis Tiant	1969
Most sacrifice hits	20	Early Wynn	1951
Most sacrifice flies	12	Early Wynn	1951
	12	Gaylord Perry	1974
Lowest ERA (LHP)	1.74	Willie Mitchell	1913
Lowest ERA (RHP)	1.16	Addie Joss	1908
Highest winning percentage	.938	Johnny Allen (15-1)	1937(c)
Lowest winning percentage	.071	Guy Morton	1914
	.071	Steven Hargan	1971
Most 1-0 games won	3	Addie Joss	1908
	3	Stan Coveleski	1917
	3	Jim Bagby, Jr.	1943
	3	Bob Feller	1946
	3	Greg Swindell	1988
Most low-hit (no-hit, one-hit) games	3	Addie Joss	1907
	3	Bob Feller	1946

(b)American League Records
(c)Ties Major League Record

Individual Fielding/Game

Most putouts, first baseman
Most putouts, second baseman .... 12, Vern Fuller, April 11, 1969 (11 innings)
11, Roy Hughes, August 4, 1937 (9 innings)
Most putouts, third baseman .... 7, Bill Bradley, Sept. 21, 1901
May 13, 1909
Most putouts, shortstop ....
Most putouts, outfielder .... 12, Harry Bary, July 19, 1904 (12 innings)
Most putouts, catcher .... 19, Joe Azcue, July 3, 1968 (10 innings)
Most putouts, pitcher .... 6, Bert Blyleven, June 24, 1984
Most assists, first baseman .... 6, Pat Tabler, June 24, 1984
Most assists, second baseman .... 13, Bobby Avila, July 1, 1952 (19 innings)
Most assists, third baseman .... 10, Ken Keltner, Sept. 13, 1948
Most assists, shortstop .... 12, Lou Boudreau, Sept. 14, 1939
Most assists, outfielder .... 4, Sam Langford, May 1, 1928
Most assists, outfielder, inning .... 2, Frank Baker, August 5, 1969
2, Gene Woodling, July 18, 1957
Most double plays, shortstop .... 5, Julio Franco, June 9, 1984(c)
Most double plays, second baseman, extra inning game .... 6, Joe Gordon, August 31, 1949
Most errors, second baseman, inning .... 3, Bill Wambsganss, May 15, 1923
Most errors, catcher, inning .... 3, John Peters, May 16, 1918

Top Fielding Percentage/Season

Position	Record	Player	Year
First baseman	.997	Boog Powell	1975
Second baseman	.988	Duane Kuiper	1979
Third baseman	.984	Willie Kamm	1933
Shortstop	.986	Frank Duffy	1973
Outfielders	1.000(b-c)	Rocky Colavito	1965
Catchers	.997	Jim Hegan	1955

Luke Easter, a power-hitting first baseman for the Indians in the 1950s, belted the longest home run ever hit in Cleveland Stadium—a shot that went 477 feet and landed in the upper deck of Section 4 of right field. He did it on June 23, 1950. Sluggers such as Mickrey Mantle, **Rocky Colavito**, and Frank Howard bounced homers near the bleacher wall, a mere 465 feet or so.

Source: Cleveland Indians

Baseball

Cincinnati Reds, The Record

Year	Position	Won	Lost	Pct.	Manager	Pennant Winner
1876	Eighth	9	56	.138	Charles H. Gould	Chicago
1877	Sixth	15	42	.253	Lipman E. Pike, Rober E. Addy	Boston
1878	Second	37	23	.617	Calvin A. McVey	Boston
1879	Fifth	38	36	.514	Calvin A. McVey, James L. White	Providence
1880	Eighth	21	59	.263	John Edgar Clapp	Chicago
1890	Fourth	78	55	.586	Thomas J. Loftus	Brooklyn
1891	Seventh	56	81	.409	Thomas J. Loftus	Boston
1892*	Fifth	82	68	.547	Charles A. Comiskey	Boston
1893*	Sixth	65	63	.508	Charles A. Comiskey	Boston
1894*	Tenth	54	75	.419	Charles A. Comiskey	Baltimore
1895*	Eighth	66	64	.508	William Ewing	Baltimore
1896*	Third	77	50	.606	William Ewing	Baltimore
1897*	Fourth	76	56	.576	William Ewing	Boston
1898*	Third	92	60	.605	William Ewing	Boston
1899*	Sixth	83	67	.553	William Ewing	Brooklyn
1900	Seventh	62	77	.446	Robert Allen	Brooklyn
1901	Eighth	52	87	.374	John (Bid) McPhee	Pittsburgh
1902	Fourth	70	70	.500	John (Bid) McPhee, Frank Bancroft, Jospeh Kelley	Pittsburgh
1903	Fourth	74	65	.532	Joseph Kelley	Pittsburgh
1904	Third	88	65	.575	Joseph Kelley	New York
1905	Fifth	79	74	.516	Joseph Kelley	New York**
1906	Sixth	64	87	.424	Edward (Ned) Hanlon	Chicago
1907	Sixth	66	87	.431	Edward (Ned) Hanlon	Chicago**
1908	Fifth	73	81	.474	John Ganzel	Chicago**
1909	Fourth	77	76	.503	Clark Griffith	Pittsburgh**
1910	Fifth	75	79	.487	Clark Griffith	Chicago
1911	Sixth	70	83	.458	Clark Griffith	New York
1912	Fourth	75	78	.490	Henry O'Day	New York
1913	Seventh	64	89	.418	Joseph Tinker	New York
1914	Eighth	60	94	.390	Charles (Buck) Herzog	Boston**
1915	Seventh	71	83	.461	Charles (Buck) Herzog	Philadelphia
1916	Seventh	60	93	.392	Charles (Buck) Herzog, Christy Mathewson	Brooklyn
1917	Foruth	78	76	.506	Christy Mathewson	New York
1918	Third	68	60	.531	Christy Mathewson, Heinie Groh	Chicago

Year	Position	Won	Lost	Pct.	Manager	Pennant Winner
1919	First	96	44	.686	Patrick Moran	Cincinnati**
1920	Third	82	71	.536	Patrick Moran	Brooklyn
1921	Sixth	70	83	.458	Patrick Moran	New York**
1922	Second	86	68	.558	Patrick Moran	New York**
1923	Second	91	63	.591	Patrick Moran	New York
1924	Fourth	83	70	.542	John (Jack) Hendricks	New York
1925	Third	80	73	.523	John (Jack) Hendricks	Pittsburgh**
1926	Second	87	67	.565	John (Jack) Hendricks	St. Louis**
1927	Fifth	75	78	.490	John (Jack) Hendricks	Pittsburgh
1928	Fifth	78	74	.513	John (Jack) Hendricks	St. Louis
1929	Seventh	66	88	.429	John (Jack) Hendricks	Chicago
1930	Seventh	59	95	.383	Dan Howley	St. Louis
1931	Eighth	58	96	.377	Dan Howley	St. Louis**
1932	Eighth	60	94	.390	Dan Howley	Chicago
1933	Eighth	58	94	.382	Owen (Donie) Bush	New York**
1934	Eighth	52	99	.344	Robert O'Farrell, Burt Shotton, Charles Dressen	St. Louis**
1935	Sixth	68	85	.444	Charles Dressen	Chicago
1936	Fifth	74	80	.481	Charles Dressen	New York
1937	Eighth	56	98	.364	Charles Dressen, Bobby Wallace	New York
1938	Fourth	82	68	.547	William McKechnie	Chicago
1939	First	97	57	.630	William McKechnie	Cincinnati
1940	First	100	53	.654	William McKechnie	Cincinnati**
1941	Third	88	66	.571	William McKechnie	Brooklyn
1942	Fourth	76	76	.500	William McKechnie	St. Louis**
1943	Second	87	67	.565	William McKechnie	St. Louis
1944	Third	89	65	.578	William McKechnie	St. Louis**
1945	Seventh	61	93	.396	William McKechnie	Chicago
1946	Sixth	67	87	.435	William McKechnie	St. Louis**
1947	Fifth	73	81	.474	John Neun	Brooklyn
1948	Seventh	64	89	.418	John Neun, William (Bucky) Walters	Boston
1949	Seventh	62	92	.403	William (Bucky) Walters	Brooklyn
1950	Sixth	66	87	.431	J. Luther (Luke) Sewell	Philadelphia
1951	Sixth	68	86	.442	J. Luther (Luke) Sewell	New York
1952	Sixth	69	85	.448	J. Luther (Luke) Sewell, Earle Brucker, Rogers Hornsby	Brooklyn
1953	Sixth	68	86	.442	Rogers Hornsby, C. Buster Mills	Brooklyn
1954	Fifth	74	80	.481	George (Birdie) Tebbetts	New York**
1955	Fifth	75	79	.487	George (Birdie) Tebbetts	Brooklyn**
1956	Third	91	63	.591	George (Birdie) Tebbetts	Brooklyn
1957	Fourth	80	74	.519	George (Birdie) Tebbetts	Milwaukee**

HOW to COPE while the REDS KEEP ON LOSING......

DON'T TAPE THE GAMES AND WAKE UP TO THEM THE NEXT MORNING.

MARV THRONEBERRY FOR MANAGER!!!

PRETEND THESE ARE THE '62 METS AND START A CULT FAN CLUB.

DEVELOP AN INTEREST IN NASHVILLE MUSIC.

PLACE YOURSELF ON THE DISABLED LIST.

WEAR A REDS UNIFORM TO THE GAME AND SEE IF YOU CAN PASS YOURSELF OFF AS A NEWLY-RECALLED PLAYER.

THINK OF THIS AS AN EXTENDED SPRING TRAINING FOR 1990.

JIM BORGMAN CINCINNATI ENQUIRER

Year	Finish	W	L	Pct.	Manager(s)	
1958	Fourth	76	78	.494	George (Birdie) Tebbetts, Jimmy Dykes	Milwaukee
1959	Fifth	74	80	.481	Mayo Smith, Fred Hutchinson	Los Angeles**
1960	Sixth	67	87	.435	Fred Hutchinson	Pittsburgh**
1961	First	93	61	.604	Fred Hutchinson	Cincinnati
1962	Third	98	64	.605	Fred Hutchinson	San Francisco
1963	Fifth	86	76	.531	Fred Hutchinson	Los Angeles**
1964	Second	92	70	.568	Fred Hutchinson, Dick Sisler	St. Louis**
1965	Fourth	89	73	.549	Dick Sisler	Los Angeles**
1966	Seventh	76	84	.475	Dick Sisler	Los Angeles
1967	Fourth	87	75	.537	Dave Bristol	St. Louis**
1968	Fourth	83	79	.512	Dave Bristol	St. Louis**
1969	Third	89	73	.549	Dave Bristol	New York**
1970	First	102	60	.628	George (Sparky) Anderson	Cincinnati
1971	Fourth	79	83	.488	George (Sparky) Anderson	Pittsburgh**
1972	First	95	59	.617	George (Sparky) Anderson	Cincinnati
1973	First	99	63	.611	George (Sparky) Anderson	New York
1974	Second	98	64	.605	George (Sparky) Anderson	Los Angeles
1975	First	108	54	.667	George (Sparky) Anderson	Cincinnati**
1976	First	102	60	.630	George (Sparky) Anderson	Cincinnati**
1977	Second	88	74	.543	George (Sparky) Anderson	Los Angeles
1978	Second	92	69	.571	George (Sparky) Anderson	Los Angeles
1979	First	90	71	.559	John McNamara	Pittsburgh**
1980	Third	89	73	.549	John McNamara	Philadelphia**
1981	See Note #	66	42	.611	John McNamara	Los Angeles**
1982	Sixth	61	101	.377	John McNamara, Russ Nixon	St. Louis**
1983	Sixth	74	88	.457	Russ Nixon	Philadelphia
1984	Fifth	70	92	.432	Vern Rapp, Pete Rose	San Diego
1985	Second	89	72	.553	Pete Rose	St. Louis
1986	Second	86	76	.531	Pete Rose	New York**
1987	Second	84	78	.519	Pete Rose	St. Louis
1988	Second	87	74	.540	Pete Rose	Los Angeles**
1989	Fifth	75	87	.463	Pete Rose, Tommy Helms	San Francisco
1990	First	91	71	.562	Lou Piniella	Cincinnati**
1991	Fifth	174	88	.457	Lou Piniella	Minnesota

All-Time Totals   **7926**   **7824**   **.503**

Finishes from 1876: First—11, Second—14, Third—12, Fourth—16, Fifth—16, Sixth—16, Seventh—11, Eighth—10, Tenth—1.
*12 Teams in National League
**World Champions
N.L. Split into two six team divisions. Reds member Western Division.
(Note: Cincinnati not member of National League 1881-1889)
 # Note: In 1981, the Reds had the best record ovrall, finishing 35-21 1st Half season, 2nd to Los Angeles and 31-21 2nd Half, 2nd to Houston.

"I WAS GOING TO BUY TWO TICKETS TO THE ALL-STAR GAME TODAY, BUT THEN I THOUGHT, 'NAW, LET'S KEEP THE HOUSE INSTEAD...'"

There was no remedy for Sparky's optimism. "If Sparky managed the Taiwanese Army," wrote Mark Purdy, "he would forecast a 10-game lead over Mainland China by August."

Sparky Anderson: The Reds' Most Successful Sack

When **Sparky Anderson** talks, grammarians gather outside the ballpark and raise picket signs. Being a retired outfielder, he can turn a double negative with the best of them. His sentences are wonderful Byzantine examples of things English coaches everywhere instruct their charges to avoid before they hit into the playing fields of language. In spite of this, he is one of baseball's most eloquent spokesmen, and even his casual utterances are possessed of wit and a rustic clarity. "How smart do I have to be?" he asks, of no one in particular. "It's a simple game."

If Anderson, was, as he would have you believe, exiled into baseball by his lack of more workaday skills, then he has, with his tenure in Cincinnati—and beyond—demonstrated an enviable mastery of "the simple game." When he was fired by the Reds in 1978, he had won four pennants in nine years, as well as two World Series, and his .596 percentage was second best among managers of the century. In 1984, when he took Detroit into the World Series, he became the only manager to win championships in both leagues, and the first to win 100 games with two different teams.

Even Anderson was astounded to find himself fired. His firing was precipitated by two-second-place finishes and he said to Dick Wagner, "Dick, wrong. It ain't no time for no change. There ain't nothing wrong with me." Wagner said the team needed a new direction. "What direction," mused Sparky, looking at the record. "Where are they going? The moon?"

While he was in town, though, it was a grand ride. Sparky was, said Red Smith, "a big-league guy with a bush-league background." But it was the bushes that cemented Sparky's sense of modesty. It was there he learned first players to the showers got the hot water. He and Roger Craig promised themselves that if they ever got to the majors, they would take a cold shower once a week, just as a reminder.

Sparky enforced the hidebound management edicts of short hair and no mustaches, and he annoyed pitchers and the fans by yanking the pitcher the moment trouble started on the mound. He pulled Don Gullet once and found out later he had been booed by even his youngest daughter, Shirlee.

"Why would you boo your father?" he asked.

"I didn't want them to know you WERE my father," she said.

They called him "Captain Hook," but he was undeterred. He handled it all: players, pitchers, newsmen, fans, the game itself. He was supremely turf-wise, having made everyone forget that before the Reds, he had only spent two years in the majors—one as a second baseman with Philadelphia in 1959 where he batted .218, the other as a coach for the Padres.

He lost his first managing job, in the minor leagues, and was selling cars when Bob Howsam, then with the Cardinals, found him and offered him a spot in the Carolina League, where Sparky won four straight pennants. In late 1969, Howsam brought him to Cincinnati; he was 35, the youngest manager in the majors.

With his grey hair and a face described by one writer as "a road map of every stretch of minor-league highway he ever traveled," he seemed older and he coached older. "We'd walk through hell in a gasoline suit for Sparky," said Pete Rose. And Sparky, always the poseur, employing artfully that Charley Ray School of Acting gesture, the digging of the toe into the infield dirt, said, "My secret was to tell players to go out and make me smart."

He did and they did and he was.

eds, World Series History

Year	Game	Date	Site	Score	Winner	Loser	Att.
1919	1	10-1	Cin.	Reds 9, White Sox 1	Ruether	Cicotte	30,511
	2	10-2	Cin.	Reds 4, White Sox 2	Sallee	Williams	29,690
	3	10-3	Chi.	White Sox 3, Reds 0	Kerr	Fisher	29,126
	4	10-4	Chi.	Reds 2, White Sox 0	Ring	Cicotte	34,363
	5	10-6	Chi.	Reds 5, White Sox 0	Eller	Williams	34,379
	6	10-7	Cin.	White Sox 5, Reds 4 (10)	Kerr	Ring	32,006
	7	10-8	Cin.	White Sox 4, Reds 1	Cicotte	Sallee	13,923
	8	10-9	Chi.	Reds 10, White Sox 5	Eller	Williams	32,930
1939	1	10-4	N.Y.	Yankees 2, Reds 1	Ruffing	Derringer	58,541
	2	10-5	N.Y.	Yankees 4, Reds 0	Pearson	Walters	59,791
	3	10-7	Cin.	Yankees 7, Reds 3	Hadley	Thompson	32,723
	4	10-8	Cin.	Yankees 7, Reds 4 (10)	Murphy	Walters	32,794
1940	1	10-2	Cin.	Tigers 7, Reds 2	Newsom	Derringer	31,793
	2	10-3	Cin.	Reds 5, Tigers 3	Walters	Rowe	30,640
	3	10-4	Det.	Tigers 7, Reds 4	Bridges	Turner	52,877
	4	10-5	Det.	Reds 5, Tigers 2	Derringer	Trout	54,093
	5	10-6	Det.	Tigers 8, Reds 0	Newsom	Thompson	55,189
	6	10-8	Cin.	Reds 4, Tigers 0	Walters	Rowe	30,481
	7	10-8	Cin.	Reds 2, Tigers 1	Derringer	Newsom	26,854
1961	1	10-4	N.Y.	Yankees 2, Reds 0	Ford	O'Toole	62,397
	2	10-5	N.Y.	Reds 6, Yankees 2	Jay	Terry	63,083
	3	10-7	Cin.	Yankees 3, Reds 2	Arroyo	Purkey	32,589
	4	10-8	Cin.	Yankees 7, Reds 0	Ford	O'Toole	32,589
	5	10-9	Cin.	Yankees 13, Reds 5	Daley	Jay	32,589
1970	1	10-10	Cin.	Orioles 4, Reds 3	Palmer	Nolan	51,531
	2	10-11	Cin.	Orioles 6, Reds 5	Phoebus	Wilcox	51,531
	3	10-13	Balt.	Orioles 9, Reds 3	McNally	Cloninger	51,773
	4	10-14	Balt.	Reds 6, Orioles 5	C. Carroll	Watt	53,007
	5	10-15	Balt.	Orioles 9, Reds 3	Cuellar	Merritt	45,341
1972	1	10-14	Cin.	Athletics 3, Reds 2	Holtzman	Nolan	52,918
	2	10-15	Cin.	Athletics 2, Reds 1	Hunter	Grimsley	53,224
	3	10-18	Oak.	Reds 1, Athletics 0	Billingham	Odom	49,410
	4	10-19	Oak.	Athletics 3, Reds 2	Fingers	C. Carroll	49,410
	5	10-20	Oak.	Reds 5, Athletics 4	Grimsley	Fingers	49,410
	6	10-21	Cin.	Reds 8, Athletics 1	Grimsley	Blue	52,737
	7	10-22	Cin.	Athletics 3, Reds 2	Hunter	Borbon	56,040
1975	1	10-11	Bos.	Red Sox 6, Reds 0	Tiant	Gullett	35,205
	2	10-12	Bos.	Reds 3, Red Sox 2	Eastwick	Drago	35,205
	3	10-14	Cin.	Reds 6, Red Sox 5 (10)	Eastwick	Willoughby	55,392
	4	10-15	Cin.	Red Sox 5, Reds 4	Tiant	Norman	55,667
	5	10-16	Cin.	Reds 6, Red Sox 2	Gullett	Cleveland	56,393
	6	10-21	Bos.	Red Sox 7, Reds 6 (12)	Wise	Darcy	35,205
	7	10-22	Bos.	Reds 4, Red Sox 3	C. Carroll	Burton	35,205
1976	1	10-16		Reds 5, Yankees 1	Gullett	Alexander	54,826
	2	10-17		Reds 4, Yankees 3	Billingham	Hunter	54,816
	3	10-19	N.Y.	Reds 6, Yankees 2	Zachry	Ellis	56,667
	4	10-21	N.Y.	Reds 7, Yankees 2	Nolan	Figueroa	56,700
1990	1	10-16	Cin.	Reds 7, Athletics 0	Rijo	Stewart	55,830
	2	10-17	Cin.	Reds 5, Athletics 4 (10)	Dibble	Eckersley	55,832
	3	10-19	Oak.	Reds 8, Athletics 3	Browning	Moore	48,269
	4	10-20	Oak.	Reds 2, Athletics 1	Rijo	Stewart	48,613

Championship Series History

Year	Game	Date	Site	Score	Winner	Loser	Att.
1970	1	10-3	Pitt.	Reds 3, Pirates 0 (10)	Nolan	Ellis	33,088
	2	10-4	Pitt.	Reds 3, Pirates 1	Merritt	Walker	39,317
	3	10-5	Cin.	Reds 3, Pirates 2	Wilcox	Moose	40,538
1972	1	10-7	Pitt.	Pirates 5, Reds 1	Blass	Gullett	50,476
	2	10-8	Pitt.	Reds 5, Pirates 3	Hall	Moose	50,584
	3	10-9	Cin.	Pirates 3, Reds 2	Kison	C. Carroll	52,420
	4	10-10	Cin.	Reds 7, Pirates 1	Grimsley	Ellis	39,447
	5	10-11	Cin.	Reds 4, Pirates 3	C. Carroll	Giusti	41,887
1973	1	10-6	Cin.	Reds 2, Mets 1	Borbon	Seaver	53,431
	2	10-7	Cin.	Mets 5, Reds 0	Matlack	Gullett	54,041
	3	10-8	N.Y.	Mets 9, Reds 2	Koosman	Grimsley	53,967
	4	10-9	N.Y.	Reds 2, Mets 1 (12)	C. Carroll	Parker	50,786
	5	10-10	N.Y.	Mets 7, Reds 2	Seaver	Billingham	50,323
1975	1	10-4	Cin.	Reds 8, Pirates 3	Gullett	Reuss	54,633
	2	10-5	Cin.	Reds 6, Pirates 1	Norman	Rooker	54,752
	3	10-7	Pitt.	Reds 5, Pirates 3 (10)	Eastwick	Hernandez	46,355
1976	1	10-9	Phil.	Reds 6, Phils 3	Gullett	Carlton	62,640
	2	10-10	Phil.	Reds 6, Phils 2	Zachry	Longborg	62,651
	3	10-12	Cin.	Reds 7, Phils 6	Eastwick	Garber	55,047
1979	1	10-2	Cin.	Pirates 5, Reds 2	Jackson	Hume	55,006
	2	10-3	Cin.	Pirates 3, Reds 2	D. Robinson	Bair	55,000
	3	10-5	Pitt.	Pirates 7, Reds 1	Blyleven	LaCoss	42,240
1990	1	10-4	Cin.	Pirates 4, Reds 3	Walk	Charlton	55,700
	2	10-5	Cin.	Reds 2, Pirates 1	Browning	Drabek	54,456
	3	10-8	Pitt.	Reds 6, Pirates 3	Jackson	Z. Smith	45,611
	4	10-9	Pitt.	Reds 5, Pirates 3	Rijo	Walk	50,461
	5	10-10	Pitt.	Pirates 3, Reds 2	Drabek	Browning	48,221
	6	10-12	Cin.	Reds 2, Pirates 1	Charlton	Z. Smith	56,079

Reds, Team Records Since 1900, Season

Most At Bats	5,767 (1968)	Most Men Left On Base	1,328 (1976)
Most Runs Scored	857 (1976)	Fewest Men Left On Base	997 (1921)
Fewest Runs Scored	488 (1908)	Most .300 Hitters	8 (1926)
Most Hits	1,599 (1976)	Most Stolen Bases	310 (1910)
Fewest Hits	1,108 (1908)	Most Caught Stealing	136 (1922)
Most Singles	1,191 (1922)	Most Double Plays	194 (1928, '31, '54)
Most Doubles	284 (1990)	Most Putouts	4,471 (1968)
Most Triples	120 (1926)	Most Assists	2,151 (1905)
Most Home Runs	221 (1956)	Most Errors	314 (1914)
Most Grand Slams	7 (1974, '80, '87)	Fewest Errors	95 (1977)
Most Home Runs By Pinch Hitters	12 (1957)	Most Consecutive Errorless Games	15 (1975)
Most Consecutive Games, One or More Home Runs	21 (1956)	Most Errorless Games	94 (1977)
Most Total Bases	2,483 (1965)	Highest Fielding Average	984 (1971, '75, '76, '77)
Most Sacrifices (Including Sacrifice Flies)	239 (1926)	Lowest Fielding Average	952 (1914)
Most Sacrifices (No Sacrifice Flies)	195 (1907)	Most Games Won	108 (1975)
Most Bases On Balls	693 (1974)	Most Games Lost	101 (1982)
Most Strikeouts	1,042 (1969)	Most Shutouts Won	23 (1919)
Fewest Strikeouts	308 (1921)	Most Shutouts Lost	24 (1908)
Most Hit Batsmen	51 (1956)	Highest Winning Percentage	686; 96-44 (1919)
Most Runs Batted In	802 (1976)	Lowest Winning Percentage	344; 52-99 (1934)
Highest Batting Average	296 (1922)	Most Games Won, One Month	24 (Aug., 1918, July, 1973)
Lowest Batting Average	227 (1908)	Most Games Lost, One Month	26 (Sept., 1914)
Highest Slugging Average	441 (1956)	Most Consecutive Games Won	19 (1914)
Lowest Slugging Average	304 (1906)	Most One-Run Games Won	41 (1940)
Most Grounded Into Double Plays	143 (1982)	Most Relief Appearances	392 (1987)
Fewest Grounded Into Double Plays	93 (1935)		

Miscellaneous Records Since 1900

Most Consecutive Hits	10

Woody Williams, 9-5-43 at St. Louis
(2nd game) & 9-6-43 at Chicago

Hitting For Cycle	1

Shared by 5 player—
Most recent—Eric Davis,
6-2-89 vs. San Diego

Most Home Runs, One Inning	2

Ray Knight, 5-13-80 vs.
New York (5th inning)

Most Home Runs Hit by a Pitcher,

Career	13

Joe Nuxhall

Most Strikeouts, One Inning, Pitcher	4

Joe Nuxhall, 8-11-59 vs.
 Milwaukee (1st game), 6th inning
Mario Soto, 5-17-84 vs. Chicago,
3rd inning
Tim Birtsas, 6-4-90 at San Francisco,
7th inning

Most Consecutive Games Played	678

Pete Rose, 4-28-73 to 5-7-78

Most Years Played	19

Pete Rose, 1963-78; 1984-86
Dave Concepcion, 1970-88

Most Consecutive Years Played	19

Dave Concepcion, 1970-88

Longest Game, Innings	21

9-1-67 at Crosley Field;
San Francisco 1-Cincinnati 0
(21 innings)

Most Home Runs in

Consecutive Games	7

Johnny Bench, 7 HR in
5 games, 5-30-72 to 6-3-72

Game Records Since 1900

Hits	6

Tony Cuccinello, 8-13-31 at Boston(1st game)
Ernie Lombardi, 5-9-37 at Philadelphia
Walker Cooper, 7-6-49 vs. Chicago

Doubles	4

Shared by several players—
Most recent—Billy Hatcher, 8-21-90 vs. Chicago

Triples	3

Shared by several players—
Most recent—Herm Winningham, 8-15-90 at St. Louis

Home Runs	3

Shared by several player—
Most recent—Eric Davis, 5-3-87 at Philadelphia

Runs Batted In	10

Walker Cooper, 7-6-49 vs. Chicago

Runs	5

Shared by several players——
Most recent—Kal Daniels, 9-6-88 at Houston

Walks	5

Hughie Critz, 5-26-28 at St. Louis
Johnny Bench, 7-22-79 at Chicago

Stolen Bases	4

Shared by several players—
Most recent—Eric Davis, 7-24-86 vs. Montreal

Strikeouts	18

Jim Maloney (11 innings), 6-14-65 vs. New York
16Frank (Noodles) Hahn (9 innings), 5-22-01 at Boston
16Jim Maloney (9 innings), 5-21-63 at Milwaukee

Hits, Team	28

5-13-02 vs. Philadelphia

Runs, Team	26

6-4-11 vs. Boston

Runs, Inning, Team	14	8-3-89 vs. Houston (1st inning)
Home Runs, Team	8	8-18-56 vs. Milwaukee

GLORY DAYS

Reds, Individual One-Season Records

Batting

Highest Batting Average	.377
J. Bentley (Cy) Seymour, 1905	
Highest Slugging Average	**.642**
Ted Kluszewski, 1954	
Most Games	**163**
Leo Cardenas, 1964; Pete Rose, 1974	
Most At Bats	680
Pete Rose, 1973	
Most Runs	134
Frank Robinson, 1962	
Most Consecutive Games Scoring Run	17
Ted Kluszewski, 1954 (24 Runs)	
Most Consecutive Games Driving In Run	10
Joe Morgan, 1975 (17 RBIs)	
Most Consecutive Games Hitting Safely	44
Pete Rose, June 14-July 31, 1978	
Most Hits	230
Pete Rose, 1973	
Most One Base Hits	181
Pete Rose, 1973	
Most Two Base Hits	
51 Frank Robinson, 1962	
51 Pete Rose, 1978	
Most Three Base Hits	23
Sam Crawford, 1902	
Most Home Runs (Left-handed Batter)	49
Ted Kluszewski, 1954	
Most Home Runs (Right-handed Batter)	52
George Foster, 1977	
Most Grand Slam Home Runs	3
Frank Robinson, 1962	
3 Lee May, 1970	
3 Ray Knight, 1980	
3 Eric Davis, 1987	
Most Home Runs At Home	34
Ted Kluszewski, 1954	
Most Home Runs On Road	31
George Foster, 1977	

Most Home Runs, Rookie	38
Frank Robinson, 1956	
Most Home Runs, One Month	14
Frank Robinson, August, 1962	
Most Extra Base Hits	92
Frank Robinson, 1962	
Most Total Bases	388
George Foster, 1977	
Most Runs Batted In	149
George Foster, 1977	
Most Game-Winning Runs Batted In	21
Eric Davis, 1988	
Most Bases On Balls	132
Joe Morgan, 1975	
Most Strikeouts	142
Lee May, 1969	
Fewest Strikeouts	13
Frank McCormick, 1941	
Most Hit By Pitch	20
Frank Robinson, 1956	
Most Sacrifices (Including Sacrifice Flies)	39
Jake Daubert, 1919	
Most Sacrifice Bunts	31
Roy McMillan, 1954	
Most Sacrifice Flies	13
Johnny Temple, 1959	
Most Stolen Bases	81
Bob Bescher, 1911	
Most Caught Stealing	28
Pat Duncan, 1922	
Most Grounded Into Double Plays	30
Ernie Lombardi, 1938	
Fewest Grounded Into Double Plays	
(150 or more games)	3
Billy Myers, 1939	
Most Pinch-Hits	19
Jerry Lynch, 1960, 1961	
Most Pinch-Hit Home Runs	5
Jerry Lynch, 1961	

Pitching

Most Victories, Right-hander	27
Dolf Luque, 1923	
27 Bucky Walters, 1939	
Most Victories, Left-hander	25
Eppa Rixey, 1922	
Most Victories, Rookie	20
Tom Browning, 1985	
Most Consecutive Victories	16
Ewell Blackwell, 1947	
Highest Percentage	.875
Tom Seaver, 1981 (14-2)	
Highest Percentage 20 Game Winner	.821
Bob Purkey, 1962 (23-5)	
Lowest Earned Run Average	1.57
Fred Toney, 1915	
Most Games Lost	25
Paul Derringer, 1933	
Most Consecutive Games Lost	12
Henry Thielman, 1902	
12 Peter J. Schneider, 1914	
12 Si Johnson, 1933	
Most Games, Right-hander	90
Wayne Granger, 1969	
Most Games, Left-hander	87
Rob Murphy, 1987	
Most Games Started	42
Frank (Noodles) Hahn, 1901	
Most Complete Games	41
Frank (Noodles) Hahn, 1901	

Most Games Finished	62
Tom Hume, 1980	
Most Saves	39
John Franco, 1988	
Most Innings Pitched	375
Frank (Noodles) Hahn, 1901	
Most Strikeouts	274
Mario Soto, 1982	
Most Strikeouts, Reliever	141
Rob Dibble, 1989	
Most Bases On Balls	162
Johnny Vander Meer, 1943	
Most Hits	368
Frank (Noodles) Hahn, 1901	
Most Runs	158
Frank (Noodles) Hahn, 1901	
Most Earned Runs	145
Herm Wehmeier, 1950	
Most Hit Batsmen	23
Jake Weimer, 1907	
Most Home Runs	36
Tom Browning, 1988	
Most Shutouts	
7 Jake Weimer, 1906	
7 Fred Toney, 1917	
7 Hod Eller, 1919	
7 Jack Billingham, 1973	
Most Wild Pitches	19
Jim Maloney, 1963 & 1965	

Good stuff

Great Moments in Cincinnati Pitching

In the 1960s, a converted short-stop named **Jim Maloney** was one of baseball's best pitchers. In 1965, he pitched two ten-inning no-hitters for the Reds within two months—losing one of them in the 11th. He pitched three no-hitters and five one-hitters. Columnist Jim Murray said Maloney's family coat of arms should be "a field of black cats rampant on a shield of snake-eyed dice."

When the NL was only in its fourth season, **Will White** set two records that will never be broken, starting 75 games and finishing them all while pitching 680 innings. He won 43 games that year, and today is 10th on the all-time list in earned run average.

A Red Stocking by the name of **Noodles Hahn** was the man who pitched the first no-hitter of the 20th century. He won 23 games as a rookie in 1899, and in 1901 he became the first southpaw to win 20 games for a last-place club, a record he held for nearly 75 years—he now shares it with Steve Carlton. Hahn allowed an average of 1.70 walks per game over 2,012 innings, and until this day, no lefty has pitched more complete games in a season—41.

In 1954, at the University of Cincinnati, **Sandy Koufax**, a freshman pitcher, struck out 16 batters in one game, 18 in another. He had been looked upon primarily as a basketball player. Basketball coach Ed Jucker later recalled his first thought of Koufax in a baseball uniform: "In the spring he told me he was a pitcher. Well, you know, practically every boy tells you he's a pitcher..." ▶

Reds All-Time Top Statistics Since 1900

Batting

Games		Doubles		Total Bases	
Rose	2,722	Rose	601	Rose	4,645
At Bats		**Triples**		**Runs Batted In**	
Rose	10,934	Roush	153	Bench	1,376
Runs		**Home Runs**		**Stolen Bases**	
Rose	1,741	Bench	389	Morgan	406
Hits		**Extra Base Hits**		**Percentage***	
Rose	3,358	Rose	868	Seymour	333

Pitching

Games		Innings Pitched		Wins	
Borbon	531	Rixey	2,890	Rixey	179
Games		**Started Strikeouts**		**Shoutouts**	
Rixey	356	Maloney	1,592	Walters	32
Complete Games		**Bases on Balls**		**ERA****	
Hahn	207	Vander Meer	1,072	Ewing	2.37

*Based on 500 or more Games
**Based on 1,000 or more Innings Pitched

The firemen

Reds All-Time Saves Leaders

John Franco	148	Ted Power	41
Clay Carroll	102	Randy Myers	31
Tom Hume	88	Will McEnaney	24
Pedro Borbon	76	Ron Robinson	19
Wayne Granger	73	Tom Hall	17
Rawly Eastwick	57	Rob Dibble	13
Doug Bair	50		

A History of Chewing in The Bigs, Especially the Queen City

Ever since man crawled out of the primordial muck and evolved moderately upright toward his finest expression—the batter's box crouch—his passage has been accompanied by a universal gesture of approbation known as The Chew. Like mastery of the strike zone, The Chew is one of humankind's fundamental idioms.

The Chew is used as a ball park divertissement, with certain unspoken rules. One is, for example, permitted to spit on shoes but not the uniform. The white shoes of sports writers are particularly fair game. **Rocky Bridges**, with the Reds in the 1950s, was considered one of the most accurate. "He's one of the best on shoes," said a compatriot. "He has what we call a soft wad. You don't feel it when he spits on your shoes."

In the old days, The Chew sometimes became part of the strategy. "You never did see a white baseball in those days," said Reds' outfielder **Edd Roush**. "All the infielders used to chew tobacco, and by the time the ball was thrown around the infield it was covered with tobacco juice. EVERYONE spit on it."

During a late 1890s game, the Reds were one run behind Chicago in the bottom of the 11th when Cincinnati's **Jake Beckley** topped a pitch and bounced it toward third base. The tying run was crossing the plate by the time the third baseman had caught up with the ball, which was slowly rolling along just inches inside the foul line. In disgust, third baseman **Harry Wolverton** took out his plug and threw it at the ground. The ball then bumped into the wad of tobacco and wobbled across the foul line. The runner was motioned back to third, Beckley returned to the batter's box where he popped up, and Chicago won the game. It was the most prominent role tobacco ever played in a major league game.

On the other hand, **Pete Rose** recalls that the Phillies' Don Lock got beaned in the jaw and the doctors said his chew saved him from being seriously hurt. **Sparky Anderson** said it was a tranquilizer. "I don't like the taste of chewing tobacco," said Sparky, "so I chew bubble gum and then wrap it around the wad of tobacco. It don't taste so good but it don't taste so bad once you get used to it. Sort of a neuter taste—ain't that the word?—something to chew on and spit out, for the nerves."

Rocky Bridges said, "I like a fat cigar," he said. "It's easier to chew. I used to have my trips measured by cigars. From Cincinnati to Long Beach was forty cigars." Someone once asked the daughter of Cincinnatian **Jim Frey**, then managing the Kansas City Royals, what he did for a living. "I don't know," she said. "All I ever see him do is spit."

A factory foreman named **Richard Plank** from Maineville, Ohio, monitored a 1987 game between the Reds and the Mets, and counted 324 spits. Mr. Plank, shocked by such liberties, complained that spitting in a public place was against the law. When asked if such an ordinance would cover baseball games, the city solicitor said, "Hyper-technically, probably."

"It's just baseball players," said **Jon Braude**, a Reds' spokesman. "People have noted it for years. I'm not personally into spitting," Braude added. "You probably expectorated me to say that."

Reds' management, however, had already taken a pro-chew stance. Visiting the Reds' workouts earlier in that year, **Siegfried Von Schotthof**, son of Schottzie, owner **Marge Schott's** mastiff mascot, ambled out and ate a discarded wad of tobacco, demonstrating conclusively that he was, indeed, one of the boys. ❿

Baseball

National Hall of Fame Members from Ohio

Name	Birthplace	Birth Date	Position	Batting Average
George Sisler	Nimisila, Ohio	March 24, 1893	First baseman	.340
Ed Delahanty	Cleveland, Ohio	October 31, 1867	Left fielder	.346
Elmer Flick	Bedford, Ohio	January 11, 1876	Right fielder	.315
Roger Bresnahan	Toledo, Ohio	June 11, 1879	Catcher	.279
Buck Ewing	Hoaglands, Ohio	October 27, 1859	Catcher	.311
Jesse Haines	Clayton, Ohio	July 22, 1893	Pitcher	3.64
Rube Marquard	Cleveland, Ohio	October 9, 1889	Pitcher	3.13
Cy Young	Gilmore, Ohio	March 29, 1867	Pitcher	2.63

Pioneers and Executives

Name	Birth place	Birth Date
Ban Johnson	Norwalk, Ohio	January 5, 1864
Kenesaw Landis	Millville, Ohio	November 20, 1866
Branch Rickey	Stockdale, Ohio	December 20, 1881

Managers

Walter Alston	Darrtown, Ohio	December 1, 1911
Miller Huggins	Cincinnati, Ohio	March 27, 1880

Ohio Baseball Hall of Fame

1976
Nick Cullop
Dean Chance
Bob Feller
Jesse Haines
Waite Hoyt
Ernie Lombardi
Mike Powers
Edd Roush
Red Ruffing
Luke Sewell
Tris Speaker
Cy Young

1977
Walter Alston
Lou Boudreau
Warren Giles
Ted Kluszewski
William McKinley
Roger Peckinpaugh
Johnny VanderMeer
Early Wynn

1978
Earl Averill
Stan Coveleski
Lefty Grove
Bob Lemon
Nap Lajoie
Al Lopez
Eddie Onslow
Satchel Paige
Branch Rickey
Frank Robinson
George Sisler
Bucky Walters

1979
Gus Bell
Rocky Colavito
Mel Harder
Tommy Henrich
Miller Huggins
Fred Hutchinson
Eppa Rixey
Joe Sewell
George Uhle
Bill Veeck

1980
Estel Crabtree
Harvey Haddix
Noodles Hahn
Joe Jackson
Kenesaw Landis
Thurman Munson
Gabe Paul
Vada Pinson
Wally Post
Vic Wertz

1981
Paul Derringer
John Galbreath
Rube Marquard
Bill McKechnie
Rocky Nelson
Al Rosen

1982
Lew Fonseca
Larry McPhail
Joe Nuxhall
Birdie Tebbetts
Gene Woodling

1983
No inductees

1984
Ethan Allen
Mike Garcia
Robert Howsam
Addie Joss
Ken Keltner
Forrest Pressnell

1985
Roger Bresnahan
Bill Mazeroski
Frank McCormick
George Sisler Jr.
Bill Wambsganss

1986
Frank Baumholtz
Woody English
Sam McDowell
Roy McMillan
Billy Southworth
Casey Stengel

1987
Burt Shotton
Ned Garver
Elmer Flick
Bob Purkey
Jim Campbell

1988
Hal Trosky
Ned Skeldon
Tony Lucadello
Brooks Lawrence
Denny Galehouse
Harold Cooper
Bobby Avila

1989
Ewell Blackwell
Larry Doby
Jim O'Toole
Charlie Root
Bob Wren

1990
Dave Dravecky
Willis Hudlin
Gene Michael
Al Oliver

1991
Johnny Bench
Roy Hughes
Sam Jethroe
"Buck" Rodgers
Moses Walker

Columbus Clippers

Year	Finish	W	L	Pct.	Manager
1932	Fourth	46	34	.517	Nemo Leibold
1933	First	101	51	.664	Ray Blades
1934	First	85	68	.556	Ray Blades
1935	Third	84	70	.545	Ray Blades
1936	Sixth	76	78	.494	Burt Shotton
1937	First	90	64	.418	Burt Shotton
1938	Seventh	64	88	.418	Burt Shotton
1939	Seventh	62	92	.403	Burt Shotton
1940	Second	90	60	.600	Burt Shotton
1941	First	95	58	.621	Burt Shotton
1942	Third	82	72	.532	Ed Dyer
1943	Third	84	67	.556	Nick Cullop
1944	Fifth	86	67	.562	Nick Cullop
1945	Eighth	63	90	.412	Charles Root
1946	Eighth	64	90	.416	Charles Root
1947	Fifth	76	78	.526	Harold Anderson
1948	Fourth	81	73	.526	Harold Anderson
1949	Seventh	70	83	.458	Harold Anderson
1950	Third	84	69	.549	Rollie Hemsley
1951	Eighth	53	101	.344	Harry Walker
1952	Seventh	68	85	.444	John Keane
1953	Seventh	64	90	.416	John Keane
1954	Fourth	77	76	.503	John Keane
1955	Seventh	64	89	.418	Nick Cullop
1956	Seventh	69	84	.451	Nick Cullop
1957	Seventh	69	85	.448	Frank Oceak
1958	Fourth	77	77	.500	Clyde King
1959	Second	84	70	.545	Cal Ermer
1960	Sixth	69	84	.451	Cal Ermer
1961	First	92	62	.597	Larry Shepard
1962	Fifth	80	74	.519	Larry Shepard
1963	Fourth	75	73	.507	Larry Shepard
1964	Sixth	69	85	.448	Larry Shepard
1965	First	85	61	.582	Larry Shepard
1966	Second	82	65	.558	Larry Shepard
1967	Fourth	69	71	.493	Harding Peterson
1968a	Second	82	65	.558	John Pesky
1969b	Fourth	74	66	.529	Don Hoak
1970c	Second	81	59	.579	Joe Morgan

1971 (No Team)
1972 (No Team)
1973 (No Team)
1974 (No Team)
1975 (No Team)
1976 (No Team)

Year	Finish	W	L	Pct.	Manager
1977	Seventh	65	75	.464	(Overall)
		54	51	.514	John Lipon
		11	24	.314	Tim Murtaugh
1978	Seventh	61	78	.439	John Lipon
1979	First	85	54	.612	Gene Michael
1980e	First	83	57	.593	Joe Altobelli
1981f	First	88	51	.633	Frank Verdi
1982g	Second	79	61	.564	Frank Verdi
1983h	First	83	57	.593	John Oates
1984i	First	82	57	.590	Stump Merrill
1985j	Third	75	64	.540	(Overall)
		65	53	.551	Stump Merrill
		10	11	.476	Doug Holmquist
1986	Sixth	62	77	.446	Barry Foote
1987k	Second	77	63	.550	Bucky Dent
1988	3 West	65	77	.458	Bucky Dent
1989	2 West	77	69	.527	(Overall)
		9	7	.563	Rick Down
		68	62	.523	Bucky Dent
1990l	1 West	87	59	.596	(Overall)
		53	34	.609	Rick Down
		34	25	.576	Stump Merril
1991m	1West	85	59	.590	Rick Down

a—Beat Rochester 3-2 in IL semifinals; lost 0-4 to Jackson in finals

b—Beat Tidewater in Governor's Cup playoff, semifinals 3 games to 1; lost to Syracuse in championship finals 4 games to 1.

c—Beat Rochester in Governor's Cup semifinal playoff, 3 games to 2; lost to Syracuse in best-of-5 championship finals, 3 games to 1.

d—Beat Tidewater in Governor's Cup semifinal playoff 3 games to 1; beatSyracuse in 7-game championship finals, 4 games to 3.

e—Beat Richmond in semifinals, 3 games to 2; beat Toledo to win Governors' Cup, 4 games to 1

f—Beat Rochester in semifinals, 3 games to 2; beat Richmond to win Governors' Cup, 2 games to 1

g—Lost to Tidewater in semifinals, 3 games to 0

h—Lost to Tidewater in semifinals, 3 games to 2

i—Lost to Pawtucket in semifinals, 3 games to 1

j—Beat Syracuse in semifinals, 3 games to 1; lost to Tidewater in finals, 3 games to 1

k—Beat Rochester in semifinals, 3 games to 0; beat Tidewater to win Governors' Cup, 3 games to 0

l—Lost Governors' Cup to Rochester, 3 games to 2

m—Beat Pawtucket to win Governors' Cup, 3 games to 0

Canton-Akron Indians

Year	Finish	League	W	L	Manager
1989a	Third	Eastern	70	69	Bob Molinaro
1990b	Third	Eastern	76	64	Ken Bolek
1991c	Fourth	Eastern	75	65	Ken Bolek

a—Lost to Harrisburg in playoffs, three games to two

b—Lost to London in playoffs, three games to two

c—Lost to Harrisburg in playoffs, three games to one

Toledo Mud Hens

Year	Finish	League	W	L	Manager(s)
1883	First	NL	56	28	Charles H. Morton
1884	Eighth	AA	46	58	Charles H. Morton
1885	Fifth	WL	9	21	Daniel O'Leary
1886	(No Team)				
1887	(No Team)				
1888	Eighth	T-SL	46	64	Harry T. Smith
					Frank H. Mountain
					Robert H. Woods
1889	Fourth	IL	54	51	Charles H. Morton
1890	Fourth	AA	68	64	Charles H. Morton
1891	(No Team)				
1892	Fourth	WL	23	22	Edward L. MacGregor
1893	Western League did not operate				
1894	Second	WL	67	55	
1895	Seventh	WL	52	72	Dennis A. Long
1896	Second	I-SL	38	30	Dennis A. Long
					F. W. Torreyson
1897	First	I-SL	83	43	C. J. Strobel
1898	Second	I-SL	84	68	C. J. Strobel
1899	Third	I-SL	82	58	C. J. Strobel
1900	Third	I-SL	81	58	C. J. Strobel
1901	Third	WA	77	61	C. J. Strobel
1902	Eighth	AA	42	98	C. J. Strobel
1903	Eighth	AA	48	91	C. J. Strobel
1904	Eighth	AA	42	109	F. C. Reisling
					H. A. Long
					W. F. Clingman
1905	Seventh	AA	60	91	Mike Finn
					J. E. Grillo
1906	Fourth	AA	79	69	J. E. Grillo
1907	Second	AA	88	66	W. R. Armour
1908	Fourth	AA	81	72	W. R. Armour
1909	Sixth	AA	80	86	F. Abbott
					R. O. Seybold
					Harry Hinchman
1910	Second	AA	91	75	Harry Hinchman
1911	Fifth	AA	78	86	Topsy Hartsel
1912	Second	AA	78	66	Topsy Hartsel
1913	Sixth	AA	69	98	H. C. Bronkie
1914	Third	SML	43	35	Topsy Hartsel
1915	Ninth	No team	9	58	
1916	Sixth	AA	78	86	Roger Bresnahan
1917	Seventh	AA	57	95	Roger Bresnahan
1918	Eighth	AA	23	54	Roger Bresnahan
1919	Seventh	AA	59	91	Roger Bresnahan
1920	Third	AA	87	79	Roger Bresnahan
1921	Seventh	AA	80	88	W. J. Clymer
					F. W. Luderus
1922	Seventh	AA	65	101	G. B. Whitted
1923	Eighth	AA	54	114	G. B. Whitted
					W. H. Terry
1924	Fifth	AA	82	83	J. T. Burke
1925	Sixth	AA	77	90	J. T. Burke
1926	Fourth	AA	87	77	Casey Stengel
1927	First	AA	101	67	Casey Stengel
1928	Fifth	AA	79	88	Casey Stengel
1929	Eighth	AA	67	100	Casey Stengel
1930	Third	AA	88	66	Casey Stengel
1931	Eighth	AA	68	100	Casey Stengel
1932	Fourth	AA	87	80	Bibb Falk
1933	Fifth	AA	70	83	Steve O'Neill
1934	Sixth	AA	68	84	Steve O'Neill
1935	Sixth	AA	64	86	Fred Haney
1936	Eighth	AA	59	92	Fred Haney
1937	Second	AA	89	65	Fred Haney

1938	Fifth	AA	79	74	Fred Haney
1939	Eighth	AA	47	107	Myles Thomas
1940	Seventh	AA	59	90	Zack Taylor
1941	Fifth	AA	82	72	Zack Taylor
					Fred Haney
1942	Fourth	AA	78	73	Fred Haney
1943	Fourth	AA	76	76	Jack Fournier
1944	Second	AA	95	58	Ollie Marquardt
1945	Sixth	AA	69	84	Ollie Marquardt
1946	Sixth	AA	69	84	Don Gutteridge
1947	Eighth	AA	61	92	Frank Snyder
1948	Seventh	AA	61	91	George Detore
1949	Eighth	AA	64	90	Eddie Mayo
1950	Seventh	AA	65	87	Eddie Mayo
1951	Sixth	AA	70	82	Jack Tighe
1952	*Franchise moved to Charleston, W. Va., in midseason*				
1953	First	AA	90	64	Tommy Holmes
					George Selkirk
1954	Sixth	AA	74	80	George Selkirk
1955	Fifth	AA	81	73	George Selkirk
1956-1964	*(No Team)*				
1965	Seventh	IL	68	78	Frank Verdi
1966	Sixth	IL	71	75	Loren Babe
1967b	Third	IL	73	66	Jack Tighe
1968c	First	IL	83	64	Jack Tighe
1969	Sixth	IL	68	72	Jack Tighe
1970	Eighth	IL	57	89	Frank Carswell
1971	Seventh	IL	60	80	Mike Roarke
1972	Fifth	IL	75	69	John Lipon
1973	Fourth	IL	65	81	Lipon Cot Deal
1974	Fifth	IL	70	74	Jim Bunning
1975	Seventh	IL	62	78	Jim Bunning
1976	Eighth	IL	55	85	Joe Sparks
1977	Eighth	IL	56	84	Jack Cassini
1978	Third	IL	74	66	Cal Ermer
1979	Seventh	IL	63	76	Cal Ermer
1980e	Second	IL	77	63	Cal Ermer
1981	Eighth	IL	53	87	Cal Ermer
1982	Seventh	IL	60	80	Cal Ermer
1983	Fifth	IL	68	72	Cal Ermer
1984	Third	IL	74	63	Cal Ermer
1985	Sixth	I	71	68	Cal Ermer
1986	Sixth	IL	62	77	Charlie Manuel
1987	Fifth	IL	71	71	Leon Roberts
1988	Fourth W. Div.	IL	58	64	Pat Corrales
1989	Fourth W. Div.	IL	69	76	John Wockenfuss
1990	Fourth W. Div.	IL	58	69	John Wockenfuss
					Tom Gamboa
1991	Third W. Div.	IL	74	70	Joe Sparks

a—Toledo won Junior World Series beating Buffalo of IL 5 games to one.

b—Toledo won Governors' Cup Playoff Championship beating Richmond 3 games to two and Columbus 4 games to one.

c-Toledo lost in first round of IL playoffs to Jacksonville 1-3 in best of five series.

d—Lost to Pawtucket in IL playoff semifinals 3 games to two.

e–Lost Governors' Cup to Columbus, 4 games to one

Prior to 1988, the Governors' Cup was the championship title for all of Triple-A minor league baseball. In 1988, the Triple-A league was split into the International League and the American Association. The Governors' Cup then became the championship for the International League, and the winner of the Governors' Cup went on to play against the American Association champion for the Triple-A Alliance Crown.

An Unlikely Port for Baseball's Most Famous Name

Where in all of baseball is there a more evocative name than the **Mud Hens** of Toledo? Answer: Nowhere. In less knowledgeable quarters, the Mud Hens are referred to as "Klinger's team," referring to Corporal Max Klinger of the TV show M*A*S*H wherein Klinger—portrayed by Toledo native **Jamie Farr**—wore a dress in his/her constant application for a Section 8 and a trip home to Toledo. This because of the show's constant references, to wit:

*

Hawkeye: Why'd you hit Zale?
Klinger: He insulted the Toledo Mud Hens.
Hawkeye: I take it that's a baseball team and not yesterday's lunch.

*

The Mud Hens, a Triple A affiliate of the Detroit Tigers, have been around for a long time, but not quite as long as professional baseball has been in Toledo, which is since 1882, in one way or another. It was Toledo—not Brooklyn—that put the first black in the major leagues. His name was **Moses (Fleet) Walker** who, in 1884 played for Toledo's American Association team. When the Chicago White Stockings came to town, their captain, Cap Anson, later admitted to the Hall of Fame, told Toledo's management he would not play "with no damned nigger," but Toledo said it would cancel the game before it would order Walker off the field. The event helped inspire the racist Anson to push for the exclusion of blacks, a sentiment that was unfortunately shared in a geography wider than Chicago and led to a white game for more than half a century.

In 1927, the Mud Hens' manager was **Casey Stengel**, who built the Yankee dynasty of the 1950s. He took the Mud Hens to the American Association pennant, an event so exciting that the season itself drew more than 324,000 and the pennant win

unleashed a three-day party in Toledo described by the Toledo Blade as "Greatest Celebration Since Armistice Day."

Veteran Mudhen watchers say that anything Stengel did with the Yankees, he did first in Toledo. Whatever the truth, he did have his entertaining moments in Ohio. One day, while being ridden tirelessly by a fan, Stengel put himself into the lineup as a pinch-hitter, hit a home run, and after touring the bases, ran straight to the loudmouth fan and shook his hand.

The Mud Hens once had a manager by the name of **Jack Cassini**, who stood on his chair at the team's opening day luncheon and promised the fans a pennant. The team, knowing better, ignored Cassini. They ignored him so roundly, they began to leave when he was around. Rather than sit with Cassini in the dugout, they sat in the stands, or squeezed into the bullpen with the pitchers. The team, meanwhile, fell desperately out of contention. "We'll still win it," said manager Cassini. His players moved farther afield. When Cassini tried to outfox them by sitting in the bullpen, they all moved back to the dugout, leaving Cassini alone, waving to his friends in the press box. The Mud Hens plunged toward the basement, where EVERYONE ended up together. Except Cassini. He became a scout for the Indians, from which geography a basement is due north.

The Mud Hens name is said to have originated before the turn of the century, when the team played at Bay View Park and wild ducks lived in the adjacent marshlands. The mud hen itself is a ducklike bird with a pointed white beak and drops in on Toledo only for a brief time on its migrations.

A fitting symbol for the peregrinations of the minor leaguer. ▶

Basketball

Cleveland Cavaliers, The Record

Year	W-L	Percent	Finish	GB	Coach
1970-71	15-67	.183	4th	27	Bill Fitch
1971-72	23-59	.280	4th	15	Bill Fitch
1972-73	32-50	.390	4th	20	Bill Fitch
1973-74	29-53	.354	4th	18	Bill Fitch
1974-75	40-42	.488	3rd	20	Bill Fitch
1975-76	49-33	.598	1st	—	Bill Fitch
1976-77	43-39	.524	4th	6	Bill Fitch
1977-78	43-39	.524	3rd	9	Bill Fitch
1978-79	30-52	.366	4th	18	Bill Fitch
1979-80	37-45	.451	5th	13	Stan Albeck
1980-81	28-54	.341	5th	32	Bill Musselman (25-46) Don Delaney (3-8)
1981-82	15-67	.183	6th	40	Don Delaney (4-13) Bob Kloppenburg (0-1 Chuck Daly (9-32) Bill Musselman (2-21)
1982-83	23-59	.280	5th	28	Tom Nissalke
1983-84	28-54	.341	4th	22	Tom Nissalke
1984-85	36-46	.439	4th	23	George Karl
1985-86	29-53	.354	5th	28	George Karl (25-42) Gene Littles (4-11)
1986-87	31-51	.378	6th	26	Lenny Wilkens
1987-88	42-40	.512	4th	12	Lenny Wilkens
1988-89	57-25	.695	2nd	6	Lenny Wilkens
1989-90	42-40	.512	4th	17	Lenny Wilkens
1990-91	33-49	.402	6th	28	Lenny Wilkens
Totals	**705-1017**	**.409**			

Cavaliers, The Statistics

1. Most points, game—Walt Wesley, 50, vs. Cincinnati, 1971
2. Most points, career—Austin Carr, 10,265
3. Highest point average, season—Mike Mitchell, 24.5, 1980-81
4. Most rebounds, game—Rick Roberson, 25, vs. Houston, 1972
5. Most rebounds, career—Jim Chones, 3,790
6. Highest rebound average, season—Rick Roberson, 12.7, 1971-72
7. Most assists, game—Geoff Huston, 27, vs. Golden Gate, 1982
8. Most games played—Bingo Smith, 720
9. Best field goal percentage, career—Mark West, .553
10. Best scoring average, career—World B. Free, 23.0
11. Most personal fouls, season—James Edwards, 347, 1981-82
12. Most steals, career—Foots Walker, 722
13. Most blocked shots, season—Larry Nance, 206, 1988-89
14. Most turnovers, career—Brad Daugherty, 1,066
15. Team points, game—154, vs. L.A. Lakers (4OT), 1980

Professional

Two professional indoor soccer leagues operate in the state of Ohio. They are the **National Professional Soccer League** and the **Major Soccer League**. The Dayton Dynamo and the Canton Invaders play in the National Professional Soccer League (as did the now defunct Columbus Capitals and the Toledo Pride) while the Cleveland Crunch plays in the Major Soccer League. While both leagues organize and supervise competition in the same sport, indoor soccer, and share similar systems of rules, they operate under different philosophies and teams from different leagues never play one another.

The Cleveland Crunch

The Major Soccer League

Year	Record	Pct.	GB
1989-90	20-32	.385	12
1990-91	29-23	.558	0

In the 1990-91 season, the Cleveland Crunch won the Eastern Division of the Major Soccer League and was defeated by San Diego (8-6) for the League Champpionship.

Canton Invaders

The Invaders are one of two remaining charter franchises, and have won five of the seven championships in league history, including three of the last four. The team was founded in 1984-85 by current National Professional Soccer League Commissioner **Steve Paxos**, along with his brothers, **Nick** and **Gus**, and Canton attorney George Trifelos. The team won regular season and playoff crowns in 1984-85 and 1985-86, plus a divisional title in 1986-87 and the Challenge Cup Tournament in 1987-88. The original owners sold the team to a group of Canton businessmen following the 1987-88 season and playoff championship under Coach **Timo Liekoski**. In 1989-90 the Invaders began with a 13-0 streak and went on to post the best single season record in professional indoor soccer history: 36-4. The Invaders then defeated Milwaukee and Dayton in the playoffs to secure their third straight title, and fifth overall. Canton lost only one game at home, in regular season and playoff games, for a home winning percentage of .849. Two members of the old group of owners, **Steve Zoumbarakis** and **Tom Schervish**, took over the club and retained Coach Liekoski and General Manager **Mike Sanger**. In 1990-91, the Invaders won the American Division Championship and also recorded the leagues's best record at 28-12. The Invaders were knocked out of the playoffs in the semi-finals by the Dayton Dynamo.

The Canton Invaders

Year	Record	Pct.	GB
1984-85	31-9	.775	—
1985-86	33-7	.825	—
1986-87	31-11	.738	—
1987-88	12-2	.500	4
Challenge Cup	9-3	.750	—
1988-89	25-15	.625	—
American Division			
1989-90	36-4	.900	—
1990-91	28-12	.700	—

Dayton Dynamo

Year	Record	Pct.	GB
1988-89	14-26	.350	11
National Division			
1989-90	21-19	.525	—
1990-91	21-19	.525	2

Golf

World Series of Golf

Firestone Country Club
Akron, Ohio
Sponsored by NEC

Year	Contestants	Scores	Prizes
1962	Jack Nicklaus	66-69—135	$50,000
	Arnold Palmer	65-75—139	$12,500
	Gary Player	69-70—139	$12,500
1963	Jack Nicklaus	70-70—140	$50,000
	Julius Boros	72-69—140	$15,000
	Arnold Palmer	71-72—143	$5,000
	Bob Charles	70-77—147	$5,000
1964	Tony Lema	70-68—138	$50,000
	Ken Venturi	69-74—143	$15,000
	Bobby Nichols	77-70—147	$5,000
	Arnold Palmer	74-74—148	$5,000
1965	Gary Player	70-69—139	$50,000
	Jack Nicklaus	71-71—142	$15,000
	Peter Thomson	73-71—144	$7,500
	Dave Marr	74-77—151	$5,000
1966	*Gene Littler	71-72—143	$50,000
	Al Geiberger	71-72—143	$11,250
	Jack Nicklaus	70-73—143	$11,250
	Billy Casper	70-74—144	$5,000
	*Won on first playoff hole		
1967	Jack Nicklaus	74-70—144	$50,000
	Gay Brewer	71-74—145	$15,000
	Roberto DeVicenzo	70-76—146	$7,500
	Don January	73-78—151	$5,000
1968	*Gary Player	71-72—143	$50,000
	Bob Goalby	72-71—143	$15,000
	Julius Boros	72-72—144	$7,500
	Lee Trevino	79-74—153	$5,000
	*Won on fourth playoff hole		
1969	Orville Moody	74-67—141	$50,000
	George Archer	74-69—143	$15,000
	Ray Floyd	72-73—145	$6,250
	Tony Jacklin	73-72—145	$6,250
1970	Jack Nicklaus	66-70—136	$50,000
	Billy Casper	71-68—139	$11,250
	Dave Stockton	69-70—139	$11,250
	Tony Jacklin	71-70—141	$5,000
1971	Charles Coody	68-73—141	$50,000
	Jack Nicklaus	71-71—142	$15,000
	Bruce Crampton	73-70—143	$7,500
	Lee Trevino	72-74—146	$5,000
1972	Gary Player	71-72—142	$50,000
	Jack Nicklaus	75-69—144	$11,250
	Lee Trevino	74-70—144	$11,250
	Gay Brewer	73-72—145	$5,000
1973	Tom Weiskopf	71-66—137	$50,000
	Johnny Miller	73-67—140	$11,250
	Jack Nicklaus	71-69—140	$11,250
	Tommy Aaron	76-73—149	$5,000
1974	*Lee Trevino	70-69—139	$50,000
	Gary Player	67-72—139	$15,000
	Bobby Nichols	71-72—148	$7,500
	Hale Irwin	76-72—143	$7,500
	*Won on seventh playoff hole		
1975	Tom Watson	69-71—140	$50,000
	Jack Nicklaus	72-70—142	$15,000
	Tom Weiskopf	75-70—145	$7,500
	Lou Graham	76-71—147	$5,000

Year	Contestants	Scores	Prizes
1976	Jack Nicklaus	68-70-69-68—275	$100,000
	Hale Irwin	71-70-71-67—279	$50,000
	Dave Hill	67-70-73-70—280	$20,000
1977	Lanny Wadkins	69-66-67-65—267	$100,000
	T-Hale Irwin	67-71-65-69—272	$35,000
	T-Tom Weiskopf	67-68-72-65—272	$35,000
1978	*Gil Morgan	71-72-67-68—278	$100,000
	Hubert Green	70-67-71-70—278	$45,000
	Tom Watson	74-70-69-67—280	$19,000
	*Won on first playoff hole		
1979	Lon Hinkle	67-67-71-67—272	$100,000
	T-Bill Rogers	69-67-67-70—273	$37,267
	T-Larry Nelson	68-67-68-70—273	$37,267
	T-Lee Trevino	67-68-72-66—273	$37,267
1980	Lon Hinkle	65-76-65-65—270	$100,000
	Ray Floyd	69-68-70-65—272	$50,000
	Jerry Pate	72-64-70-67—273	$34,500
1981	Bill Rogers	68-69-71-67—275	$100,000
	Tom Kite	72-71-66-67—276	$55,000
	T-Hale Irwin	68-68-70-72—278	$27,850
	T-Isao Aoki	74-65-72-67—278	$27,850
1982	*Craig Stadler	70-68-75-65—278	$100,000
	Ray Floyd	69-71-68-70—278	$55,000
	Isao Aoki	77-66-70-67—280	$34,500
	*Won on fourth playoff hole		
1983	Nick Price	66-68-69-67—270	$100,000
	Jack Nicklaus	67-73-69-65—274	$60,000
	Johnny Miller	71-69-68-67—275	$40,000
1984	Denis Watson	69-62-70-70—271	$126,000
	Bruce Lietzke	66-68-69-70—273	$75,600
	T-Bob Eastwood	70-70-66-69—275	$40,600
	T-Peter Jacobsen	70-67-69-69—275	$40,600
1985	Rogger Maltbie	65-69-68-66—268	$126,000
	Denis Watson	65-71-66-70—272	$75,600
	T-Tom Kite	67-68-70-68—273	$40,600
	T-Calvin Peete	66-69-71-67—273	$40,600
1986	Dan Pohl	69-66-71-71—277	$126,000
	Lanny Wadkins	68-68-70-72—278	$75,600
	Bobby Cole	74-67-68-70—279	$47,600
1987	Curtis Strange	70-66-68-71—275	$144,000
	Fulton Allen	71-70-67-70—278	$86,400
	Mac O'Grady	69-72-69-69—279	$54,400
1988	*Mike Reid	70-65-71-69—275	$162,000
	Tom Watson	74-69-64-68—275	$97,200
	Ian Baker-Finch	68-67-71-71—277	$52,200
	*Won on first playoff hole		
1989	*David Frost	70-68-69-69—276	$180,000
	Ben Crenshaw	64-72-72-68—276	$108,000
	Payne Stewart	72-67-68-71—278	$68,000
	*Won on second playoff hole		
1990	Jose Maria Olazabal	61-67-67-67—262	*$198,000
	Lanny Wadkins	70-68-70-66—274	$118,600
	Hale Irwin	70-67-66-74-277	$74,600
	*Olazabal's round of 61 and four-round total of 262 are tournament and course records.		
1991	*Tom Purtzer	72-69-67-71—279	$216,000
	Davis Love III	72-66-72-69—279	$105,600
	Jim Gallagher, Jr.	72-68-70-69—279	$105,600
	*Won on second playoff hole		

Memorial Tournament

Muirfield Village Golf Club
Dublin, Ohio

Year	Winners	Scores	Earnings
1976	*Roger Maltbie	71-71-70-76—288	$40,000
	Hale Irwin	71-74-74-69—288	$22,800
	Don Bies	68-75-71-75—289	$14,200

*Won in a three-hole playoff at stroke play followed by sudden death

Year	Winners	Scores	Earnings
1977	Jack Nicklaus	72-68-70-71—281	$45,000
	Hubert Green	71-71-72-69—283	$25,650
	Tom Watson	71-70-73-71—285	$15,975
1978	Jim Simons	68-69-73-74—284	$50,000
	Bill Kratzert	72-70-69-74—285	$28,500
	Fuzzy Zoeller	71-73-73-70—287	$17,750
1979	Tom Watson	73-69-72-71—285	$54,000
	Miller Barber	74-73-71-70—288	$32,400
	Bob Gilder	74-80-68-69—291	$20,400
1980	David Graham	73-67-70-70—280	$54,000
	Tom Watson	74-67-69-71—281	$32,400
	Mike Reid	69-73-70-70—282	$20,400
1981	Keith Fergus	71-68-74-71—284	$63,000
	Jack Renner	75-70-69-71—285	$37,800
	Tom Watson	72-72-69-74—287	$16,800
1982	Ray Floyd	74-69-67-71—281	$63,000
	Wayne Levi	74-70-69-70—283	$23,100
	Peter Jacobsen	74-69-68-72—283	$23,100
1983	Hale Irwin	71-71-70-69—281	$72,000
	Ben Crenshaw	67-71-73-71—282	$35,200
	David Graham	72-67-69-74—282	$35,200
1984	*Jack Nicklaus	69-70-71-70—280	$90,000
	Andy Bean	71-75-67-67—280	$54,000
	Roger Maltbie	70-73-73-67—283	$26,000

* Won on the third playoff hole

Year	Winners	Scores	Earnings
1985	Hale Irwin	68-68-73-72—281	$100,000
	Lanny Wadkins	69-72-67-74—282	$60,000
	Bill Kratzert	69-71-71-73—284	$37,780
1986	Hal Sutton	68-69-66-68—271	$100,000
	Don Pooley	69-67-70-69—275	$60,000
	Johnny Miller	70-69-69-68—276	$32,225
1987	Don Pooley	70-67-65-70—272	$140,000
	Curt Byrum	64-71-69-71—275	$84,000
	Denis Watson	75-66-65-70—276	$40,443
1988	Curtis Strange	73-70-64-67—274	$160,000
	Hale Irwin	70-68-68-70—276	$78,220
	David Frost	69-70-68-69—276	$78,220
1989	Bob Tway	71-69-68-69—277	$160,000
	Fuzzy Zoeller	69-66-72-72—279	$96,000
	Payne Stewart	70-73-73-65—281	$60,440
1990	Greg Norman	73-74-69—216	$180,000
	Payne Stewart	74-74-69—217	$108,000
	Mark Brooks	76-70-72—218	$48,000
	Brad Faxon	77-69-72—218	$48,000
	Fred Couples	69-74-75—218	$48,000
	Don Pooley	73-71-74—218	$48,000
1991	*Kenny Perry	70-63-69-71—273	$216,000
	Hale Irwin	73-69-65-66—273	$129,600
	Corey Pavin	66-71-67-71—275	$81,600

*Won on the fifteenth playoff hole

Source: The Memorial Tournament

Kroger Senior Golf Classic

Jack Nicklaus Sports Center, Mason, Ohio

Year	Winners	Scores	Earnings
1990*	Jim Dent	67-66	$90,000
	Harold Henning	70-64	$53,500
	Charles Coody	67-68	$42,500
1991	Al Geiberger	66-69-68—203	$90,000
	Larry Laoretti	67-70-67—204	$51,200
	Miller Barber	71-67-67—205	$35,083.34

* The tournament was rained out before the final round.

Source: Jack Nicklaus Sports Center

Jamie Farr Toledo Classic

Toledo, Ohio

Year	Winner	Score	Earnings
1984	Lauri Peterson	278	$26,250
1985	Penny Hammel	278	$26,250
1986	No Tournament		
1987	Jane Geddes	280	$33,750
1988	Laura Davies	277	$41,250
1989	Penny Hammel	206	$41,250
1990	Tina Purtzer	205	$48,750
1991	Alice Miller	206	$52,200

Source: Jamie Farr Toledo Classic

LPGA Phar-Mor Tournament

Youngstown, Ohio

Year	Winner	Score	Earnings
1990	Beth Daniel	207	$60,000
1991	Deb Richard	207	$75,000

Source: Ladies Professional Golf Association

JIM BORGMAN
The CINCINNATI
ENQUIRER 1989

" IT WAS ANNOUNCED TODAY IN STOCKHOLM THAT WALTER PFLEGELMAN OF PRICE HILL
HAS BEEN AWARDED THE 1989 NOBEL PRIZE IN BOWLING...."

Bowling

Firestone Tournament of Champions

Firestone Tournament of Champions

The world's most prestigious bowling event is the Firestone Tournament of Champions. This "crown jewel" of Professional Bowlers Association (PBA) tournaments has been held in the Akron area since its inception in 1965.

Year	Winner	Year	Winner	Year	Winner
1965	Billy Hardwick	1975	Dave Davis	1985	Mark Williams
1966	Wayne Zahn	1976	Marshall Holman	1986	Marshall Holman
1967	Jim Stefanich	1977	Mike Berlin	1987	Peter Weber
1968	Dave Davis	1978	Earl Anthony	1988	Mark Williams
1969	Jim Godman	1979	George Pappas	1989	Del Ballard, Jr.
1970	Don Johnson	1980	Wayne Webb	1990	Dave Ferraro
1971	Johnny Petraglia	1981	Steve Cook	1991	David Ozio
1972	Mike Durbin	1982	Mike Durbin		
1973	Jim Godman	1983	Joe Berardi	Source: Professional Bowlers Association, Inc.	
1974	Earl Anthony	1984	Mike Durbin		

PBA National Championship

The national championship tournament of the Professional Bowlers Association (PBA) began in Memphis, Tennessee in 1960. The event has been held in Toledo since 1981.

Year	Winner	Year	Winner	Year	Winner
1960	Don Carter	1971	Mike Lemongello	1982	Earl Anthony
1961	Dave Soutar	1972	Johnny Guenther	1983	Earl Anthony
1962	Carmen Salvino	1973	Earl Anthony	1984	Bob Chamberlain
1963	Billy Hardwick	1974	Earl Anthony	1985	Mike Aulby
1964	Bob Strampe	1975	Earl Anthony	1986	Tom Crites
1965	Dave Davis	1976	Paul Colwell	1987	Randy Pedersen
1966	Wayne Zahn	1977	Tommy Hudson	1988	Brian Voss
1967	Dave Davis	1978	Warren Nelson	1989	Peter Weber
1968	Wayne Zahn	1979	Mike Aulby	1990	Jim Pencak
1969	Mike McGrath	1980	Johnny Petraglia	1991	Mike Miller
1970	Mike McGrath	1981	Earl Anthony		

Ohio State Bowling Champions, Men's

Started in 1904, the Ohio State Bowling Association is affiliated with the American Bowling Congress. The Ohio State Bowling Association's state champion tournament is held annually at various locations throughout Ohio, and the bowler who wins the All Events category represents Ohio in national competition at the annual American Bowling Congress Masters Tournament.

	Year	Actual Champion	Handicap Champion
Team	1980	Len Immeke Buick, Columbus	C.R. Paving, Wilmington
Doubles		Ron Bell/Rick Davis, Kent	Ron Bell/Rick Davis, Kent
Singles		Jeff Magas, Wickliffe	Dan Hunsicker, Middletown
All Events		Jeff Thielson, Columbus	
Team	1981	Kent Lincoln-Mercury, Kent	Kent Lincoln-Mercury, Kent
Doubles		Doug Jackson/Mark Moore, Columbus	Doug Jackson/Mark Moore,
Columbus			
Singles		Pebo Church, Brunswick	Pebo Church, Brunswick
All Events		Dan Stelter, Cleveland	
Team	1982	Commercial Enterprises, Cleveland	Commercial Enterprises, Cleveland
Doubles		Lee Dannemiller/Ken Smythe, Orrville	Dave Brough/Greg McFarlane, Oak
Harbor			
Singles		Rick Frederick, Mansfield	Ken Rahm, Cleveland
All Events		John Gant, Cincinnati	
Team	1983	Cherokee Bowl, Independence	Vault Fun Center, Waverly
Doubles		Jeff White/Bob Kussmaul, Zanesville	Jeff White/Bob Kussmaul, Zanesville
Singles		Jim Smith, Kent	Jim Smith, Kent
All Events		John Gant, Independence	
Team	1984	Twin Lanes, Cleveland	Friendly Bowling Center, East
Liverpool			
Doubles		Dave Oesch/Dan Lucas, Akron	Dave Oesch/Dan Lucas, Akron
Singles		Frank Zitnik, Jr., Hubbard	Frank Zitnik, Jr., Hubbard
All Events		Todd Martin, Newark	
Team	1985	Terry's Pro Shop, Sagamore Hills	Terry's Pro Shop, Sagamore Hills
Doubles		Dave Hines/Wendall Spencer, Cincinnati	Darrell Brown/Don Hartness,
Middletown			
Singles		Rob Theis, Youngstown	Rob Theis, Youngstown
All Events		Rick Martin, Cincinnati	
Team	1986	Dayton Band, Dayton	Dayton Band, Dayton
Doubles		Joe Nuzzo/Charles Lias, Youngstown	Joe Nuzzo/Charles Lias, Youngstown
Singles		Bob Fitt, Akron	Randy Parriott, Hebron
All Events		Joe Nuzzo, Youngstown	
Team	1987	Plaza Lanes, Dayton	Fairfield Lanes, Hamilton
Doubles		Bob Bures/Marty Freed, Cleveland	Bob Bures/Marty Freed, Cleveland
Singles		Sam Stump, Columbus	Sam Stump, Columbus
All Events		Bob Bures, Cleveland	
Team	1988	Browning Pontiac, Cincinnati	Browning Pontiac, Cincinnati
Doubles		Clarence Caldwell/Walter Price, Euclid	Clarence Caldwell/Walter Price,
Euclid			
Singles		Rocky Heater, Akron	Rocky Heater, Akron
			Cliff Turner, Euclid
All Events		Dale Parker, Toledo	
		Sonny Goldstein, Columbus	
Team	1989	Fairborn Camera & Video, Fairborn	Bert's Car Wash, Hamden
Doubles		Jim Beatty/Bobby Moore, Columbus	Brent F. Daniels/Victor Casey, Sr.,
Springfield			
Singles		Jake Mullet, Plain City	Jake Mullet, Plain City
All Events		Rick Theberge, Brookpark	
Team	1990	Rick Starbuck's Pro Shop, Beavercreek	Dick's Party Shop, Midland
Doubles		Wyatt Kosier/Ken Dudley, Toledo	Loren Nicol/Tom Rausch, Marysville
Singles		Patrick Hughes, Fairfield	Richard Schneider, Wapakoneta
All Events		Brad Fazio, Canal Winchester	

Team	1991	Redskin Lanes #1, Utica	Advantage Display, Montpelier
Doubles		Rick Graham/Larry Neff, Bellefontaine	Rick Graham/Larry Neff, Bellefontaine
Singles		Pat Mercer, Dayton	Steve Storer, Wilmington
All Events		Pat Mercer, Dayton	

Source: Ohio Bowling Association

Ohio State Bowling Champions, Women's

Founded in Toledo by ten women in 1925, the Ohio Women's Bowling Association (OWBA) now has 195,000 members, making it the nation's fourth largest state organization of women bowlers. OWBA is affiliated with the Women's International Bowling Congress, and OWBA's state championship tournament is held annually in various locations throughout Ohio.

	Year	Actual Champion	Handicap Champion
Team	1980	King Pin Classic, Cincinnati	Braidich Trucking, Cleveland
Doubles		Nancy Amlung Fehr/Diane Felton, Cincinnati	Kathryn Funk/Olive Ruehle,
Tiffin			
Singles		Nancy Moore, Dayton	Jane Shoemaker, Findlay
All Events		Diane Felton, Cincinnati	
Team	1981	Sillias Pro Shop, Cleveland	Babbs Sheet Metal, Wilmington
			Agnes Provision, Massillon
			Spencer House Inn, Lima
Doubles		Jeanne Maiden/Kitty Kumher, Cleveland	Sandra Elser/Luinda Young,
Warren			
Singles		Rosemary Williams, Cleveland	Rosemary Williams, Cleveland
All Events		Madeline Kivett, Cincinnati	
Team	1982	Hudepohl Beer, Cincinnati	Jim Back Construction,
Cincinnati			
Doubles		Lois Schiml/Ruby Whited, Dayton	Kim Jadwin/Bonnie Reed,
Chillicothe			
Singles		Fran Kurjan, Lorain	Fran Kurjan, Lorain
All Events		Terri Stauffer, Canton	
Team	1983	Savoy Beverage, Cleveland	Rockdale Metal, Steubenville
Doubles		Diane Cushman/Elizabeth Baude, Cincinnati	Pam Engstrom/Ruth Smith,
Bryan			
Singles		Maxine Dillard, Columbus	
All Events		Elizabeth Baude, Cincinnati	
Team	1984	Mentor Pro Shop, Cleveland	Willow Lanes, Marietta
Doubles		Becky Hart, Columbus/Linda Kelly, Dayton	Lillian Cicotte/Penny
		Dannenberg, Hamler-Deshler District	
			Becky Hart, Columbus/Linda
		Kelly, Dayton	
Singles		Lorraine Anderson, Canton	Connie Myers, Hamilton
All Events		Mary Slawinski, Wauseon	
Team	1985	No State Tournament Held	
Doubles			
Singles			
All Events			
Team	1986	Plaza Lanes, Dayton	Jim Foreman Pontiac-Nissan,
Springfield			
Doubles		Rhoda Barnett/DeCinda Shattuck, Youngstown	Shirley Shonkwiler/Joan Fisher,
Dayton			
Singles		Helen Zamborsky, East Liverpool	Mary C. Boysel, Springfield
All Events		Rose Kotnik, Cleveland	
Team	1987	Plaza Lanes, Dayton	Sam's Carpet, Lancaster
Doubles		Marge Gullatta/Debbie Rainone, Cleveland	Barbara Kidder/Ann Wells,
Springfield			
Singles		Marian Workman, Cleveland	Cheryl Harder
All Events		Ronnie Kirby, Akron	

Team	1988	National Medicine Homecare, Dayton	Hydra Clean 11, Akron
Doubles		Gwen Robinson/Mandy Wilson, Dayton	Rhonda Evans/Tina Callahan,
Wellston			
Singles		Tammy Burtscher, Sandusky	Glenna McGonical, Springfield
All Events		Debbie Bennett, Akron	
		Loretta Gedeon, Akron	
Team	1989	Plaza Lanes, Dayton	Proud Pony, Cleveland
Doubles		Cindy Russell/Sue Chenea, Columbus	Paula M. Leonard/Debby
Schade, Findlay			
Singles		Mandy Wilson, Dayton	April Roush, Gallipolis
All Events		Mandy Wilson, Dayton	
Team	1990	Sportman Shop, Springfield	Fremont Athletic Supply,
Fremont			
Doubles		Linda Kelly, Dayton/Debbie Bennett, Akron	Sara Higgins/Nancy Gerschutz,
Defiance			
			Judy Gore/Maxine Petranyi,
Elyria			
Singles		Ronnie Kirby, Akron	Carolyn Lewandowski, Toledo
All Events		Debbie Bennett, Akron	
Team	1991	Plaza Lanes, Dayton	Deshler Car Wash, Napoleon
Doubles		Linda Kelly, Dayton/Debbie Bennett, Akron	Tina Saunders/Cornelia Walker,
Columbus			
Singles		Kitty Kumher, Cleveland	Dianne Moses, Springfield
All Events		Jennifer Rayman, Akron	

Source: Ohio Women's Bowling Association

Bowling for dollars

Down Ohio's Favorite Alleys

Site of the PBA National Championship—Imperial Lanes, Toledo

Site of the PBA Firestone Tournament of Champions—Riviera Lanes, Fairlawn

Recognized as bowling's equivalent of the major leagues, the Professional Bowlers Association of America (PBA) was founded by Akron attorney **Eddie Elias** in 1958. The first PBA tour consisted of only three cities—Albany, New York, Paramus, New Jersey, and Dayton, Ohio—and offered a mere $49,500 in prize money. Today, the PBA boasts some 3400 members and more than 30 major tournaments throughout the U.S. that award millions of dollars annually. It was Mr. Elias who first sought television contracts to broadcast PBA events, thus increasing the popularity of professional bowling and assuring the success of the association. ABC began televising the "Pro Bowlers Tour" in 1962, and it is now second only to NCAA football as network television's longest-running live sports series. The headquarters of the PBA, which is also the home of the professional bowling hall of fame, is located in Akron. ▶

Horse Racing

Little Brown Jug

Delaware, Ohio

The Little Brown Jug is the nation's most prestigious harness race for three-year-old standardbred colts. Named via a newspaper contest in the 1940s, the pacing classic takes place annually at the Delaware County Fairgrounds. Along with The Cane Pace at Yonkers Raceway and the Messenger Stake at Roosevelt Raceway, it comprises the Triple Crown of Pacing.

Year	Winning Horse	Driver	Winning Time	Winner's Purse
1946	Ensign Hanover	Wayne Smart	2:03.1	$17,679.32
1947	Forbes Chief	Del Cameron	2:05	$19,100
1948	Knight Dream	Frank Safford	2:07.1	$22,746.29
1949	Good Time	Frank Ervin	2:03.2	$23,312.53
1950	Dudley Hanover	Delvin Miller	2:02.3	$28,262.75
1951	Tar Heel	Del Cameron	2:00	$33,140.27
1952	Meadow Rice	Wayne Smart	2:01.3	$30,231.66
1953	Keystoner	Frank Ervin	2:03.3	$21,255.92
1954	Adios Harry	Morris MacDonald	2:01.3	$26.346.19
1955	Quick Chief	William Haughton	2:01	$24,645.24
1956	Noble Adios	John Simpson, Sr.	2:00.4	$29,602.97
1957	Torpid	John Simpson, Sr.	2:00.4	$27,205.41
1958	Shadow Wave	Joe O'Brien	2:01	$36.592.64
1959	Adios Butler	Clint Hodgins	1:59.2	$28,335.34
1960	Bullet Hanover	John Simpson, Sr.	1:58.3	$29,264.79
1961	Henry T. Adios	Stanley Dancer	1:58.4	$21,721.43
1962	Lehigh Hanover	Stanley Dancer	1:58.4	$27.764.36
1963	Overtrick	John Patterson	1:57.1	$38,245.14
1964	Vicar Hanover	William Haughton	2:01	$24,638.57
1965	Bret Hanover	Frank Ervin	1:57	$40,010.32
1966	Romeo Hanover	George Sholty	1:59.3	$41,785
1967	Best of All	James Hackett	1:59.1	$42,954.41
1968	Rum Customer	William Haughton	1:59.3	$38,563.72
1969	Laverne Hanover	William Haughton	2:00.2	$43,892.52
1970	Most Happy Fella	Stanley Dancer	1:57.1	$53,392.03
1971	Nansemond	Herve Filion	1:57.2	$31,919.09
1972	Strike Out	Keith Waples	1:56.3	$52,982.58
1973	Melvin's Woe	Joe O'Brien	1:57.3	$44,400
1974	Armbro Omaha	William Haughton	1:57	$49,073.10
1975	Seatrain	Ben Webster	1:57	$54,609.82
1976	Keystone Ore	Stanley Dancer	1:57	$56,905.64
1977	Governor Skipper	John Chapman	1:56.1	$75,750
1978	Happy Escort	William Popfinger	1:57.2	$49,492
1979	Hot Hitter	Herve Filion	1:55.3	$83,788
1980	Niatross	Clint Galbraith	1:54.4	$104,717
1981	Fan Hanover	Glen Garnsey	1:56.3	$90,198
1982	Merger	John Campbell	1:56.3	$99,492
1983	Ralph Hanover	Ron Waples	1;55.3	$108,537
1984	Colt Fortysix	Chris Boring	1:55	$110,931
1985	Nihilator	William O'Donnell	1:52.1	$129,770
1986	Barberry Spur	William O'Donnell	1:52.4	$150,841
1987	Jaguar Spur	Dick Stillings	1:55.3	$124,729.84
1988	B.J. Scoot	Michel Lachance	1:52.3	$147,030
1989	Goalie Jeff	Michel Lachance	1:54.1	$151,310
1990	Beach Towel	Ray Remmen	1:53.3	$149,955
1991	Precious Bunny	Jack Moiseyev	1.55	$228,334

Source: Little Brown Jug Society

Ohio Derby

The state's oldest and most esteemed thoroughbred race began in Cincinnati in 1876. Today, the three-year-olds compete annually for a $300,000 purse at the Thistledown track southeast of Cleveland.

Year	Winning Horse	Jockey	Winner's Purse	Track
1876	Bombay	Walker	$1,000	Chester Park
1877	McWhirter	James	$975	Chester Park
1878	Harper	McLellan	$1,025	Chester Park
1879	Ben Hill	Shauer	$750	Chester Park
1880	Mary Anderson	n/a	$600	Chester Park
1881	Bootjack	Allen	$550	Chester Park
1882	Babcock	Kelso	$950	Chester Park
1883	Pilot	Watkins	$1,100	Chester Park
1884-1923	No Race			
1924	Black Gold	J.D. Mooney	$4,000	Maple Heights
1925	Millwick	K. Noe	$7,320	Maple Heights
1926	Boot To Boot	A. Johnson	$7,320	Maple Heights
1927	No Race			
1928	Sunfire	B. Leonard	$9,350	Bainbridge
1929	Thistle Fyrn	V. Smith	$11,880	Bainbridge
1930	Culloden	P. Gross	$10,480	Bainbridge
1931	A La Carte	F. Catrone	$11,580	Bainbridge
1932	Economic	F. Horn	$7,760	Bainbridge
1933-1934	No Race			
1935	Paradisical	L. Hardy	$4,250	Thistledown
1936-1951	No Race			
1952	Carter's Pride	S. Bielen	$3,783	Cranwood
1953	Find	E. Guerin	$18,988	Thistledown
1954	Timely Tip	P.A. Ward	$18,703	Thistledown
1955	Traffic Judge	E. Arcaro	$28,938	Thistledown
1956	Born Mighty	J. Choquette	$29,041	Thistledown
1957	Manteau	K. Church	$19,840	Thistledown
1958	Terra Firma	L.C. Cook	$19,980	Thistledown
1959	On-And-On	S. Brooks	$19,730	Thistledown
1960	Playgoer	C. Meaux	$11,757	Thistledown
1961	Gay's Pal	G. Smithson	$12,477	Randall Park
1962	Gushing Wind	R.L. Baird	$15,616	Randall Park
1963	Lemon Twist	S. LeJeune	$20,572	Thistledown
1964	National	P. Anderson	$19,435	Thistledown
1965	Terra Hi	R.J. Campbell	$21,020	Thistledown
1966	War Censor	D. Kassen	$22,320	Thistledown
1967	Out The Window	B. Wall	$21,000	Thistledown
1968	Te Vega	M. Manganello	$19,075	Thistledown
1969	Berkley Prince	J. Giovanni	$22,450	Thistledown
1970	Climber	H. Gustines	$25,641	Thistledown
1971	Twist The Axe	R. Woodhouse	$36,256.50	Thistledown
1972	Freetex	J. Moseley	$64,134	Thistledown
1973	Our Native	A. Rini	$63,882	Thistledown
1974	Stonewalk	M.A. Rivera	$63,000	Thistledown
1975	Brent's Prince	B.R. Feliciano	$66,780	Thistledown
1976	Return of A Native	Garth Patterson	$75,000	Thistledown
1977	Silver Series	Larry Snyder	$90,000	Thistledown
1978	Special Honor	Robert Breen	$90,000	Thistledown
1979	Smarten	Sam Maple	$90,000	Thistledown
1980	Stone Manor	Pat Day	$90,000	Thistledown
1981	Pass The Tab	Antonio Graell	$90,000	Thistledown
1982	Spanish Drums	J. Vasquez	$90,000	Thistledown
1983	Pax Nobiscum	R. Platts	$90,000	Thistledown
1984	At The Threshold	Garth Patterson	$120,000	Thistledown
1985	Skip Trial	J.L. Samyn	$120,000	Thistledown
1986	Broad Brush	G.L. Stevens	$150,000	Thistledown
1987	Lost Code	Gene St. Leon	$150,000	Thistledown
1988	Jim's Orbit	Shane Romero	$150,000	Thistledown
1989	King Glorious	Chris McCarron	$180,000	Thistledown
1990	Private School	J. Vasquez	$180,000	Thistledown
1991	Private Man	John Velazquez	$180,000	Thistledown

Source: Thistledown Racing Club, Inc.

Budweiser Cleveland Grand Prix

One of 17 professional races on the CART/PPG (Championship Auto Racing Teams/Pittsburgh Plate Glass) Indy Car World Series circuit, the Cleveland Grand Prix is held annually at Burke Lakefront Airport in Cleveland.

Year	Winner	Average speed	Earnings
1982	Bobby Rahal	101.234 mph	$42,341
1983	Al Unser. Sr.	108.202	$44,340
1984	Danny Sullivan	118.734	$33,150
1985	Al Unser, Jr.	124.081	$50,094
1986	Danny Sullivan	127.106	$57,160
1987	Emerson Fittipaldi	128.421	$46,410
1988	Mario Andretti	124.295	$45,660
1989	Emerson Fittipaldi	128.072	$45,160
1990	Danny Sullivan	112.483	$81,628
1991	Michael Andretti	117.763	$78,922

Source: Indy Car Grand Prix, Inc.

Pioneer Electronics 200

*Held annually at the Mid-Ohio Sports Car Course in Lexington, Ohio, the Pioneer Electronics 200 is on the CART/PPG (Championship Auto Racing
Teams/Pittsburgh Plate Glass) Indy Car World Series professional racing circuit.*

Year	Winner	Average speed	Earnings
1980	Johnny Rutherford	86.601 mph	$22,178
1981	No Race		
1982	No Race		
1983	Teo Fabi	98.755	$38,680
1984	Mario Andretti	100.388	$46,970
1985	Bobby Rahal	107.041	$53,484
1986	Bobby Rahal	103.430	$56,910
1987	Roberto Guerrero	107.431	$67,410
1988	Emerson Fittipaldi	89.570	$58,160
1989	Teo Fabi	104.820	$53,160
1990	Michael Andretti	85.751	$80,655
1991	Michael Andretti	99.789	$83,700

Source: TrueSports Inc.; Championship Auto Racing Teams

Nissan Grand Prix of Ohio Camel GT Event

The Nissan Grand Prix of Ohio is on the International Motor Sports Association (IMSA) circuit of professional sports car races and is held annually at the Mid-Ohio Sports Car Course in Lexington, Ohio.

Year	Winner	Average speed
1975	Al Holbert (Race 1)	89.858 mph
	Al Holbert/Elliott Forbes-Robinson(Race 2)	87.74
1976	Mike Keyser (Race 1)	89.98
	Jim Busby (Race 2)	88.47
1977	David Hobbs (Race 1)	91.476
	Peter Gregg (Race 2)	88.338
1978	Bill Whittington/Jim Busby	90.058
1979	Peter Gregg/Hurley Haywood	90.575
1980	No Race	
1981	Brian Redman	94.023
1982	John Fitzpatrick (Race 1)	96.079
	John Fitzpatrick/David Hobbs (Race 2)	92.133
1983	Bobby Rahal/Doc Bundy/Jim Trueman	84.614
1984	Al Holbert/Derek Bell	90.477
1985	Al Holbert/Derek Bell	97.980
1986	Al Holbert/Derek Bell	98.855
1987	Jochen Mass/Bobby Rahal	101.518
1988	Geoff Brabham/Tom Gloy	100.351
1989	Geoff Brabham/Chip Robinson	96.458
1990	Geoff Brabham/Derek Daly	103.455
1991	Davy Jones	107.275

Source: TrueSports Inc.; The International Motor Sports Association

All-American Soap Box Derby Champions

Year	Champions	Age	Year	Champions	Age
1934	Robert Turner, Muncie, Indiana	11	1973	Bret Yarborough, Elk Grove, California	11
1935	Maurice Bale, Jr., Anderson, Indiana	14	1974	Curt Yarborough, Elk Grove, California	11
1936	Herbert Muench, Jr., St. Louis, Missouri	14	1975	Karren Stead, Lower Bucks County, Pennsylvania	11
1937	Robert Ballard, White Plains, New York	12	1976	Phil Raber, Sugarcreek, Ohio (Junior)	11
1938	Robert Berger, Omaha, Nebraska	14		Joan Ferdinand, Canton, Ohio (Senior)	14
1939	Clifton Hardesty, White Plains, New York	11	1977	Mark Ferdinand, Canton, Ohio (Junior)	10
1940	Thomas Fisher, Detroit, Michigan	12		Steve Washburn, Bristol, Connecticut (Senior)	15
1941	Claude Smith, Akron, Ohio	14	1978	Darren Hart, Salem, Oregon (Junior)	11
1946	Gilbert Klecan, San Diego, California	14		Greg Cardinal, Flint, Michigan (Senior)	13
1947	Kenneth Holmboe, Charleston, West Virginia	14	1979	Russell Yurk, Flint, Michigan (Junior)	10
1948	Donald Strub, Akron, Ohio	14		Craig Kitchen, Akron, Ohio (Senior)	14
1949	Fred Derks, Akron, Ohio	15	1980	Chris Fulton, Indianapolis, Indiana (Junior)	11
1950	Harold Williamson, Charleston, West Virginia	15		Dan Purol, Northern California (Senior)	12
1951	Darwin Cooper, Williamsport, Pennsylvania	15	1981	Howie Fraley, Portsmouth, Ohio (Junior)	11
1952	Joe Lunn, Columbus, Georgia	11		Tonia Schlegel, Hamilton, Ohio (Senior)	13
1953	Fred Mohler, Muncie, Indiana	14	1982	Carol Ann Sullivan, New Hampshire St. (Junior)	10
1954	Richard Kemp, Los Angeles, California	14		Matt Wolfgang, Lehigh Valley, Pa. (Senior)	12
1955	Richard Rohrer, Rochester, New York	14	1983	Tony Carlini, Southern California (Junior)	10
1956	Norman Westfall, Rochester, New York	14		Mike Burdgick, Flint, Michigan (Senior)	14
1957	Terry Townsend, Anderson, Indiana	14	1984	Christopher Hess, Hamilton, Ohio (Junior)	11
1958	James Miley, Muncie, Indiana	15		Anita Jackson, St. Louis, Missouri (Senior)	15
1959	Barney Townsend, Anderson, Indiana	13	1985	Michael Gallo, Danbury, Connecticut (Junior)	12
1960	Fredric Lake, South Bend, Indiana	11		Matt Sheffer, York, Pennsylvania (Senior)	14
1961	Dick Dawson, Wichita, Kansas	13	1986	Marc Behan, New Hampshire St. (Junior)	9
1962	David Mann, Gary, Indiana	14		Tami Jo Sullivan, Lancaster, Ohio (Senior)	13
1963	Harold Conrad, Duluth, Minnesota	12	1987	Matt Margules, Danbury, Connecticut (Junior)	11
1964	Gregory Schumacher, Tacoma, Washington	14		Brian Drinkwater, Bristol, Connecticut (Senior)	14
1965	Robert Logan, Santa Ana, California	12	1988	Jason Lamb, Des Moines, Iowa (Junior)	10
1966	David Krussow, Tacoma, Washington	12		David Duffield, Kansas City, Mo. (Senior)	13
1967	Kenneth Cline, Lincoln, Nebraska	13	1989	David Schiller, Dayton, Ohio (Kit car)	12
1968	Branch Lew, Muncie, Indiana	11		Faith Chavarria, Tri-County California (Masters)	12
1969	Steve Souter, Midland, Texas	12	1990	Mark Mihal, Valparaiso, Indiana (Kit car)	12
1970	Samuel Gupton, Durham, North Carolina	13		Sami Jones, Salem, Oregon (Masters)	13
1971	Larry Blair, Oroville, California	13	1991	Paul Greenwald, Saginaw, Michigan (Kit car)	13
1972	Robert Lange, Jr., Boulder, Colorado	14		Danny Garland, San Diego, California	14

The derby

Soap Box Derby Gets Inspired Start on Neighborhood Hill in Dayton

The Soap Box Derby, an enduring bit of Middle Americana, was the brainchild of a Dayton Daily News feature writer in 1933. **Myron Scott** was driving around town when he spotted some boys racing down Big Hill Road in Oakwood, in handmade "cars." Scott told the kids to get all the other kids in the neighborhood to show up the following week, and he would present the winner a trophy. Scott returned to find the hill aswarm with kids piloting the oddest contraptions he'd ever seen. He took a picture of young Bob Gravett's number 7—it became later the official symbol—and ran a coupon in the paper asking kids to sign up for a bigger derby, on Burkhardt Hill in East Dayton. On race day in August, the crowds were so big, Scott himself had trouble getting close: 40,000 people had come out to see boys run down a hill in handmade cars. The crowd was so large it trampled lawns and spectators sitting on a garage roof collapsed the whole building. The Daily News gave Scott $200 to promote the next derby, which became in 1934 the first All-American Soap Box Derby. The Derby was destined for larger things and when Akron offered to build a hill for a permanent track, it moved north where it has been ever since. ▶

Trapshooting

Grand Americans Handicap Champions

Year	Entries	Name/Residence	Yds.	Bk.
1900	74	R. O. Heikes, Dayton, Ohio	22	91
1901	75	E. C. Griffith, Pascoaq, Rhode Island	19	95
1902	91	C. W. Floyd, New York, New York	18	94
1903	180	Martin Diefenderfer, Wood River, Nebraska	16	94
1904	317	R. D. Guptil, Aitken, Minnesota	19	96
1905	333	R. R. Barber, Paulina, Iowa	16	99
1906	290	F. E. Rogers, St. Louis, Missouri	17	94
1907	495	J. J. Blanks, Trezevant, Tennessee	17	96
1908	362	Fred Harlow, Newark, Ohio	16	92
1909	457	Fred Shatluck, Columbus, Ohio	18	99
1910	383	Riley Thompson, Coinsville, Missouri	19	100
1911	418	Harvey Dixon, Oronogo, Missouri	20	99
1912	377	W. E. Phillips, Chicago, Illinois	19	96
1913	501	M. S. Hootman, Edgerton, Ohio	17	97
1914	515	Woolfolk Henderson, Lexington, Kentucky	22	98
1915	884	L. B. Clarke, Chicago, Illinois	18	96
1916	683	J. F. Wulf, Milwaukee, Wisconsin	19	99
1917	808	C. H. Larson, Waupaca, Wisconsin	20	98
1918	620	J. D. Henry, Elkhart, Indiana	16	97
1919	848	G. W. Lorimer, Piqua, Ohio	18	98
1920	715	A. L. Ivins, Red Bank, New Jersey	19	99
1921	637	E. F. Haak, Canton, Ohio	21	97
1922	588	J. S. Frink, Worthington, Minnesota	22	96
1923	513	Mark Arie, Champaign, Illinois	23	96
1924	528	H. C. Deck, Plymouth, Ohio	16	97
1925	710	E. C. Starner, Ithaca, New York	17	98
1926	932	C. A. Young, Springfield, Ohio	23	100
1927	873	Otto Newlin, Georgetown, Illinois	20	98
1928	891	Isaac Andrews, Spartanburg, South Carolina	20	95
1929	1,100	Mose Newman, Sweetwater, Texas	20	98
1930	966	Alfred Rufus King, Wichita Falls, Texas	16	97
1931	938	Garrison Roebuck, McClure, Ohio	17	96
1932	722	A. E. Sheffield, Dixon, Illinois	21	98
1933	597	Walter Beaver, Berwyn, Pennsylvania	25	98
1934	612	L. G. Dana, Derrick City, Pennsylvania	17	98
1935	608	J. B. Royall, Tallahassee, Florida	20	98
1936	704	B. F. Cheek, Clinton, Indiana	16	98
1937	932	F. G. Carroll, Brecksville, Ohio	19	100
1938	814	O. W. West, Coschocton, Ohio	20	99
1939	757	D. L. Ritchie, Goshen, Ohio	22	99
1940	820	E. H. Wolfe, Charleston, West Virginia	23	98
1941	1,108	Walter Tulburt, Detroit, Michigan	18	99
1942	910	J. F. Holderman, Morris, Illinois	20	193
1943	810	Jasper Rogers, Dayton, Ohio	18	97
1944	865	L. C. Jepson, Dwight, Illinois	19	97
1945	828	Don Englebry, Vermillion, Ohio	23	99
1946	1,478	Capt. F. J. Bennett, Miami, Florida	18	98
1947	1,786	H. H. Crossen, Gardiner, Montana	22	99
1948	1,678	John W. Schenk, Sharpsburg, Pennsylvania	20	99
1949	1,758	Pete Donat, Antwerp, Ohio	20	100
1950	1,737	Oscar Scheske, Jr., Belleville, Illinois	19	100
1951	1,682	E. Michael Wayland, Washington, Kansas	21	99
1952	1,727	Orval E. Voorhees, Grand Island, Nebraska	18	98
1953	1,949	Raymond Williams, Eaton, Ohio	19	98
1954	2,009	Nick Egan, New York, New York	19	99
1955	2,025	Logan Bennett, Hodgeville, Kentucky	19	99
1956	2,136	C. W. Brown, Dayton, Ohio	19	99
1957	2,129	C. R. Crawford, Maywood, Illinois	22	98
1958	2,202	Emerson Clark, Preston, Ontario	20	98
1959	2,392	Clyde Bailey, Oquawka, Illinois	21	99
1960	2,429	Roy Foxworthy, Indianapolis, Indiana	20	100
1961	2,353	Steve Barringer, Russell, Kansas	20	99
1962	2,414	Milton Young, Chicago, Illinois	20	99

1963	2,527	Albert Kees, Richmond, Indiana	21	100
1964	2,688	W. E. Duggan, Delphos, Ohio	20	99
1965	3,031	Daniel C. Paulter, Alden, New York	20	99
1966	3,464	Delbert Grim, Lincoln, Nebraska	23	100
1967	2,930	Herman Welch, Downers Grove, Illinois	20	100
1968	3,111	Denton Childers, Rochester, Michigan	21 1/2	100
1969	2,881	Bernard Bonn, Jr., Fairborn, Ohio	19	99
1970	2,953	Charles Harvey, Oskaloosa, Iowa	24	98
1971	3,047	Ralph Davis, Lorton, Virginia	20 1/2	98
1972	3,326	George Mushrush, Fairfield, Ohio	22	99
1973	3,421	Dennis Taylor, Muscoda, Wisconsin	22	99
1974	3,932	John Steffen, Minneapolis, Minnesota	24 1/2	99
1975	3,718	Wayne Hegwood, Jackson, Mississippi	23	99
1976	3,925	Frank Crevatin, Tecumseh, Ontario, Canada	21 1/2	99
1977	3,996	James Edwards, Fairfield, Ohio	19 1/2	99
1978	4,073	Reggie Jachimowski, Antioch, Illinois	27	100
1979	3,863	Dean Shanahan, Dubuque, Louisiana	21 1/2	100
1980	3,674	William Hazlett, Sarver, Pennsylvania	22 1/2	99
1981	3,762	Claude Kolbe, Sheboygan, Wisconsin	22	100
1982	3,617	Chet Hendrickson, Olive Hill, Kentucky	19	100
1983	3,708	Roger Smith, Wichita, Kansas	27	100
1984	3,550	John McQuade, Elburn, Illinois	21	100
1985	3,584	Artis Roy, Russell Springs, Kentucky	22	100
1986	3,697	Lawrence Evans, Ionia, New York	22	100
1987	4,080	Roger Stiles, Campbellsville, Kentucky	20 1/2	99
1988	4,237	Britt Robinson, Tahoka, Texas	27	100
1989	4,505	Jack Titus, Bradford, Pennsylvania	22 1/2	100
1990	4,558	Richard (Pat) Neff, Middletown, Ohio	26	100
1991	4,450	Frederic Kaschak	24 1/2	100

Auto Racing

Burke Lakefront Airport, Cleveland
Phone: (216) 781-3500
Location: On Lake Erie in downtown Cleveland, three minutes from the business district
Main Events: Budweiser Cleveland Grand Prix (CART PPG Indy Car World Series and SCCA Trans-Am Championship)

The track at Burke Lakefront is a temporary road course averaging between two and three miles. It operates three days a year.

Eldora Speedway
Phone: (513) 338-8511
Location: Almost three miles north of Rossburg on State Route 118
Main Events: 4-Crown Nationals (USAC Silver Crown)

The track at Eldora Speedway is a dirt oval measuring half a mile.

Marion County International Raceway
Phone: (614) 499-3666
Location: Three miles south of LaRue on S.R. 37 (2454 Richwood-LaRue Rd.)
Main Events: Sports Nationals (IHRA)

The raceway is a 1/4-mile area of asphalt and concrete.

Mid-Ohio Sports Car Course
Phone: (419) 884-4000
Location: Off S.R. 314 on Steam Corners Road in Lexington, about fifteen miles from S.R. 95 and 314.
Main Events: Pioneer 200 (CART PPG Indy Car World Series), Mid-Ohio Trans-Am (SCCA), Nissan Grand Prix of Ohio (IMSA Camel GT)

The Mid-Ohio Sports Car Course is a 2.24 mile track for CART and a 2.4 mile, 15-turn road course for IMSA and SCCA.

National Trail Raceway
Phone: (614) 587-1005
Location: Off I-70 at exit 126 (Rte. 37), one mile west of Rts. 37 and 40
Main Events: Oldsmobile Springnationals (NHRA)

National Trail is a quarter-mile strip of track.

Norwalk Raceway Park
Phone: (419) 668-5555
Location: In Norwalk, five miles south of Ohio Turnpike Exit 7 on US 250
Main Events: World Nationals (NHRA)

The raceway is a 1/4-mile area of asphalt and concrete.

Pro Team Sports

Beeghly Center
Phone: (216) 743-8111
Location: 410 Wick Avenue in Youngstown
Main Events: Youngstown Pride World Basketball League team. Games broadcast by WKBN (570 AM). Youngstown State University basketball (Mid-Continent Conference (men); North Star Conference (women) beginning in Fall '92, NCAA Division I)

The Youngstown Pride have been playing in Beeghly Center since they joined the World Basketball League in 1988. Seating capacity at Beeghly is 6,896. The largest crowd ever recorded for a Pride game was 7,148 on September 1, 1989.
The YSU Penguins (men's and women's basketball) also play at Beeghly. Check the Youngstown State University entry for more information on YSU sports.

Cleveland Stadium
Phone: (216) 861-1200 (Indians), (216) 696-3800 (Browns)
Location: On Boudreau Boulevard in Cleveland
Main Events: Cleveland Indians Major League ball club. Games also broadcast by WWWE (1100 AM), WUAB (TV 45, Fox), and SportsChannel Ohio. Cleveland Browns American Football Conference franchise. Games also broadcast by WHK (1420 AM) and WMMS (100.7 FM)

Foul line to foul line, Cleveland Stadium is the largest ballpark in the American League; it is so large, in fact, that no ball has ever been hit into the centerfield bleachers. The stadium has three message boards (with accompanying state of the art sound system) and a seating capacity of 74,483 (including 108 private, air conditioned boxes). Tickets range from $11.00 for box seats to $4.00 for bleacher seats.

The stadium is also the largest facility in the nation housing both a Major League ball team and a Pro-Football team. During the Browns season, seating capacity at Cleveland Stadium increases to 80,098 with the opening of the centerfield seats closed for baseball season. Tickets for a Browns game range from $17 to $30.

Cleveland Stadium has also seen its share of sports and non-sports related activities including the Schmeling vs. Stribling fight for the heavy-weight championship of the world and performances by the Beatles and the Metropolitan Opera.

Cooper Stadium
Phone: (614) 462-5250
Location: 1155 W. Mound Street in Columbus
Main Events: Columbus Clippers Triple-A Minor League ball club (affiliated with the New York Yankees); games also broadcast by WBNS (1460 AM)

Cooper has a seating capacity of 15,000 and parking for 3,500 cars and buses. The Columbus Clippers play all regular season home games here. The largest crowd ever recorded at Cooper Stadium was on June 17, 1980, when 20,131 fans jammed into the park to see Columbus take on fellow Ohio minor leaguers, the Toledo Mud Hens.

Ervin J. Nutter Center
Phone: (513) 429-4000 (Wings), (513) 885-3267 (Dynamo), (513) 873-2771 (WSU)
Location: Off I-675 where North Fairfield Rd. meets Col. Glenn Highway in Dayton, adjacent to the campus of Wright State University
Main Events: Dayton Wings World Basketball League team. Games broadcast by WONE (980 AM). Dayton Dynamo National Professional Soccer League team. Wright State University sports (Mid-Continent Conference, men, North Star Conference, women) including basketball (NCAA Division I)

The 10,464 seat Nutter Center is the home of the Dayton Dynamo, the Dayton Wings, Wright State NCAA Division I basketball, and other indoor college sports.

Fairgrounds Coliseum at the Ohio Exposition Center
Phone: (614) 299-2100 (Columbus Horizon)
Location: On 632 East 11th Ave. in Columbus
Main Events: Columbus Horizon Continental Basketball Association team (affiliated with Houston Rockets, Cleveland Cavaliers). Games broadcast by WCOL (1230 AM)

Average attendance for a Columbus Horizon game was 3,260 in the 5,750 seat Coliseum for 1990-91, a record for the Continental Basketball Association.

Ned Skeldon Stadium
Phone: (419) 893-9483
Location: 2901 Key Street in Maumee
Main Events: Toledo Mud Hens Triple-A Minor League baseball club (affiliated with Detroit Tigers). Games also broadcast by WMTR (96.1 FM)

Home of the Toledo Mud Hens, Ned Skeldon Stadium has a seating capacity of over 10,000. Regular season attendance has been known to reach over 160,000.

Riverfront Stadium
Phone: (513) 421-4510 (Reds), (513) 621-3550 (Bengals)
Location: 100 Riverfront Stadium in Cincinnati
Main Events: Cincinnati Reds Major League ball club. Games also broadcast by WLW (700 AM), WLWT (TV 5). Cincinnati Bengals American Football Conference franchise. Games also broadcast by WKRC (550 AM) and affiliates

Seating capacity at Riverfront is 52,952 including 10,383 box seats adjacent to the infield. Tickets range from $3.50 to $10.00. Since its opening on June 30, 1970 (the same day Hank Aaron hit Riverfront's first homerun), millions of fans have been there to see some of the finest moments in baseball, including Pete Rose's record breaking 4,192nd hit.

During football season, seating capacity at Riverfront increases to 60,389. The largest crowd ever at the stadium was there on October 17,

*1971, when 60,284 football fans packed in to
see the Bengals take on the Browns.*

Thurman Munson Memorial Stadium
Phone: (216) 456-5100
Location: Two miles south of downtown Canton
at 2501 Allen Ave., SE
Main Events: Canton-Akron Indians Double-
A Minor League baseball club (affiliated with
Cleveland Indians). Games broadcast by WOAC
(TV 67 Cable)
*The Canton-Akron Indians have only been
playing at the 5,700 seat Thurman Munson
Stadium since 1989, the year the franchise
moved there from Vermont. In that short time,
however, the "Little Wahoos" have not only set a
team record for single-season attendance
(204,189 in 1990), but also subsequently broke
that record (217,347 in 1991).*

Richfield Coliseum
Phone: (216) 659-9100 (Cavaliers), (216) 349-
2090 (Crunch)
Location: At 2923 Streetsboro Road in Richfield
near Cleveland
Main Events: Cleveland Cavaliers NBA franchise.
Games also broadcast by WOIO (TV 19)
and SportsChannel Ohio. Cleveland Crunch
Major League Soccer franchise. Games also
broadcast by WERE (1300 AM)

*The Richfield Coliseum has a regulation-
sized basketball court for regular season Cavs
games, a full-sized tennis court and health club,
92 private loge boxes, as well as saunas, lounges
and two restaurants on its upper two levels.
Tickets to a Cavaliers regular season game range
from $9 to $32. In addition to being the home of
the Cavaliers and the Major Soccer League's
Cleveland Crunch, the Coliseum hosts professional boxing, wrestling, tennis and other sports
as well as concerts, ice shows and exhibition
events.*

Bowling

Imperial Lanes
Phone: (419) 531-5338
Location: On 5505 West Central in Toledo
Main Events: Professional Bowlers Association
National Championship

Riviera Lanes
Phone: (216) 836-7985
Location: At 20 South Miller Road in Akron
Main Events: Professional Bowlers Association
Firestone Tournament of Champions

Yorktown Lanes
Phone: (216) 886-5300
Location: At 6218 Pearl Road in Parma Heights
Main Events: Professional Bowlers Association
Bud Light Open

College Sports

Bowling Green State University (**Doyt L. Perry
Field** and **Anderson Arena**)
Phone: (419) 372-2401
Location: on the campus of Bowling Green State
University, twenty miles south of Toledo
Main Events: BGSU sports including football and
basketball (Mid-American Conference)

*Doyt L. Perry Field has a seating capacity of
30,500; Anderson Arena, 5,200*

Cleveland State University (**Physical Education
Center**)
Phone: (216) 687-4800
Location: on the campus of CSU, 10900 Euclid
Avenue, Cleveland.
Main Events: CSU sports including basketball
(Mid-Continent Conference (men), North
Star Conference (women) Division I)

*The Physical Education Center at CSU seats
3,000.*

Kent State University (**Dix Stadium** and the
**Memorial Athletic and Convocation
Center**)
Phone: (216) 672-3120
Location: On the Kent State University campus,
Kent
Main Events: Kent State sports including Mid-
American Conference basketball and
football

*In addition to hosting men's basketball, the
6,034 seat Memorial Athletic Convocation
Center is home to Kent's womens team who
were runners-up for the MAC tournament title in
'92. Dix stadium, home of Kent State Golden
Flashes football, seats 30,520.*

Miami University (**Millett Hall** and **Yager Stadium**)
Phone: (513) 529-3113
Location: On the campus of Miami University in Oxford, 30 miles from Cincinnati
Main Events: Miami University sports including Mid-American Conference football and basketball (NCAA Division I)

Yager Stadium has a seating capacity of 25,500. Millet Hall (home of Miami Redskins basketball who won the MAC League and Tournament Championships and made it to the first round of the NCAA Tournament in 1992) seats 9,200.

Ohio State University (**Ohio Stadium** and **St. John Arena**)
Phone: (614) 292-7572 (OSU Sports Information)
Location: On the campus of OSU, on Woody Hayes Drive in Columbus
Main Events: OSU sports including Big Ten Conference football and basketball (NCAA Division I) Ohio Glory, World Football League. OSU games broadcast by all major networks and several radio station as well as campus radio and television station, WOSU

A perennial leader nationally in home game attendance, Ohio Stadium has been visited by over 30,000,000 fans in its 70 years for an average of 70,000 per game. The horseshoe-shaped stadium features a $2.6 million state-of-the-art scoreboard and seating for 86,071 and is listed in the National Register of Historic Places. St. John Arena has seen more than 5,000,000 fans pass through its doors since its opening in 1956, an average of just under 12,000 per game. A large main scoreboard, smaller corner scoreboards, and a new lighting system were installed in the arena for the 1988 season. Of St. John's 13,276 seats, the most distant one is only 155 feet from the center ring.

Ohio University (**Don Peden Stadium** and **Ohio University Convocation Center**
Phone: (614) 593-1174
Location: On the campus of Ohio University in Athens
Main Events: Ohio University sports (Mid-American Conference) including football and basketball

Don Peden Stadium has a seating capacity of 20,000; the Convocation Center, 13,000

University of Akron (**Rubber Bowl** and **James A. Rhodes Arena**)
Phone: (216) 972-7080
Location: On the campus of the University of Akron
Main Events: University of Akron sports (Mid-Continent Conference (men) and North Star Conference (women)) including football and basketball

The Rubber Bowl has a seating capacity of 35,482; JAR Arena, 7,000.

University of Cincinnati (**Nippert Stadium** and **The Myrl Shoemaker Center**)
Phone: (513) 556-5191
Location: On the campus of the University of Cincinnati
Main Events: University of Cincinnati sports (Great Midwest Conference) including football and basketball (NCAA Division I)

After renovation, Nippert Stadium will open with a seating capacity of 35,000 for the 1992 football season. The Myrl Shoemaker Center, home of championship class UC basketball, seats 13,176.

University of Dayton (**Welcome Stadium** and **UD Arena**)
Phone: (513) 229-4421
Location: On the University of Dayton campus
Main Events: University of Dayton sports (Midwestern Collegiate Conference) including football (NCAA Division III) and basketball (NCAA Division I)

In addition to hosting the Midwestern Collegiate Conference men's and women's post-season championship tournaments for the last three years, the 13,455 seat UD Arena has been the host of thirteen NCAA tournament Main Events including first and second round games of the 1992 men's basketball tournament. Welcome Stadium, home of Flyer Football (who have been to the Division III championship game five times since 1980), seats 11,000 and is within walking distance of the Arena.

University of Toledo (**Glass Bowl** and **Savage Hall**)
Phone: (419) 537-4184
Location: On the University of Toledo Campus, 2801 West Bancroft Street
Main Events: University of Toledo sports (Mid-American Conference) including football and basketball (NCAA Division I)

The Glass Bowl has a seating capacity of 26,248. Savage Hall, home of Lady Rockets basketball (who won the MAC championship and were invited to the NCAA Division I women's tournament in '92), seats 9,200.

Wright State University (see **Ervin J. Nutter Center** entry)

Xavier University (**Corcoran Field, Cincinnati Gardens, Schmidt Field House, Hayden Field**)
Phone: (513) 745-3413
Location: On the Xavier campus on Victory Parkway in Cincinnati (except the Cincinnati Gardens located at 2250 Seymour Avenue)
Main Events: Xavier University sports (Midwestern Collegiate Conference, men; North Star Conference, women) including basketball, soccer, and baseball

Schmidt Field House with its capacity of 3,000 is the site of most games by the women's basketball team, who recorded the North Star Conference's best ever win-loss record in 1992 and were runners-up for the tournament championship. Hayden Field seats 600 and is the site of Xavier University baseball and softball. Men's and women's soccer play at Corcoran Field, capacity—500. Xavier University men's basketball plays at the Cincinnati Gardens with a seating capacity of 10,400.

Youngstown State University (**Stambaugh Stadium** and **Beeghly Center**)
Phone: (216) 742-3192
Location: 410 Wick Avenue in Youngstown.
Main Events: Youngstown State University sports (no conference) including football and basketball (NCAA Division I).

Beeghly Center, home of YSU Basketball and the Youngstown Pride (World Basketball League), has a seating capacity of 7,200. Stambaugh Stadium has a capacity of 16,000.

Halls of Fame

National Football Foundation's **College Football Hall of Fame**
Phone: (513) 398-5410
Location: At Kings Island

This establishment honors inductees into the College Football Hall of Fame from its inception in 1951 to the present time. Services include computer access to short biographies on every player enshrined, a 45-seat theater-locker room where audiences view a recreation of Knute Rockne's "Win One for the Gipper" speech, a room recreating the atmosphere of an actual college football game (including noisy fans) where visitors can attempt a field goal, and much more.

Pro Football Hall of Fame
Phone: (216) 456-8207
Location: At 2121 George Halas Drive, N.W., Canton

The Pro Football Hall of Fame honors professional players and administrative agents who have either had outstanding careers or left a lasting impression on the game of football. Inductees from Ohio include Paul Brown, Lou Groza, Roger Staubach, Paul Warfield, and several others.

Trapshooting Hall of Fame
Phone: (513) 898-1945
Location: 601 West National Road in Vandalia, three miles east of the Dayton International Airport

The Trapshooting Hall of Fame honors people who have made significant contributions to the growth of the sport and shooters who have made impressive records. Candidates are eligible for induction after 25 years of participation. The Hall of Fame also houses a trapshooting reference library and one of the largest collections of target shooting artifacts in the world.

Golf, PGA/LPGA

Firestone Country Club
Phone: (216) 644-8441
Location: On 452 East Warner Road in Akron
Main Events: NEC World Series of Golf

Firestone is a 72-hole club.

Highland Meadows Golf Club
Phone: (419) 882-4040
Location: On 7455 Erie Street in Sylvania
Main Events: LPGA Jamie Farr Toledo Classic

Highland meadows is a 54-hole club.

Muirfield Village Golf Club
Phone: (614) 889-6700
Location: On 5750 Memorial Drive in Dublin
Main Events: PGA Memorial Tournament

Muirfield is a 72-hole club.

Squaw Creek Country Club
Phone: (216) 539-5008
Location: On 761 Youngstown-Kingsville Road
in Vienna
Main Events: LPGA Phar-Mor in Youngstown

Squaw Creek is a 54-hole club.

The Grizzley Course, Bruin Course
Phone: (513) 398-5200
Location: At the Jack Nicklaus Sports Center on
6042 Fairway Dr., Mason, OH
Main Events: PGA Kroger Senior Classic,
Grizzley Course;

The Grizzley Course has 54 holes.

Thoroughbred Racing

B e u lah Park
Phone: (614) 871-9600
Location: On 3664 Grant Avenue in Grove City

River Downs
Phone: (513) 232-8000
Location: On 6301 Kellogg Avenue in Cincinnati

Thistledown
Phone: (216) 662-8600
Location: At 21501 Emery Rd. in North Randall

Harness Racing

Lebanon Raceway
Phone: (513) 932-4936
Location: On the Warren County Fairgrounds on
State Rte. 48 in Lebanon

Northfield Park
Phone: (216) 467-4101
Location: On State Rte. 8 in Northfield

Raceway Park
Phone: (419) 476-7751
Location: On 5700 Telegraph Rd. in Toledo

Scioto Downs
Phone: (614) 491-2515
Location: At 6000 South High St. in Columbus